The James Jones Reader

The JAMES

OUTSTANDING SELECTIONS

Including
From Here to Eternity,
The Thin Red Line,
and *Whistle*

A Birch Lane Press Book

JONES Reader

FROM HIS WAR WRITINGS

Edited by
James R. Giles
and
J. Michael Lennon

Published by Carol Publishing Group

A Birch Lane Press Book. Published by Carol Publishing Group.
Birch Lane Press is a registered trademark of Carol
Communications, Inc. Editorial Offices 600 Madison Avenue, New
York, NY 10022. Sales & Distribution Offices 120 Enterprise
Avenue, Secaucus, NJ 07094. In Canada: Musson Book Company, a
division of General Publishing Co. Limited. All rights reserved. No
part of this book may be reproduced in any form, except by a
newspaper or magazine reviewer who wishes to quote brief passages
in connection with a review. Queries regarding rights and
permission should be addressed to Carol Publishing Group, 600
Madison Avenue, New York, NY 10022. Manufactured in the United
States of America.

10 9 8 7 6 5 4 3 2 1

Library of Congress Cataloging-in-Publication Data

Jones, James, 1921–1977.
  [Novels, Selections]
  The James Jones reader : outstanding selections from his war
writings / edited by James R. Giles and J. Michael Lennon.
    p. cm.
  "Including From here to eternity, The thin red line, and Whistle."
  "A Birch Lane Press book."
  ISBN 1-55972-066-2
  I. Giles, James Richard, 1937–   . II. Lennon, J. Michael.
III. Title.
PS3560.O49A6 1991
813'.54—dc20   90-29104
                                                    CIP

Contents

One day one of their number would write a book about all this, but none of them would believe it, because none of them would remember it that way.

—From *The Thin Red Line*

The James Jones Reader

Introduction

December 7, 1991, marks the fiftieth anniversary of the Japanese bombing of the United States naval installations at Pearl Harbor and this country's subsequent entry into World War II. Americans now remember that massive conflict as the last "good war," the last armed struggle in which the morality of the cause and the justice of eventual victory seemed unambiguous. World War II was a stupendous human event, a cultural watershed of unprecedented significance that completed a profound and irreversible loss of American innocence that began in World War I. We could no longer pretend to be aloof from international affairs. The horrors of years of war, culminating in the Holocaust, Hiroshima, and Nagasaki, forced us into a new and terrifying realization of the insignificance of the individual. Since 1945, human existence has been defined by a pervasive absurdity, a sense of the fundamental disparity between humanity's spiritual aspirations and the ever-present possibility of self-inflicted annihilation.

In the United States, two groups of novelists brought their special visions and fictional techniques to World War II. First, a group of writers working in realistic and naturalistic modes began publishing immediately after the war. Over a decade later, another group interpreted the war from surrealistic and absurdist perspectives. Norman Mailer, Irwin Shaw, John Horne Burns, Harry Joe Brown, and James Jones were the major figures in the first group, while Joseph Heller, Thomas Pynchon, and Kurt Vonnegut, Jr., typified the second. Of all these writers, none evoked the war and its cultural aftermath with the totality of vision that distinguished the work of Jones. His war narratives—four novels, a small group of stories, some essays and a work of nonfiction—constitute our most important literary account of World War II. His encyclopedic treatment of the suffering of the enlisted man before, during, and after combat is unmatched in American literature.

The descendant of a once-prominent small-town Illinois family who had fallen on hard times, James Jones joined the old peacetime United States Army out of economic necessity, just after graduating from high school in 1939. Initially, he belonged to the United States Army Air Corps, but he soon transferred to the infantry. Stationed in Hawaii, he experienced, as a private, the degrading caste system of the peacetime army with its spoiled officer class and exploited mass of enlisted men. Then, in 1941, two events changed his life. First, he read Thomas Wolfe in the Schofield Barracks post library, an experience which made him understand that he had "been a writer all along without really having realized it." Second, also at Schofield Barracks, Jones saw the waves of attacking Japanese planes. Later, he wrote about that day:

> I remembered thinking with a sense of the profoundest awe that none of our lives would ever be the same...and I wondered how many of us would survive to see the end results. I had just turned twenty, the month before.

Some years later, he would begin the task of translating his Hawaiian army experiences into a book which, in 1951, would become his first published novel, *From Here to Eternity*. It is unique in being the only World War II novel written by someone who served in the peacetime U.S. Army and personally witnessed the Japanese attack on Pearl Harbor. The attack on Pearl Harbor is retold five times, in five ways, in this anthology. It is clearly the event that mobilized Jones's nascent novelistic imagination, just as it mobilized the United States, blasting the country out of isolationism to center stage in world affairs.

In late 1942, Jones's unit was sent to Guadalcanal to help capture that remote island in the Solomons from the occupying Japanese. There, the future novelist was initiated into impersonal technological combat. He struggled to make the first essential adjustment in a process that he later called "the evolution of a soldier"—the acceptance of the inevitability and insignificance of his own death. His artistic ambitions fought against such an acceptance, however. He later wrote, "I simply did not want to die and not be remembered for it. Or not be remembered at all." One especially horrible combat experience affected him in another way: In unexpected hand-to-hand combat, he was forced to kill a young Japanese soldier. While Jones never discussed this incident in his autobiographical accounts of the war, he does treat it twice in his fiction. Apparently, the indirection of fiction was necessary for him to be able to write about killing a man by touch. Jones was a warm, friendly man. It is not difficult to imagine him in later life remembering the intimacy of that struggle; this soldier was, for him, like Thomas Hardy's "Man He Killed," someone "You'd treat if met where any bar is, / Or help to half-a-crown." But they met, like the victims in the Hardy poem, in infantries, and there was the necessity that one of them die. Jones was himself wounded on Guadalcanal and evacuated to the United States. His experiences in the Pacific provided the material for his brilliant 1962 novel, *The Thin Red Line*.

When Jones returned to the States in 1943, the still-young man was more psychologically than physically damaged. He was haunted by the memories of combat and enraged by the changes that had taken place at home. In 1943, he saw the birth of a new American society devoted solely to material gain. Recuperating in a Memphis, Tennessee, army hospital, he was enraged by the loose money and selfishness he saw all around him. In a 1978 memoir, *James Jones: A Friendship*, Willie Morris recalls what Jones told him about the country in 1943:

> It was a different America altogether from the one so many of them [the American military] had left before the war. There was an unexpected affluence everywhere. Everyone had a cynical, knowing grin. Everyone seemed to be getting rich.

"Everyone" but the soldiers dying ugly, anonymous deaths in combat overseas. Jones wrote eloquently and angrily about the hedonism of the homefront. He first tried to develop this vision in a novel begun while he was stationed at Camp Campbell, Kentucky, after his release from the Memphis military hospital. His anger was still too great and his experience as a writer too limited, however, for that initial effort at fiction, entitled *They Shall Inherit the Laughter*, to succeed, and it was never published. But the vision of a war-profiteering homefront stayed with him for the rest of his life and ultimately was transformed into fiction in his posthumous novel, *Whistle* (1978).

Jones, though a young, frustrated, inexperienced writer in 1943, realized the underlying concept of what he would call his "army trilogy" (*From Here to Eternity*, *The Thin Red Line*, and *Whistle*) at the very beginning of his literary career. It took over twenty-five years for the trilogy to be written, but what emerged was true to his original vision. In the first selection of this anthology, "A Note by the Author" from *Whistle*, Jones compares his army trilogy to John Dos Passos's *U.S.A.*, but says correctly that each of his three novels stands alone as fully realized work to a degree unmatched by the three novels of Dos Passos's trilogy. Jones's three volumes are long, fully realized studies of the old peacetime army and the attack on Pearl Harbor; the brutal ugliness of combat; and the American soldier returning to an affluent, cynical postwar society. The army trilogy is unique in another way. In it, the author develops three "character types" whose names changed in each novel. The name changes were necessitated by the death of the protagonist, Private Robert E. Lee Prewitt, in *From Here to Eternity*. But in the course of the three novels, the changes are, ironically, justified by what happens to the three. Combat transforms the three characters into different men than they had been, and alienation from, and anger at, a selfish homefront changes them again. Thus, the "romantic bolshevik" private, Robert E. Lee Prewitt of *From Here to Eternity*, is reduced to the cunning and implacably stubborn Witt in *The Thin Red Line*, and finally to the physically and emotionally crippled Prell of *Whistle*. First Sergeant Milt Warden of *From Here to Eternity*, who hides his own idealism behind a mask of cynicism, evolves into *The Thin Red Line's* "Mad" Welsh, who desperately adopts a mask of insanity to accept the impossibility of protecting his men in combat; and then, in *Whistle*, into Matt Winch, who surrenders at last to a real madness. *From Here to Eternity's* Maylon Stark, mess sergeant and sexual adventurer, becomes *The Thin Red Line's* Storm, selflessly obsessed with feeding his men despite the chaos of combat, and then John Strange of *Whistle*, who commits suicide rather than take part in the Normandy invasion.

Profound and defining as they are, though, these three novels do not represent all of Jones's World War II writing. In 1959, he published *The Pistol*, a tightly structured novella that focuses on the terror and desperation of Private Richard Mast in Schofield

Barracks during and after the December 7, 1941, attack. Mast accidentally comes into possession of an army pistol (as did Jones), and desperately clings to it as a talisman. Jones's friend Irwin Shaw insisted that *The Pistol* should be viewed, along with *From Here to Eternity*, *The Thin Red Line*, and *Whistle*, as part of an "army quartet." Jones never thought of it that way, perhaps because it does not treat his three recurrent character types or because it is so short; but *The Pistol* unquestionably constitutes an impressive part of his World War II work. In addition to the trilogy and *The Pistol*, Jones wrote several powerful short stories about the war that he included in his 1968 collection *The Ice-Cream Headache and Other Stories*. Three of these are included in this volume.

WWII, a tightly written infantryman's history of the big war, was the result of a request to write the commentary for a book of reproductions of World War II graphic art. Published in 1975, it is one of his finest works. It is in *WWII* that Jones fully develops his concept of the evolution of a soldier, which underlies the army trilogy. The process of psychological evolution involves essentially two distinct stages. In order to stand the anonymous horror of combat, the soldier had to accept the inevitability of his own death. It was this crucial first step in the process that Jones said he was unable to take on Guadalcanal; but those who did manage it were transformed into a new kind of human being:

> [The combat soldier] was about the foulest-mouthed individual who ever existed on earth....And internally, his soul was as foul and cynical as his mouth....He had pared his dreams and ambitions down to no more than relief and a few days away from the line, and a bottle of booze, a woman and a bath.

It was an article of faith for Jones that combat numbed and then destroyed minds as well as bodies, yet this numbing was a necessary psychological protection. Of course, if it went too far, it resulted in a debilitating fatalism, and soldiers acted in bizarre, foolhardy, and doomed ways.

The second stage in the soldier's transformation was no easier. If the combat veteran did somehow survive, he returned as a spiritually and psychologically dead man, suddenly forced back to a country devoted exclusively to acquisition and consumption. One of the walking dead, he found himself in an alien nation that, even if it had tried, could not even begin to understand him. Thus, even if physically sound, the returning soldier was a new kind of war casualty, one who would frighten himself and those at home who "knew" him. In *WWII*, Jones wrote:

> Men still woke up in the middle of the night, thrashing around and trying to get their hands on their wives' throats. Men still rolled out from a dead sleep, and hit the dirt with a crash on the bedroom floor, huddling against the bed to evade the aerial bomb or the artillery shells they had dreamed they heard coming. While their wives sat straight up in bed in their new frilly nightgowns bought for the homecoming, wide-eyed and staring, horrified. An old buddy would have roared with laughter. There is no telling what the divorce rate was then, in the early year or two. Certainly a lot higher than was ever admitted.

Jones's attitude toward war was inevitably complex. He hated it, but he was obsessed with it; it was, in fact, something of a grand passion for him. He collected knives and Civil War books and talked about writing a Civil War novel. The earliest piece in this collection is a previously unpublished book report on *The Red Badge of Courage*. Moreover, he dedicated *Eternity* to the U.S. Army, *Thin Red Line* to war and warfare, and *Whistle* to all who served in World War II. Jones's treatment of Americans in combat is not limited to the Second World War, however. In Chapter 2 of *From Here to Eternity*, Jones recalls World War I and the Moro revolt in the Philippines earlier in this century. A tableau of freezing combat in Korea ends his 1958 novel, *Some Came Running*. And in *Viet Journal* (1974), he recounts his visit to that war-torn country before the American forces pulled out in 1973. It ends with his finest essay, an account of his return to Hawaii, three decades after Pearl Harbor.

Jones was fifty-two and suffering from congestive heart disease when he became a war correspondent. While in Vietnam, he went to some lengths *not* to stay out of danger as he zoomed around the country in a helicopter. At that time the liberal establishment at home was unified in hatred of the war, and some even included U.S. soldiers in the condemnation that was voiced throughout the country. But Jones felt he had to see this generation of American soldiers for himself; for if James Jones hated war, he loved the U.S. Army, especially its enlisted men, and did not want to believe that they had degenerated into mere murderers and rapers of civilians. He did not deny horrors such as My Lai, but he felt instinctively that such hideousness had to be aberrational. Jones agreed that United States military intervention was a mistake, but he refused to go so far as many at-home war critics who considered United States soldiers brutal exploiters of a helpless people; nor did he believe that the Viet Cong were universally noble, innocent peasant-patriots. His book got an unfavorable reception from the liberal intellectual establishments at home and in Europe. Now, it seems obviously more right than not—it is as if Jones could see further than the other writers of the sixties, perhaps far enough to anticipate the clarifications and moderations of such works as *The Deer Hunter*, *Dispatches*, *Coming Home*, and "China Beach." If he were alive today, and able, he would undoubtedly be pondering the problems of another generation of GIs in the sands of Arabia.

Jones's depiction of Americans in combat covers three-quarters of a century, from World War I to Vietnam, a time of armed and bloody combat. In this panoramic achievement, his perspective is nearly always that of the enlisted man, the privates and sergeants confronting death on the line day after endless day. Loving the U.S. Army as the first real "home" he had ever known, he wanted, nevertheless, to demythologize war, to destroy its associations with nobility and grandeur. The overriding project of his life was to show that the product of modern technological combat was nothing more than sordid and anonymous annihilation and to serve as a voice for someone he called the proletarian enlisted man. Although Jones once applied for Officer Candidate School, with a few exceptions he had little interest in, or sympathy for, officers. As he says in *WWII*, the twentieth-century enlisted man is a special kind of exploited worker. Finally, it is necessary to say that the writer who so loved the U.S. Army, and who so powerfully reported on his nation's century-long involvement in war, had some deeply pacific elements in his personality. He was a mid-twentieth-century American stoic, akin to Marcus Aurelius in his long apprenticeship to war, suffering, and the effort to bear it all. Of course, he did cry out, was afraid. But like earlier stoics, he tried always to effect a comprehension of war and suffering, a framework of understanding. This means he was unable to turn away from the worst recognition: that if war is sometimes a treat for the senses, it is still horrible, the worst thing humanly invented. He understood the inevitability of World War II but profoundly believed, despite his grand passion, that anyone who would glorify the idea of war was guilty of blasphemy. For Jones, all other obscenities were as nothing compared to the deaths of the innocent.

Jones's reputation as a writer went through more than its share of ups and downs. While always commercially successful, he was not always accepted by the critics. It is a considerable understatement to say that his career began well. Forty years later, it is perhaps difficult to appreciate the kind of sensation aroused by *From Here to Eternity*. With its sexual explicitness and frankness of language, *Eternity* shocked a lot of people in 1951. This was, of course, the beginning of a smug, reactionary decade in American history, and only three years earlier Norman Mailer's soldiers on his fictional island of Anopopei had been forced to say *fug* for the commonest slang term for having sex. *Eternity* transcended scandal, however. The public and the critics were amazed at its scope and its unforgettable characters. They understood that American literature had gained an important new voice. But the critics were decidedly cruel to Jones's second novel, *Some Came Running*, and while several of his later books received favorable reviews, by the late sixties he was increasingly considered an old-fashioned writer. This view was largely due to the triumph of postmodernism in American literature and to Jones's unshakable commitment to traditional realism.

For James Jones was a stubborn man. He did not follow—he hardly noticed—trends. Usually, he seemed in conflict with the spirit of the times; one critic noted that *From Here to Eternity*, a tragic novel devoted to the depression-era U.S. Army, appeared at a time when the United States was awash in postwar optimism and expansion. *The Thin Red Line* appeared the same year as *Catch-22*; black humor, not classic realism, was in vogue in 1962. And *WWII* and *Whistle*, published in the 1970s, came out when America was years away from overcoming its revulsion for the recent war in Vietnam.

If Jones was rarely in step with trends and currents, it was because he was faithful to his own vision of war. Combat marked Jones in more than the ordinary ways and his attitude toward it, as noted earlier, was complex, ranging from the exultant to the pacifistic. But there was this constant: he was never emotionally detached from it. His fidelity is reflected in the hovering, sympathetic, brooding narrative consciousness of all his novels. Jones gets as close to his characters as he can without formally relinquishing his third-person perspective. Identification and emotional commitment were what he sought. He recalls Walt Whitman: "I am the man, I suffered, I was there." Jones, wounded at Guadalcanal, recipient of the Purple Heart and the Bronze Star, witness bearer to unknown soldiers, was there; he was writing as he lay dying, dictating, taping the words of those he kept alive for thirty-four years of his short life. And if some critics of his time had their doubts about Jones's fiction, other, quite important readers were always with him, for Jones was a writer's writer. Norman Mailer has said that *From Here to Eternity* was the most important postwar American novel. The list of other writers of his era who have admired his writing include William Styron, Saul Bellow, and Irwin Shaw. In later years, Joan Didion, Larry Heinemann, Joseph Heller, Willie Morris, George Plimpton, and Kurt Vonnegut, Jr., have praised Jones's fiction. It is the purpose of this collection to demonstrate that James Jones continues to be one of the most important voices in twentieth-century American literature and that no American writer of any century has written about war and the soldier as compellingly as he did. As Irwin Shaw said in his eulogy for Jones, "From the stink of the battlefield and the barracks came a bracing, clear wind of truth. To use a military term, he walked point for his company."

NOTE: Of the sixty-seven excerpts that follow, twenty-seven carry Jones's original titles. The remainder were supplied by the editors and are enclosed in brackets. The selections are given in the order they appeared in Jones's individual books. The chronological order of the books themselves has been shuffled, however, and is somewhat arbitrary. The chief reason for this is to present Jones's four war novels in one narrative cluster.

Acknowledgments

For their sustaining friendship and for support of this project, we thank Gloria Jones and her children, Kaylie Jones and Jamie Jones.

The editors also thank Northern Illinois University and Sangamon State University for supporting the development of this book, and the following individuals for support, assistance, and advice: John Bowers, Wanda H. Giles, Mark Goldman, George Hendrick, Marilyn Huff, Cherrill Kimbro, Donna P. Lennon, Peter K. Lennon, Robert F. Lucid, Norman Mailer, Glenn Meeter, Joe Mitchell, James Norris, Larry Shiner, Gloria Taylor, and Tom Woods.

A Note by the Author
(from *Whistle*)

I FIRST BEGAN ACTUAL WORK ON *Whistle* in 1968, but the book goes back a much longer time than that. It was conceived as far back as 1947, when I was still first writing to Maxwell Perkins about my characters Warden and Prewitt, and the book I wanted to write about World War II. When I was beginning *From Here to Eternity*, then still untitled, I meant for that book to carry its people from the peacetime Army on through Guadalcanal and New Georgia, to the return of the wounded to the United States. A time span corresponding to my own experience. But long before I reached the middle of it I realized such an ambitious scope of such dimension wasn't practicable. Neither the dramatic necessities of the novel itself, nor the amount of sheer space required, would allow such a plan.

The idea of a trilogy occurred to me then. *Whistle*, still untitled and—as a novel—unconceived, was a part of it. So when I began *The Thin Red Line* (some eleven years later) the plan for a trilogy was already there. And *Whistle*, as a concept, would be the third part of it.

Which of course it should be. It was always my intention with this trilogy that each novel should stand by itself as a work alone. In a way that, for example, John Dos Passos' three novels in his fine *USA* trilogy do not. *The 42nd Parallel*, *1919*, and *The Big Money* will not stand alone as novels. *USA* is one large novel, not a trilogy.

I intended to write the third volume immediately after I finished *The Thin Red Line*. Other things, other novels, got in the way. Each time I put it aside it seemed to further refine itself. So that each time I took it up again I had to begin all over. My own personal experiments with style and viewpoint affected the actual writing itself.

One of the problems I came up against, with the trilogy as a whole, appeared as soon as I began *The Thin Red Line* in 1959. In the original conception, first as a single novel, and then as a trilogy, the major characters such as 1st/Sgt Warden, Pvt Prewitt and Mess/Sgt Stark were meant to continue throughout the entire work. Unfortunately the dramatic structure—I might even say, the spiritual content—of the first book demanded that Prewitt be killed in the end of it. The import of the book would have been emasculated if Prewitt did not die.

When the smoke cleared, and I wrote End to *From Here to Eternity*, the only end it seemed to me it could have had, there I stood with no Prewitt character.

It may seem like a silly problem now. It wasn't then. Prewitt was meant from the beginning to carry an important role in the second book, and in the third. I could not just resurrect him. And have him there again, in the flesh, wearing the same name.

I solved the problem by changing the names. All of the names. But I changed them in such a way that a cryptic key, a marked similarity, continued to exist, as a reference point, with the old set of names. It seems like an easy solution now, but it was not at the time.

So in *The Thin Red Line* 1st/Sgt Warden became 1st/Sgt Welsh, Pvt Prewitt became Pvt Witt, Mess/Sgt Stark became Mess/Sgt Storm. While remaining the same people as before. In *Whistle* Welsh becomes Mart Winch, Witt becomes Bobby Prell, Storm becomes John Strange.

After publication of *The Thin Red Line*, a few astute readers noted the similarity of names, and wrote to ask me if the similarity was intentional. When they did, I wrote back saying that it was, and explaining why. So far as I know, no critic and no book reviewer ever noticed the name similarity.

There is not much else to add. Except to say that when *Whistle* is completed, it will surely be the end of something. At least for me. The publication of *Whistle* will mark the end of a long job of work for me. Conceived in 1946, and begun in the spring of 1947, it will have taken me nearly thirty years to complete. It will say just about everything I have ever had to say, or will ever have to say, on the human condition of war and what it means to us, as against what we claim it means to us.

Paris, 15 November 1973

From Here to Eternity

(1951)

The conclusion of Jones's first published novel—the Japanese attack on Pearl Harbor—was the beginning of his combat experience. He was the only future novelist of note on active duty on December 7, 1941. But *From Here to Eternity* is not a combat novel. It is an army novel, perhaps the finest ever written by an American, and is in fact dedicated to the United States Army. Most of the novel's action takes place at Schofield Barracks, where Jones served until shipping out in 1942 for Guadalcanal, where he was wounded. *Eternity* is the first of a trilogy of novels that follows an infantry company from the caste-ridden, authoritarian peacetime army through Pearl Harbor, ferocious combat in the South Pacific, and back to military hospitals in the United States.

"Authenticity" is the word used over and over in reviews and essays on the novel. This is a tribute, in part, to Jones's massive documentation of the gear, tackle, drills, bugle calls, boredom, KP, masochism and camaraderie—in short, all facets of barracks, bivouac, and stockade life in the "old" army. Although *Eternity* (860 pages) is clearly a novel of saturation in the Dreiserian tradition, it rarely flags. Its narrative drive and pace are tremendous. Jones writes with the classic realistic novelist's confidence that the world can be understood and explained. His epigraph from Emerson notes that "the whole of history is in one man." Jones's man is Pvt. Robert E. Lee Prewitt, a romantic rebel whom he first described as

"a small man standing on the edge of the ocean shaking his fist."
Maxwell Perkins, legendary Scribner's editor of Fitzgerald, Hemingway, and Wolfe, liked Jones's description of Prewitt and the plan
to make him the tragic hero/scapegoat of a peacetime army novel.
In February 1945, he asked Jones to drop work on his first novel,
They Shall Inherit the Laughter (see Appendix), and begin work on
what became *From Here to Eternity*. With the encouragement of
Perkins, and (after Perkins's death in 1947) Scribner's editors
Burroughs Mitchell and John Hall Wheelock, Jones worked on his
huge manuscript for over five years. He was also aided immensely
by a couple in his hometown of Robinson, Illinois, Harry and
Lowney Handy, who added a room to their house for Jones to live
and work in.

In 1951, after a big publicity campaign, the novel was published
and soon rose to the top of the best-seller list. It remained there for
months, despite, and partly because of, what the *Saturday Review*
called its "spectacularly indecent vocabulary." Praise came from
established writers such as John Dos Passos and John P. Marquand
and from the young author of *The Naked and the Dead* (1948), until
then the most successful World War II novel. Norman Mailer called
Eternity "a big fist of a book," and said it was "one of the best of the
'war novels,' and in certain facets is perhaps the best." In 1952 it
won the National Book Award; in 1953 it was made into a
fabulously successful movie that won eight Academy Awards,
including Best Picture.

The majority of the ten excerpts from *Eternity* that follow deal
with Prewitt. First Sgt. Milton Anthony Warden and Mess Sgt.
Maylon Stark, the other two characters Jones carries through the
trilogy, also appear several times, and the longest single excerpt in
the anthology—Jones's magnificent account of the Japanese strafing
runs on Schofield Barracks—is given from Warden's point of view.
But Prewitt is the central figure, as Jones's previously unpublished
notes to the novel confirm (see Appendix), and his decline,
degradation, and death comprise the essential action of these
excerpts. Even so, not every key linkage—his killing of Fatso
Judson, for example—could be included. Prewitt's fate is also tied
in with several other important characters who are presented here,
more or less: Karen Holmes, Capt. "Dynamite" Holmes, Chief
Choate, Ike Galovitch, Jack Malloy and the indestructible Angelo
Maggio, "formerly of Gimbel's Basement." He was able to make so

much of these characters and their life in D Quad and the stone quarry and the bars and brothels of Honolulu because, as Joan Didion has put it, "James Jones had known a great simple truth: the Army was nothing less than life itself."

[The Profession: Prewitt]

ROBERT E. LEE PREWITT had learned to play a guitar long before he ever learned to bugle or to box. He learned it as a boy, and with it he learned a lot of blues songs and laments. In the Kentucky Mountains along the West Virginia Line life led him swiftly to that type of music. And this was long before he ever seriously considered becoming a member of The Profession.

In the Kentucky Mountains along the West Virginia Line guitar playing is not considered the accomplishment it is in most places. Every wellbred boy learns to chord a guitar when he is still small enough to hold it like a string bass. The boy Prewitt loved the songs because they gave him something, an understanding, a first hint that pain might not be pointless if you could only turn it into something. The songs stayed with him, but the guitar playing did not give him anything. It left him cold. He had no call for it at all.

He had no call for boxing either. But he was very fast and had an incredible punch, developed by necessity on the bum, before he entered The Profession. People always find those things out. They tend to become manifest. Especially in The Profession where sports are the nourishment of life and boxing is the most manly sport. Beer, in The Profession, is the wine of life.

To tell the truth, he had no call for The Profession. At least not then. As a dissatisfied son of a Harlan County miner he just naturally gravitated toward it, the only profession open to him.

He really had no call for anything until the first time he handled a bugle.

It started as a joke on a battalion beer convention and he only held it and blew a couple of bleats, but he knew at once that this was something different. It was somehow something sacred, the way you sit out at night and watch the stars and your eye consciously spans that distance and you wonder if you're sitting on an electron that revolves around a proton in a series of infinite universes, and you suddenly see how strange a tree would look to one who had never lived upon the earth.

He had wild visions, for a moment, of having once played a herald's trumpet for the coronations and of having called the legions to bed down around the smoking campfires in the long blue evenings of old Palestine. It was then he remembered that hint about pointlessness that the blues songs and laments had given him; he knew then that if he could play a bugle the way he thought a bugle he would have found his justification. He even realized, all at once, holding the bugle, the reason why he had ever got into The Profession at all, a problem that had stumped him up till then. That was actually how much it meant to him. He recognized he had a call.

He had heard a lot about The Profession as a boy. He would sit on the railless porch with the men when the long tired, dirty-faced evening rolled down the narrow valley, thankfully blotting out the streets of shacks, and listen to them talk. His Uncle John Turner, tall, raw-boned and spare, had run away as a boy and joined The Profession, to find Adventure. He had been a corporal in the Philippine Insurrection.

The boy Prewitt's father and the others had never been beyond the hills, and in the boy's mind, already even then bludgeoning instinctively against the propaganda of the walls of slag as the foetus kicks frantically against the propaganda of the womb, this fact of The Profession gave to Uncle John Turner a distinction no one else could claim.

The tall man would squat on his hams in the little yard—the coal dirt was too thick on all the ground to sit—and in an abortive effort to dispel the taste of what the Encyclopedias call "Black Gold" he would tell them stories that proved conclusively there was a world beyond the slag heaps and these trees whose leaves were always coated black.

Uncle John would tell about the Moro juramentados, how their native Moslem datu would call the single volunteer up before the tribe and anoint him and consecrate him to the heaven he was getting ready to attend and then, practically, bind his balls and pecker with wet rawhide before he ran amok, so that the pain of the contraction of the drying leather would keep him going. That was why, said Uncle John, the Army first adopted the .45. Because six slugs from a .38 Special would not knock a juramentado down. And, in his condition, obviously, you had to knock him down to stop him. The .45 was guaranteed to knock any man off his feet, if it only hit the tip of his little finger, or your money back. And the Army, said Uncle John, had been using it effectively ever since.

The boy Prewitt doubted that about the little finger, but he liked the story. It impressed him with a sense of seeing history made, as did the stories of young Hugh Drum and young John Pershing and the expedition on Mindanao and the trek around the edge of Lake Lanao. They proved the Moros were good men, worthy opponents of his Uncle John. Sometimes when his Uncle John had swilled enough white lightning he would sing the song about the "monkeys have no tails in Zamboanga" that had been his Regimental song. And he would alternate the Philippines with Mexico and stories of an older, much less informal Blackjack and of young Sandy Patch, not yet too great a man to be informal.

But Uncle John always made it plain, especially to the boy, the reason why he had come home in 1916 and stayed in Harlan mining coal all during the World War. Uncle John wanted to be a farmer, and it was probably this that kept him from acquiring that Great, American, Retrospective Spirit of Romance.

It would be nice to think of a grubby miner's son with a dirt-rimmed mouth possessed of so burning a dream to see the world and help make history, via The Profession, that he refused to have it thwarted. But Uncle John Turner was not the kind of man who'd let his nephew dream of a life of adventure, via The Profession, and have it on his conscience.

It happened quite, quite differently.

When the boy Prewitt was in the seventh grade his mother died of the consumption. There was a big strike on that winter and she died in the middle of it. If she had had her choice, she could have picked a better time. Her husband, who was a striker, was in the county jail with two stab wounds in his chest and a fractured skull.

And her brother, Uncle John, was dead, having been shot by several deputies. Years later there was a lament written and sung about that day. They said blood actually ran like rainwater in the gutters of Harlan that day. They gave Uncle John Turner the top billing, a thing he doubtless would have decried with vigor.

The boy Prewitt saw that battle, at least as near as any man can ever come to seeing any battle. The only thing he saw and could remember was his Uncle John. He and two other boys stood in a yard to watch until one of the other boys got hit with a stray bullet, then they ran home and did not watch the rest.

Uncle John had had his .45 and he shot three deputies, two of them as he was going down. He only got to fire three times. The boy was interested in proving the guarantee of the .45, but since all the deputies were hit in the head they would have gone down anyway. Uncle John did not hit any of them on the tip of the little finger.

So when his mother died there was nobody to stop him except his father in the jail, and since his father had beaten him again just two days before the battle he did not figure his father counted either. Having made up his mind, he took the two dollars that was in the grocery jar, telling himself his mother would not need it and it would be good enough for his father and would help to put them square, and he left. The neighbors took up a collection for his mother's funeral but he did not want to see it.

The disintegration of a family, where the family still has meaning, emotes tragedy in every one. Its consolatory picture is of the surviving member freed to follow his lifelong ambition, a sort of Dick Whittington with a bandanna tied to a stick but no cat. But it was not this with him either, any more than it was the burning dream to see the world and help make history. He had never heard of a Lord Mayor and he had no ambition. The Profession, and the bugle, came much later.

As she was dying his mother made him promise her one thing. "Promise me one thing, Robert," she wheezed at him. "From your father you got pride and endurance and I knowed that you would need it. But one of you would have kilt the other if it hatn't of been for me. And now, I wont be standin atween you no more."

"I'll promise anything you want, ma, whatever you say for me to promise, whatever it is you say," the boy, watching her die in front of him, looking at her above his haze of disbelief for signs of immortality, said woodenly.

"A deathbed promise is the most sacred one there is," she hawked at him from the lungs that were almost, but not quite, filled up yet, "and I want you to make me this promise on my deathbed: Promise me you wont never hurt nobody unless its absolute a must, unless you jist have to do it."

"I promise you," he vowed to her, still waiting for the angels to appear. "Are you afraid?" he said.

"Give me your hand on it, boy. It is a deathbed promise, and you'll never break it."

"Yes maam," he said, giving her his hand, drawing it back quickly, afraid to touch the death he saw in her, unable to find anything beautiful or edifying or spiritually uplifting in this return to God. He watched a while longer for signs of immortality. No angels came, however, there was no earthquake, no cataclysm, and it was not until he had thought over often this first death that he had had a part in that he discovered the single uplifting thing about it, that being the fact that in this last great period of fear her thought had been upon his future, rather than her own. He wondered often after that about his own death, how it would come, how it would feel, what it would be like to know that this breath, now, was the last one. It was hard to accept that he, who was the hub of this known universe, would cease to exist, but it was an inevitability and he did not shun it. He only hoped that he would meet it with the same magnificent indifference with which she who had been his mother met it. Because it was there, he felt, that the immortality he had not seen was hidden.

She was a women of an older time set down in a later world and walled off from knowing it by mountains. If she had known the effect of the promise she exacted from her son, upon his life, she would not have asked it of him. Such promises belong in an older, simpler, less complex and more naïve, forgotten time.

Three days after he was seventeen he got accepted for enlistment. Having been used to certain elemental comforts back in Harlan, he had already been turned down a number of times all over the country because he was too young. Then he would go back on the bum awhile and try some other city. He was on the East Coast at the time he was accepted and they sent him to Fort Myer. That was in 1936. There were lots of other men enlisting then.

It was at Myer he learned to box, as distinguished from fight. He was really very fast, even for a bantamweight, and with that punch, all out of proportion to his size, he found he might have a future in The Profession. It got him a PFC in the first year of his hitch, a thing that, in 1936, when getting any rating at all in your first hitch was considered a sin that made for laxity of character by every soldier who had begun his second three-year term, bespoke his talent.

It was also at Myer where he first handled the bugle. It made a change in him right away and he dropped out of the boxing squad to get himself apprenticed to the Bugle Corps. When he truly found a thing he never wasted time, and since he was still a long ways from being a Class I fighter then the coach did not think it worth his while to hold him. The whole squad watched him go without any sense of loss, figuring that he did not have the staying power, that the going was too rough, that he would never be a champion like Lew Jenkins from Fort Bliss, as they would be, and marked him off the list.

He was too busy then to care much what they thought. With the call driving him he worked hard for a year and a half and earned himself another, totally different reputation. At the end of that year and a half he had earned himself a rating of First and Third and he was good, good enough to play the Armistice Day Taps at Arlington, the Mecca of all Army buglers. He really had a call.

Arlington was the high point and it was a great experience. He had finally found his place and he was satisfied to settle into it. His enlistment was almost up by then and he planned to re-enlist at Myer. He planned to stay there in that Bugle Corps for his full thirty years. He could see ahead down the line, obviously, and quite clearly, how smoothly it would go and the fullness it would be. That was before the other people began to come into it.

Up until then it had only been himself. Up to then it had been a private wrestle between him and himself. Nobody else much entered into it. After the people came into it he was, of course, a different man. Everything changed then and he was no longer the virgin, with the virgin's right to insist upon platonic love. Life, in time, takes every maidenhead, even if it has to dry it up; it does not matter how the owner wants to keep it. Up to then he had been the young idealist. But he could not stay there. Not after the other people entered into it.

At Myer all the boys hung out in Washington on their passes and he hung out there too. That was where he met the society girl. He picked her up at a bar, or she picked him up. It was his first introduction into the haute monde, outside of the movies, and she was good looking and definitely high class, was going to college there, to be a journalist. It was not a great love or anything like that; half of it, for him, for both of them, was that the miner's son was dining at the Ritz, just like the movies said. She was a nice kid but very bitter and they had a satisfying affair. They had no poor little rich girl trouble because he did not mind spending her money and they did not worry and stew about an unladylike marriage. They had good fun for six months, up until she gave him the clap.

When he got out of the GU Clinic his job was gone and his rating with it. The army did not have sulfa then, it could not make up its mind to adopt the doubtful stuff until the war, and it was a long and painful process, getting cured, with lots of long-handled barbs and cutters. One boy he met there was on his fourth trip through the Clinic.

Unofficially, nobody really minded the clap. It was a joke to those who had never had it and to those who had been over it for a little while. No worse than a bad cold, they said. Apparently the only time it was not a joke was when you had it. And instead of hurting your unofficial reputation it boosted you a notch, it was like getting a wound stripe. They said that in Nicaragua they used to give out Purple Hearts.

But officially it hurt your Service Record, and it automatically lost you your rating. On your papers it put a stigma on you. When he put in to get back in the Bugle Corps, he found that while he was away they had suddenly gone overstrength. He went back on straight duty for the rest of his enlistment.

Already the other people were beginning to come into it. It seemed that any man could drive a car, but the only man who never had a wreck was the guy who drove not only for himself but for the other driver too.

When his time was up they tried to re-enlist him for the same outfit, there at Myer. He wanted that hundred and fifty dollar bonus, but he wanted to get as far away from there as he could go. That was why he picked Hawaii.

He went up once, to see his society girl before he left. He had heard guys say they would kill any woman who gave them the clap; or they would go out and give it to every woman they could lay; or they would beat her up until she wished she had of died. But having the clap did not make him bitter against all women or anything like that. It was a chance you took with every woman, white, black or yellow. What disillusioned him, what he did not understand, was that this dose of the clap should have cost him his bugle when he still could play it just as well as ever, and also that a society girl had given it to him. And what made him mad was that she did not tell him first and leave it up to him to choose, then it would not have been her fault. He found out, that last time he went to see her, after he had convinced her he was not going to beat her up, that she had not known she had it. After she saw he wouldn't hit her, she cried and she was very sorry. It was a society boy she had known since she was a kid. She was disillusioned, too. And she was having a hell of a time getting herself cured, and on the sly, so her parents would not know. And she was truly very sorry.

When he arrived in Schofield Barracks he was still very bitter about the bugle. It was this that made him go back to fighting, here in the Pineapple Army where fighting was even more prolific than it was at Myer. That was his error, but it did not seem so then. The bitterness about the bugle, added to all the other bitternesses, gave him something. Also he had put on more weight and filled out more until he was a welterweight. He won the Company Smoker championship of the 27th and for that he got a corporalcy. Then he went on, when the Division season opened, to make Schofield Class I and become the runner-up in the welterweight division. For that, and because they expected him to win it the next year, he got a sergeantcy. Also, the bitternesses in some subtle way seemed to make him more likeable to everyone, although he never did quite figure that one out.

Everything would probably have gone on like that indefinitely, since he had convinced himself that bugling was nothing, had it not been for that deathbed promise to his mother and for Dixie Wells. And actually it happened after the season was over. Perhaps it was his temperament, but he seemed to have a very close working alliance with irony.

Dixie Wells was a middleweight who loved boxing and lived for boxing. He had enlisted because business was not so good for fighters during the Depression, and because he wanted time to mature his style and season it without being overmatched in some ham and egger, and without having to live on the beans a ham and egger has to eat while he is trying to work up to the big time. He planned to come out of the Army and go right into the upper brackets. A lot of people on the Outside had their eye on him and he was already having fights downtown in Honolulu at the Civic Auditorium.

Dixie liked to work with Prewitt because of the other's speed and Prewitt learned a lot from Dixie. They worked together often. Dixie was a heavy middle, but then Prewitt was a heavy welter. They are very professional about those things in the Army; they keep every pound that they can squeeze; they always figure a man for ten pounds more than what he weighs in at when they match him; they dry him out and then after he had weighed in they feed him steak and lots of water.

It was Dixie who asked him to work this time, because he had a fight coming up downtown. Also, it was Dixie who wanted to use the six ounce gloves, and they never wore headgear anyway.

Things like that happen more often than any one suspects. Prew knew that, and there was no reason why he should feel guilty. He had known a wizard lightweight at Myer who also had a future. Until he went into a civilian gym half-tight one night and wanted to put them on. They used new gloves, and the man who tied them on forgot to cut the metal tips off the laces. Gloves often come untied. This was like the old kid game of crack the whip, a wrist flick drove the metal into the wizard lightweight's eye like an arrow into a target. The fluid of his eye ran down over his cheek and he had to buy a glass one, and as a wizard lightweight he was through. Things like that just happen, every now and then.

Prew was set, flat on his feet when he caught Dixie wide with this no more than ordinarily solid cross. Dixie just happened to be standing solid too. Maybe he had heard something. From the way he fell, dead weight, a falling ingot or a sack of meal dropped from the haymow that shudders the barn and bursts its own seams, Prew knew. Dixie lit square on his face and did not roll over. Fighters do not light on their faces any more than judo men. Prew jerked back his hand and stared at it, like a kid who touched the stove. Then he went downstairs to get the Doc.

Dixie Wells was in a coma for a week but he finally came out of it. The only thing was that he was blind. The doctor at the Station Hospital said something about concussion and a fracture, a pressure on or injury to a nerve. Prew went up to see him twice but after the second time he could not go back. The second time they got to talking about fighting and Dixie cried. It was seeing the tears coming out of those eyes that could not see that made him stay away.

Dixie did not hate him, nor was he bitter, he was just unhappy. As soon as he was able, he told Prew that last time, they would ship him back to the States, to an old soldier's home, or to one of Hines's VA hospitals which was even worse.

Prew had seen a lot of those things happen. If you hang around any profession long enough you will learn about the things the brethren never talk about to the public. But just seeing them had been like it is with getting wounded, this man's handless arms have no relation to yourself, it happens to the other guy, but never you.

He felt a great deal like an amnesia case must feel, upon waking in some foreign land where he had never been and hears the language that he cannot understand, having only a vague, dream-haunted picture of how he ever got there. How came you here? he asks himself, among these strange outlandish people? but is afraid to listen to the answer himself gives him back.

My god! he wondered. Are you a misfit? What happened to you does not bother any of these others. Why should you be so different? But fighting had never been his calling, bugling was his calling. For what reason then was he here, posing as a fighter?

It would probably, after Dixie Wells, have been the same whether or not he had been haunted by his promise to his mother. But the old, ingenuous, Baptist-like promise was the clincher. Because the uninitiated boy had taken it, not like a Baptist, but literally.

One way, he thought, the whole thing of ring fighting was hurting somebody else, deliberately, and particularly when it was not necessary. Two men who have nothing against each other get in a ring and try to hurt each other, to provide vicarious fear for people with less guts than themselves. And to cover it up they called it sport and gambled on it. He had never looked at it that way before, and if there was any single thing he could not endure it was to be a dupe.

Since the boxing season was already over he could have waited until next December before he told them his decision. He could have kept his mouth shut and rested on his hard-earned laurels, until the time came round again to prove his right to them. But he was not honest enough to do a thing like that. He was not honest enough to dupe them, when he himself refused to be their dupe. He had not the makings of that honest man to whom success comes naturally.

At first when he told them why he was quitting they would not believe him. Then, later when they saw that it was true, they decided he had only been in the sport for what he could get out of it and did not love it like they did, and with righteous indignation had him busted. Then, still later, when he did not come around, they really did not understand it. They began to build him up then, they began to heckle him, they called him in and talked to him man to man, told him how good he was, explained what hope we have in you and are you going to let us down, enumerated what he owed the regiment, showed him how he ought to be ashamed. It was then they really began not to let him alone. And it was then he transferred.

He transferred to this other regiment because it had the best Bugle Corps in the Lower Post. He did not have any trouble. As soon as they heard him play they got him transferred quick. They had really, truly, wanted a good bugler there.

(Chapter 2)

[Reporting In]

"PRIVATE PREWITT reporting to the Company Commander as ordered, Sir," he mouthed the formula, whatever humanness there was inside him falling out, leaving only a juiceless meatless shell.

Capt Dynamite Holmes, who was a favorite with the Islands sport fans, directed his long, high-foreheaded face with its high cheekbones and eagle's nose and the hair combed sideways across the just beginning bald spot, sternly at the man before him and picked up the Special Orders that announced the transfer without looking at them.

"At ease," he said.

His desk was right before the door, and at right angles on the left was the First Sergeant's desk, where Milt Warden sat with folded elbows leaning on it. As he moved his left foot and crossed his hands behind his back, Prew spared him one swift glance. Warden stared back at him, half-gleefully, half-foreboding; he seemed to be poised and waiting for his chance.

Capt Holmes swung his swivel chair to the right and stared sternly out the window for a moment, offering Prew a profile of the jutting jaw, grim mouth, and sharp commanding nose. Then suddenly he swung back around, the swivel creaking, and began to speak.

"I always make it a policy to talk to my new men, Prewitt," he said sternly. "I dont know what you've been used to in the Bugle Corps, but in my outfit we run it by the book. Any man who fucksup gets broken—quick and hard. The Stockade is the place for fuckups until they learn to soldier."

He paused and stared at Prewitt sternly, and crossed his booted legs whose spurs jangled punctuation to the warning. Capt Holmes was warming to his subject. Here, said the long boned, eagle's face to Prew, is a soldier who is not afraid to talk to his men in their own language, who does not mince the words, and who understands his men.

"I have," he said, "a damned fine smoothrunning outfit. I do not allow anything to bitch it up. But—if a man does his work, and keeps his nose clean, does as I say, he'll get along. Plenty of room for advancement here, because in this organization there is no favoritism. I make it my business to see that each man gets just what he earns. No more, no less.

"You start with a clean slate, Prewitt. What you do with it is up to you.

"Understood?"

"Yes, Sir," Prew said.

"Good," said Capt Holmes, and nodded sternly.

Milt Warden, at his own desk, was watching the progress of this conference that was not new to him with acumen. Crap! cried the king, he thought, and twenty thousand royal subjects squatted and strained, for in those days the king's word was law! His face straight, he grinned at Prew with his eyebrows, and a devilish pixy peered out from behind his face with unholy glee.

"To get a rating in my Company," Capt Holmes was saying sternly, "a man has got to know his stuff. He has to soldier. He has to show me he's got it on the ball." He looked up sharply.

"Understood?"

"Yes, Sir," Prew said.

"Good," said Capt Holmes. "Understood. Its always important for an officer and his men to understand each other." Then he pushed his chair back and smiled at Prewitt, handsomely. "Glad to have you aboard, Prewitt," he smiled, "as our colleagues in the navy say. I can always use a good man in my outfit and I'm glad to have you."

"Thank you, Sir," Prew said.

"How would you like to be my Company bugler, temporarily?" Holmes paused to light himself a cigarette. "I saw your fight with Connors of the 8th Field in the Bowl last year," he said. "A damned fine show. Damned fine. With any luck you should have won it. I thought for a while in there, in the second round, you were going to knock him out."

"Thank you, Sir," Prew said. Capt Holmes was talking almost joyously now. Here it comes, Prew told himself; well, bud, you asked for it, now figure it out. Figure it out yourself, he thought. Better yet, just let him figure it out.

"If I'd known you were in the Regiment last December when the season started I'd have looked you up," Holmes smiled.

Prew said nothing. On his left he could feel, not hear, The Warden snorting softly with disgust as he began to study a sheaf of papers with the elaborate I'm-not-with-him air of a sober man whose friend is drunk.

"I can use a good bugler, Prewitt," Holmes smiled. "My regular Company bugler hasnt the experience. And his apprentice only has his job because he's such a fuckup I was afraid he'd shoot somebody on a problem." He laughed and looked at Prew, inviting him to join it.

Milt Warden, who was the one who had suggested Salvatore Clark for the apprentice bugler, after Clark almost shot himself on guard, went on studying his papers, but his eyebrows quivered.

"A Pfc rating goes with the job," Holmes said to Prew. "I'll have Sergeant Warden post the order, first thing tomorrow."

He waited then, but Prew said nothing, watching the dry ironic sunlight coming through the open window, wondering how long now it would take him to catch on, unable to believe that they had not heard it all before, and feeling how his uniform that had been fresh at eight o'clock was damp and musty now with sweat, beginning to be soaked.

"I realize," Holmes smiled indulgently, "a Pfc isnt very much, but our TO quota of noncoms is all filled up. We have two noncoms who are shorttimers though," he said. "They'll be leaving on next month's boat.

"Its too bad the season's almost over or you could start training this afternoon, but the schedule ends the last of February. But then," he smiled, "if you dont fight Regimental this year, you'll be eligible for Company Smokers in the fall.

"Have you seen any of our boys in the Bowl this year?" he asked. "We've got some good ones, I'm confident we'll keep the trophy. I'd like to get your opinion on a couple of them."

"I havent been to any of the fights this year, Sir," Prew said.

"What?" Holmes said, not believing it. "You havent?" He stared at Prew a moment curiously, then looked at Warden knowingly. He picked up a freshly sharpened pencil from his desk and studied it. "Why is it," Capt Holmes said softly, "that you've been in the Regiment a whole year, Prewitt, and nobody knew a thing about it? I should have thought you would have come around to see me, since I am the boxing coach and since we're the Division champions."

Prew moved his weight from one foot to the other and took one deep breath. "I was afraid you'd want me to go out for the squad, Sir," he said. There it is, he thought, its out now, you've got it now. Now he can carry the ball. He felt relieved.

"Of course," Holmes said. "Why not? We can use a man as good as you are. Especially since you're a welterweight. We're poor in that division. If we lose the championship this year, it will be because we lost the welterweight division."

"Because I left the 27th because I had quit fighting, Sir," Prew said.

Again Holmes looked at Warden knowingly, this time apologetically, as if now he could believe it since he'd heard it from the man himself, before he spoke. "Quit fighting?" he said. "What for?"

"Maybe you heard about what happened with Dixie Wells, Sir,"

Prew said, hearing Warden lay his papers down, feeling Warden grinning.

Holmes stared at him innocently, eyes wide with it. "Why, no," he said. "What was that?"

Prew went through the story for him, for both of them, standing there with his feet one foot apart and his hands clasped behind his back, and feeling all the time he spoke it was superfluous, that both of them already knew all about the deal already, yet forced to play the role that Holmes had set for him.

"Thats too bad," Holmes said, when he had finished. "I can understand why you might feel that way. But those things happen, in this game. A man has got to accept that possibility when he fights."

"Thats one reason why I decided I would quit, Sir," Prew said.

"But on the other hand," Holmes said, much less warmly now, "look at it this way. What if all fighters felt like that?"

"They dont, Sir," Prew said.

"I know," Holmes said, much less warmly still. "What would you have us do? Disband our fighting program because one man got hurt?"

"No, Sir," Prew said. "I didnt say..."

"You might as well," Holmes said, "say stop war because one man got killed. Our fighting season is the best morale builder that we have off here away from home."

"I dont want it disbanded, Sir," Prew said, and then felt the absurdity to which he had been forced. "But I dont see," he went on doggedly, "why any man should fight unless he wanted to."

Holmes studied him with eyes that had grown curiously flat, and were growing flatter. "And that was why you left the 27th?"

"Yes, Sir. Because they tried to make me go on fighting."

"I see." Capt Holmes seemed all at once to have lost interest in this interview. He looked down at his watch, remembering suddenly he had a riding date with Major Thompson's wife at 12:30. He stood up and picked up his hat from the IN file on his desk.

It was a fine hat, a soft expensive unblocked Stetson, with its brim bent up fore and aft, its four dents creased to a sharp point at the peak, and it bore the wide chinstrap of the Cavalry, instead of the thin strap authorized for the Infantry that went behind the head. Beside it lay his riding crop he always carried. He picked that up, too. He had not always been an Infantryman.

"Well," he said, with very little interest, "theres nothing in the ARs that says a man must be a boxer if he doesnt want to. You'll find that we wont put any pressure on you here, like they did in the 27th. I dont believe in that sort of thing. If you dont want to fight we dont want you on our squad." He walked to the door and then turned back sharply.

"Why did you leave the Bugle Corps?"

"It was a personal matter, Sir," Prew said, taking refuge in the taboo that says a man's, even a private's, personal matters are his own affair.

"But you were transferred at the Chief Bugler's request," Holmes told him. "What kind of trouble was it you were in, over there?"

"No, Sir," Prew said. "No trouble. It was a personal matter," he repeated.

"Oh," Holmes said, "I see." That it might be a personal matter he had not considered and he looked uneasily at Warden, not sure of how to approach this angle, but Warden, who had been following everything with interest, was suddenly staring unconcernedly at the wall. Holmes cleared his throat, but Warden did not get it.

"Have you anything you wish to add, Sergeant?" he had to ask him, finally.

"Who? me? Why, yes, Sir," exploded Warden with that sudden violence. He was, quite suddenly, in a state of indignation. His brows hooked upward, two harriers ready to pounce upon the rabbit.

"What kind of rating you have in the Bugle Corps, Prewitt?"

"First and Fourth," Prew said, looking at him steadily.

Warden looked at Holmes and raised his eyebrows eloquently.

"You mean," he said, astounded, "you took a bust from First-Fourth to transfer to a rifle company as a buckass private, just because you like to hike?"

"I didnt have no trouble," Prew said stolidly, "if thats what you mean."

"Or," Warden grinned, "was it just because you couldnt stand to bugle?"

"It was a personal matter," Prew said.

"That's up to the Compny Commander's discretion to decide," Warden corrected instantly. Holmes nodded. And Warden grinned at Prewitt velvetly. "Then you didnt transfer because Mr Houston made young MacIntosh First Bugler? Over you?"

"I was transferred," Prew said, staring at the other. "It was a personal matter."

Warden leaned back in his chair and snorted softly. "What a helluva thing to transfer over. Kids in the Army we got now. Someday you punks will learn that good jobs dont grow on trees."

In the electric antagonism that flashed between the two of them and hung heavy like ozone in the air Capt Holmes had been forgotten. He broke in now, as was his right.

"It looks to me," he said indifferently, "as if you were fast acquiring a reputation as a bolshevik, Prewitt. Bolsheviks never get anywhere in the Army. You'll find that straight duty in this outfit is considerably tougher than SD in the Bugle Corps."

"I've done straight duty before, Sir," Prew said. "In the Infantry. I dont mind doing it again." You liar, he told himself, like hell you do not mind it. How is it that people make you lie so easily?

"Well," Holmes said, pausing for the effect, "it looks as though you'll get a chance to do it." But he was no longer jocular. "You're not a recruit and you should know that in the Army its not the individual that counts. Every man has certain responsibilities to fulfill. Moral responsibilities that go beyond the ARs' regulations. It might look as though I were a free agent, but I'm not. No matter how high you get there is always somebody over you, and who knows more about it all than you do.

"Sergeant Warden will take care of you and get you assigned to a squad." Nothing more was said about the Company bugler's job. He turned to Warden. "Is there anything else for me to take care of today, Sergeant?"

"Yes, Sir," Warden, who had been listening to this abstract conversation, said violently. "The Compny Fund Report has got to be checked and made out. Its due tomorrow morning."

"You make it out," Holmes said, undisturbed by the regulation that says no one but an officer may touch the Company Fund. "Fix it up and I'll be in early tomorrow to sign it. I havent time to bother with details. Is that all?"

"*No*, Sir," Warden said vehemently.

"Well, whatever it is, you fix it. If theres anything that has to go in this afternoon, sign my name. I wont be back." He looked at Warden angrily and turned back to the door, ignoring Prewitt.

"Yes, *Sir*," Warden raged. "Ten-nsh-HUT!" he bawled, bellowing it at the top of his lungs in the smallness of the room.

"Carry on," Holmes said. He touched his crop to hat brim and disappeared. A moment later his voice came in the open window.

"Sergeant Warden!"

"*Yes*, Sir!" Warden bellowed, jumping to the window.

"Whats the matter with this outfit? This place needs policing. Look there. And there. And over by the garbage rack. Is this a barracks or a pigpen? I want it policed up! Immediately!"

"Yes, *Sir*!" bellowed Warden, "Maggio!"

Maggio's gnomelike body bobbed up in its undershirt before the window. "Yesser."

"Maggio," said Capt Holmes. "Wheres your goddam fatigue blouse? Get your blouse and put it on. This is no goddamned bathing beach."

"Yessir," Maggio said. "I'll get it, Sir."

"Maggio," Warden bellowed. "Get the other KPs and police the goddam area. Dint you hear what the Compny Commander said?"

"Okay, Sarge," said Maggio resignedly.

Warden leaned his elbows on the sill and watched Holmes's broad back move through the midst of Dog Company, called to attention by their duty sergeant. "Carry on," Holmes thundered. After Holmes had passed, the blue-dressed figures sat back down to go on with their stoppage drill.

"The hell for leather Cavalryman," Warden muttered. "Errol Flynn with fifty extra pounds." He walked deliberately over to his desk and smashed his fist into his own rigidly blocked, flat-peaked issue hat hanging on the wall. "The son of a bitch'd try to ship me down if I bent up my hat like his." Then he went back to the window.

Holmes was climbing the outside stair to Regimental Hq, going up to Col Delbert's office. Warden had a theory about officers: Being an officer would make a son of a bitch out of Christ himself. And they had you by the nuts. You couldnt do a thing. That was why they were such ones.

But beyond the Hq stairs the bedroom window of Holmes's house peered at him coyly through the truck entrance. And maybe right now, behind that unrevealing window, she was languorously undressing the long flowing milk of that blonde body, garment by garment like a stripper in a honkytonk, to take a bath or something. Maybe she had a man in there with her now.

Warden felt his chest swelling potently with maleness, as if a great balloon were being blown up inside him. He turned from the window and sat back down.

Prew was waiting for him, standing quietly before the desk, feeling worn out now and very tired, feeling the sweat still dripping slowly from his armpits with the strain of subduing his own fear and disagreeing with authority. The collar of the shirt that had been fresh at eight o'clock was wilted and the sweat had soaked clear through the back. Only a little more of this and you are through, he told himself. Then you can relax.

Warden picked up a paper from his desk and began to read it, as if he were alone. When he finally looked up there was hurt surprise and indignation on his face, as if wondering how this man had got into his office uninvited and without his knowing it.

"Well?" Milt Warden said. "What the hell do you want?"

Prew stared at him levelly, not answering, not disconcerted. And for a time both were silent, studying each other, like two opposing checker\players taking each other's measure before the game began. There was no open dislike in the face of either, only a sort of cold inherent antagonism. They were like two philosophers starting from the same initial premise of life and each, by irrefutable argument, arriving at a diametrically opposite conclusion. Yet these two conclusions were like twin brothers of the same flesh and heritage and blood.

Warden broke the spell. "You havent changed a bit, have you, Prewitt?" he said sarcastically. "Havent learned a thing. Fools rush in where angels fear to re-enlist, as some great wit once said. All a man has to do is to leave it up to you and you'll put your own head in the noose for him."

"A man like you, you mean," Prew said.

"No, not me. I like you."

"I love you too," Prew said. "And you aint changed none either."

"Put his own head in the noose," Warden shook his head sorrowfully. "Thats what you did just now; you know that, dont you? When you turned down Dynamite's Boxing Squad?"

"I thought you didnt like jockstraps and SD men," Prew said.

"I don't," Warden said. "But did it ever occur to you that in a way I'm an SD man myself? I dont do straight duty."

"Yeah," Prew said. "I've thought of that. Thats why I couldnt see why you hated us guys in the Bugle Corps so much."

"Because," Warden grinned, "SD men and jockstraps are all the same, fugitives from straight duty. They aint got what it takes so they ride the gravytrain."

"And make life a hellhole for every one they can, like you."

"No," Warden said. "Guess again. I dont make hell for nobody. I'm only the instrument of a laughing Providence. Sometimes I dont like it myself, but I couldnt help it if I was born smart."

"We cant all be smart," Prew said.

"Thats right," Warden nodded. "We cant. Its a shame too. You been in the army what now? Five years? Fivenahalf? Its about time for you to get over being a punk ree-croot and begin to get smart, aint it? That is, if you're ever goin to."

"Maybe I'd ruther not be smart."

Warden unfolded his arms and proceeded to light a cigaret, lazily, taking his time. "You had a soft deal as a bugler," he said, "but you toss it up because Queer Houston hurt your feelins. And then you turn Holmes down when he wants you for his boxing squad," he said, mincing the words. "You should of took him up, Prewitt. You wont like straight duty in my compny."

"I can soljer with any man," Prew said. "I'll take my chances."

"Okay," Warden said. "So what? Since when has bein a good soljer had anything to do with the Army? Do you think bein a good soljer will get you a sergeant's rating in this outfit? after what you just pulled? It wont even get you Pfc.

"You're the kind of soljer ought to be jockstrappin, Prewitt. Then you could get your name in all the Honolulu papers and be a hero. Because you'll never make a real soljer. Never in God's world.

"When you change your mind and decide you might as well jockstrap for Dynamite after all, remember this: the jockstraps dont run this compny—in spite of Holmes.

"This aint A Compny now, Prewitt. This is G Compny, of which I am First Sergeant. I run this compny. Holmes is the CO, but he is like the rest of the officer class: a dumb bastard that signs papers an rides horses an wears spurs an gets stinking drunk up at the stinking Officers' Club. I'm the guy that runs this compny."

"Yeah?" Prew grinned. "Well, you aint doin a very goddam good job of it, buddy. If you run this outfit, how come Preem's the mess sergeant? And how come O'Hayer's the supply sergeant, when Leva does the work? And how come most every noncom in 'your compny' is one of Holmes's punchies? Dont give me that crap."

The whites of Warden's eyes turned slowly red. "You dont know the half of it yet, kid," he grinned. "Wait till you been here for a while. Theres a lot more yet. You dont know Galovitch, and Henderson, and Dhom, the duty sergeant."

He removed the cigaret from the corner of his mouth and knocked it with deliberate slowness on the ashtray. "But the point is, Holmes would strangle on his own spit if I wasnt here to swab out his throat for him." He stuffed the burning coal out savagely and then rose languidly like a stretching cat. "So at least we know where we stand," he said, "dont we, kid?"

(from Chapter 4)

[Warden and Karen Holmes]

SOMEBODY CALLED TO HIM from Choy's but he only waved and went on, out the front of the sallyport, crossing Waianae Avenue to the officers' quarters, walking along it through the rain till he came to the alley behind Holmes's corner house. He stopped under the shelter of a big old elm, grinning to himself because he was breathing so heavy, feeling the autumnal chill creep up to him under his raincoat when he stopped, thinking this was a fine day for it and that if she had taken all the others there was no reason why she shouldnt take him too, before he went up finally and knocked on the door.

Inside a longlegged black shadow moved across the dimness of the livingroom doorway cutting off the light, and he caught the scissor-flash of naked legs cutting the light and opening again in another step and his breath seemed to go very deep in his chest.

"Mrs Holmes," he called, knocking, his head pulled down between his shoulders in the rain.

The shadow moved again inside without sound and stepped through the door into the kitchen to become Karen Holmes in shorts and halter.

"What is it?" she said. "Oh. If it isnt Sergeant Warden. Hello,

Sergeant. You better step inside or you'll get wet. If you're looking for my husband, he isnt here."

"Oh," Warden said, opening the screendoor and jumping in past the water that ran off the eave. "And if I'm not looking for him?" he said.

"He still isnt here," Karen Holmes said. "If that does you any good."

"Well, I'm looking for him. You know where he is?"

"I havent the slightest idea. Perhaps at the Club, having a drink or two," she smiled thinly. "Or was it snort? I guess it was snort you said, wasnt it?"

"Ah," Warden said. "The Club. Why didnt I think of that? I got some papers its important for him to sign today."

He eyed her openly, traveling up the length of leg in the very short homemade-looking trunks, to the hollow of the hidden navel, to the breasts tight against the halter, to the woman's eyes that were watching his progress and his open admiration indifferently, without interest.

"Kind of chilly for trunks, aint it?" he said.

"Yes." Karen Holmes looked at him unsmiling. "Its cool today. Sometimes its very hard to keep warm, isnt it?" she said. "What is it you want, Sergeant?"

Warden felt his breath come in very slowly, and go very deep, clear down into his scrotum.

"I want to go to bed with you," he said, conversationally. That was how he had planned it, how he had wanted to say it, but now hearing it it sounded very foolish to him. He watched the eyes, in the unchanged face, widen only a little, so little that he almost missed it. A cool cool customer, Milton, he said to himself.

"All right," Karen Holmes said disinterestedly.

With Warden, standing dripping on the porch, it was as if he was listening to her but he did not hear her.

"What are the papers?" she said then, reaching for them. "Let me see them. Maybe I can help you."

Warden pulled them back, grinning, feeling the grin stiff on his face, masklike. "You wouldnt know anything about them. These are business."

"I always take an interest in my husband's business," Karen Holmes said.

"Yes," Warden grinned. "Yes, I sure bet you do. Does he take as big an interest in your business?"

"Do you want me to help you with them?"

"Can you sign his name?"

"Yes."

"So it looks like his own signature?"

"I dont know about that," she said, still not smiling. "I never tried."

"Well I can," Warden said. "I can do everything for him but wear his goddamned bars. At that I draw the line. But these papers go to Division and he's got to sign them himself."

"Then I'd better call the Club," she said, "hadnt I? That is where he is."

"Having a drink or two," Warden said.

"But I'll be glad to call him for you, Sergeant."

"To hell with that. I never like to disturb a man drinking. I could use a drink myself right now. Bad."

"But if its business," Karen Holmes said.

"Anyway, I dont think you'll find him at the Club. I got a faint suspicion he went to town with Colonel Delbert," Warden grinned at her.

Karen Holmes did not answer. She stared at him unsmiling from a cold reflective face that did not know he still was there.

"Well," he said. "Aint you going to ask me in?"

"Why, yes, Sergeant," Karen Holmes said. "Come right in."

She moved then, slowly, as if her joints had got rusty from standing still so long, and stepped back up the single step into the kitchen to let him in.

"What kind of drink do you want, Sergeant?"

"I dont care," he said. "Any drink'll do."

"You dont want a drink," Karen Holmes said. "You dont really want a drink. What you really want is this," she said, looking down at her own body and moving her hands out sideways like a sinner at the altar. "Thats what you really want. Isnt it? Thats what you all want. All all of you ever want."

Warden felt a shiver of fear run down his spine. What the hell is this, Milton? "Yes," he said. "Thats what I really want. But I'll take a drink too," he said.

"All right. But I wont mix it for you. You can mix it yourself or you can drink it straight." She sat down in a chair beside the enameled kitchen table and looked at him.

"Straight's all right," he said.

"The bottle's there," she pointed to a cupboard. "Get it yourself. I wont get it for you." She laid her hand flat on the cool smoothness of the table. "You can have it, Sergeant, but you'll have to do the work yourself."

Warden laid the papers on the table and got the bottle from the cupboard, thinking I can match that, baby. "You want one too?" he said. "You just wait," he said. "You'll help me."

"I dont think I want a drink," Karen Holmes said. Then, "Yes, perhaps I'd better. I'll probably need it, dont you think?"

"Yes," he said. "You probly will." There were glasses on the sink and he took two and poured them both half full, wondering what kind of a woman this one was anyway.

"Here," he said. "To the end of virginity."

"I'll drink to that," she raised her glass. She made a face from the liquor as she set it down. "You're taking an awful chance, you know," she said. "Do you really think its worth it? What if Dana should come home? I'm safe you know: my word is always better than an EM's word. I'd holler rape and you'd get twenty years, at Leavenworth."

"He wont," Warden grinned, repouring in her glass. "I know where he is. He probly wont be home at all tonight. Besides," he said, looking up from filling his own glass, "I got two buddies from PI at Leavenworth, I'd be among friends."

"What happened to them?" she asked, drinking what was in her glass, making another face at it.

"They got caught in a buggy with a colonel's wife by one of MacArthur's gook boy scouts."

"Both of them?"

He nodded. "And with the same dame. She picked them up, they said, but they still got twenty years. The gook was the colonel's orderly. But I've heard it said he did it out of jealousy."

Karen Holmes smiled tolerantly, but she did not laugh. "I think you're bitter, Sergeant." She set down her empty glass and lay back in the chair, sprawled. "My maid is liable to be home any time you know."

Warden shook his head, seeing in his mind a picture of her lying on a bed inviting him, now that his first insecurity was gone. "No she wont," he said. "Thursday's her day off. Today is Thursday."

"You think of everything, dont you, Sergeant?"

"I try," he said. "In my position you have to."

Karen Holmes picked up the papers from the table. "I guess we can dispense with these now, cant we? They're nothing, are they?"

"Yes, they are," he said. "They're letters. You dont think I'd bring something worthless, do you? so Holmes might see them? so you might use them as evidence when you turned me in? And you can call me Milt, now we're intimate."

"Thats what I like about you, Sergeant: You have confidence. Its also what I dislike about you." Slowly she tore the papers into little bits and dropped them in the wastebasket behind her. "Men and their confidence. You can consider these as the payment you had to make. You always pay, dont you?"

"Not if I can help it," Warden said, wondering again what all this amounted to anyway, not expecting anything like this. "I got carbons of those back at the office," he grinned, "so it wont be much work to fix them up."

"At least your confidence is real," she said. "Not false confidence, or bravado—many men have that. Pour me another drink. Tell me, how did you acquire it?"

"My brother is a priest," he said, reaching for the bottle.

"Well?"

"Thats all she wrote," he said.

"What has that to do with it?"

"Everything, baby. In the first place it isnt confidence, its honesty. Being a priest, he believes in celibacy. He has a very heavy beard shaved very close and he believes in mortal sin and he is worshipped by his adoring flock. Makes a very good living at it."

"Well?" she said.

"Whata ya mean, well? After watching him a while, I decided to believe in honesty, which means the opposite of celibacy. Because I did not want to hate myself and everybody else, like him. That was my first mistake, from then on it was easy.

"I decided to not believe in mortal sin, since obviously no Creator who was Just would condemn His creations to eternal hellfire and brimstone for possessing hungers He created in them. He might penalize them fifteen yards for clipping, but He wouldnt stop the ball game. Now would He?"

"You wouldnt think so," Karen said. "But where does that leave you? if there is no such a thing as punishment for sins?"

"Ah," Warden grinned. "You went right to the heart. I dont like this word 'sin.' But since there is obviously punishment, I was forced by irrefutable logic to accept the weird outlandish idea of reincarnation. That was when my brother and I parted. I had to beat him up, to prove my theory; it was the only way. And, to date, the reincarnation is as far as my philosophy has gotten. What do you say we have another drink?"

"Then I take it you dont believe in sin at all?" Karen Holmes said, a kind of interest flickering for the first time in her eyes.

Warden sighed. "I believe the only sin is a conscious waste of energy. I believe all conscious dishonesty, such as religion, politics and the real estate business, are a conscious waste of energy. I believe that at a remarkable cost in energy people agree to pretend to believe each other's lies so they can prove to themselves their own lies are the truth, like my brother. Since I cannot forget what the truth is, I gravitated, naturally, along with the rest of the social misfits who are honest into the Army as an EM. Now what do you say we have another drink? Since we've settled the problems of God, Society, and the Individual I really think we rate another drink."

"Well," the woman smiled, and the momentary flick of interest had gone out, replaced by the old flip and coldness. "He's smart as well as virile. Lucky little female, to be allowed to enclose the erect pride of such virility. But since you believe the conscious waste of energy is a sin, dont you believe the loss of semen is a sin? unless accompanied by impregnation?"

Warden grinned and dipped the bottle in salute, bowing over it. "Madam, you have touched the weak spot in my philosophy. Far be it from me to snow you. All I can say is—not as long as it is not cast out on the ground, or paid for, and sometimes even then. (Have you ever served in the field?) All I can say is—not as long as it is useful."

Karen Holmes emptied her glass and set it on the table, with finality. "Useful. Now we're getting into dialectic."

"Dont such talk always?"

"And I do not believe in dalectic. I dont want to listen to your definition of what useful means."

She put one hand behind her and flipped the snap of her halter and tossed it to the floor. Staring at him with eyes of liquid smoke in which there was a curious and great disinterest she unzipped her shorts and shucked out of them without moving from the chair and dropped them with the halter.

"There," she said. "That is what you want. Thats what all the talk's about. Thats what all you virile men, you intellectual men, always want. Isnt it? You big strong male men who are virile and intelligent, but who are helpless as babies without a fragile female body to root around on."

Warden found himself staring at the twisted navel and the ridge of scar-tissue that ran down from it, disappearing in the hairy mattress, and that was so old now as to almost be a shadow.

"Pretty, isn't it?" she said. "And its a symbol, too. A symbol of the waste of energy."

Warden set his glass down carefully. He moved toward her on the chair, seeing the nipples wrinkled tightly like flowers closed for night, seeing the feminine grossness that he loved, that was always there, that he always knew was there, hidden maybe behind perfume, unmentioned, unacknowledged, even denied, but still always there, existing, the beautiful lovely grossness of the lioness and the honest bitch dog, that no matter how much, shrinking, they tried to say it wasnt so, in the end always had to be admitted.

"Wait," she said. "Not here, you greedy little boy. Come in the bedroom."

He followed, angry at the "greedy little boy" but knowing it was true, and wondering wonderingly what kind of creature this one was with all the buried darknesses.

He wasnt wearing anything under his CKCs and she shut the door, turning to him blindly, her arms out, raising the roundnesses of her breasts and making hollows beside her arms.

"Now," she said. "Here. Now. Here and now and now."

"Which bed is Holmes's?" he said.

"The other one."

"Then you just move over there."

"All right," she said. She laughed, the first time, richly. "You take your cuckoldry seriously dont you, Milt?"

"Where Holmes is concerned I take everything seriously."

"And so do I."

(from Chapter 9)

[Warden and Stark]

MAYLON STARK stood in the Orderly Room during the whole of Capt Holmes's lecture, after he and Holmes had shaken hands and Holmes had beamed his pleasure at him, with his hands easily behind his back, his campaign hat dangling from them, staring at Holmes reflectively. He expressed his gratitude perfunctorily and said nothing else. At the end of the lecture, still staring reflectively at his new commander, he saluted precisely and withdrew immediately.

Maylon Stark was medium-built and husky. That was the only word to fit him, husky. He had a husky face, and the nose on it was badly bent and flattened huskily. His voice was husky. His head sat huskily on his neck, the way a fighter carries his chin pulled in from habit. It was the huskiness of a man who hunches up his shoulders and hangs on hard with both hands. And with it Maylon Stark had a peculiar perpetual expression, like that of a man who is hanging hard onto the earth to keep it from moving away, out from under him. The line from the right side of his flattened nose to the corner of his mouth was three times as deep as the same line on the left side; his mouth did not curl, but the deepness of this line made him look like he was about to smile sardonically, or cry wearily, or sneer belligerently. You never knew which. And you never found out which. Because Maylon Stark never did any of them.

"He's a good man, Sergeant Warden," Holmes insisted, after Stark had left. There was a puzzled, not quite satisfied look on his face. "I can always tell a good man when I see one. Stark'll make me one damn fine cook."

"Yes, Sir," Warden said. "I think he will."

"You do?" Holmes said, surprised. "Well. Well, its like I say, real soldiers dont grow on trees, and you have to look hard before you find one."

Warden did not bother to answer this one. Dynamite had said the same thing about Ike Galovitch, when he made him sergeant, except that he had not looked puzzled.

Capt Holmes cleared his throat and reset his face and began to dictate next week's Drill Schedule to Mazzioli, who had come in while the lecture had been on. Mazzioli stopped his filing to type the Drill Schedule for the Captain. The Captain walked back and forth, his hands behind his back, his head thrown back thoughtfully, dictating slowly so Mazzioli could get it with the typewriter.

Mazzioli typed disgustedly, knowing that later The Warden would haul out his FMs and change the schedule all around and then he would have to type it up again. And Dynamite would sign it without noticing the difference.

As soon as Holmes was gone, Warden beat it out to the cooks' room, almost unhinged by Dynamite's eternal piddling rumination of the Schedule, feeling he had suddenly escaped from an airtight bottle, breathing joyously, and wondering what Holmes would do if he ever realized his own uselessness and the finicking he hid it with; dont worry, he thought, he never will; it would kill him; but mostly hoping Holmes's dawdling had not given any of the cook force time to get back before he got to see Stark alone.

"Come on upstairs," he said, finding Stark was still alone, doubtfully holding up a pair of the old outmoded suntan breeches that he hated to throw away but had no use for any more. "To my room. I got talkin to do thats private. And I dont want none of them cooks around to see me with you."

"Okay, First," Stark said, answering the urgency in his voice, and got up still holding out the breeches. "I had these breeches ever since the year my sis got married."

"Throw them out," Warden decided for him. "When this war comes and we move out you wont have room for half of what you got thats useful."

"Thats right," Stark said. He tossed them on the growing pile of refuse by the door implacably and looked around the tiny room, and at the three barracks bags that held seven years' accumulation of a way of life.

"Aint much, is it?" Warden said.

"Enough, I guess."

"Footlockers aint got room for memories," Warden said. "And barracks bags even less. Hell, I even use to keep a diary. Still dont know what happened to it."

Stark took a leather framed picture of a young woman and three boys from the satchel and set it open on his wall locker shelf. "Well," he said, "I'm home."

"This is important," Warden said. "Lets go."

"I'm with you, First," Stark said, and picked up the pile of castoffs and the breeches. "Ony time I ever got around to clearin out is when I move," he said apologetically.

On the porch he dropped it all into a GI trash can without breaking stride, following Warden up the stairs, but at the landing he looked back at it, once, at the breeches leg with its thin round GI laces whose metal tips had been lost long ago, dangling outside the can.

"Sit down," Warden said, indicating old Pete's bunk. Stark sat down without speaking. Warden sat on his own bunk facing him, and lit a cigaret. Stark rolled one.

"You want a tailormade?"

"I like these better. I awys smoke Golden Grain," Stark said, eyeing him reflectively, but waiting coolly, "if I can get it. If I cant get Golden Grain, I rather smoke Country Gentleman than tailormades."

Warden set the battered ashtray on the floor between them. "I play them straight, Stark. Five cards face up."

"Thats the way I like them."

"You had two strikes on you when you got here, as far as I'm concerned. Because you served with Holmes at Bliss."

"I figured that," Stark said.

"You from Texas, aint you?"

"Thats right. Borned in Sweetwater."

"How come you to leave Fort Kam?"

"Didnt like it."

"Didnt like it," Warden said, almost caressingly. He went to his wall locker and fished around down behind his diddy box till he brought up a fifth of Lord Calvert. "They never inspect my room on Saturday," he said. "Drink?"

"Sure," Stark said. "A breath." He took the bottle and looked at the label, inspecting the longhaired dandy the way a man sweats out his hole card in a big game too rich for his blood, then upended it and drank.

"You ever handled a Mess, Stark?"

Stark's adam's apple paused. "Sure," he said around the bottle and went on with his drink. "I was runnin one in Kam."

"I mean really run one."

"Sure. Thats what I mean. I was acting bellyrobber on one stripe. Ony I was never acting."

"How about menus and marketing?"

"Sure," Stark said. "All that." He handed the bottle back reluctantly. "Good," he said.

"What kind of rating did you say?" Warden said, not bothering to drink now.

"Pfc. I was up for a Sixth Class, ony I never got it. I was Second Cook on the TO, but without the money. I ran the mess without even being acting. I did everything but wear the stripes and draw the money."

"And you didnt like it," Warden grinned, repeating back, saying it almost chortlingly.

Stark stared at him reflectively, that peculiar about to laugh, about to cry, about to sneer expression on his face. "The setup? no," he said. "The work? yes. Thats my job," he said.

"Good," Warden said happily and took a drink now. "I need a good man in my Mess, one I can depend on, one *with* the rating. How about First and Fourth, to start with?"

Stark looked at him reflectively. "Sounds reasonable," he said. "If I get it. What then?"

"The Rating," Warden said. "Preem's Rating."

Stark talked it over with his cigaret. "I dont know you," he said, "but I'll call you, First."

"Heres the deal. Theres four men from your old outfit at Bliss in this Compny. They're all four sergeants. You got no trouble there."

Stark nodded. "I can see that far."

"The rest is simple. All you got to do is keep your nose clean and show you're a better man than Preem. You're a First Cook with a First and Fourth, as of today. All you got to do is step in and take over whenever Preem dont show, which is just about every day."

"I'm a new man here. Kitchen crews is clannish people. And Preem's got The Rating."

"Dont worry about The Rating. You dont need The Rating. I'll take care of that end. When you have trouble in the kitchen, come to me. The cooks'll give you lip for a while, especially this fat guy

Willard. He's a First Cook and he's bucking for Preem's job. But Dynamite dont like Willard.

"You'll get lots of lip, but dont argue. Be chickenshit. Bring it to me. It'll be all your way."

"Its goin to sure be tough on poor old Preem," Stark said, accepting the bottle Warden was offering him again.

"Have you seen him yet?"

"Not since Bliss." Stark handed the bottle back reluctantly. "Good," he said.

"I like it some myself," Warden said, wiping his mouth with the back of his hand. "Preem likes it too. Preem married it. Preem looks like a man who either seen a miracle, or was hit at the base of the skull with a rubber hammer."

"He was an awful quiet guy when I knew him. Kind of guy to go off and get drunk all by himself."

"He's still that way. Except now he has to go off and get sober by himself."

"Quiet guys like that are bad. The ones that get drunk by theirselves. They awys flip their lid."

"You think so?" Warden said, suddenly narrowly, that other part of his mind tuning in and clocking up the platitude, and reminding him that where theres smoke theres fire and where theres platitude theres liar. "Some of them dont."

Stark shrugged. "Theres just one thing, First. If I take your kitchen, I run it my way. Nobody sings and nobody squares. There'll be no backseat driving from the Orderly Room if I take your kitchen. Otherwise no soap."

"Forget it," Warden said. "You run it right and its your baby."

"That aint what I said," Stark said doggedly. "I said its all my baby. Right *or* wrong. And the Office keeps its nose out. Or else I dont want any part of it."

Warden grinned at him slyly, the pixy's eyebrows quivering, thinking that he couldnt be *too* dumb. "Fine," he said. Why cant you just be honest once? he thought, just make one promise without keeping your fingers crossed, you bastard.

"Okay," Stark said, with finality. "How about a nuther drink?"

Warden handed him the bottle. The hand was over now, the cards were being collected by the dealer. The spontaneous conversation of relaxed tension broke out bubbling.

"What I dont see," Stark said conversationally, "is what you make on this deal."

"I make nothing," Warden grinned. "You ever hear of the man with the whip? Well, I'm the guy. Holmes only thinks this is his Compny."

The bottle worked back and forth now like a shuttle, weaving brilliant colors, over and under, around the strings of words.

"How many guys from Bliss in the Compny now?"

"Five, counting you. 'Champ' Wilson has the First Platoon," Warden said, skewering the word. "Preem the Mess. Two platoon guides, Henderson and Old Ike Galovitch."

"Ike Galovitch! Jesus Christ! He was our boiler orderly at Bliss, couldnt even speak plain English."

"Thats the boy. He still cant speak it. And he's Dynamite's Close Order expert."

"My God!" Stark said. He was sincerely shocked.

"You see what I'm up against?" Warden grinned happily, watching the lovely beautiful brilliant shuttling of the bottle as it wove and wound and spun the web of unreality, of talk about them both, relaxing into it.

"...But you're all right. You were at Bliss and that puts you on the inside track."...

"These cooks wont like it though."...

"To hell with them. Long as I like it, you got no worry."...

"Okay, First. You lead the band."...

"You goddam right I do...."

"...the setup in the Regiment. Holmes and Colonel Delbert are just like that, see? They..."

"...what I got to work with."...

"They's two men you can depend on...."

"...and heres the setup in the Compny. Strickly a jockstrap outfit, see? Dhom is the Staff because he's trainer for Dynamite's squad, but he's as far as he will ever get and..."

The soldier's greatest hobby, he thought as he listened to his own voice talking, the bull session, add a bottle and you have his greatest joy, also his greatest escape, he thought. The unofficial institution that is the first-string substitute for women and the ageold conversation where the man explains his ideals and his hopes for his life and the woman listens and agrees and tells him how wonderful he is. But soldiers are men without women, he thought, and they cannot hold each other's heads upon their breasts and pat each other's hair. But they escape just as well, the other part reminded him.

Ah, if you could only lose this other part of your mind too, like Stark is doing, not lose but forget it for a little while, without thinking about the women, or the men, or all the other angles.

"Gimme a drink," Stark said. "Is that tall blonde wife of his still around?"

"Who?" Warden said.

"His wife," Stark said. "Whats her name. Karen. Is he still married to her?"

"Oh her," Warden said.

Maybe its better for you you cant deliberately distract that other part, he thought. More painful, surely. But maybe in the long run better. Provided, of course, that you can stand it. There is courage, he thought, and then theres courage.

"Yeah," he said, "he's still married to her. She comes over here ever once in a while. Why?"

"I just wondered," Stark said, mellow now and feeling philo-sophical. "I dunno, I awys figure Holmes would of left her before now. She was a regular bitch in heat at Bliss, when I knew her, but mean like, as if she really hated it and all the ones she gave it to. They said she laid half the EM on the Post at Bliss."

"They did?" Warden said.

"Hell yes. I heard she even got the clap down there. Ony thing kept her from bein out and out a whore was she was married."

"You mean she kept her amateur standing," Warden said.

Stark threw back his head and laughed. "Thats it."

"I dont put much stock in stories like that though," Warden said, carefully casual. "You hear them about every woman that lives on a Army Post. Mostly wishful thinking, you ask me."

"Oh yeah?" Stark said indignantly. "Well this aint no story. I fucked her myself, at Bliss. So I know it aint no story."

"Come to think of it," Warden said. "I been hearin some pretty rough stories about her around here." What was it she had said, that afternoon, in the house, with the rain dripping sounding softly at the open window, what was it? Now he had it. She said, *Dont you want me either?*

"You can probly," Stark said, whiskily innocent, "believe them all. Because she's rough. I can see a single woman sleepin around some," he said; "I can even see a married woman steppin out on her old man. But I dont like to see any woman, specially if she's married, just layin for any guy comes along. A whore's a whore, thats how she makes her livin. But theys somethin wrong with a woman who does it for fun, and then dont like it."

"You think thats what she does?" Warden said. "Holmes's wife, I mean?"

"Hell yes. Why should she of laid me down there at Bliss? a buckass private in the rear rank, who didnt even have no dough to spend on her?"

Warden shrugged. "What the hell?" he said. "Its nothing to me. Maybe I can get some of it myself, sometime."

"If you're smart," Stark said, "you'll leave it alone. She's nothin but a topflight bitch. She's coldern hardern any whore I ever saw." His face was adamant, convincing.

"Here," Warden said. "Have another drink. Dont let it get you down, for Christ sake."

Stark took the bottle without looking at it. "I done seen too many of these rich women. They worse than queers. And I dont like them."

"Neither do I," Warden said. If she had as many . . . , Leva had said, she'd be a porcupine, he thought, listening to Stark's voice going on to something else and his own voice answering. And they're both smart boys, he thought, they know their way around, they aint punk kids.

But Leva's only giving you hearsay, he's had no personal experience with her. And Stark was five years younger then, a mere nineteen, a kid, when he had his experience with her. That must have been an experience, he thought, that must really have been quite an experience, to make him talk the way he does now, five years later. Remember he was a juicy green young kid serving his first hitch.

But would the woman who went on the moonlight swimming party have done that? would she have laid for half the EM at Bliss? What do you say? I dont know. Yes, you dont know; and here are two men who do know. But can you trust their judgment? No, you cant. You cant accept what they know, and you dont know. Where does that leave you?

He wanted to take the bottle and rise up and smash it down on this talking, jawbone wagging skull, flatten it out on the floor until the jawbone jutted out of the pancaked matter and ceased wagging. Not because of what Stark had told him, and not because he'd laid this woman he himself had laid (you shy away from the Word, dont you?), no not because of that; he felt almost a curious friendliness and comradeship for him because of that, like two men who use the same toothbrush. Did two men ever use the same toothbrush? No, he wanted to flatten out this wagging skull with this bottle simply because it happened to be here, and he, absurdly, for no reason, felt the need of smashing something. Because what right have you to be mad at Stark because she laid for him? or for all the EM on the Post at Bliss, for that matter?

"... I think we can make it work," Stark was saying. "We got all the cards."

"Right." Warden caught the shuttle in midpassage and returned it to his footlocker. "You wont see me around after this, Maylon," he said. Might as well call him by his first name, he's practically your brother, it looks as though you've got a lot of brothers. "Bring your troubles to the Orderly Room," he said, listening to the tones of his own voice carefully. "You'll have plenty of them. But after Retreat you dont know me any better than you do any other noncom in this outfit."

Stark nodded at this wisdom. "Okay, First," he said.

"You better get back down and get that stuff cleaned up now," Warden said, astounded, maybe even proud, at how cool he could make his own voice sound.

"Christ," Stark said getting up. "I forgotten all about it."

Warden grinned, it felt as if his face was cracking, and waited till he left. Then he lay down on his bunk and put his arms behind his head. And with the other part, that came forward now, that always came forward when he was alone, thinking about it, consciously, like a man who cant quit biting on a sore tooth but wont go to the dentist.

He could see it all in his mind, just the way it must have happened, with Stark holding her, her lying on the bed as he himself had seen her, every secret open and unveiled, the heavy breathing like a distance runner, the eyelids shuddering closed at that moment when you went clear out of your own body and you knew nothing and knew everything, you a long ways off with only a slim silver cord attaching you to yourself back there. Maybe Stark gave her more pleasure than you gave her, he thought, biting on the tooth that was unbearable, maybe all of them gave her more pleasure than you gave her, maybe even Holmes gave her more pleasure than you gave her. He had never thought about Holmes sleeping with her before. But now he thought about it. Now he wondered if she might not be sleeping with Holmes all along, all this time.

Whats the matter with you? he thought, what is it to you? You're not in love with her. Its nothing to you who she sleeps with. You're not even going to see her anymore anyway. You made your mind up to that the night of the swimming party, didnt you?

He would, he decided after a while, just keep that next date, after all. Theres no sense in turning down a piece of free stuff, when it costs three bucks at Mrs Kipfer's. Besides, he would like to find out the true answer to this puzzle, just to satisfy his curiosity, his intellectual curiosity.

I think, piped up the other part of his mind suddenly, *I* think you wanted to keep it all along, meant to keep it all along.

Maybe, he admitted. But anyway I didnt blow this transfer deal, did I? I could have, but I didn't. This deal should pan out all right now, if we have any luck, dont you think?

Dont change the subject on me, the other part insisted. *I* think you meant to keep that date even then, that same night, when you went down to Wu Fat's and got drunk, looking for sympathy.

All right, he said to it, but go away. Do you always have to be checking up on me too? like you do with everybody else? Cant you even trust your own flesh and blood?

How much do you know about families? it said to him disgusted, and you ask me that? You're the one I should trust the least.

Listen, he said, I got work to do. This kitchen deal is going to be touch and go for a while, and we'll need all our luck, but I think we can swing it, if we have the luck. So dont bother me with theory. This is practical. And he got up quickly off the bed and went downstairs to make out Stark's promotion, before it had a chance to answer.

They had the luck. Capt Holmes found the order on his desk that night, when he stopped in a minute on his way up to the Club for dinner, and he signed it. It made Stark a First Cook with a First and Fourth, dropped Willard back to Second Cook and First and Sixth, and sent Pfc Sims back to straight duty shorn of his Sixth Class. It was just the way Holmes had planned it, except he had not meant to let Sims keep his Pfc, and he was surprised to find it there like that because he had expected to have trouble out of Warden when he put it through. Nothing serious, just some of Warden's childish balking, and he was glad now, as he signed it, that there would be no argument because he always hated to have to pull his rank, even when it was for the good of his Company.

The rest of it was just as easy as that. It was so ridiculously easy that it seemed incredible. Stark had the anticipated trouble with the cooks. They balked at the assumed authority of the newcomer. Fat Willard, watching the wind change and seeing his own star set, was the ringleader. He agitated brilliantly and complained superlatively until Stark took him out on the green and beat him up so bad he was afraid to speak at all. When the rest of them impeded progress Stark took it to the Orderly Room. Warden gave his decision and Stark departed. By the end of a week Capt Holmes was so sure he had discovered a kitchen genius that he pointed out to Warden the vast importance of proper early training for recruits.

Stark loved his kitchen, it was already "his," with the single-mindedness women have been taught to dream of and expect, demand, and decry when attached to anything but love. Stark drove himself as hard or harder than he drove the cooks and the KPs. The dormant Company Fund was brought into the light, and Stark bought new silverware, he recommended the purchase of newer better equipment. There were even fresh flowers on the tables now and then, a unique experience in G Company. Sloppiness in eating was no longer allowed, and Stark enforced this new rule like a tyrant. A man who slopped catsup over his plate onto the oilcloth would suddenly find himself outside the door in the middle of a meal. The KPs lived a life of hell on earth, yet the reflective eyes in Stark's sad sneering laughing face were always soft and no KP could force himself to hate him. They saw him working just as hard as they did, and they chortled at the way he rode the cooks. Even fat Willard was forced to work.

In less than two weeks, before the end of March, the tall cadaverous Sergeant Preem was broken to a private. Capt Holmes could be as hard as the next man, when it was necessary. He called Preem in and told him bluntly and militarily. Because after all, it was Preem's own fault, nobody could have given him more of a chance than Capt Holmes. If another man was the better man, then by rights he should have the job. He gave Preem a choice between transferring to another company in the Regiment, or transferring to another regiment, because you cant let a former high-ranking noncom stay in his outfit as a private, its bad for discipline.

Preem, who had been rising every day at noon, oozing that stale mushy smell of a middle-aged drunk, and wandering out dazedly through his now bustling sparkling kitchen where there was no room for him, chose the other regiment because he was ashamed. He said nothing. There was nothing he could say. He was through and he knew it. His gravytrain days were over. He heard his fate with a face that was as much dazed as it was impassive. He was a broken man.

"Captain," Warden said, after he had left, "how you want me to make this order out? Busted for 'Inefficiency'?"

"Why, yes," Holmes said. "How else would one make it?"

"Well, I thought maybe we might make it 'Insubordination.' Everybody gets busted for insubordination sometime or other. A man who aint been busted for insubordination aint a soldier yet. But 'Inefficiency,' a man who's got that on his record's done."

"Why, yes, Sergeant," Holmes said. "Make it 'Insubordination.' I dont guess anybody'll know, will they? Preem ought to have a break, as long as it doesnt interfere with the efficiency of my Company. After all, he served with me in Bliss."

"Yes, Sir," Warden said.

The order was made out that way, but he knew it was a futile gesture. The minute Preem appeared at his new outfit with his rubber hammer look they would know the story.

That night Stark bought the traditional boxes of cigars and passed them out at chow. Everybody was happy with the new food, new management, and new rating. Pvt Preem ate in obscurity at a back table, already completely forgotten, displaying that most touching mark in soldiering: the dark spots on his sleeves from which the stripes had been removed.

(from Chapter 12)

[Prewitt Plays Taps]

"THAT WAS NO WAY to play Tattoo," Prew said to Andy, with the indisputable air of an expert. "Tattoo wants to be staccato. Short, and snappy. You dont waste a second on the long notes. Tattoo is urgent. You're telling them to get them goddam lights out and you dont want argument. So it has to be precise and fast, without slurring the notes. And yet a little sad underneath, because you hate to have to do it."

"We cant all be good," Andy said. "I'm a git-tar player. You stick to the bugle and I'll stick to the git-tar."

"Okay," Prew said. "Here." He handed over the new guitar that was not very new any more but was still Andy's private guitar.

Andy took it and picked up the melody from Friday, still watching Prew's face in the darkness.

"You wanta take my Taps?" he offered. "You can take them tonight if you want."

Prew thought it over. "You sure you dont care?"

"Naw. I aint no bugler, I'm a guitarman, like I said. Go ahead and take them. I never could play them anyway."

"Okay. Gimme the horn. Heres your mouthpiece. I got mine with me. Just happened to have it."

He took the tarnished guard bugle and rubbed at it a little, held it in his lap then, as they sat on in the cool darkness, playing softly and talking a little, but mostly listening, Stark not talking any but only listening, gladly but sullenly. Once a couple of men wandering by stopped to listen for a minute, caught by the haunting hope without hope that sang out in the set blues rhythm. But the silent Stark was alert. He flipped his cigaret viciously out into the street, at them, the falling coal shattering at their feet and showering sparks. It was as if an unseen hand had pushed them away and they went on, but they were strangely lifted.

At five of eleven they stopped and all got up, the four of them walking out to the megaphone in the corner, leaving Stark leaning against the wall still smoking sullenly, tacitly accepting his aloofness, him rolling them and smoking and silently taking it all in, not missing anything.

Prew took his quartz mouthpiece from his pocket and inserted it. He stood before the big tin megaphone, fiddling nervously, testing his lips. He blew two soft tentative tones, then wiped the mouthpiece out angrily and rubbed his lips vigorously.

"My lip's off," he said nervously. "I aint touched a horn in months. I wont be able to play them for nothing. Lip's soft as hell."

He stood there in the moonlight, shifting nervously from one foot to the other, fiddling with the bugle, shaking it angrily, testing it against his lips.

"Christ," he said. "I cant play them like they ought to be played. Taps is special."

"Oh, go ahead, for God sake," Andy said. "You know you can play them."

"All right," he said angrily. "All right. I dint say I wasnt gonna play them, did I? You never get nervous, do you?"

"Never," Andy said.

"Then you aint got no goddam sensitivity," Prew said angrily. "Nor sympathy, nor understanding."

"Not for you," Andy said.

"Well for Christ's sake shut up then," he said angrily nervously.

He looked at his watch and as the second hand touched the top stepped up and raised the bugle to the megaphone, and the nervousness dropped from him like a discarded blouse, and he was suddenly alone, gone away from the rest of them.

The first note was clear and absolutely certain. There was no question or stumbling in this bugle. It swept across the quadrangle positively, held just a fraction longer than most buglers hold it. Held long like the length of time, stretching away from weary day to weary day. Held long like thirty years. The second note was short, almost too short, abrupt. Cut short and too soon gone, like the minutes with a whore. Short like a ten minute break is short. And then the last note of the first phrase rose triumphantly from the slightly broken rhythm, triumphantly high on an untouchable level of pride above the humiliations, the degradations.

He played it all that way, with a paused then hurried rhythm that no metronome could follow. There was no placid regimented tempo to this Taps. The notes rose high in the air and hung above the quadrangle. They vibrated there, caressingly, filled with an infinite sadness, an endless patience, a pointless pride, the requiem and epitaph of the common soldier, who smelled like a common soldier, as a woman once had told him. They hovered like halos over the heads of the sleeping men in the darkened barracks, turning all grossness to the beauty that is the beauty of sympathy and understanding. Here we are, they said, you made us, now see us, dont close your eyes and shudder at it; this beauty, and this sorrow, of things as they are. This is the true song, the song of the ruck, not of battle heroes; the song of the Stockade prisoners itchily stinking sweating under coats of grey rock dust; the song of the mucky KPs, of the men without women who collect the bloody menstrual rags of the officers' wives, who come to scour the Officers' Club—after the parties are over. This is the song of the scum, the Aqua-Velva drinkers, the shameless ones who greedily drain the half filled glasses, some of them lipsticksmeared, that the party-ers can afford to leave unfinished.

This is the song of the men who have no place, played by a man who has never had a place, and can therefore play it. Listen to it. You know this song, remember? This is the song you close your ears to every night, so you can sleep. This is the song you drink five martinis every evening not to hear. This is the song of the Great Loneliness, that creeps in like the desert wind and dehydrates the soul. This is the song you'll listen to on the day you die. When you lay there in the bed and sweat it out, and know that all the doctors and nurses and weeping friends dont mean a thing and cant help you any, cant save you one small bitter taste of it, because you are the one thats dying and not them; when you wait for it to come and know that sleep will not evade it and martinis will not put it off and conversation will not circumvent it and hobbies will not help you to escape it; then you will hear this song and, remembering, recognize it. This song is Reality. Remember? Surely you remember?

> "Day   is done...
> Gone   the sun...
> From-the-lake
> From-the-hill
> From-the-sky
> Rest in peace
> Sol jer brave
> God   is   nigh..."

And as the last note quivered to prideful silence, and the bugler swung the megaphone for the traditional repeat, figures appeared in the lighted sallyport from inside of Choy's. "I told you it was Prewitt," a voice carried faintly across the quadrangle in the tone of a man who has won a bet. And then the repeat rose to join her quivering tearful sister. The clear proud notes reverberating back and forth across the silent quad. Men had come from the Dayrooms to the porches to listen in the darkness, feeling the sudden choking kinship bred of fear that supersedes all personal tastes. They stood in the darkness of the porches, listening, feeling suddenly very near the man beside them, who also was a soldier, who also must die. Then as silent as they had come, they filed back inside with lowered eyes, suddenly ashamed of their own emotion, and of seeing a man's naked soul.

Maylon Stark, leaning silent against his kitchen wall, looked at his cigaret with a set twisted mouth that looked about to cry, about to laugh, about to sneer. Ashamed. Ashamed of his own good luck that had given him back his purpose and his meaning. Ashamed that this other man had lost his own. He pinched the inoffensive coal between his fingers, relishing the sting, and threw it on the ground with all his strength, throwing with it all the overpowering injustice of the world that he could not stomach nor understand nor explain nor change.

Prewitt lowered the bugle slowly and let the megaphone rest in its swivel. Reluctantly he withdrew his mouthpiece and gave the bugle back to Andy. His lips were pinched and red from the playing.

"Christ," he said huskily. "Jesus Christ. I need a drink a water. I'm tired. Me and Stark goin to town. Wheres Stark?" and fingering his mouthpiece he went vaguely toward the barracks in the darkness, not proud but innocently unaware as yet of what he had created.

"Boy," Maggio said as they watched him go. "That guy kin really play a bugle. Whynt he never play? He should ought to be in the Bugle Corps."

"He was, you jerk," Andy said scornfully. "He quit. He wouldnt play in this old Corps. He played a Taps at Arlington."

"Yeah?" Maggio said. He peered after the retreating figure. "Well," he said. "Well what do you know."

(from Chapter 15)

[Kolekole Pass]

IT WAS NOT, STRANGELY, until Capt Dynamite Holmes came bouncing in from across the quad, freshly showered, shaved, shampooed, and shined, his big boots gleaming—it was not till then that all these things suddenly got under Prewitt's skin.

"Hello there, Sergeant Galovitch," Holmes grinned, stopping in the doorway.

"Atten HUT," Ike bawled, making two distinct words of it, and bracing his bigfooted longarmed missinglink's body into an archbacked travesty of it proudly. The men went on working.

"Everything under control, Sergeant?" Holmes said fondly. "Are you getting this place slicked up for me tomorrow?"

"Yes, *Serr,*" Ike grunted, uncomfortably because still bracing solidly, his thumbs along the seams of his trousers, somewhere down around his knees. "Slickem up. Everyting I am doing just like the Gomny Gmandr saying."

"Good," Holmes grinned fondly. "Fine." Still grinning fondly, he stepped over to inspect the wall, and nodded. "Looks fine, Sergeant Galovitch, A-1. Keep up the good work."

"Yes, *Serr,*" Ike grunted worshipfully, still bracing. The narrow shouldered barrel ape's chest expanded out until it looked about to burst and Ike saluted, stiffly, grotesquely, looking as if the hand would knock his eye clear out.

"Well," Holmes grinned fondly. "Carry on then, Sergeant." He went on into the orderly room grinning and Old Ike bawled "*Atten HUT*" again, making it two words again, and the men still went on working.

Prew went on rubbing his rag over the pebbly plaster he had just washed and that suddenly sickened him now, feeling his jaws tighten reasonlessly. He felt as if he had just witnessed the sodomitic seduction of a virgin brunser who had liked it.

"All right, you men there," Ike hollered proudly, moving slabfooted up and down behind them. "You men I want on the ball to get, see? Just begause da Gomny Gmandr comes around is to stop working no escuse. Dis a fatigue, not vacation."

The men still went on working, wearily ignoring this new outburst because they had been expecting it, as they wearily ignored the other outbursts, and Prew went with them, suddenly suffocating in the wet plaster smell that enveloped him. He wished he had a pair of bright and shining boots.

"You Prewitt," Ike hollered angrily, not finding anything else to criticize. "Lets looking a life. Dis a fatigue, not vacation for a seminaries of lady. I got to tell you all ready times too many. Now looking a life."

If Ike had not mentioned him by name, with Holmes in there listening taking it all in, he could still have stomached it. But quite suddenly the words were beating against his ears, on and on, so that instinctively he wanted to shake his head to clear it.

"What the hell do you want, me to grow a couple more arms for Chrisake?" he said violently suddenly, hearing his own voice outhollering Ike's astoundedly, yet seeing in his mind the Great God Holmes sitting grinning at his desk listening relishingly to his favorite sergeant. For once maybe The Man might like to hear what his men thought of his favorite sergeant, for a change.

"How?" Ike said flabbergastedly. "What?"

"Yas, what," Prew sneered. "You want this job done so perfect and so fast why dont you grab a bush yourself? Instead of standing around giving orders nobody listens to."

The men stopped mechanically washing and all stared at him, just as mechanically, and he looked at them, the rage filling him, now knowing why. He knew it was senseless, absolutely senseless, even dangerous, but for a moment he was wildly proud.

"Now listen," Ike said, thinking hard. "This back talk are you giving me do I not want. To work get back on the lip shut button."

"Oh blow it out your ass," he said savagely, still mechanically scrubbing with his rag, "I'm working. What do you think, I'm floggin my doggin?"

"What," Ike gasped. "What."

"*AT EASE!*" roared Capt Holmes, appearing in the door. "What the hell is all this racket, Prewitt?"

"Yes, *Serr,*" Ike grunted, popping to attention. "Dis man bolshevik da back talk is giving to a noncom."

"Whats the matter with you, Prewitt?" Capt Holmes said sternly, ignoring the momentarily shattered illusion of his favorite sergeant. "You know better than to talk back to a noncommissioned officer, and in that tone of voice."

"To a noncom, *yes*, Sir," Prew grinned savagely, aware now of the watching eight wide pairs of eyes. "But I have never liked being pissed on, Sir. Even by a noncommissioned officer," he said, twisting the phrase.

The Warden appeared in the door behind Holmes and stood looking at all of them, his eyes narrowed thoughtfully, himself aloof from it.

Holmes looked as if someone had dashed a glass of ice water in his face absolutely without reason. His brows were up with disbelief and his eyes were wide with hurt and his mouth was open with surprise. When he spoke his voice quivered openly with both rage and start.

"Private Prewitt, I think you owe both Sergeant Galovitch and myself an apology." He paused and waited.

Prew did not answer. He felt a shrinking in his belly at the thought of what this stupidity would do to his chances Payday, wondering what in hell had possessed him to do a thing like that.

"Well?" Holmes said authoritatively. He was as surprised by it as any of them, as surprised as Prewitt even, and had said the first thing that came into his head but he could not show that. He had to back it up. "Apologize, Prewitt."

"I dont think I owe anybody any apology," Prew said savagely doggedly. "In fact, if apologies are in order, I think they're owed to me," he went on recklessly, wanting suddenly to laugh at the comedy of it, like a mother chastening a child to bring it back in line. But then thats the way they always treat us, isnt it?

"What!" Holmes said. It had not occurred to him that an EM could refuse. He was as much at a loss now as Old Ike had been before and his eyes that had become almost normal size now got wider even than before. He looked at Galovitch, as if for help, then he turned and looked at Warden behind him, then he turned and looked vaguely out the corridor doorway. Corporal Paluso, a second-string Regimental tackle with a big flat murderous face that he tried to make people forget by adopting a heavy-handed bull-laughing sense of humor, and who had not missed a chance to work on Prew at drill all morning, was sitting on one of the backless chairs out on the porch and had turned and looked inside, his hard eyes in the murderous face as wide now as any of the others, as wide as Holmes's.

"Corporal Paluso," Holmes roared, in his battalion close order voice, which was the best in the Regiment.

"Yes, Sir," Paluso said, and jumped up as if stabbed.

"Take this man upstairs and have him roll a full field pack, a complete full field, extra shoes helmet and all, and then take a bicycle and hike him up to Kolekole Pass and back. And see that he hikes all the way. And when he gets back, bring him to me." It was a pretty long speech for his battalion close order voice that had been developed more for short commands.

"Yes, Sir," Paluso said. "Come on, Prewitt."

Prew climbed down meekly off the board without a word. The Warden turned around and disgustedly went back inside. Paluso led him to the stairs and a still-shocked silence reached out after them from the corridor like a cloud.

Prew bit his lips. He got his envelope roll out of the wall locker and the combat pack off the bed foot. He laid them on the floor and opened the light pack. Everyone in the squadroom sat up and watched him silently and speculatively, as they might watch a sick horse upon whose time to die they had gotten up a pool.

"Dont forget the shoes," Paluso said apologetically, in the voice one uses in the presence of a corpse.

He got them off the rack under the footlocker and had to unroll the roll to put them in and then build the whole thing up from scratch in the deadness of the silence.

"Dont forget the helmet," Paluso said apologetically.

He hung it under the snap of the meat can carrier, and picked the whole solid-heavy mess of straps and buckles up and shouldered into it and went to get his rifle from the racks, wanting only to get out of this sad, shocked silence.

"Wait'll I get a bike," Paluso said apologetically, as they came down the stairs.

He stood in the grass and waited. The sixty-five or seventy pounds of pack dragged at his back, already starting to cut in on the circulation of his arms. It was just about five miles to the top of the pass. In the corridor the great silence still reigned.

"Okay," Paluso said, using his clipped official voice because they were downstairs now. "Lets shove."

He slung his rifle and they went out the truck entrance, still followed by the silence. Outside of the quad the rest of the Post

moved busily, just as if there had not been a cataclysm. They passed
Theater #1, on past the Post gym, past the Regimental drill field,
and went on up the road, into the sun, Paluso riding embarrassedly
beside him, the front wheel wobbling precariously at the slowness
of the pace.

"You want a cigaret?" Paluso offered apologetically.

Prew shook his head.

"Go ahead and have one. Hell," Paluso said, "theres no reason to
be mad at me. I dont like this any better than you do."

"I aint mad at you."

"Then have a cigaret."

"Okay." He took a cigaret.

Paluso, looking relieved, started off ahead on the bike. He cut
capers on it and looked back grinning with the big murderous face,
trying to make him laugh. Prew grinned weakly for him. Paluso
gave it up and settled down to the monotony, wobbling along beside
him. Then he had another idea. He rode off a hundred yards ahead
and then circled back, riding fast, a hundred yards behind, waving
as he went by, and then circled back up, pumping as hard as his legs
would go, to skid the brakes and slide alongside Prewitt. When this
bored him he got off and walked a while.

They passed the golf course, went on past the officers' bridle
path, past the Packtrain, past the gas chamber, last outpost of the
Reservation, and Prew plodded on concentrating on the old hiking
rhythm, swing up and drop, swing up and drop, using only the
thigh muscles on the upswing, not using the calf or ankle or foot
muscles at all but letting the feet hit willy-nilly, the body's
momentum carrying it forward as the thigh muscles tensed for the
next swing up, that he had learned from the old timers at Myer a
long time ago. Hell, he could do ten miles standing on his head
carrying two packs, he cursed, as the sweat began to run in bigger
rivulets down his spine and legs and drip from under his arms and
down in his eyes off his face.

When they reached the last steep rise that curved left up to the
top of the pass, Paluso stopped and got off his bike.

"We might as well turn back here. Theres no use to go up to the
crest. He'll never know it anyway."

"To hell with him," Prew said grimly, plodding on. "He said the
pass. The pass it is." He looked over at the Stockade rock quarry
cut back into the side of the hill on the right of the curve. Thats

where you'll be tomorrow this time. All right. So fine. Fuck em all but six and save them for the pallbearers.

"Whats the matter with you?" Paluso said angrily dumbfoundly. "You're crazy."

"Sure," he called back.

"I aint going to walk this bike up there," Paluso said. "I'll wait on you here."

The prisoners, working in the heavy dust with the big white capital P on the backs of their blue jackets standing out like targets, whooped at the two of them, razzing about the extra duty and the hard life of the Army. Until the big MP guards cursed them down and shut them up and put them back to work.

Paluso waited, smoking disgustedly, at the bottom of the rise and he climbed it doggedly by himself, sweating heavier now on the steeper rise, until at the top the big never-flagging breeze hit him and chilled him and he could look down the steep-dropping snake of road, dropping way down, at least a thousand feet, among the great sharp lava crags, down to Waianae where they had gone last September, where they went every September, for the machinegun training that he liked, fitting the heavy link-curling web belts of identical clinking cartridges every fifth one painted red into the block and touching the trigger lightly between thumb and forefinger and feeling the pistol grip buck against your hand as the belts bobbed through, firing off across the empty western water at the towed targets, the tracers making flat meteor flights of light in the night firing. He breathed some of the stiffness of the breeze. Then he turned around and went back down, the wind dying suddenly, to where Paluso was waiting.

When they got back to the barracks his jacket and his pants down to his knees were soaked clear through. Paluso said, *"Wait here,"* and went in to report and Capt Holmes came back out with him, and he unslung his rifle and came to attention and rendered a smart rifle salute.

"Well," Holmes said deeply, humorously. Sharp lines of lenient humor cut indulgent planes and angles in the handsome aquiline face. "Do you still feel you need to offer advice to the noncoms about how to manage details, Prewitt?"

Prew did not answer. In the first place, he had not expected humor, even indulgent humor, and inside in the corridor they were still scrubbing down the walls, exactly as they had two hours ago, and they looked very safe and secure in their weary bored monotony.

"Then I take it," Holmes said humorously, "that you are ready to apologize to Sergeant Galovitch and myself now, arent you."

"No, Sir, I'm not." Why did he have to say that? why couldnt he just have left it? why did he have to demand it all? couldnt he see what he was doing, how impossible that was.

Paluso made a startled noise behind him that was followed by a very guilty silence. Holmes's eyes only widened imperceptibly, he had better control this time, he knew more what to expect. The indulgent planes and angles of his face shifted, subtly and were neither humorous nor indulgent any more.

Holmes jerked his head at the pass. "Take him back up there again, Paluso. He hasnt had enough yet."

"Yes, Sir," Paluso said, letting go of the handlebars with one hand to salute.

"We'll see how he answers next time," Holmes said narrowly. The red was beginning to mount in his face again. "I dont have a thing planned for all night tonight," he added.

"Yes, Sir," Paluso said. "Come on, Prewitt."

Prew turned and followed him again, feeling bottomlessly sick inside, and feeling tired, feeling very tired.

"Goddam," Paluso protested, as soon as they were out of sight, "you're nuts. Plain crazy. Dont you know you're ony cuttin your own throat? If you dont give a damn about yourself, at least think about me. My legs is gettin tard," he grinned apologetically.

Prew did not even manage a weak grin this time. He knew that, if there had been any chance within the indulgent humor, it was gone now, that this was it, this was how you went to the Stockade. He hiked the ten miles carrying the sixty-five or seventy pounds of pack with that knowledge making an added weight inside of him.

What he did not know was what had happened in the orderly room to put Holmes in the indulgent mood, nor what happened this time, the second time.

The Man's face was congested a brick red when he stomped back inside, the anger he had managed to conceal in front of Prewitt backing up now like a flood behind a bridge.

"You and your bright ideas of leadership," he raged at Warden. "You and your brilliant ideas of how to handle bolsheviks."

Warden was still standing by the window. He had watched all of it. Now he turned around, wishing The Mouth, or would you say The Sword, The Flaming Sword, would step outside to talk to Ike, so The Warden could open up the file cabinet and get a drink.

"Sergeant Warden," The Man said thickly, "I want you to prepare court martial papers for Prewitt. Insubordination and refusing a direct order of an officer. I want them now."

"Yes, Sir," The Warden said.

"I want them to go in to Regiment this afternoon," The Man said.

"Yes, Sir," The Warden said. He went to the blank forms file, where the useless bottle was. He got out four of the long double sheets of the forms and shut the drawer on the bottle and took the papers to the typewriter.

"You cant be decent to a man like that," The Man said thickly. "He has been a troublemaker ever since he hit this outfit. Its time he had a lesson. They tame the lions in the Army, not appease them."

"You want it recommended for a Summary? or a Special," The Warden said indifferently.

"Special," The Man said. His face got redder. "I'd like to make it a goddamned General. I would, if I could. You and your bright ideas."

"Its nothing to me," The Warden shrugged, beginning to type. "All I said was, we've had three court martials in the last six weeks and it might not look so good on the records."

"Then to hell with the records," The Man almost, but not quite, shouted. It was the peak. He sat down in his swivel chair exhausted and leaned back and stared broodingly at the door into the corridor that he had carefully closed.

"Thats all right with me," The Warden said, still typing.

The Man did not appear to hear, but The Warden, typing, still watched him, gauging carefully, making sure it *was* the peak. You could not handle this time like the last time. This was stronger. This was the last time squared, and you would have to square the strength of your approach, and then if you waited till the other's peak was past, then logically you would have it made, but was it worth it? Hell no, it wasnt worth it, not when you might crimp your own concatenation, what was it to you if some damned son of a bitching stupid fool of an antediluvian got himself beheaded by a progressive world by going around in a dream world and trying to live up to a romantic, backward ideal of individual integrity? You could go doing things for a jerk like that forever, and never help him any. It was never worth it, but it would really be a feather in your cap if you could pull it off again now, this time. That would be worth a try, just for the hell of it. If he was doing this, it was not because it was his responsibility to knock himself out taking care of headless chickens who refuse to become modern and grow a head, it was just for the fun of seeing if he could pull it off, not for no stupid ass who still believed in probity.

"Too bad you got to lose a welterweight like that," The Warden said indifferently, after The Man had brooded on the door a while in silence. He took the sheets out of the machine and began to rearrange the carbons for the second page.

"What?" The Man said, looking up. "What do you mean?"

"Well, he'll still be in hock when Compny Smokers comes up, wont he?" The Warden said indifferently.

"To hell with the Company Smokers," The Man said. "All right," he said. "Make it a Summary then."

"But I already got this typed up," The Warden said.

"Then change it, Sergeant," The Man said. "Would you let your laziness make a difference of five months in the Stockade to a man?"

"Jesus Christ," The Warden said. He tore the papers up and went to get some blank ones. "These Kentucky mountain hardheads cause a man more trouble than a regiment of niggers. Might as well leave it as a Special for all the good a break will do a man like that."

"He needs to be taught a lesson," said The Man.

"He sure as hell does," The Warden said fervently. "The only trouble with them guys, they never learn. I've seen too many of them go into the hockshop, and all they make is work. They aint out two weeks before they're right back in again. They had rather let you kill them, than admit they're wrong. No more sense than a goddam GI mule. About the time you get him groomed up for Regimental next December, he'll pull some hair brained deal and get himself right back in hock, just to get even with you. I seen too many of them mountain boys. They're a threat to the freedom of this whole country."

"I dont give a goddam what he does," The Man yelled, sitting up. "Fuck the Regimentals, and fuck the fucking championship. I dont have to stand for insolence like that. I dont have to take it. I'm an officer in this Army, not a boiler orderly." The red outrage of affront was back in his face. He glared at The Warden.

The Warden waited, timing it exactly to the color in the face, before he empathetically told The Man what The Man was thinking.

"You dont mean that, Captain," The Warden said softly, in horror. "You're just mad. You wouldnt say a thing like that, if you werent mad. You dont want to take a chance on losing your championship next winter, just for being mad."

"Mad!" The Man said. "Mad? Mad, he says. Jesus H Christ, Sergeant!" He rubbed his hands over his face, tentatively feeling of the congestion. "All right," he said. "I guess you're right. Theres no sense in losing your head and going off half cocked and cutting off your nose to spite your face. Maybe he didnt even mean any disrespect at all." The Man sighed. "Have you started on those new forms yet?"

"Not yet, Sir," The Warden said.

"Then put them back," said The Man. "I guess."

"Well at least give him a good stiff company punishment," The Warden said.

"Ha," The Man said vehemently. "If I wasnt the boxing coach of this outfit, I'd give him something," he said. "He's getting off damned easy. Okay, you enter it in the Company Punishment Book, will you? Three weeks restriction to quarters. I'm going home now. Home," he said, as if to himself. "Call him in tomorrow and I'll talk to him and initial the book."

"All right, Sir," The Warden said. "If you think thats the way to handle it." He got the stiff leather-bound Company Punishment Book out of his desk and opened it up and got his pen. The Man smiled at him wearily and left, and he closed the book and put it away again and stepped to the window to watch the Captain cross the quad through the lengthening evening shadows, going home. In a way he almost felt sorry for him, any more. But then he asked for everything he got.

The next day when Holmes asked for the book he got it out and opened it. Then he discovered the page was still blank. Shamefacedly he explained how he had had to do some other things. He had forgotten it. The Man was on his way to the Club, he was in a hurry. He told The Warden to have it ready for him tomorrow.

"Yes, *Sir*," The Warden told him. "I'll do it right away." He got his pen out. The Man left. He put his pen away.

The next day even Holmes had forgotten all about it, under the stress of more recent things.

(from Chapter 19)

[The Stockade, 1]

IN THE CENTER OF the bulletin board, holding the place of honor among the mimeographed memorandums and sheets of detailed instructions about inspections, was a Robert Ripley "Believe It Or Not" that had been clipped from a newspaper. The clipping was brittle and yellow with age. It had been mounted on cardboard to preserve it, and there was a black border of cardboard around it. On the bulletin board it caught the eye instantly.

Hanson and Turnipseed were grinning down at him proudly, like the old nigger guides conducting a party around the sacred environs of Mount Vernon Virginia as if they personally owned it. Prew stepped up to the board.

The chief subject of the clipping was a bust drawing in the familiar style of Mr Ripley, of John Dillinger grinning behind his dark moustache he had grown shortly before he died. Under it was the legend, in Mr Ripley's familiar block printing and equally familiar Gabriel Heatterish style.

THE FIRST PLACE WHERE FORMER PUBLIC ENEMY #1 JOHN DILLINGER EVER SERVED TIME IN PRISON WAS IN THE POST STOCKADE AT SCHOFIELD BARRACKS IN THE TERRITORY OF HAWAII, WHERE THE SCHOFIELD BARRACKS MILITARY POLICE COMPANY RUNS WHAT IS SAID TO BE THE TOUGHEST JAIL IN THE U S ARMY. IT WAS SO TOUGH THAT JOHN DILLINGER UPON BEING RELEASED FROM IT SWORE TO HAVE VEN-

GEANCE UPON THE WHOLE UNITED STATES SOME-
DAY, EVEN IF IT KILLED HIM.

Under this, neatly printed in small letters with a pencil, were
the words

WHICH IT DID

Prew looked again at the pencilled words *"which it did"* and the
black border of one inch cardboard. A flaming rage burned up
fiercely through him like fire sucked up a flue, burning out the soot
and cleansing it so it will draw well. There was a cool calm solace of
protection in the unreasoning rage. But his mind was functioning
enough to recognize it was a false protection.

The two giants still grinned down at him, waiting. He felt he
must not say something debasing.

"Great stuff," he said. "Why show it to me?"

"Show it to every new man," Hanson grinned. "Major
Thompson's orders."

"You'd be surprised," Turnipseed grinned, "all the differnt
reactions we get from this clipping."

"Very illuminatin," Hanson grinned. "Some guys fly into a
reglar fit and cuss and fart and snort like a stud bull in the pasture."

"On the other hand," Turnipseed grinned, "other guys actually
get the shakes."

"Major Thompson must be quite a guy," Prew said. "To put that
up there. I wonder where he got hold of it."

"Hell, he dint put it there," Turnipseed said indignantly. "I been
here longer than he has, and it was there when I come here."

"I been here longer than you have," Hanson said. "And it was
here when I first come here."

"Well," Prew said, "you've showed it to me. Where to now?"

"Take you in for your visit with the Major," Hanson grinned,
"then we'll take you out to work."

Prew studied him. There was no malice in that odd grin, only a
humor of amusement, like when you watch a child mispronounce a
word too big for it. It seemed to be a stiff grin.

"Well, lets go," he said. "What're we waitin for?"

"Major Thompson's very proud of that clipping," Turnipseed
said. "You'd almost think it was his. He claims you can tell just

what kind of prisoner a guy will make just by the way he reacts to it."

"Well, lets shove," Hanson grinned friendlily. "From now on you're marching at attention, bud," he added.

As they rounded the corner back down the long gleaming corridor to the outside door they had first entered by, Hanson made the old familiar quick shuffle movement with his feet, like a sliding boxer, to pick up the step. Their footsteps in unison reverberated crashingly ahead of them down the long hall.

"Prisoner, column right, harch!" Hanson said, when they reached the first door on the right, and both giants marked time while Prew cut the pivot and then followed him in one pace behind him, half a step on his right and left.

"Prisoner, halt!" Hanson said from his left. It was a beautiful movement, beautifully executed with professional precision. Prew was standing two paces from the mission oak desk of Major Thompson and bracketed exactly between the two statues of the gleaming giant MPs.

Major Thompson looked at them approvingly. Then he picked up the sheaf of papers on his desk and looked at them through his gold rimmed spectacles.

Major Thompson was a short barrelchested man whose OD blouse and summer pinks fitted like a glove. On his chest was a World War Victory ribbon with three stars and a Legion of Merit ribbon, joined on the same steel band. He peered myopically from his gold rimmed spectacles. He had the ruddy complexion and close cropped gray hair common to Regular Army officers on long service. He had evidently been an officer ever since 1918.

"I see you are from Harlan Kentucky," Major Thompson said. "We get quite a few boys from Kentucky and West Virginia here. I could almost say they are our chief stock in trade. Most of them is coal miners," he said, "but you dont look big enough to be a coal miner."

"I'm not a coal miner," Prew said. "I never was a—"

The butt of a grub hoe handle thudded into the small of his back above the kidney on the left side and he was afraid for a second he would vomit.

"—Sir," he said quickly.

Major Thompson nodded at him from behind his gold rimmed

spectacles. "Much better," he said. "Our purpose here is to re-educate men to both the manual skills and right mental thinking of soldiers, and to reinstill in them (or teach them, if they never have learned) the desire to soldier. You dont want to get off on the wrong foot, do you?"

Prew did not answer. His back ached and he thought the question was purely rhetorical. The butt of the grub hoe handle whacked into the small of his back in the same spot making his testicles ache, informing him differently.

"Do you?" Major Thompson said.

"No, Sir," Prew said quickly. He was catching on.

"We feel here," Major Thompson said, "that if you men had not mislaid either your manual skills of soldiering, or your mental conditioning, or your desire to soldier, you would not be here. Whatever the legal reason for your restriction. So our every effort is bent toward reaching the objective of re-education with the minimum of wasted time and the maximum of efficiency. Both to the men personally and to the government. We all owe that much to the American taxpayers who support our Army, dont we?"

"Yes, Sir," Prew said quickly, and was rewarded by hearing a rustle subside behind his left. That would be Hanson, he thought, my old pal Pfc Hanson.

"I think you will make a model prisoner," Major Thompson said, and paused.

"Sir, I hope so," Prew said quickly into the breach.

"We may appear to be unduly harsh in our methods," Major Thompson said. "But the quickest, efficientest, least expensive way to educate a man is to make it painful for him when he is wrong, the same as with any other animal. Then he will learn to be right. Its the same way you train yourself a birddog. Our country is at present building a rather reluctant civilian army with which to defend itself in the greatest war in history. The only way to do that is to make the men want to soldier. To be a good soldier a man has to want to soldier more than he wants not to soldier.

"Chaplains' talks on patriotism and indoctrination films are not enough. Perhaps if there was less egotistical selfishness and more willing sacrifice in the world it would work. But it dont. This policy works. We wont talk to you about patriotism here. We will make not wanting to soldier so painful you will prefer to soldier. We

mean to see when a man gets out of this Stockade he will be willing
to do anything not to get back into it again, even die. Are you
following me?"

"Yes, Sir," Prew said quickly. The nausea in his stomach was
beginning to subside a little.

"There is always some men," Major Thompson said, "who
because of psychological shortcomings and poor home training who
will never be good soldiers. If there are men like that here we want
to find out about it. If its more painful for them to soldier than to
stay in this Stockade then they are useless, and we want to get rid of
them before they taint the men around them. They will be
discharged as unfit for service. We are not concerned with individual soldiers, we're concerned with the Army. But we want to be
quite sure they really dont want to soldier, and are not just
goldbricking. You see what I mean?"

"Yes, Sir," Prew said quickly.

"We have the perfect system to carry out this policy," Major
Thompson said. "You cant beat it. We'll find out if you really dont
want to soldier or not." He turned in his chair toward the other
desk. "Wont we, Sgt Judson?"

"Yes, Sir," rumbled the man behind the other desk. Prew turned
his head to look at him and the butt of the omniscient grub hoe
handle immediately thudded into his back in the same place that
had grown very sensitive now, nauseating him sickly. He snapped
his head back to the front, but not before he had seen an enormous
head and hogshead chest with deep concentric layers of fat over the
even deeper layers of muscle that made S/Sgt Judson somewhat
resemble Porky Pig in the Walt Disney cartoons. S/Sgt Judson was
staring at him with the deadest eyes he had ever seen in a human
being. They looked like two beads of caviar spaced far apart on a
great white plate.

"Theres a few rules," Major Thompson said. "All of them is
designed toward the single objective of seeing how bad a man wants
not to soldier. For instance," he said, "when in the presence of
superiors, prisoners move only on command. Especially in this
office," he said.

"Yes, sir," Prew said quickly. "I'm sorry, Sir." The nausea had
come back full force, worse than before, and he wanted to take his
hands and knead and massage the place on his back that had

become so sensitive now that it seemed to have a mind of its own with which to anticipate the grub hoe handle.

When Major Thompson did not acknowledge his apology but went right on naming off rules, the spot on his back seemed to leap quiveringly in its own private panic for fear he had made another mistake in talking when not asked, but the omniscient grub hoe handle did not fall. He waited for it eternally, while trying to listen to the rules Major Thompson was naming.

"Prisoners are not allowed to have visitors, and they are not allowed to have tailormade cigarettes," Major Thompson said. "Prisoners are issued one bag of Duke's Mixture a day and any other tobacco, either tailormade plug or pipe, found in the possession of a prisoner earns him an immediate demerit."

Prew felt he was beginning to learn what a demerit was finally. It seemed to be a very elastic medium that covered a multitude of sins.

"We have barracks inspection daily," Major Thompson said, "instead of just on Saturday, and any discrepancy of personal equipment earns a prisoner an immediate demerit. Repeated infractions of any rule gets solitary confinement.

"While here," Major Thompson said, "every internee is called by the title of 'Prisoner.' Men serving time in this Stockade have lost their rights to the title of rank, and to the complimentary title of 'Soldier.'

"S/Sgt Judson here is the second in command. In the event of my absence his decision will be final. Is that understood?"

"Yes, Sir," Prew said quickly.

"Then I think thats all," Major Thompson said. "Any questions, Prisoner?"

"No, Sir," Prew said quickly.

"Then thats all. Pfc Hanson will take you out to work."

"Yes, Sir," Prew said, and snapped out a salute. The butt of the grub hoe handle slammed into the small of his back above the kidney in the same spot with the precision of a clock, the Godlike reprimand of a schoolteacher's ruler.

"Prisoners do not salute," Major Thompson said. "Only soldiers have got the right to the mutual compliment of the salute."

"Yes, Sir," Prew said thickly through the sickness in his belly.

"Thats all," Major Thompson said. "Prisoner, about face! Prisoner, forward march!"

At the door Hanson took over and gave him a column right and they were headed for the outside door they had first come in by. Prew's back hurt sickly all the way down to his knees and his mind was in a delirium of rage. He did not notice where Turnipseed went, or when. Hanson halted him at the tool room, next to the locked weapons room. Another trustee handed him out a 16 pound sledgehammer. Then Hanson stopped him at the weapons room and exchanged his grub hoe handle for a riot gun with the armed sentry who stayed locked inside, before he took him on outside to the 2½ ton waiting just inside the gate.

"You done pretty fair," Hanson grinned, as they climbed in the thick-dusty back and he signaled the driver. "What was it, only four wasnt it?"

"Just four," Prew said.

"Hell, thats good," Hanson grinned. "I've seen them get as many as ten or twelve, during their first session. I've even seen a couple of them that clean lost their head and had to actually be carried out finally they got so fuckedup. I think the least I ever seen is two, and that was Jack Malloy who's a three time loser. You really done exceptional."

"Thats good," Prew said grimly, "I was beginning to think for a minute there I'd failed my first examination."

"Naw," Hanson grinned. "I was real proud of you. Four is fine. The saluting always gets one, so it was really only three. Even Jack Malloy got one on the salute, a guy just does it by instinct."

"That makes me feel better," Prew said, as he watched the gates close behind them and felt the air and saw the Waianae Range up there at Kolekole where they were going.

"You'll be all right," Hanson grinned.

(from Chapter 36)

[The Stockade, 2]

IT WAS DURING THE MONTH after Angelo had gone to the hosp and before Stonewall Jackson came back with news of him, that the young Indiana farmboy Prew had seen beaned in Number Three was transferred into Number Two. Of all the men that had been in Number Three with Prew he was the one Prew would have picked as least likely to succeed, but he came in with them after his three day jaunt in the Hole as mildly affable as ever.

They had been expecting him since before Angelo had gone in the Hole. Apparently, after that first spell of lapse that resulted from the beaning itself and had lasted only one day, the Indiana farmboy had started having them more and more often and for longer and longer periods. When he was normal, he was the same old mild uncomplaining self; when he was in one of the lapses, he was the same docile dreamy idiot Prew had seen. But every time he came out of a period of lapse he went crazy fighting mad and attacked whatever happened to be closest to him. Twice he had attacked guards on the rockpile. Once in the messhall he had emptied his plate of catsup and beans over the head of the man eating next to him and started sawing on him with the dull edge of his table knife; the only thing that saved the man was the fact that the GI cutlery would hardly cut butter. He got three days in the Hole for that one, served them uncomplainingly affably, and the day after he got out tried to brain the man next to him on the rockpile with a medium-sized boulder. A number of times at night in the barracks some man in Number Three would wake to find a crazy-faced demon wildly choking his neck and grapple with him until three or four others, roused by the scuffle, would come to his aid and sit on the Indiana farmboy until he was all right again. The boys in Number Three loyally covered these up for him and finally set up a system of guard duty in which there was always one man awake at night to keep an eye on him. But finally he went after Fatso himself one day in the messhall. He was beaned with a grub hoe handle again for his trouble, and it was decided he was worthy Number Two Material.

The truth was, he was not. He was as out of place in Number Two as a white chicken amongst a black flock. But he accepted this with the same equanimity that he accepted everything else. He remembered Prew and eagerly made friends with him, and he quickly arrived at a worship of Jack Malloy that surpassed even that of Blues Berry and came very close to the point of embarrassment the way he followed Jack around like a puppy. When they came to playing games in the evenings he tried as hard with that as he tried with everything else, when he was normal, and suffered the knee-punctures and burned hands of Indian-wrassle and the sore ribs of The Game as uncomplainingly as he suffered everything else. Once, he even managed to stay up at The Game through the five smallest men and was cheered roundly. He achieved the distinction of being the first man in the history of Number Two who was ever offered exemption from playing games, but he refused to sit on the sidelines and not play, although he was never known to have won any game from anybody, up to the time they all started taking it easy on him.

They took him under their wing and looked after him and adopted him as a sort of a mascot. His crazy spells when he was coming out of one of his lapses did not bother them and they did not need to set up a guard system because without exception they were all adepts at rough and tumble fighting and had been since childhood. If one of them woke up to find him choking on him he would wrassle loose from him, knock him out, and then put him back to bed where he would wake up in the morning his old mild affable self again. None of them in Number Two, in fact nobody in the Stockade, considered him even remotely dangerous. Even a mind like Jack Malloy could not have seen danger in such an ineffectually murderous Indiana farmboy. That he would ever be the match that would touch off the fuse that would blow apart the tautly balanced status quo of the Stockade as a whole and Number Two in particular, and alter the whole lives of several of them, even unto the Outside, was frankly laughable.

It happened without warning or expectation, out on the rockpile one afternoon. Since he had come into Number Two, the Indiana farmboy had gradually grown more and more bitter about life in an affable sort of a way. It was not like him, and nobody ever knew afterwards if it was because he was trying to emulate his new heroes, or if it was because his spells had cost him his time-off-for-good-behavior and, with his final removal to Number Two, lengthened his one-month sentence into a two-month one.

That afternoon he was in one of his dreamy lapses. Prew was working between Blues Berry and Stonewall Jackson when he came out of it. They had been watching for the signs, and no sooner had the Indiana farmboy dropped his hammer and looked up wildly than the three of them fell on him and held him down until he was all right again. Then they all four went on back to work without thinking anything much about it since they were all used to the procedure by now.

But a little while later the Indiana farmboy stepped over to them with an unusually affably resolute look and asked if one of them would break his arm for him.

"What the hell for, Francis?" Prew wanted to know.

"Because I want to go to the hospital," the Indiana farmboy explained.

"What do you want to go to the hospital for?"

"Because I'm sick and tired of this goddam hole," the Indiana farmboy said affably. "I've pulled my whole month's sentence and I've still got twenty-six days to do. Twenty-six more days."

"How would you like to have six months to do, like me?" Jackson said.

"I wouldnt like it," the Indiana farmboy said.

"Breaking your arm wont help you to get out any quicker," Prew said reasonably.

"It'll get me two or three weeks in the hospital though."

"Anyway, how the hell could we break your arm? Take it over our knee like a stick and break it?" Prew said. "An arm's hard to break, Francis."

"I've already thought of that," the Indiana farmboy said triumphantly. "I can lay my arm down between two rocks and one of you can hit it with a sledgehammer. That would break it quick and easy and give me at least two weeks vacation in the hospital."

"I dont want to do it, Francis," Prew said, suddenly feeling a little bit queasy.

"Will you do it for me, Stonewall?" the Indiana farmboy said.

"What the hell do you want to go to the hospital for?" Jackson evaded. "It aint no better than here. I've been there, and I'm telling you true. It aint a dam bit bettern here."

"Well, at least there wont be no Fatso there, and you wont have to work in this goddam sun breaking rocks with a hammer."

"No," Jackson said, "but you'll sit around on your dead ass looking out through them goddam chainmesh grids till you'll wish to hell you was breaking rocks with a hammer."

"At least the food will be better."

"Its better," Jackson admitted. "But you'll get just as sick of it anyway."

"Then you wont do it for me? Even as a favor?" the Indiana farmboy said reproachfully.

"Oh, I guess I'd do it for you," Jackson said reluctantly squeamishly, "but I'd a hell of a lot rather not, Francis."

"I'll do it," Blues Berry grinned. "Any old time you want it done, Francis. If you really want to do it, that is."

"I want to do it," the Indiana farmboy said affably firmly.

"Well, wheres some rocks?" Berry said.

"Theres a couple over here where I'm working that'll do just fine."

"Okay," Berry said. "Lets go." Then he paused and turned back to the others. "You guys dont care if I do it for him, do you? I mean, what the hell? If he's that sick of it. I can see how I might want somebody to do it for me sometime maybe."

"No," Prew said reluctantly. "I dont care. Its none of my affair. I just dont want to do it, thats all."

"Thats the way I feel," Jackson said queasily.

"Okay, I'll be right back," Berry said. "Keep an eye out for them guards."

The guard down in the pit was clear out of sight, but the two guards up on the cliff were both in position to see them.

"You better watch them up there," Prew said.

"Hell, if I waited till they got out of sight, I'd wait till the earth looked level."

"They probly move off a piece in a little bit," Prew suggested.

"Ahh, hell with them," Berry said disgustedly. "They too blind to see anything anyway."

He took his hammer and followed the Indiana farmboy off about five yards where Francis pointed out two rocks he had selected, two smooth flat-topped ones about six or eight inches apart and three or four inches off the ground. The Indiana farmboy knelt down and laid his left arm out across the rocks with his elbow and upper forearm on one and his wrist out onto the other.

"This way, you see, it wont break any joints," he explained affably. "I figured my left arm because I'm righthanded. It'll be easier to eat with and I can still write letters home to the family. Okay," he said. "Hit it."

"All right, here goes," Berry said. He stepped up and measured the swing with the head of his hammer and then swung, back over his head, a full double-armed swing, and hit the arm between the two rocks with all the force and accuracy of an expert axman notching a tree.

Francis the Indiana farmboy screamed with just as much surprise as if he had not been expecting it, like a man who had been shot by a sniper he didnt see. If there was any sound of bone breaking, the scream smothered it. He stayed on his knees a few seconds, looking whitefaced and faint, then he got up and came over to show it to them. In the middle of his forearm where the line should have run straight there was a kind of square-cornered offset. In the few seconds it took him to cross the five yards it had already started to swell. As they watched it, it swelled until the recessed part of the offset was filled out level again and there was only a big bulge on the bottom.

"I think its broke in two places," Francis said happily. "Hell, that ought to get me at least three whole weeks. Maybe more." He broke off strangeledly and got down on his knees, holding his left arm gingerly with his right, and vomited.

"Boy, it sure hurts," he said proudly, getting back up. "I sure didnt think it would hurt that much," he said, with the same astounded surprise that had been in his scream. "Thanks a hell of a lot, Berry."

"Think nothing of it," Berry grinned. "Glad to help out."

"Well, I think I'll go on down and show this to the guard," Francis said happily. "See you guys later." He went off down the hill still holding his left arm gingerly with his right.

"Jesus!" Prew said, feeling an unusually cool trickle of sweat down his back.

"Man, he can have it," Jackson said. "I dont want any of that. Not even if it would get me clear out of the Stockade."

"What the hell?" Berry grinned. "You hear about criminals

operatin on themself all a time to get bullets out. Thats lots worse then this."

"I never heard about it anywheres outside of the movies," Prew said.

"Me neither," Jackson said. "I never seen it."

"Hell, it was easy," Berry grinned at them. "There wasnt nothing to it."

Between hammerswings they watched the guard on the road make a call in from the box while the Indiana farmboy stood beside him happily, holding his left arm gingerly in his right. Then pretty soon the truck came up for him and he climbed in the back, still holding his left arm gingerly in his right.

"See?" Berry said. "Easy as pie. Hell, I got a goddam good notion to do it myself."

"If two guys showed up with broken arms, they'd sure as hell suspect something then," Prew said.

"I know it," Berry grinned wolfishly. "Thats why I aint. But thats about the ony goddam reason."

That evening when they came in from work they learned that Francis Murdock the Indiana farmboy was already in the prison ward with a certified broken arm from a fall on the rockpile. It was, however, only broken in one place, instead of two as he had hoped.

Nothing was said about it and no questions were asked and it appeared as if it had all gone off like clockwork. Evening chow went off just as usual.

But after chow, shortly before lights out, Fatso and Major Thompson himself came into Number Two with the grub hoe handles and looking madder than hell.

It was almost like an inspection. They lined them up at attention by their bunks and the two riot-gunned guards stood just inside with the third guard standing outside holding the key to the locked door. Major Thompson looked as if he had just caught his wife in bed with a private.

"Young Murdock broke his arm out on the rockpile this afternoon," the Major said crisply. "He claimed it was broke by a fall. He went to the hospital with that disposition because we like to keep our fights in the family here. But just between us, somebody broke that arm for him. Murdock and the man who broke it for him are both guilty of malingering. We do not tolerate malingering in this Stockade. Murdock's sentence is going to be lengthened, and when he comes back from the hospital he's going to find it pretty tough around here. Now I want the man who broke Murdock's arm to step forward."

Nobody moved. Nobody answered.

"All right," the Major said crisply. "We can play hard too. You men are in Number Two because you are recalcitrants. I dont have no sympathy for any of you. You've been getting away with murder lately and its about time all of you learned who runs this Stockade. I'll give the man one last chance to step forward."

Nobody moved.

"All right, Sergeant," the Major said crisply and nodded at Fatso.

S/Sgt Judson stepped up to the first man and said, "Who broke Murdock's arm?" The man was a skinny little old-timer from the 8th Field with a craggy lined face that portrayed absolute cynicism and eyes that stared straight ahead as immovably as two stones. He had been clear over at the other side of the quarry but he already knew the whole story. He said, "I dont know, Sergeant" and Fatso rapped him across the shins with the grub hoe handle and asked him again. The craggy face never moved and the solid stone eyes neither wavered nor flickered. He said, "I dont know, Sergeant" again and Fatso slammed him with the head in the belly and asked him again. He got exactly the same results.

It was the same way all up and down the line. Fatso started methodically at one end and worked his way diligently down and back up to the other. He asked each man the same question "Who broke Murdock's arm?" five times. Not a figure moved and not an eye flickered or wavered and nothing but infinite contempt for Fatso's hard methods and Fatso himself showed on any face. This was not Number Three; this was Number Two. And Number Two was as solidly together as a morticed stone wall.

Neither the contempt nor the unbreakability bothered Fatso. His business was to ask each man the question and hit him if he gave the wrong answer, not to worry about the results, and he did his job thoroughly and methodically. When he had worked his way through the line, he came back to the Major and they both went down the line and stopped in front of Blues Berry.

"Who broke Murdock's arm for him?" Major Thompson said.

Everybody knew they knew, then.

Berry stared straight ahead without answering.

Fatso hit him.

"Did you break Murdock's arm for him?" Major Thompson said.

Berry stared straight ahead, at attention, without answering.

Fatso hit him.

"It just happens," the Major smiled, "that we already know you was the man who broke Murdock's arm for him."

Berry grinned.

Fatso hit him.

"Step forward," Major Thompson said.

Berry took two paces forward, still grinning.

Fatso hit him across the bridge of the nose with the head of the grub hoe handle. Berry went down to his knees. He stayed there several seconds, nobody helping him, before he got back up shakily. Blood was pouring out of his nose, but he did not raise his hands or move his eyes from the wall. He licked his lips with the tip of his tongue and grinned at the Major.

"I'm going to make an example out of you, Berry," Major Thompson said crisply. "You're too big for your pants. I'm going to cut you down till you fit them. I'm going to show these men what happens to a man who gets too big for his pants and thinks he's too tough. Did you break Murdock's arm?"

"Fuck you," Berry said huskily.

This time Fatso hit him in the mouth with the head of the grub hoe handle. Berry's knees went loose but he did not quite go down. His eyes came unfocused but he did not move them from the wall. When he straightened up, he worked his mouth a little and spat two teeth out at Fatso's feet contemptuously and grinned at him.

"And I'm going to kill you, Fatso," he grinned. "If I ever get out of here, I'm going to hunt you down and kill you. So you better get me first. Because if I ever get out, I'll kill you."

Fatso was as unmoved by this as he had been by the general contempt and uncooperativeness. He raised his grub hoe handle again, methodically, diligently, impassively, but Major Thompson stopped him.

"Take him down to the gym," the Major said. "I dont want to dirty the barracks up any more than necessary. Some of you men clean this mess up."

Fatso took Berry by the arm and started to lead him to the door but Berry jerked his arm loose and said, "Keep your fat paws off of me. I can still walk," and walked to the door by himself. The guard outside unlocked the door. Berry walked through it. Fatso and the Major and then the two guards followed him.

"The crazy son of a bitch," Jack Malloy said contortedly. "Thats not the way to handle them. I told him thats not the way to handle them."

"Maybe he's tired of handling them," Prew said narrowly.

"He'll be tireder," Malloy said unforgivingly. "They're serious."

It was the first time any of them had ever heard a man scream when he was in the gym getting a workout. The fact that it was Blues Berry whom they heard screaming proved they were serious, that this time the Major and Fatso were out to make it or break it, showdown or else. In Number Two they cleaned up the floor and settled down to wait. It was already after nine-thirty, and the fact that the lights were still on showed this was really going to be an occasion. They managed to find out from Pfc Hanson who passed by the door under arms hurriedly, that it was one of the guards up on the cliff who had seen him.

It was eleven-thirty when Major Thompson, wearing his side-arms, came for them with the guards. There were ten guards, each wearing sidearms and carrying a riotgun.

They were lined up in a column of twos and marched down to the gym. The guards were spaced along the walls with their riotguns at port arms. More guards lined the walls of the gym. Apparently, every guard on the place had been called out tonight. The column from Number Two was marched into the gym and distributed around three of the walls with the guards in back of them.

Blues Berry stood against one of the side walls in his GI shorts under the lights, still trying to grin with a mouth that was too swollen to do more than twist. He was barely recognizable. His broken nose had swollen and was still running blood in a stream. Blood was also flowing out of his mouth, whenever he coughed. His eyes were practically closed. Blows from the grub hoe handles had torn the upper half of both ears loose from his head. Blood from his nose and mouth, and the ears which were not bleeding much, had spotted his chest and the white drawers.

"He's dead," somebody whispered behind Prew with finality.

Fatso and two other guards, Turnipseed and Angelo Maggio's old friend Brownie, all looking exhausted, stood near him. Major Thompson, wearing his sidearms, stood off by himself near the corner.

"We want to show you men what happens to men who think they can run the Army," he said crisply. "Sergeant," he nodded.

"Turn around," S/Sgt Judson said. "Put your nose and toes against the wall."

"You better kill me, Fatso," Berry whispered. "You better do a good job. If you dont, I'll kill you. If I ever get out of here, I'll kill you."

S/Sgt Judson stepped up and drove his knee up into Berry's testicles. Berry screamed.

"Turn around," S/Sgt Judson said. "Put your nose and toes against the wall."

Berry turned around and put his nose and toes to the wall. "You son of a bitch," he whispered, "you fathog son of a bitch. You better kill me. If you dont, I'll kill you. You better kill me." It was as if it was the one solitary idea he had left and he had fixed his mind on it to keep something with him. He said it over and over.

"Did you break Murdock's arm for him, Berry?" S/Sgt Judson said.

Berry went on whispering his passion to himself.

"Berry, can you hear me?" S/Sgt Judson said. "Did you break Murdock's arm?"

"I can hear you," Berry whispered. "You better kill me, Fatso, thats all. If you dont, I'll kill you. You better kill me."

"Brown," Fatso said. He nodded at Berry. "Take him."

Cpl Brown stepped into position like a man stepping into the batter's box at the plate and swung his grub hoe handle with both hands into the small of Berry's back. Berry screamed. Then he coughed, and some more blood splashed down from his mouth.

There are two kinds of grub hoe handles, curved ones and straight ones. The straight ones are longer and heavier than the curved ones. A pick handle is longer and heavier than any ax handle, and a grub hoe handle is longer and heavier than a pick handle. A straight grub hoe handle is about four inches longer than a pick handle and around a pound heavier in weight and can be recognized by the double hump at the head end. The steel head of a grub hoe, which is like the mattock half of a pick-mattock with the pick half left off the other end, fits between these two humps on the handle and makes the grub hoe a fine tool for clearing brushy root-matted ground.

"Did you break Murdock's arm?" Fatso said.

"Fuck you," Berry whispered. "You better kill me. If you dont, I'll kill you. You better kill me."

They kept them there fifteen mintes. Then they marched them back between the lines of guards to the barrack and turned off the lights. The occasional screams from the gym did not stop however, and there was not much sleep. But in the morning they were got up at 4:45 just the same.

At chow they learned that at one-thirty Blues Berry, unable to urinate and with his ears knocked half loose from his head, had been taken up to the prison ward of the Station Hospital for treatment of a fall from the back of a truck.

He died the next day about noon, "from massive cerebral hemorrhage and internal injuries," the report was quoted as stating, "probably caused by a fall from a truck traveling at high speed."

(from Chapter 43)

[December Seventh]

MILT WARDEN did not really get up early the morning of the big day. He just had not been to bed.

He had gone around to the Blue Chancre, after Karen had gone home at 9:30, on a vague hunch that Prewitt might be there. Karen had asked him about him again and they had discussed him a long time. Prewitt hadnt been there, but he ran into Old Pete and the Chief; Pete was helping the Chief to celebrate his last night in town before going back into his garrison headquarters at Choy's. They had already made their bomb run on the whorehouses and dropped their load on Mrs Kipfer's New Congress. After Charlie Chan closed up the Blue Chancre, the four of them had sat out in the back room and played stud poker for a penny a chip while drinking Charlie's bar whiskey.

It was always a dull game; Charlie could not play poker for peanuts; but he always let them have the whiskey at regular wholesale prices and if they complained loud enough he would even go in on it and pay a full share, although he drank very little. So they were always willing to suffer his poker playing. They would always overplay a hand to him now and then to keep him from finding out how lousy he was.

When they had drunk as much as they could hold without passing out, it was so late the Schofield cabs had stopped running. They had hired a city cab to take them back because there was nowhere else to go at 6:30 on Sunday morning.

Besides, Stark always had hotcakes-and-eggs and fresh milk on Sundays. There is nothing as good for a hangover as a big meal of hotcakes-and-eggs and fresh milk just before going to bed.

They were too late to eat early chow in the kitchen, and the chow line was already moving slowly past the two griddles. Happily drunkenly undismayed, the three of them bucked the line amid the ripple of curses from the privates, and carried their plates in to eat at the First-Three-Graders' table at the head of the room.

It was almost like a family party. All the platoon sergeants were there, and Stark was there in his sweated undershirt after getting the cooks started, and Malleaux the supply sergeant. Even Baldy Dhom was there, having been run out by his wife for getting drunk last night at the NCO Club. All of this in itself did not happen often, and today being Sunday, nobody was less than half tight and since there had been a big shindig dance at the Officers' Club last night none of the officers had shown up, so that they did not have to be polite.

The conversation was mostly about Mrs Kipfer's. That was where Pete and the Chief had wound up last night, and most of the others had gone there. Mrs Kipfer had just got in a shipment of four new beaves, to help take care of the influx of draftees that was raising Company strengths all over Schofield. One was a shy dark-haired little thing who was apparently appearing professionally for the first time, and who showed promise of someday stepping into Lorene's shoes when Lorene went back home. Her name was Jeanette and she was variously recommended back and forth across the table.

At least one officer was always required to eat the men's food in the messhall, either Lt Ross, or Chicken Culpepper, or else one of the three new ROTC boys the Company had been issued during the last week; the five of them passed the detail around among them; but whichever one got it, it was still always the same and put a damper over the noncoms' table. But today it was just like a big family party. Minus the mother-in-law.

Stark was the only one, outside of Warden and Baldy, who had not been around to Mrs Kipfer's last night. But he was drunk, too. Stark had picked himself off a shackjob down at the Wailupe Naval Radio Station while they had had the CP out at Hanauma Bay. Some of them had seen her, and she was a hot-looking, wild, I'll-go-as-far-as-you-will wahine, but Stark would not talk about her. So he did not enter the conversation much at the table; but he listened. He had not spoken to Warden since the night at Hickam Field except in the line of duty, and at the table he ignored Warden and Warden ignored him.

It was a typical Sunday morning breakfast, for the first weekend after payday. At least a third of the Company was not home. Another third was still in bed asleep. But the last third more than made up for the absences in the loudness of their drunken laughter and horseplay and the clashing of cutlery and halfpint milk bottles.

Warden was just going back for seconds on both hotcakes and eggs, with that voracious appetite he always had when he was drunk, when this blast shuddered by under the floor and rattled the cups on the tables and then rolled on off across the quad like a high wave at sea in a storm.

He stopped in the doorway of the KP room and looked back at the messhall. He remembered the picture the rest of his life. It had become very quiet and everybody had stopped eating and looked up at each other.

"Must be doin some dynamitin down to Wheeler Field," somebody said tentatively.

"I heard they was clearin some ground for a new fighter strip," somebody else agreed.

That seemed to satisfy everybody. They went back to their eating. Warden heard a laugh ring out above the hungry gnashings of cutlery on china, as he turned back into the KP room. The tail of the chow line was still moving past the two griddles, and he made a mental note to go behind the cooks' serving table when he bucked the line this time, so as not to make it so obvious.

That was when the second blast came. He could hear it a long way off coming toward them under the ground; then it was there before he could move, rattling the cups and plates in the KP sinks and the rinsing racks; then it was gone and he could hear it going away northeast toward the 21st Infantry's football field. Both the KPs were looking at him.

He reached out to put his plate on the nearest flat surface, holding it carefully in both hands so it would not get broken while he congratulated himself on his presence of mind, and then turned back to the messhall, the KPs still watching him.

As there was nothing under the plate, it fell on the floor and crashed in the silence, but nobody heard it because the third groundswell of blast had already reached the PX and was just about to them. It passed under, rattling everything, just as he got back to the NCOs' table.

"This is it," somebody said quite simply.

Warden found that his eyes and Stark's eyes were looking into each other. There was nothing on Stark's face, except the slack relaxed peaceful look of drunkenness, and Warden felt there must not be anything on his either. He pulled his mouth up and showed his teeth in a grin, and Stark's face pulled up his mouth in an identical grin. Their eyes were still looking into each other.

Warden grabbed his coffee cup in one hand and his halfpint of milk in the other and ran out through the messhall screendoor onto the porch. The far door, into the dayroom, was already so crowded he could not have pushed through. He ran down the porch and turned into the corridor that ran through to the street and beat them all outside but for one or two. When he stopped and looked back he saw Pete Karelsen and Chief Choate and Stark were all right behind him. Chief Choate had his plate of hotcakes-and-eggs in his left hand and his fork in the other. He took a big bite. Warden turned back and swallowed some coffee.

Down the street over the trees a big column of black smoke was mushrooming up into the sky. The men behind were crowding out the door and pushing those in front out into the street. Almost everybody had brought his bottle of milk to keep from getting it stolen, and a few had brought their coffee too. From the middle of the street Warden could not see any more than he had seen from the edge, just the same big column of black smoke mushrooming up into the sky from down around Wheeler Field. He took a drink of his coffee and pulled the cap off his milk bottle.

"Gimme some of that coffee," Stark said in a dead voice behind him, and held up his own cup. "Mine was empty."

He turned around to hand him the cup and when he turned back a big tall thin red-headed boy who had not been there before was running down the street toward them, his red hair flapping in his self-induced breeze, and his knees coming up to his chin with every step. He looked like he was about to fall over backwards.

"Whats up, Red?" Warden hollered at him. "Whats happening? Wait a minute! Whats going on?"

The red-headed boy went on running down the street concentratedly, his eyes glaring whitely wildly at them.

"The Japs is bombing Wheeler Field!" he hollered over his shoulder. "The Japs is bombing Wheeler Field! I seen the red circles on the wings!"

He went on running down the middle of the street, and quite suddenly right behind him came a big roaring, getting bigger and bigger; behind the roaring came an airplane, leaping out suddenly over the trees.

Warden, along with the rest of them, watched it coming with his milk bottle still at his lips and the twin red flashes winking out from the nose. It came over and down and up and away and was gone, and the stones in the asphalt pavement at his feet popped up in a long curving line that led up the curb and puffs of dust came up from the grass and a line of cement popped out of the wall to the roof, then back down the wall to the grass and off out across the street again in a big S-shaped curve.

With a belated reflex, the crowd of men swept back in a wave toward the door, after the plane was already gone, and then swept right back out again pushing the ones in front into the street again.

Above the street between the trees Warden could see other planes down near the smoke column. They flashed silver like mirrors. Some of them began suddenly to grow larger. His shin hurt from where a stone out of the pavement had popped him.

"All right, you stupid fucks!" he bellowed. "Get back inside! You want to get your ass shot off?"

Down the street the red-haired boy lay sprawled out floppy-haired, wild-eyed, and silent, in the middle of the pavement. The etched line on the asphalt ran up to him and continued on on the other side of him and then stopped.

"See that?" Warden bawled. "This aint jawbone, this is for record. Thems real bullets that guy was usin."

The crowd moved reluctantly back toward the dayroom door.

But one man ran to the wall and started probing with his pocketknife in one of the holes and came out with a bullet. It was a .50 caliber. Then another man ran out in the street and picked up something which turned out to be three open-end metal links. The middle one still had a .50 caliber casing in it. The general movement toward the dayroom stopped.

"Say! Thats pretty clever," somebody said. "Our planes is still usin web machinegun belts that they got to carry back home!" The two men started showing their finds to the men around them. A couple of other men ran out into the street hurriedly.

"This'll make me a good souvenir," the man with the bullet said contentedly. "A bullet from a Jap plane on the day the war started."

"Give me back my goddam coffee!" Warden hollered at Stark. "And help me shoo these dumb bastards back inside!"

"What you want me to do?" Chief Choate asked. He was still holding his plate and fork and chewing excitedly on a big bite.

"Help me get em inside," Warden hollered.

Another plane, on which they could see the red discs, came skidding over the trees firing and saved him the trouble. The two men hunting for metal links in the street sprinted breathlessly. The crowd moved back in a wave to the door, and stayed there. The plane flashed past, the helmeted head with the square goggles over the slant eyes and the long scarf rippling out behind it and the grin on the face as he waved, all clearly visible for the space of a wink, like a traveltalk slide flashed on and then off of a screen.

Warden, Stark, Pete and the Chief descended on them as the crowd started to wave outward again, blocking them off and forcing the whole bunch back inside the dayroom.

The crowd milled indignantly in the small dayroom, everybody talking excitedly. Stark posted himself huskily in the doorway with Pete and the Chief flanking him. Warden gulped off the rest of his coffee and set the cup on the magazine rack and pushed his way down to the other end and climbed up on the pingpong table.

"All right, all right, you men. Quiet down. Quiet down. Its only a war. Aint you ever been in a war before?"

The word war had the proper effect. They began to yell at each other to shut up and listen.

"I want every man to go upstairs to his bunk and stay there," Warden said. "Each man report to his squad leader. Squad leaders keep your men together at their bunks until you get orders what to do."

The earth shudders rolling up from Wheeler Field were already a commonplace now. Above it, they heard another plane go roaring machinegun-rattling over.

"The CQ will unlock the rifle racks and every man get his rifle and hang onto it. *But stay inside at your bunks.* This aint no maneuvers. You go runnin around outside you'll get your ass shot off. And you cant do no good anyway. You want to be heroes, you'll get plenty chances later; from now on. You'll probly have Japs right in your laps, by time we get down to beach positions.

"Stay off the porches. Stay *inside*. I'm making each squad leader responsible to keep his men *inside*. If you have to use a rifle butt to do it, thats okay too."

There was a mutter of indignant protest.

"You heard me!" Warden hollered. "You men want souvenirs, buy them off the widows of the men who went out after them. If I catch anybody runnin around outside, I'll personally beat his head in, and then see he gets a goddam general court martial."

There was another indignant mutter of protest.

"What if the fuckers bomb us?" somebody hollered.

"If you hear a bomb coming, you're free to take off for the brush," Warden said. "But not unless you do. I dont think they will. If they was going to bomb us, they would of started with it already. They probly concentratin all their bombs on the Air Corps and Pearl Harbor."

There was another indignant chorus.

"Yeah," somebody hollered, "but what if they aint?"

"Then you're shit out of luck," Warden said. "If they *do* start to bomb, get everybody outside—on the side *away* from the quad—not *into* the quad—and disperse; *away* from the big buildings."

"That wont do us no good if they've already laid one on the roof," somebody yelled.

"All right," Warden hollered, "can the chatter. Lets move. We're wasting time. Squad leaders get these men upstairs. BAR men, platoon leaders and first-three-graders report to me here."

With the corporals and buck sergeants haranguing them, the troops gradually began to sift out through the corridor to the porch stairs. Outside another plane went over. Then another, and another.

Then what sounded like three planes together. The platoon leaders and guides and BAR men pushed their way down to the pingpong table that Warden jumped down off of.

"What you want me to do, First?" Stark said; his face still had the same expression of blank, flat refusal—like a stomach flatly refusing food—that he had had in the messhall; "what about the kitchen force? I'm pretty drunk, but I can still shoot a BAR."

"I want you to get your ass in the kitchen with every man you got and start packing up," Warden said, looking at him. He rubbed his hand hard over his own face. "We'll be movin out for the beach as soon as this tapers off a little, and I want that kitchen all packed and ready to roll. Full field. Stoves and all. While you're doin that, make a big pot of coffee on the big stove. Use the biggest #18 pot you got."

"Right," Stark said, and took off for the door into the messhall.

"Wait!" Warden hollered. "On second thought, make two pots. The two biggest you got. We're going to need it."

"Right," Stark said, and went on. His voice was not blank, his voice was crisp. It was just his face, that was blank.

"The rest of you guys," Warden said.

Seeing their faces, he broke off and rubbed his own face again. It didnt do any good. As soon as he stopped rubbing it settled right back into it, like a campaign hat that had been blocked a certain way.

"I want the BAR men to report to the supplyroom right now and get their weapons and all the loaded clips they can find and go up on the roof. When you see a Jap plane, shoot at it. Dont worry about wasting ammo. Remember to take a big lead. Thats all. Get moving."

"The rest of you guys," Warden said, as the BAR men moved away at a run. "The rest of you guys. The first thing. The main thing. Every platoon leader is responsible to me personally to see that all of his men stay inside, except the BAR men up on the roof. A rifleman's about as much good against a low flying pursuit ship as a boy scout with a slingshot. And we're going to need every man we can muster when we get down to beach positions. I dont want none of them wasted here, by runnin outside to shoot rifles at airplanes. Or by goin souvenir huntin. The men stay inside. Got it?"

There was a chorus of hurried vacant nods. Most of the heads were on one side, listening to the planes going over and over in ones twos and threes. It looked peculiar to see them all nodding on one side like that. Warden found himself wanting to laugh excitedly.

"The BARs will be up on the roof," he said. "They can do all the shooting that we can supply ammo for. Anybody else will just be getting in the way."

"What about my MGs, Milt?" Pete Karelsen asked him.

The easy coolness in old Pete's voice shocked Warden to a full stop. Drunk or not, Pete seemed to be the only one who sounded relaxed, and Warden remembered his two years in France.

"Whatever you think, Pete," he said.

"I'll take one. They couldnt load belts fast enough to handle more than one. I'll take Mikeovitch and Grenelli up with me to handle it."

"Can you get the muzzle up high enough on those ground tripods?"

"We'll put the tripod over a chimney," Pete said. "And then hold her down by the legs."

"Whatever you think, Pete," Warden said, thinking momentarily how wonderful it was to be able to say that.

"Come on, you two," Pete said, almost boredly, to his two section leaders. "We'll take Grenelli's because we worked on it last."

"Remember," Warden said to the rest of them as Pete left with his two machinegunners. "The men stay inside. I dont care how you handle it. Thats up to you. I'm going to be up on the roof with a BAR. If you want to get in on the fun, go yourself. Thats where I'm going to be. But make damn sure your men are going to stay *inside*, off the porches, before you go up."

"Like hell!" Liddell Henderson said. "You aint goin to catch this Texan up on no roof. Ah'll stay down with ma men."

"Okay," Warden said, jabbing a finger at him. "Then you are hereby placed in charge of the loading detail. Get ten or twelve men, as many as you can get in the supplyroom, and put them to loading BAR clips and MG belts. We're going to need all the ammo we can get. Anybody else dont want to go up?"

"I'll stay down with Liddell," Champ Wilson said.

"Then you're second-in-command of the loading detail," Warden said. "All right, lets go. If anybody's got a bottle laying around, bring it up with you. I'm bringing mine."

When they got out to the porch, they found a knot of men arguing violently with S/Sgt Malleaux in front of the supplyroom.

"I dont give a damn," Malleaux said. "Thats my orders. I cant issue any live ammo without a signed order from an officer."

"But there aint no goddamned officers, you jerk!" somebody protested angrily.

"Then there aint no live ammo," Malleaux said.

"The officers may not get here till noon!"

"I'm sorry, fellows," Malleaux said. "Thats my orders. Lt Ross give them to me himself. No signed order, no ammo."

"What the fuckin hell is all this?" Warden said.

"He wont let us have any ammo, Top," a man said.

"He's got it locked up and the keys in his pocket," another one said.

"Gimme them keys," Warden said.

"Thats my orders, Sergeant," Malleaux said, shaking his head. "I got to have a signed order from an officer before I can issue any live ammo to an enlisted man."

Pete Karelsen came out of the kitchen and across the porch wiping his mouth off with the back of his hand. From the screendoor Stark disappeared inside putting a pint bottle back into his hip pocket under his apron.

"What the hells the matter?" Pete asked his two machinegunners happily.

"He wont give us no ammo, Pete," Grenelli said indignantly.

"Well for—Jesus Christ!" Pete said disgustedly.

"Thats my orders, Sergeant," Malleaux said irrefragably.

From the southeast corner of the quad a plane came over firing, the tracers leading irrevocably in under the porch and up the wall as he flashed over, and the knot of men dived for the stairway.

"Fuck your orders!" Warden bawled. "Gimme them goddam keys!"

Malleaux put his hand in his pocket protectively. "I cant do that, Sergeant. I got my orders, from Lt Ross himself."

"Okay," Warden said happily. "Chief, bust the door down." To Malleaux he said, "Get the hell out of the way."

Choate, and Mikeovitch and Grenelli the two machinegunners, got back for a run at the door, the Chief's big bulk towering over the two lightly built machinegunners.

Malleaux stepped in front of the door. "You cant get by with this, Sergeant," he told Warden.

"Go ahead," Warden grinned happily at the Chief. "Bust it down. He'll get out of the way." Across the quad, there were already two men up on top of the Headquarters Building.

Chief Choate and the two machinegunners launched themselves at the supplyroom door like three blocking backs bearing down on an end. Malleaux stepped out of the way. The door rattled ponderously.

"This is your responsibility, Sergeant," Malleaux said to Warden. "I did my best."

"Okay," Warden said. "I'll see you get a medal."

"Remember I warned you, Sergeant," Malleaux said.

"Get the fuck out of my way," Warden said.

It took three tries to break the wood screws loose enough to let the Yale night lock come open. Warden was the first one in. The two machinegunners were right behind him, Mikeovitch burrowing into a stack of empty belt boxes looking for full ones while Grenelli got his gun lovingly out of the MG rack. There were men up on both the 3rd and 1st Battalion roofs by now, to meet the planes as they came winging back, on first one then the other of the cross legs of their long figure 8.

Warden grabbed a BAR from the rack and passed it out with a full bag of clips. Somebody grabbed it and took off for the roof, and somebody else stepped up to receive one. Warden passed out three of them from the rack, each with a full bag of clips, before he realized what he was doing.

"To hell with this noise," he said to Grenelli who was unstrapping his tripod on his way out the door. "I could stand here and hand these out all day and never get up on the roof."

He grabbed a BAR and clip bag for himself and pushed out the door, making a mental note to eat Malleaux's ass out. There were a dozen bags of full clips in there, left over from the BAR practice firing in August. They should have been unloaded and greased months ago.

Outside, he stopped beside Henderson. Pete, Grenelli and Mikeovitch were already rounding the stair landing out of sight with the MG and eight belt boxes.

"Get your ass in there and start passing them out," Warden told

Henderson, "and start loading clips. And belts. Have Wilson go up and get a detail of men. Soons you get a batch loaded send a couple men up with them. Put three men on belts, the rest on BAR clips."

"Yes, Sir," Henderson said nervously.

Warden took off for the stairs. On the way up he stopped off at his room to get the full bottle that he kept in his footlocker for emergencies.

In the squadroom men were sitting on their bunks with their helmets on holding their empty rifles in black despair. They looked up hopefully and called to him as he passed.

"What gives, Sarge?" "Whats the deal, First?" "Are we going up on the roofs now?" "Where the hells the ammunition, Top?" "These guns aint worth nothing without no ammunition." "Hell of a note to sit on your bunk with an empty rifle and no ammunition while they blow your guts out." "Are we soljers? or boy-scouts?"

Other men, the ones who had slept through breakfast and were now getting up tousle-headed and wide-eyed, stopped dressing and looked up hopefully to see what he'd say.

"Get into field uniforms," Warden said, realizing he had to say something. "Start rolling full field packs," he told them ruthlessly in an iron voice. "We're moving out in fifteen minutes. Full field equipment."

Several men threw their rifles on their beds disgustedly.

"Then what the hell're you doin with a BAR?" somebody hollered.

"Field uniforms," Warden said pitilessly, and went on across the squadroom. "Full field equipment. Squad leaders, get them moving."

Disgustedly, the squad leaders began to harangue them to work.

In the far doorway onto the outside porch Warden stopped. In the corner under an empty bunk that had three extra mattresses piled on it, S/Sgt Turp Thornhill from Mississippi lay on the cement floor in his underwear with his helmet on hugging his empty rifle.

"You'll catch a cold, Turp," Warden said.

"Dont go out there, First Sergeant!" Turp pleaded. "You'll be killed! They shootin it up! You'll be dead! You'll not be alive any more! Dont go out there!"

"You better put your pants on," Warden said.

In his room on the porch splinters of broken glass lay all over

Warden's floor, and a line of bullet holes was stitched across the top
of his footlocker and up the side of Pete's locker and across its top.
Under Pete's locker was a puddle and the smell of whiskey fumes
was strong in the air. Cursing savagely, Warden unlocked his
footlocker and flung back the lid. A book in the tray had a slanting
hole drilled right through its center. His plastic razor box was
smashed and the steel safety razor bent almost double. Savagely he
jerked the tray out and threw it on the floor. In the bottom of the
locker two .30 caliber bullets were nestled in the padding of rolled
socks and stacked underwear, one on either side of the brown quart
bottle.

The bottle was safe.

Warden dropped the two bullets into his pocket and got the
unbroken bottle out tenderly and looked in his wall locker to make
sure his recordplayer and records were safe. Then he hit the floor
in the broken glass, holding the bottle carefully and under him, as
another plane went over going east over the quad.

As he beat it back out through the squadroom the men were
beginning bitterly to roll full field packs. All except Turp Thornhill, who was still under the bunk and four mattresses in his helmet
and underwear; and Private Ike Galovitch, who was lying on top
his bunk with his rifle along his side and his head under his pillow.

On the empty second floor, from which men were hurriedly
carrying their full field equipment downstairs to roll into packs, at
the south end of the porch by the latrine Readall Treadwell was
going up the ladder in the latrine-supplies closet to the roof hatch
carrying a BAR and grinning from ear to ear.

"First time in my goddam life," he yelled down; "I'm really goin
to git to shoot a BAR, by god. I wount never of believe it."

He disappeared through the hatch and Warden followed him on
up, and out into the open. Across G Company's section of roof most
of G Company's first-three-graders were waiting to meet the enemy
from behind one of the four chimneys, or else down on their knees
in one of the corners, the BAR forearms propped on the crotch-
high wall, or a chimney top, their muzzles looking eagerly into the
sky, and their bottles of whiskey sitting beside them close up
against the wall. Reedy Treadwell, who did not have a bottle, was
just dropping down happily beside Chief Choate, who did. Two of
the first-three-graders had hopped across the wall onto F Company's roof and were standing behind two of their chimneys. A

knot of first-three-graders from F Co were just coming up through their own hatch. They crossed the roof and began to argue violently with the two first-three-graders from G Co, demanding their chimneys. All down the 2nd Battalion roof, and on the 1st and 3rd Battalion roofs, first-three-graders were coming up through the hatches eagerly with BARs, rifles, pistols, and here and there a single MG. There were a few buck sergeants visible among them, but the only privates visible anywhere were Readall Treadwell and the two other BAR men from G Co.

"Throw your empty clips down into the Compny Yard," Warden hollered as he moved down the roof. "Pass it along. Throw your empty clips down in the Compny Yard. The loading detail will pick em up. Throw your empty—"

A V of three planes came winging over from the southeast firing full blast, and the waiting shooters cheered happily like a mob of hobos about to sit down to their first big meal in years. All the artillery on all the roofs cut loose in a deafening roar and the earth stopped. The argument on F Co's roof also stopped, while both sides all dived behind the same chimney. Warden turned without thinking, standing in his tracks, and fired from the shoulder without a rest, the bottle clutched tightly between his knees.

The big BAR punched his shoulder in a series of lightning left jabs.

On his right Pete Karelsen was happily firing the little air-cooled .30 caliber from behind the chimney while Mikeovitch and Grenelli hung grimly onto the bucking legs of the tripod laid over the chimney, bouncing like two balls on two strings.

The planes sliced on over, unscathed, winging on down to come back up the other leg of the big figure 8. Everybody cheered again anyway, as the firing stopped.

"Holymarymotherofgod," Chief Choate boomed in his star basso that always took the break-line of the Regimental song uncontested. "I aint had so much fun since granmaw got her tit caught in the ringer."

"Shit!" old Pete said disgustedly in a low voice behind Warden. "He was on too much of an angle. Led him too far."

Warden lowered his BAR, his belly and throat tightening with a desire to let loose a high hoarse senseless yell of pure glee. This is *my* outfit. These are *my* boys. He got his bottle from between his knees and took a drink that was not a drink but an expression of feeling. The whiskey burned his throat savagely joyously.

"Hey, Milt!" Pete called him. "You can come over here with us if you want. We got enough room for you and the bottle."

"Be right with you!" Warden roared. Gradually his ears had become aware of a bugle blowing somewhere insistently, the same call over and over. He stepped to the inside edge of the roof and looked down over the wall.

In the corner of the quad at the megaphone, among all the men running back and forth, the guard bugler was blowing The Charge.

"What the fuck are *you* doing," Warden bellowed.

The bugler stopped and looked up and shrugged sheepishly. "You got me," he yelled back. "Colonel's orders." He went on blowing.

"Here they come, Pete!" Grenelli hollered. "Here comes one!" His voice went off up into falsetto excitedly.

It was a single, coming in from the northeast on the down leg of the 8. The voice of every gun on the roofs rose to challenge his passage, blending together in one deafening roar like the call of a lynch mob. Down below, the running men melted away and the bugler stopped blowing and ran back under the E Company porch. Warden screwed the cap back on his bottle and ran crouching over to Pete's chimney and swung around to fire, again with no rest. His burst curved off in tracer smoke lines well behind the swift-sliding ship that was up, over, and then gone. Got to take more lead.

"Wouldnt you know it?" Pete said tragically. "Shot clear behind that one.

"Here, Mike," he said. "Move back a little and make room for the 1st/Sgt so he can fire off the corner for a rest. You can set the bottle down right here, Milt. Here," he said, "I'll take it for you."

"Have a drink first," Warden said happily.

"Okay." Pete wiped his soot-rimmed mouth with the back of his sleeve. There were soot flecks on his teeth when he grinned. "Did you see what they done to our room?"

"I seen what they done to your locker," Warden said.

From down below came the voice of the bugle blowing The Charge again.

"Listen to that stupid bastard," Warden said. "Colonel Delbert's orders."

"I dint think the Colonel'd be up this early," Pete said.

"Old Jake must of served his first hitch in the Cavalry," Warden said.

"Say, listen," Grenelli said, "listen, Pete. When you going to let me take it a while?"

"Pretty soon," Pete said, "pretty soon."

"Throw your empty clips down in the Compny Yard, you guys!" Warden yelled around the roof. "Throw your empty clips down in the Compny Yard. Pass it along, you guys."

Down along the roof men yelled at each other to throw the empties down into the yard and went right on piling them up beside them.

"God damn it!" Warden roared, and moved out from behind the chimney. He walked down along behind them like a quarterback bolstering up his linemen. "Throw them clips down, goddam you Frank. Throw your clips down, Teddy."

"Come on, Pete," Grenelli said behind him. "Let me take it a while now, will you?"

"I got firsts on it," Mikeovitch said.

"Like hell!" Grenelli said. "Its my gun, aint it?"

"Shut up," Pete said. "Both of you. You'll both get your chance. Pretty soon."

Warden was behind the Chief and Reedy Treadwell on the inside edge when the next ones came in, a double flying in in echelon from the northeast like the single, and he dropped down beside them. Down below the bugler stopped blowing and ran back in under the E Company porch again.

Straight across from Warden on the roof of the Headquarters Building there were only two men up. One of them he recognized as M/Sgt Big John Deterling, the enlisted football coach. Big John had a .30 caliber water-cooled with no tripod, holding it cradled in his left arm and firing it with his right. When he fired a burst, the recoil staggered him all over the roof.

The winking noseguns of the incoming planes cut two foot-wide swathes raising dust across the quad and up the wall and over the D Co roof like a wagon road through a pasture. Warden couldnt fire at them from laughing at Big John Deterling on the Headquarters Roof. This time Big John came very near to falling down and spraying the roof. The other man up over there had wisely put the chimney between him and Big John, instead of between him and the planes.

"Look at that son of a bitch," Warden said, when he could stop laughing.

Down below the loading detail dived out to pick up the clips in the lull, and the bugler ran back to the megaphone.

"I been watching him," Chief grinned. "The son of a bitch is drunk as a coot. He was down to Mrs Kipfer's last night when me and Pete was there."

"I hope his wife dont find out," Warden said.

"He ought to have a medal," Chief said still laughing.

"He probly will," Warden grinned.

As it turned out, later, he did. M/Sgt John L. Deterling; the Silver Star; for unexampled heroism in action.

Another V of three flashed sliding in from the southeast and Warden turned and ran back to Pete's chimney as everybody opened up with a joyous roar. Firing with the BAR forearm resting on his hand on the chimney corner, he watched his tracers get lost in the cloud of tracers around the lead plane spraying the nose, spraying the cockpit, and on back into the tail assembly. The plane shivered like a man trying to get out from under a cold shower and the pilot jumped in his seat twice like a man tied to a hot stove. They saw him throw up his arms helplessly in a useless try to ward it off, to stop it pouring in on him. There was a prolonged cheer. A hundred yards beyond the quad, with all of them watching it now in anticipatory silence, the little Zero began to fall off on one wing and slid down a long hill of air onto one of the goalposts of the 19th Infantry football field. It crashed into flames. A vast happy college-yell cheer went up from the quad and helmets were thrown into the air and backs were slapped as if our side had just made a touchdown against Notre Dame.

Then, as another V of three came in from the northeast, there was a wild scramble for helmets.

"You got him, Pete!" Grenelli yelled, bobbing around on the bucking tripod leg, "you got him!"

"Got him hell," Pete said without stopping firing. "Nobody'll ever know who got that guy."

"Hey, Milt!"

In the lull, Chief Choate was yelling at him from the roof edge.

"Hey, Milt! Somebody's yellin for you down below."

"Comin up!" Warden bawled. Behind him as he ran, Grenelli was pleading:

"Come on, Pete. Let me take it for a while now. You got one already."

"In a minute," Pete said. "In a minute. I just want to try one more."

Looking down over the wall, Warden saw Lt Ross standing in the yard looking up angrily, large bags under his eyes, a field cap on his uncombed head, his pants still unbuttoned, and his shoes untied and his belt unbuckled. He started buttoning his pants without looking down.

"What the hell are you doing up there, Sergeant?" he yelled. "Why arent you down here taking care of the Company? We're going to move out for the beach in less than an hour. Its probably alive with Japs already."

"Its all taken care of," Warden yelled down. "The men are rolling full field packs right now in the squadroom."

"But we've got to get the kitchen and supply ready to move, too, goddam it," Lt Ross yelled up.

"The kitchen is bein pack," Warden yelled down. "I gave Stark the orders and he's doing it now. Should be all ready in fifteen minutes."

"But the supply—" Lt Ross started to yell up.

"They're loading clips and belts for us," Warden yelled down. "All they got to do is carry the water-cooled MGs for the beach out to the trucks and throw in Leva's old field repair kit and they ready to go.

"And," he yelled, "they making coffee and sandwidges in the kitchen. Everything's all taken care of. Whynt you get a BAR and come on up?"

"There arent any left," Lt Ross yelled up angrily.

"Then get the hell under cover," Warden yelled down as he looked up. "Here they come."

Lt Ross dived under the porch for the supplyroom as another single came blasting in from the southeast and the roaring umbrella of fire rose from the roofs to engulf it. It seemed impossible that he could fly right through it and come out untouched. But he did.

Right behind him, but flying due north along Waianae Avenue

and the Hq Building, came another plane; and the umbrella swung that way without even letting go of its triggers.

The plane's gastank exploded immediately into flames that engulfed the whole cockpit and the plane veered off down on the right wing, still going at top speed. As the belly and left under-wing came up into view, the blue circle with the white star in it showed plainly in the bright sunlight. Then it was gone, off down through some trees that sheered off the wings, and the fuselage, still going at top speed, exploded into some unlucky married officer's house quarters with everyone watching it.

"That was one of ours!" Reedy Treadwell said in a small still voice. "That was an American plane!"

"Tough," Warden said, without stopping firing at the new double coming in from the northeast. "The son of a bitch dint have no business there."

After the Jap double had flashed past, unscathed, Warden turned back and made another circuit up and down the roof, his eyes screwed up into that strained look of having been slapped in the face that he sometimes got, and that made a man not want to look at him.

"Be careful, you guys," he said. Up the roof. Down the roof. "That last one was one of ours. Try and be careful. Try and get a look at them before you shoot. Them stupid bastards from Wheeler liable to fly right over here. So try and be careful after this." Up the roof. Down the roof. The same strained squint was in his voice as was in his eyes.

"Sergeant Warden!" Lt Ross roared up from down below. "God damn it! Sergeant *Warden!*"

He ran back to the roof edge. "What now?"

"I want you down here, god damn it!" Lt Ross yelled up. He had his belt buckled and his shoes tied now and was smoothing back his hair with his fingers under his cap. "I want you to help me get this orderly room ready to move out! You have no business up there! Come down!"

"Goddam it, I'm busy!" Warden yelled. "Get Rosenberry. Theres a goddam war on, Lieutenant."

"I've just come from Col Delbert," Lt Ross yelled up. "And he has given orders we're to move out as soon as this aerial attack is over."

"G Compny's ready to move now," Warden yelled down. "And I'm busy. Tell that goddam Henderson to send up some clips and belts."

Lt Ross ran back under the porch and then ran back out again. This time he had a helmet on.

"I told him," he yelled up.

"And tell Stark to send us up some coffee."

"*God damn it!*" Lt Ross raged up at him. "What is this? a Company picnic? Come down here, Sergeant! I want you! Thats an order! Come down here immediately! You hear me? thats an order! All Company Commanders have orders from Col Delbert personally to get ready to move out within the hour!"

"Whats that?" Warden yelled. "I cant hear you."

"I said, we're moving out within the hour."

"What?" Warden yelled. "What? Look out," he yelled; "here they come again!"

Lt Ross dove for the supplyroom and the two ammo carriers ducked their heads back down through the hatch.

Warden ran crouching back to Pete's chimney and rested his BAR on the corner and fired a burst at the V of three that flashed past.

"Get that goddam ammo up here!" he roared at them in the hatchway.

"Milt!" Chief Choate yelled. "Milt Warden! They want you downstairs."

"You cant find me," Warden yelled. "I've gone someplace else."

Chief nodded and relayed it down over the edge. "I cant find him, Lootenant. He's gone off someplace else." He listened dutifully down over the edge and then turned back to Warden. "Lt Ross says tell you we're moving out within the hour," he yelled.

"You cant find me," Warden yelled.

"Here they come!" Grenelli yelled from the tripod.

They did not move out within the hour. It was almost another hour before the attack was all over. And they did not move out until early afternoon three and a half hours after the attack was over. G Company was ready, but it was the only company in the Regiment that was.

Warden stayed up on the roof, by one subterfuge or another, until the attack was over. Lt Ross, it turned out, stayed down in the supplyroom and helped load ammunition. The Regimental fire umbrella claimed one more positive, and two possibles that might have been hit by the 27th and already going down when they passed over the quad. Stark himself, personally, with two of the KPs, brought them up coffee once, and then still later brought up coffee and sandwiches. In gratitude for which, Pete Karelsen let him take the MG for a while.

After it was all over, and the dead silence which no sound seemed able to penetrate reigned, they all smoked a last cigarette up on the roof and then, dirty-faced, red-eyed, tired happy and let-down, they trooped down reluctantly into the new pandemonium that was just beginning below and went to roll their full field packs. Nobody had even been scratched. But they could not seem to get outside of the ear-ringing dead silence. Even the pandemonium of moving out could not penetrate it.

Warden, instead of rolling his pack, went straight to the orderly room. In the three and a half hours before they finally left he was in the orderly room all the time, getting it packed up. Lt Ross, whose Company was the only one that was ready ahead of time, had already forgotten to be angry and came in and helped him. So did Rosenberry. Warden had plenty of time and to spare, to pack the orderly room. But he did not have any time left to roll his full field pack or change into a field uniform. Or, if he did, he forgot it.

The result of this was that he had to sleep in the popcorn vender's wagon at Hanauma Bay without blankets for five days before he could get back up to Schofield to get his stuff, and he would have welcomed even a woolen OD field-uniform shirt. He did not see how the hell he could have possibly have forgotten that.

One by one, each company's consignment of trucks lined up before its barracks in a double file and settled down to wait. One by one, the platoons of troops filed out into their company yards and sat down on their packs holding their rifles and looked at the waiting trucks. The Regiment moved as a unit.

No two companies were going to the same place. And when they got there each company would be a separate unit on its own. But one company, that was ready, did not leave out by itself for its beach positions ahead of the other companies, that were not ready. The Regiment moved as a unit.

Everywhere trucks. Everywhere troops sitting on their packs. The quad filled up with trucks until even the Colonel's jeep could not worm through between them. The yards filled up with troops until even the Colonel's adjutants and messengers could not work through them. There was much swearing and sweaty disgust. The Regiment moved as a unit.

And in the G Co orderly room, Warden chortled to himself smugly, as he worked.

Once, when Lt Ross had gone to the supplyroom, Maylon Stark stuck his head in at the door. "The kitchen truck's loaded and ready to roll."

"Right," Warden said, without looking up.

"I want you to know I think you done a hell of a swell job," Stark said reluctantly strangledly. "It'll be two hours, anyway, before any other kitchen in this outfit is ready; and some of them probly have to stay behind to get loaded and come down later."

"You done a good job yourself," Warden said, still not looking up.

"It wasnt me," Stark said. "It was you. And I just want you to know I think you done a hell of a job."

"Okay," Warden said, "thanks," and went on working without looking up.

He rode down in the jeep at the head of the Company's convoy with Lt Ross, Weary Russell driving. There was terrific traffic. The roads were alive with trucks and taxis as far as the eye could see, bumper to bumper. The trucks were taking them down, to beach positions; the taxis were taking them up, to Schofield, where their outfits would already be gone. Recons and jeeps slithered in and out among the long lines of trucks, but the big two-and-a-halfs could only lumber on, a few feet at a time, stopping when the truck in front of stopped in back of the truck in front of him, waiting to move on until the truck in front of them moved on a little in back of the truck in front of him.

The trucks had been stripped of their tarps and one man with his BAR or machinegun mounted over the cab rode standing on the truckbed wall. Helmeted heads were poked above the naked ribs watching the sky like visitors inspecting the dinosaur's skeleton in the Smithsonian Institute.

In the jeep, riding up and down haranguing on the road shoulder alongside the Company's column, Warden saw them all, a lot of times. Their faces were changed and they did not look the same any more. It was somewhat the same look as Stark had had in the messhall, only the drunkenness was evaporating out of it leaving only the hard set of the dry plaster. Out here on the highway, lost among hundreds of other outfits, the idea was not only clearer but bigger, much bigger, than back at your home barracks in your own quad. Chief Choate, riding with a BAR up, looked down at him from above his truck cab and Warden looked back.

They had all left everything behind, civilian clothes, garrison shoes and uniforms, campaign hat collections, insignia collections, photograph albums, private papers. To hell with all that. This was war. We wont need that. They brought nothing but the skeletal field living equipment, and the only man who packed in anything comfortable to bring with him was Pete Karelsen. Pete had been in France.

Gradually, foot by foot, the trucks moved on down toward Honolulu and whatever waited on the beaches. Up till now it had been a day off, it had been fun.

Pearl Harbor, when they passed it, was a shambles. Wheeler Field had been bad, but Pearl Harbor numbed the brain. Pearl Harbor made a queasiness in the testicles. Wheeler Field was set back quite a ways from the road, but parts of Pearl Harbor were right on the highway. Up till then it had been a big lark, a picnic; they had fired from the roofs and been fired at from the planes and the cooks had served them coffee and sandwiches and the supply detail had brought them up ammo and they had got two or three planes and only one man in the whole Regiment had been hit (with a .50 caliber in the fleshy part of his calf, didnt even hit a bone, he walked up to the dispensary by himself), and he was getting himself a big Purple Heart. Almost everybody had had a bottle and they all had been half-drunk anyway when it started and it had all been a sort of super-range-season with live targets to shoot at. The most exciting kind: Men. But now the bottles were fast wearing off and there was no immediate prospect of getting any more and there were no live targets to shoot at. Now they were thinking. Why, it might be months—even years—before they could get hold of a bottle again! This was a big war.

As the trucks passed through the new, Married NCO Quarters that had been added onto Pearl Harbor recently, women and children and an occasional old man standing in the yards cheered them. The troops rode on through in silence, staring at them dully.

Going through the back streets of town, all along the route, men, women and children stood on porches fences cartops and roofs and cheered them roundly. They waved Winnie Churchill's V-for-Victory sign at them, and held their thumbs up in the air. Young girls threw them kisses. Mothers of young girls, with tears in their eyes, urged their daughters to throw them more kisses.

The troops, looking wistfully at all this ripe young stuff running around loose that they could not get into, and remembering the old days when civilian girls were not allowed—and did not desire—to speak to soldiers on the street in broad daylight let alone at night in a bar, gave them back the old one-finger salute of the clenched fist jabbing the stiff middle finger into the air. They returned Winnie Churchill's V-for-Victory sign with an even older one of their own, in which the fist is clenched and the middle finger and thumb are extended and pinched repeatedly together.

The ecstatic civilians, who did not know that this was the Old Army sign for the female, or that the first meant "Fuck you!" cheered them even more roundly and the troops, for the first time since they'd left Schofield, grinned a little bit at each other, slyly, and redoubled with their saluting.

From Waikiki on east, the trucks in the Company's convoy began to peel off to deliver the various three- and four-man details each with its noncom to their various beach positions. By the time they reached the rise up over the Koko Head saddle where the road turned off down to the CP at Hanauma Bay, there were only four trucks left. The two for Position 28 at Makapuu Head, one for the CP personnel and Position 27, and the kitchen truck. The first two, the CP truck and the kitchen truck, pulled off onto the side road and stopped and the last two bound for Makapuu went on, then, past them. They had all had their big day with the civilians, which most of them had waited from two to five years for, and now they were preparing to pay for it.

Among the troops in the trucks there was a certain high fervor of defense and patriotism that exploded into a weak feeble cheer in the heavy perpetual wind, as they passed Lt Ross and The Warden who had climbed out of the jeep on the road-shoulder to watch them go past. A few fists were shaken in the air up between the bare truck ribs and Friday Clark, current-rifleman and ex-apprentice-Company-bugler, shook a wildly promising two-finger V-for-Victory sign at Lt Ross from over the tailgate of the last truck as they pulled on away.

This general patriotic enthusiasm lasted about three days.

Lt Ross, standing beside his jeep to watch his men go off to possible maiming and death, certainly off to a war that would last a long time, looked at Friday sadly and without acknowledgment from across a great gulf of years pity and superior knowledge, his eyes set in a powerful emotion, a look of great age and fearful responsibility on his face.

1st/Sgt Warden, standing beside his Company Commander and watching his face, wanted to boot his Company Commander hard in the ass.

It was perhaps the stringing of the barbed wire, more than anything else, that ate into the patriotism of the troops in the next few days. The men who had acquired the new unknown disease of aching veins in their arm joints from the building of these positions now found it coming back on them doubly powerfully from putting up barbed wire to protect these position. So that even when they were not pulling guard at night, they couldnt sleep anyway. The stringing of the barbed wire, after the first day, was an even more powerful astringent to the patriotism than their getting crummy with no prospect of a shower, or their getting itchy with beard and no prospect of a shave, or their having to sleep on the rocks with nothing but a single shelterhalf and two blankets over them when it rained.

Actually, this war that had started out so well Sunday morning and given them such high hopes of the future was turning out to be nothing more than an extended maneuvers. With the single difference that this showed no prospects of ending.

It was five days before things were organized enough to allow the sending of a detail back to Schofield for the rest of their stuff, that they had not thought they'd need, and the Company's quota of pyramidal tents. But even these didnt do the men at Makapuu any good since out there there werent any trees to set them up under.

Warden, armed with the request list of each man which altogether covered an entire pad of legal-size scratch paper, led the detail of three trucks. Pete Karelsen, who was the only man in the Company who had been anywhere near comfortable in the five days, was his second-in-command. They pulled into the quad with their three trucks to find another outfit already moved into the barracks and the footlockers and wall lockers of G Company thoroughly rifled. Their lists were useless. Pete Karelsen, again, had been practically the only man in the Company who had bothered to lock either his footlocker or wall locker that Sunday morning. But even Pete's extra set of false teeth, which had been out on the table, were gone.

And, of course, none of the new tenants they talked to knew a damn thing about it.

Warden's records and player were gone, also his $120 Brooks Bros. suit, saddle-stitched Forstmann jacket, and the white dinner jacket and tux pants he had bought but never worn yet, together with all of his uniforms. Also, the brand new $260 electric guitar, still less than half paid for, that Andy and Friday had bought while Prew was in the Stockade, was gone too, speaker jackplug and all.

If it had not been for 1st/Sgt Dedrick of A Company, who was about his size and had remembered to lock his wall locker, he would not have even been able to scare up two whole field uniforms. Just about the only thing that had been left untouched were the folded pyramidal tents in the supply room.

By the end of the seventh day, when they had got the tents back downtown and distributed out to the positions and set up ready to occupy, every man on the Company roster—including the two men serving time in the Stockade who had been released with the rest of the prisoners—had shown up and reported for duty. With the single exception of Prewitt.

(Chapter 50)

[The Death of Prewitt]

FROM OUTSIDE THE HOUSE looked full dark as if there was not a soul home. He stood a minute happily and looked back at it, still feeling a little drunk although he had not had a drink since around three o'clock, feeling free.

She would get over it in a couple days. He knew that. When he got a pass and came back up she would be as glad to see him as ever. He was not worried about her going back to the States.

One good thing about the Army. It kept you separated from your women so much they never had the chance to get sick of you. And vice versa.

After he had gone a block he stopped and took the pistol out of his belt and put it in his pants pocket. Then he went on. The pistol, and the shells in the other pocket, dragged at his thighs as he walked. The pistol especially was very bulky.

There was always the chance he could talk them out of it.

But no bunch of lousy MPs were going to take him in and keep him from getting back to the Company. He had made up his mind.

It would be best to follow Sierra down into Kaimuki. Wilhelmina was shorter. But most of the houses were close to the street on Sierra. So were their garages. And the yards were all terraced with brick or stone walls. There were more dark nooks and niches among the fairy tale houses of Sierra. He was not worried about after he got out of Kaimuki.

When he got out of Kaimuki he would cross Waialae Avenue and go over into the Waialae Golf Course.

The Waialae Golf Course was a strip of dull barren but slightly higher ground between the Highway and the beach, treeless and all sand hills and scrubgrass, which had never been good for anything else but a golf course. Where Waialae Avenue that ran through Kaimuki met Kealaolu Avenue it changed its name and became the Kalanianaole Highway to Makapuu Head, and the resulting triangle between the two avenues and the beach was the Waialae Golf Course. He knew the Waialae Golf Course like the back of his hand. They had used to meet a couple of gook maids on the 5th Tee every night, last year during maneuvers. Going through the golf course meant he would have to cross the Highway twice because at its eastern end the Highway narrowed in almost to the beach. But going through the golf course, which he knew, was worth the risk of crossing the Highway twice.

After that, the only hard thing was the causeway over the salt marsh clear out just this side of Koko Head. The causeway was about half a mile long and he would probly have to sprint it. But after that, it was made.

All the beach positions along here belonged to G Company and he could have turned in at any one of them. But he did not want to turn in to one of the beach positions. He wanted to turn in at the CP at Hanauma Bay. Under his own power.

The trip through the golf course was something like the wild loud nightmare of the long walk to Alma's after Fatso had cut him. And it was something like the dreamy stillness of the stalk through Waikiki the night he had hunted Angelo Maggio drunkenly down Kalakaua. There was no sound except his breathing and the scuff of his shoes in the sand. Not a living soul moved anywhere in the blackness. He was completely alone in a world as soundproofed and as black as the inside of a coal mine. There was not a single light to be seen anywhere. No windows. No streetlights. No neon on the juke joints. Not even car headlights. Hawaii had gone to war. He was glad to be getting back.

Once, over on the Highway as he moved east he saw one patrol car with blue headlights rolling slowly west in the opposite direction. It excited him strangely. He stopped for a minute to watch it. He had been very careful when he crossed Waialae the first time. He had waited a long time and made very sure there was nothing on the Highway. Those blue headlights were supposed to be invisible from the air and maybe they were. But on the ground you could see them a mile away.

He was just as careful when he came up to the second crossing, near the end of the golf course. He was coming down from higher ground with no obstructions and he could see almost half a mile each way and there was not a blue light anywhere. So he did not stop. He just started on across. If there had been a patrol car with its light on anywhere within a mile he could have seen it easily.

What he could not have seen easily, if at all, was a patrol car with its lights off. But he was not expecting to see any patrol cars with their lights off. So he did not look for any.

It was sitting about thirty yards to the west of him in the middle of the Highway.

As he came up onto the shoulder and stepped out on to the asphalt it turned its lights on, the two blue headlights and one spot that was a much lighter blue, almost white. He saw it then. He was caught square in the center of the beam. If he had crossed a hundred yards back or fifty yards further on, it might not have heard him, even though he was not trying to move quietly.

His first instinct was to run but he choked it off. It wouldnt have done any good anyway. He was almost in the middle of the Highway, with flat open ground on both sides of it. Besides, there was still always the chance he might talk them out of it, before he had to make the break.

"Halt!" a voice erupted at him nervously.

But he was already halted. It made him think of the night Warden had halted him, that time at Hickam Field, and he wanted to laugh wildly. Oh, the bastards, the bastards, the smart smug bastards. Sitting there with their lights off. Just when it was all going so good. They would have to pull a smart one like that.

The patrol car, it was a jeep, pulled up slowly and cautiously to within ten yards of him. There were four scared MPs in it; he could see their blue faces and the blue light reflecting from the white letters of their brassards. They all had helmets on. The one beside the driver was standing up staring at him over a Thompson gun above the windshield; he could see the bulge of the Cutts Comp on the muzzle.

"Who goes there?"

"A friend," he said.

The two in the back, who doubtless considered the answer to be a stock reply to a stock question, were climbing out over the side reluctantly slowly. They were covering him with pistols.

"Advance, friend, and be recognized," said the bigger one squeakily. Then he cleared his throat.

And he, Prewitt that is, the unrecognized friend, came toward them slowly. Thinking how now, for a split minute out of the time run, by a happenstance of smartness on their part and dumbness on his, they held it all in their hands. A thing that had started almost a year ago, with Chief Bugler Houston, and led up through Dynamite Holmes and the boxing into The Treatment and Ike Galovitch and from there to the Stockade and Jack Malloy and the late Fatso Judson, and a lot of other things both before and after, to finally here, where, for this split minute that was the current point of time in the line of time which was not a line but an infinite series of points, four strangers held it all in their hands without even knowing it.

"Halt!" the bigger one said again. With four eyes and two pistol holes the two of them looked him over cautiously.

"Its all right, Harry," said the bigger one, a little more confidently. "He's a GI."

Well, at least there was that, anyway.

The man standing up staring at him over the Thompson gun sat back down, and there was an unheard sound of a great relaxing, like a vast sigh of relief.

"Douse that spot," called the bigger one. In the dimmer light the two of them came up to him.

"What the hell you doin out here, Mack?" said the bigger one indignantly. He was a S/Sgt. The other was a Cpl. "You like to scared the livin shit out of us. We get a call from Position Sixteen somebody moving aroun out on the golf course and we think we got a whole battalion of parachutists in our lap."

He understood it then. Somebody had seen his silhouette against the blue headlights of the patrol car he had stood in the golf course and watched. Somebody from G Company. But you'd think a goddam man who claimed to be such a hotshot Infantry soldier would have remembered that.

"I'm going back to my position," he said.

"Yeah. What position."

"Number Eighteen. Down the road."

"Eighteen, hunh. What outfit."

"G Company, —th Infantry."

The S/Sgt relaxed a little bit more. "Dont G Company —th Infantry know theres a goddam curfew on?"

"Yes."

"Then what the hell you doin off your position?"

"I'm just goin home from seein my wahine. She lives right over there," he nodded across the golf course.

"You got a pass?"

"No."

"No pass," said the other one with finality. "Come on, lets take him in and get it over with." He was being tough. He had relaxed some too now. He had been bad scared and now he was being tough. He had put his pistol back in the holster.

"Just hold your horses, Corprl Oliver," said the S/Sgt.

"Its immaterial to me," said the Cpl.

"Who's in charge of Position Eighteen, friend?" said the S/Sgt.

"S/Sgt Choate."

The two MPs looked at each other.

"You know who's in charge of Eighteen, Harry?" the S/Sgt called back to the jeep.

In the jeep there was a consultation. "No," Harry said. "But we can sures hell find out in a minute."

"Okay," said the S/Sgt. "Lets run him down there."

"Its immaterial to me," said the Cpl. "But I say take him down to the Station. I dont like his looks, Fred. Look at that uniform. Its garrison, and starched neat as a pin. Whats he doin in a garrison uniform? There aint no barricksbag press on that uniform. That uniform aint seen the inside of a barricksbag since it was last to the cleaners."

"It wont hurt to run him down there," said the S/Sgt.

"Its immaterial to me," the Cpl said. "But it might hurt a lot. If he taken off on us."

"How the hell is he going to taken off on four of us, for Chrisake?"

"What if he just happen to of stole that nice clean uniform?" said the Cpl. "He might be a sabatoor. And his buddies waitin down the road to cut us down. Its immaterial to me. But how do we know he aint a spy or something?"

"How about that, friend?" said the S/Sgt. "You got buddies waitin down the road to cut us down?"

"I aint no spy, for Christ's sake. Do I look like a spy?" That was one he had not anticipated. To be taken in for a possible spy. The would really be good.

"But how the hell *we* know you aint a spy?" said the Cpl. "Its immaterial to me."

"Thats right," said the S/Sgt. "You might be Tojo for all we know."

"Maybe he's gettin ready to blow up the Governor's Mansion," said the Cpl. "Or something. Its immaterial to me. But I say take him down to the Station. Then it aint our responsiblity."

"Ah, he aint no spy," said the S/Sgt disgustedly. He had not put his pistol away, but it was hanging down at arm's length by his side. "You got any identification on you, Mack? So we could tell who you are?"

"No."

"Aint you got nothing?"

"No."

"Then I'm afraid we'll have to taken you in, friend," the S/Sgt said. "You ought to have some kind of identification. I hate to do it. But then we just cant let every son of a bitch and his brother go runnin around all over at night without no identification like they was generals, either."

Well, it was what he had expected. It had only been a shot in the dark anyway. But the S/Sgt was a pretty good joe and had come so near there for a minute. He made a try.

"Wait a minute. Listen you guys. You guys know I aint no spy. I been in this man's Army six years. And plan to stay in twenty-four more. But you know what the Provost will do if you taken me in. He have me in the Stockade sure as you're born. Theres a goddam war on and the whole Army needs ever man it can lay hands on. It wont do the war no good to send me to the Stockade. And I been waitin six years for this war. Please, give me a break."

"You shoulda thoughta all that before you taken off," said the Cpl.

"If there was any chance of me bein a spy, it would be differnt. But you guys know I aint no spy or nothing like that."

"You knew what the orders was," said the Cpl. "You knew there was a curfew. So you taken off to see your shackjob. Okay. You knew what you'd get if you got caught.

"Besides, how we suppose to know who you are. Its immaterial to me. But you could say you're anything. Everybody knows G Company of the —th is all down along here."

"Shut up, Oliver," said the S/Sgt. "Who's in charge of this detail, me or you? That what you said about the Stockade," he said. "Thats true as Christ's cross. There aint no sense in throwin a man in there where he's useless when theres a war on for some little thing like this here. Its a waste of valuble manpower. Its stupid."

"Of course its stupid!"

"But at the same time, I got to be *sure*. Aint you got *no* kind of identification on you, Mack? If you just had *some* kind of identification on you. So we could be sure. Any old thing, that would identify you."

"No," he lied, "not a thing," fingering with his left hand in his pocket among the cartridges the old, green, frayed, SP Card. The used-to-be passport. The once-was visa. Back into the promised land, that everybody always acted like was the desert and made like they wanted to get out of. The last year's membership card. That would not get you into the Clubroom this year why the hell dint you remember to keep up your dues this card and five cents will get you a good nickel cigar. And that, because everybody who was not over the hill had had to turn theirs in a month ago, was now not only useless, but actively dangerous, to show. There was a good one for you. There was the best one yet. The Warden would *really* love that one.

"Then we'll just *have* to take you in," the S/Sgt said.

He tried one more time.

"You could take me down to Position Eighteen? and let them identify me?"

"Yeh, I could do that," the S/Sgt said.

"I swear to you they know me there," he swore to them. Because he would settle for that. He hadnt wanted to. But he would. Gladly. He wasnt proud. What difference did it make? if Chief Choate sent him on down to the CP after he'd lied the MPs off? or if he went there under his own power? What did he care?

"You aint got the right to take the chance, Fred," said the Cpl. "Its immaterial to me. But this guy."

"He's right there," Fred said. "My job is to not take no chances whatever. If you aint got no identification, I'm afraid we'll have to take you down."

"Well for Christ's sake do something," Harry called indifferently from the jeep. "Time's a wastin."

"You shut up," Fred the S/Sgt hollered. "Its my job, I got to answer for it. Not you.

"I'm afraid we'll have to take you down, Mack," he said reluctantly. He raised his pistol that was still hanging at arm length and made a half-hearted shooing motion toward the jeep.

"Dont *you* know I aint a spy?"

"Sure. I know it. But."

"And take your goddam hands out of your pockets," said the Cpl disgustedly. "Its immaterial to me. But how the hell long you been in the Army, friend? to keep your hands in your pockets?"

"Lets go, Mack," said the S/Sgt.

Well, then that was the way it was then. Okay. Then so be it. He could still work back up and around them. There was only four. And sneak past across the Highway. They wouldnt look for him on the other side of the Highway. And work on east from there. So thats what the matter. They werent going to take this one back. They'd never take this one back.

"Come on, Mack," the S/Sgt said, still shooing half-heartedly. "Lets go."

He let the mind, which at a great cost in Kentucky pride had been kept loose and open with the mineral oil of belief, constipate itself and close down into the old, narrow, clear, hard, crystal something which was the trademark of Harlan Kentucky and which was the only gift his father had ever given him in his whole life, and even that unwittingly, or he would probly tried to take it back.

"I said take your goddam hands out of your pockets," the Cpl said disgustedly.

He jerked his hands out of his pockets, Alma's Police .38 in the right one, and with the left one snatched the S/Sgt's still shooing pistol and threw it sailing heavily across on the other side of the road, and with the right one bent the barrel of the .38 over the jaw of the helmeted Cpl.

And Prewitt, feeling airishly free in the arms and legs, without ropes, without handcuffs, without shackles, free to breathe too, without a strait jacket, feeling so free all over he was almost able to believe he was free, was running freely and without restriction into the night, into the levelness, into the darkness, of the Territory of Hawaii's Waialae Golf Course. Treelessness, sand hills, scrubgrass, and all. There was a big sandtrap right around here someplace.

Running hard, sprinting, he flashed a look back over his shoulder and saw the two of them still there in the blue light of the headlights. They never should have done that, his mind registered automatically, they should have headed for the darkness first thing, he could shoot them both, even with this gun he did not know.

Then, in the middle of the split flash of the glance, he realized they did not know yet he had a gun, and were therefore not technically guilty of a mistake. At least not a reckless mistake. That made his sense of priority feel a little less offended. Mistakes in knowledge were at least excusable. But a good soldier should never make a *reck*less mistake.

Fred the S/Sgt was yelling. "Back down to the corner. Theres a field phone station there." The Cpl, his left hand holding his jaw, was just coming up shakily off his knees and there was the big red merry wink of his .45, before he was even clear up yet.

Prewitt quit looking and stopped sprinting and started the skirmisher's zigzag, wanting to grin. They would measure up all right. Except for that one mistake of not getting out of the light, they were doing fine. And doing it fast. Where the hell was that sandtrap?

"All the men they got available," Fred the S/Sgt was still yelling. "And alert all the beach positions. This guy wasnt no soldier." The motor of the jeep roared. "No, not now, you fool!" Fred the S/Sgt yelled. "The light, first! The spot. Turn on the spot."

Off to his left not far Prew saw the sandtrap.

Then the spotlight went on.

He stopped and turned around facing them.

Almost simultaneously, from the rider's seat of the jeep, Harry's Thompson gun batted its one big eye in a series of winks that had all the false coy merriness of a bloodshot one-eyed bar pickup.

Prewitt was standing facing them, almost on the lip of his sandtrap.

Maybe it was what Fred the S/Sgt yelled about alerting the beach positions. He had the Infantryman's abhorrence of being shot at by his own outfit. Or maybe it was that about getting out every man available. There was still yet the causeway over the salt marsh and he saw in his mind the blue-lighted jeeps crowding on it waiting, till it looked like a rich man's Christmas Tree in the front yard and he had been running from them a long time now he was out of breath now. Or perhaps it might have been because he felt such a strong affection for them suddenly the way they were handling it, almost proud of them, a confidence in them, they were really handling it well, it was a sound competent piece of work. He could not have done better himself. They were competent. Or, maybe it was just, simply, that last thing the S/Sgt had yelled: "*This guy wasnt no soldier.*"

Perhaps it was only a mechanical thing caused by the going on of the spotlight, the instinctive move of the Kentuckian who, unlike the Infantryman, is used to being shot at by friends, but has an almost religious abhorrence of being shot in the back.

Anyway, he knew Harry's Thompson gun was winking at him, as he turned around.

Standing there, in that couple of seconds, he could have fired twice with the .38 and killed two of them, Fred and the Cpl, standing there in the light of the headlights, they were perfect targets, but he did not shoot. He did not even want to shoot. He hardly even thought about shooting. They were the Army, too.

And how could a man kill a soldier for just simply doing a sound competent job? It was still the rottenest word in the language. He had killed once. It did not do any good. Even though it was justified, and he did not regret it, it still did not do any good. Maybe it never did any good. The other still went right on. And if he could not kill the other, he would kill nothing. You could kill and kill and kill. He would not become a Disciple of the Word. And these were the Army, too. It was not true that all men killed the things they loved. What was true was that all things killed the men who loved them. Which, after all, was as it should be.

Three somethings rent their way agonizingly through his chest in echelon and he fell over backwards into the sandtrap and Harry's Thompson gun ceased its short burst that had been going on for what seemed such a long time.

Well, I learned it, Jack. I learned it. The sandtrap was deep and the slope was steep and he had fallen on a downhill lie and had bounced over onto his face in the sand of the bottom. His chest hurt numbly, but it was not especially uncomfortable. But he could hear them coming up, and he did not want them to see him like this. Not facedown in the sand. His legs would not work, but using his elbows a little he managed to roll himself over downhillwards onto his back and to pull himself on down out onto the sand where it was level. Then he was done. Well, Jack, I learned it.

(from Chapter 52)

The Pistol

(1959)

After completing the huge *Some Came Running* (1266 pages), Jones wanted to try his hand at a short, symbolic novel. At 148 pages, *The Pistol* is his shortest book. Set in wartime Hawaii, it begins where *From Here to Eternity* ends: the Japanese attack on Pearl Harbor. The central character is Pfc. Richard Mast, who like Jones was on guard duty when the attack came and kept the .45 pistol he was wearing. The novel details the persistent efforts of Mast's fellow soldiers to get the pistol from him by hook or by crook. They all believe that it is the only effective defense against a Japanese Samurai saber. Despite the urgency of their various beliefs in the pistol's talismanic qualities, and Mast's almost heroic stubbornness in resisting them, it is in the end repossessed by the long, bureaucratic arm of the army.

Jones wrote *The Pistol* after moving to New York City in 1957, completing it in five weeks. It was published by Scribner's. He had moved there with his wife of one year, the former Gloria Mosolino, after breaking with Lowney Handy in Illinois. The novel received, for the most part, excellent reviews; its success gave Jones energy for the intense effort required to write the second novel of his trilogy, *The Thin Red Line*. While *The Pistol* is not formally a part of the trilogy, it is fair to call it a pendant to it. Mast appears to be a preparation for Pfc. Doll in *The Thin Red Line*, and First Sgt. Wycoff, "a big man in his thirties," might even be confused with Sgt. Warden-Welch-Winch.

[The Japanese Attack]

WHEN THE FIRST BOMBS lit at Wheeler Field on December 7, 1941, Pfc Richard Mast was eating breakfast. He was also wearing a pistol. From where Mast sat, amidst the bent heads, quiet murmur, and soft, cutlery-against-china sounds of breakfast, in a small company mess in one of the infantry quadrangles of Schofield Barracks, it was perhaps a mile to Wheeler Field, and it took several seconds for the sound of the explosions, followed soon after by the shockwave through the earth, to reach his ears. Obviously, as far as Mast was concerned during those few seconds, the United States was still at peace, although in actual fact she was already, even then, at war. Consequently, during those moments, Mast had no idea at all of getting to keep the pistol he was wearing.

In one way it was unusual for a soldier in peacetime to be wearing a pistol at breakfast, but in another way it was not. The day before, on Saturday's duty roster, Mast and three other men had been named to go on Interior Guard duty. This guard duty lasted from four in the afternoon to four in the afternoon, twenty-four hours, and the men assigned to it daily from the various companies drew pistols, pistol belts, arm brassards and pistol lanyards from their company supply rooms. They were required to sign for these, required to wear them at all times when they were not actually sleeping, and twenty-four hours later when they came off guard, required to turn them back immediately. This was a strict rule. No exceptions to it were allowed in any form. There was a good reason for it.

In our Army, back in those now-dead, very far off times, pistols were at a premium. The regulation .45 caliber automatic pistol adopted by the Army was a beautiful thing; it was also a potent weapon at close range. But perhaps even more important, it was small enough to steal. It would be pretty hard for any soldier who was being discharged to steal a rifle, even if he dismantled it completely. Not so with the pistol, and any man would have dearly loved to get his hands on a loose one, without signed records following it around. This, however, was next to impossible to do. Not only was very careful track kept of them, but they were also very scarce in an infantry regiment, since they were only issued to Headquarters personnel, officers, and members of machinegun squads. As a result, about the only time a straight duty rifle private like Mast ever got to put his hands on one, was the twenty-four hours when he went on guard.

All this, of course, went into Mast's enjoyment of wearing, handling and possessing, for twenty-four hours at least, a pistol. But for Mast, who was nineteen and imaginative, there was an even greater pleasure in it. Wearing a pistol on his hip made him feel more like a real soldier, seemed to give him an unbroken lineal connection with the Army of the days of the west and Custer's Cavalry, made him feel that he was really in the Army, a feeling Mast did not often have in what to himself he termed this crumby, lazy outfit. It was almost enough to offset his irritation at having his weekend pass spoiled by guard duty on Sunday.

After the first rack of bombs went off and the sound and shockwave reached the little company mess, there was almost a full minute of thoughtful silence during which everyone looked at everyone else. "Dynamiting?" somebody said. Then another rack fell and exploded and at the same time the first plane came screeching over the quadrangle, its machineguns going full blast. After that there wasn't any doubt and the entire mess jumped up to rush outside.

Mast, being careful to catch up his Sunday half pint of milk so no one could steal it, went too, his pistol riding reassuringly on his hip. A pistol obviously wasn't much good against strafing airplanes, but just the same it felt good to him to have it. It gave Mast a sort of swaggery confidence. He wished rather wistfully, as he watched the next plane come over, that he did not have to turn it in tonight when he went off guard.

It was pretty exciting outside the quadrangle in the street. Out here you could see a big column of black smoke beginning to rise up through the bright, morning air from down at Wheeler Field where they were bombing the planes. You could see them twinkling up there in the sun. They looked innocent, as though they had nothing to do with the destruction going on below.

Every few minutes a fighter with the red discs painted on the wings and fuselage would come screeching and blasting over, his MG fire raking the street. Then everyone would surge back against the building. As soon as he was gone, they would surge right back out again and stand staring at the smoke column as if they were personally responsible for it and proud of their achievement. They looked as though they wanted to take credit for the whole thing themselves, without giving the Japs any at all.

Mast, surging backward and forward with them, had an excited feeling of being in on history, of actually seeing history made, and he wondered if any of the other men felt that way. But Mast doubted if they did. Most of them weren't too bright, or very educated.

Mast happened to be one of three high school graduates in his company, and this fact often worked against him, in many ways. Of the other two, one was company clerk and a sergeant, and the other had been carried off on special duty to work in battalion intelligence and was a tech sergeant. But Mast had steadfastly refused to be inveigled into any such job. If he had wanted to be a clerk, he could have enlisted in the Air Corps. As a result, Mast was the only high school graduate doing straight duty as a rifle private in his company, and in a company like this, where almost nobody had completed grade school, almost no one liked or trusted a man who had finished high school.

For a moment, excitedly, Mast thought of drawing his pistol and taking a few blasts at the low-flying planes as they came over, but he was afraid of looking absurd or ridiculous so he didn't. Even though he had made Expert in pistol on the range, he was reasonably sure he would never hit one. But, boy! Mast thought, what if he did hit one? did bring one down single-handed all by himself with his pistol? What a hero he would be, and at only nineteen! Hell, maybe he'd even get a medal. He could imagine the whole thing in his mind as he allowed himself to be jostled by the men in front as another plane screamed over: the general, the regimental band playing the parade on the division parade ground, the whole business. Boy, what would they think about *that* back home in Miseryville? Even so, he was still too embarrassed, too afraid of being laughed at, to haul the pistol out.

Actually, Mast was the only man present with a weapon, since the other three men on guard with him had to stay over at the guardhouse and sleep there. That was where Mast himself would have been, if he had not been picked as orderly at guardmount yesterday. Wishing he dared draw it, Mast let his hand fall down to his side and massaged the holster flap of his pistol he knew he would have to turn back this evening.

Just then a heavy hand was laid on his shoulder. Startled, Mast turned around to see First Sergeant Wycoff, a big man in his thirties, looking at him with angry eyes and the same numb, stupid, half-grinning expression on his face that all the others had, including his own.

"Mast, aren't you on guard orderly today?"

"What? Oh. Yeah, Yeah, I am."

"Then you better get your tail on over to Headquarters and report," the First Sergeant said, not unkindly. "They'll probably be needing you for carrying messages."

"Okay," Mast said; "yes, sir," and began to shoulder his way back inside through the press, finishing his bottle of milk as he went. Now why the hell hadn't he thought of that himself? he wondered.

Inside the quadrangle, after he had gone back through the building, Mast found men were running everywhere. Whenever a plane came roaring, sliding over they broke and scattered like bowling pins. Then they would get back up and go back to their running. Mast saw one man actually get shot in the leg. It was unbelievable. He simply fell down and lay there with his head up beating his fists on the ground, whether in anger or anguish Mast could not tell. After the plane passed he was helped to the sidelines by two men who ran out, dragging his leg for all the world like an injured football player being helped out of the game.

Up on the roofs of the quadrangle men had begun to appear with machineguns and BARs and were now firing back at the planes as they came over, and from his vantage point under the porch Mast watched them, envying them hungrily. Of all days, he would have to be on guard today; and not only that, would have to get himself picked as guard orderly.

Mast had been on guard plenty of times in the past, but he had never before been chosen orderly. This was because he always became nervous when it came to answering the General Orders questions. He always looked as polished at inspection as everyone else, and he had the General Orders memorized. But whenever the Officer of the Day asked him the questions he would freeze, and his mind would go blank.

And now today of all days, Mast thought regretfully, he would have to make it for orderly. Usually it was the most coveted job, because all you had to do was sit around Headquarters all day outside the Colonel's office and you got your whole night off to yourself, while the rest of them had to stand two hours on and four off, around the clock.

Well, that was just about what he might have expected, Mast thought sadly, have figured on, his customary luck: guard orderly on the day the dirty Japs attacked Oahu.

Standing in under the covered porch and watching the scene before him, a sad, bitter melancholy crept over Mast. It was a feeling that even the longest life was short and the end of it was death and extinction and then rotting away, and that about all a man could expect along the way was frustration, and bitterness, and phoniness in everybody, and hatred. Perhaps being a high school graduate in a company of oafs contributed to it a little bit.

Disdaining to run like the rest of them, even though he could not help feeling a certain nervousness, Mast composed his face into a contemptuous smirk and came out from under the protection of the porch and walked slowly around the square, his pistol swaying bravely on his hip. Twice as he walked flame-spitting planes came sliding over, churning up twin rows of dust across the grass and richocheting screamingly off the brick, and Mast could feel the muscles of his back twitch, but he refused to let himself run or even walk faster.

From under one of the porches of the 3rd Battalion an officer yelled at him, angrily, indignantly, outraged: "Hey, you silly son of a bitch! Get out of there! Are you crazy? Move! Run! That's an order!"

Mast turned his head to look at him, but he did not stop or change his gait. Then suddenly emotion spurted out of him like blood gushing out of a wound. "Go to hell!" he shouted happily, knowing that for once he was invulnerable even to an officer. Just then a third plane came screeching, blasting over and his eyes began to blink themselves rapidly, as if that act in itself would offer him protection. Then it was gone, just like that, off over the quad. In some odd way of possessive ownership, of just knowing it was there, the pistol on his hip helped shore up Mast's courage. He sure wished he didn't have to turn it in tonight. It wasn't like a rifle. Didn't give you the same feeling at all. What the damned government *ought* to do was issue every trooper a rifle and pistol both. They used to. In the Cavalry.

(from Chapter 1)

[The Pistol as Talisman]

MAST'S EYES FOLLOWED Musso, almost hypnotized. He could not help seeing the Italian oldtimer as his personal and vindictive enemy. If Mast's pistol was his savior, and his potential salvation, then Musso was Satan, the Devil, come to take it away. Mast could only hate him; viciously, bitterly, terrifiedly and with horror. On the other hand, Musso was a visitor to the position from the outside world beyond the wire, contact with which had been denied them except for the kitchen trucks, and Mast's instinct was to rush up to him and shake his hand happily and ask him what news there was, how was it going in the Philippines? The two emotions pushed and shoved at each other inside Mast, battling each other over the no-man's land of his body, while Mast himself only stood and stared, transfixed, hypnotized, by this Evil that was climbing the hill with long-legged strides toward the lieutenant's hole, and at the same time there appeared in front of his face that other face of the man from the 8th Field Artillery talking cunningly and grinning slyly as he tried to milk another five dollars out of Mast for the pistol.

There was, of course, only one thing for him to do. That was to get out of sight and keep out of sight until Musso left. Re-enforcing this highly sensible decision, there was running through Mast's mind still another picture, like a short strip of movie film being run over and over and over again without pause, and this was the antithetical filming of his salvation by pistol: the same Jap major was once again rushing down on him with the same bejeweled, gleaming, beautiful Samurai sword through the same jungle on the same unknown island, and the same Mast lay, alone, with the same wound, and missing the same lost rifle, only this time there was no pistol. As a result, as Mast watched the other Mast struggle up to a sitting position, the Jap major, leaping astraddle the wounded legs, his two-handed saber describing a flashing gleaming beautiful arc and striking just beside the neck, clove the sitting Mast splitting him in two to the waist as Mast had seen done to Chinese prisoners in news photos, and the still-living Mast looked down and with anguish watched one half of his own body fall away from the other half while Mast himself anguishedly watched him. Over and over the little film vignette entilted *Ordeal Without Pistol* ran itself through his mind without pause, and Mast stood hopelessly and watched himself divided by saber uncounted numbers of times.

But where was he to get out of sight? The quickest would be to go right back down into number six hole where he had just been relieved, but to do that would be to invite all kinds of suspicion. No man in his right mind would remain in one of these wretched holes and sit and chat with his relief after he had been relieved. The only other alternative was to go down to the number four hole, Mast's home hole where all his gear was, and sit there on his barracks bag and hope no one called him.

It was an unsatisfactory alternative, but it was the only one. Of course he did not make it. Even if there had been enough time to get there without being seen, he had already sacrificed it by standing and staring at Musso and the picture of his, Mast's, own frightful future. Long before he had climbed down to the entrance of the number four hole he was spotted by old Sergeant Pender, the chief noncom of the position, and called down to help unload the machineguns, as he had known he would be.

Reluctantly, miserably, but with no alternative left him now, Mast climbed down past the already lost security of the number four hole, which he looked at longingly, to where the five or six men who had been called out to help unload the guns were converging on the weapons carrier. As he scrambled down over the rough rocks, it seemed to Mast that all his life as far back as he could remember he had lived the life of a doomed and guilty man, for some obscure reason he had never been able to isolate, and that this was just one more classic example of it: These other five or six men, they had nothing to be frightened or afraid of or guilty about in going to help unload the carrier; only he, Mast, did. They could approach it happily or cheerfully or laughing or joking without guilty consciences; only he, Mast, could not. And almost every event that had happened to him in his life had been the same way, and never once had any of them been his own fault. Any more than this one now was his own fault: he had not stolen the pistol. Why this was so, Mast could not understand; but it always had been, and Mast could not help wondering with the apathy of despair, as he approached the weapons carrier down on the level ground, if it would continue to be so through the rest of his life, too. Must he always be doomed and guilty and if so, why? Mast wondered as he approached them.

It was an ordeal the like of which Mast hoped never to have to go through again in his life, that unloading. Musso did not recognize the pistol, in fact he apparently did not even see it, but that did not mean that at the very next moment he might not do so. So for the forty-five minutes it took to unload the two heavy guns from the little truck and carefully cart them and their tripods up the rough, rocky hillside and set them up in the holes to which they had been assigned, Mast existed in a state of suspense that all but unmanned him. As he first came up Musso grinned and said hello to him, and he said hello to Musso. There wasn't much choice. And after that he tried always to unobtrusively keep someone or some thing between himself and Musso. Musso stood beside the truck with old Sergeant Pender, leaning on it and supervising everything and making sure they were careful not to drop or dent or scratch his precious new guns, and after they got them off the truck and began struggling up the treacherous slope with them, he followed them there too, doing the same thing. And to Mast's eyes, which to Mast seemed to bulge and roll around giddily with this unbearable suspense, Musso with his thin, cynical, Italian old-soldier's face was the living picture of Evil. To say that Mast hated him would be such an understatement as to lose all conveyance of meaning. Mast hated him viciously, murderously, with the white purity of Galahad and every fiber of his existence.

It was only some time, a full half hour at least, after Musso left, and after Mast himself had gone off by himself and sat with his head in his hands on a rock, that Mast was actually able to realize he still had his pistol after all. He was so shaken by his ordeal that, even when he did realize it, it did not mean anything. Finally, though, he was able to appreciate it: He had gone through the ordeal, and now his salvation was his. *Truly* his. His pistol was his, free and clear.

Obviously, the paper he had signed had been lost, perhaps in the packing and moving out from Schofield. Or maybe it had been lost after they got down here. But the requisition obviously had to be lost. And just as obviously, Musso himself had clearly forgotten all about it. Mast had walked right past him with it hanging on his hip and Musso had looked right at it and hadn't noticed or remembered.

So his pistol was his, truly and actually his, perhaps for the first time. Once again the face of the man from the 8th Field Artillery from whom he had bought it, and the scene where he had bought it, and the conversation of the transaction itself, all unfolded itself in his mind. It was living proof that it was his, now; that he had bought it after all. When Mast raised his head from his hands, the whole world had taken on a different look, a new look, as if he had never seen it before, or as if it were sparkling cheerfully after a clean, refreshing rain.

Mast's salvation, Mast's chance of surviving, Mast's little margin of safety which riflemen without pistols did not have, just as machinegunners with pistols but without rifles did not have it either, was Mast's again, really Mast's. Now all he had to do was keep it. Keep it away from these maniacal wolves on this Makapoo beach position who wanted to take it from him.

(from Chapter 4)

[Paoli and Pender]

MAST DID NOT have long to wait for the next assault against his salvation to take place, once he arrived back at Makapoo. Less than a week, in fact. He had been tricked, lied to and cheated, bribed, and manhandled, in that order. He thought he knew, and had become experienced in, just about every method. But there was one he had never considered: the honest man. In many ways this one was the worst.

But out of it came something else, something good for Mast. And that was confidence: for the first time, real, genuine confidence.

It was now more than three months since the Pearl Harbor attack and Mast's arrival at Makapuu Head with the pistol. During that three months, in which Mast had battled so desperately to keep it, two things had emerged. One was that no one had ever actually assaulted him physically and taken it from him by force; even Grace hadn't done that. And no one had tried to kill him for it. Not that, Mast suspected, someone wouldn't have been willing to try. But the efficiency of Authority precluded that. There was hope to be seen in this, Mast felt.

The second thing which had emerged during the three desperate months was that never yet had anyone gone to higher authority, such as the lieutenant or the two platoon sergeants, about the pistol. Apparently none of these three, neither the lieutenant nor Sergeants Pender and Cowder, knew anything at all about Mast's loose pistol. With all the pistol's changing of hands, the attempted thefts, the jockeyings for position, the angers and rages and fights and near-fights, never did the three position commanders find out about it. With the wisdom of soldiers, or people under the hand of Authority anywhere, all this was carefully kept from them. And not once during all this time had anyone, not even Mast though he had contemplated it, as had some of the others probably, deliberately gone to them and told them about it. That distinction was reserved for Sergeant Paoli, the honest man.

Paoli came up to Mast one afternoon four days after he had returned from Marconi Pass. Short, chunky, dark, a former butcher from Brooklyn, he was a section sergeant in the machinegun platoon under Sergeant Pender and thus wore a pistol himself. Always a 'book soldier' and known laughingly in Mast's company as 'The Book Says' Paoli, he was stupid, unimaginative, mechanically a genius with a machinegun, and short with words.

"I see you got a pistol," he said to Mast, who was working quietly on a detail that was putting up siding on another new hutment. "I seen you walking around here with it long time now, pretty cocky. I know some the stuff that's went on with it."

"Yeah?" said Mast, who did not like Paoli. "So what?"

"It's screwing up the whole position. That's what. It's causing all kinds a trouble and in-efficiency round here. That's what."

"Nobody else has noticed any inefficiency that I know of."

"Yeah?" Paoli folded his chunky arms authoritatively. "The book says—"

"I know what the book says, Paoli," Mast said.

"The book says," Paoli said doggedly, nevertheless, "riflemen carry rifles. It don't say they carry pistols. Machinegunners carry pistols."

"Okay, so what?"

Paoli jerked his head backwards, at the command post hole behind him. "I'm taking that pistol. And I'm turning it in to Sergeant Pender."

"You're not taking this pistol anywhere, Paoli," Mast said quite positively. "And neither is anybody else. Nobody's taking this pistol off of me."

"Yes. I am," Paoli said. "And that's an order."

"Order be damned. Nobody's taking this pistol off me except an officer or Sergeant Pender himself. I've had that stuff pulled on me before."

"You won't obey my order?"

"That order, no."

"The book says—" Paoli began.

"To hell with the book!" Mast said fierily.

"The book says," Paoli said anyway, "to refuse to obey a order of a noncom is a courtmartial offense." Again he jerked his head backward at the CP hole. "You come with me."

"Sure," Mast said. "Any old time." But the confidence that sounded in his voice was not inside him. Here, now, descending upon him, was the thing he had dreaded most: To be turned in with the pistol: He stood and watched the event shaping itself in time; even though it hadn't happened yet he was already now into the sequence, and it would happen, and nothing could prevent it. It twisted his stomach crampingly. Once again his old friend the Jap major charged down on him screaming, saber high, while he sat and watched him, pistolless. And after all of this, after all of what he had gone through, it would have to be Paoli who would be the agent. He followed Paoli to the hole.

"Tell you something, Mast." Paoli slowed his pace. They threaded their way between two outcroppings. "You got no right to have a pistol. Where you get it?"

"I bought it," Mast said wearily. "From a guy in the 8th Field."

"Well, you got no right to it. And somebody stole it. You're a buyer a stolen equipment. That's bad. And how you think I feel? Me and my boys in my section? We got pistols. We was issued them. But we ain't got rifles. You got a rifle. You was issued it. But you wasn't issued a pistol. Yet you got one. You got a rifle and pistol both." His voice was accusing.

"So has Sergeant Pender," Mast said. "And so has the First Sergeant."

"They're first-three-graders," Paoli said. "You're a private. Everybody knows the pistol's the best defense against them Samurai sabers. Okay. But what about the defense against a rifleman? For that you need a rifle. I ain't got a rifle. Me and my boys in my section. All we got is pistols. But you got a rifle."

"In other words, if you can't have a rifle, I can't have a pistol?" Mast said.

"That's it," Paoli said.

"Why don't you buy yourself a rifle?"

"Where?"

"Anywhere. Look around." But Paoli, having had his say, characteristically did not answer this and clumped on.

They found old Sergeant Pender sitting outside on a rock outcropping scratching himself in the sun. He looked up at Paoli noncommittally as they came up.

"This man refused to obey a direct order, Sergeant," Paoli said without preamble.

"Yeah?" Pender said. "Well. What was the order?"

"I ordered him to give me that pistol. So I could turn it in to you. He refused, Sergeant."

"Well," Pender said. He scratched his three day stubble of beard.

"He says he bought it off a guy in the 8th Field," Paoli said stolidly. "So it's stolen equipment. He's a buyer of stolen equipment."

"Looks like that, doesn't it?" Pender said thoughtfully.

"That's a courtmartial offense," Paoli said, and Mast looked at him, at his dull, perpetually injured face, at his bulling-head stolidity, that did not know it was injuring Mast, or anybody or anything else in the world for that matter. It merely went bulling ahead. Mast hated him. He stood and thrust hate at him as if it were sacks of cement, or bricks.

"That's right, it is," Sergeant Pender said.

"And he refused to obey a direct order from me," Paoli said. "I want to turn him in to you for that too. The book says—"

"I know what the book says, too, Paoli," Pender said.

"Yes, Sergeant," Paoli said.

"Mast's not in your section, is he?"

"No, Sergeant. He's in a rifle platoon. But he's got a pistol."

"If he's not in your section, why'd you take it on yourself to turn him in, Paoli?"

"Because he's got a pistol. That's what. The book says riflemen supposed to have rifles but not pistols."

"Okay, Paoli," Sergeant Pender said. "Thanks. I'll take care of it. You can go."

"Yes, Sergeant," Paoli said, and turned on his heel and left, the set of his chunkily muscled back showing how well he thought he had done his duty. Pender stared after him thoughtfully.

"Well, Mast," the old sergeant said, and scratched his stubble again. He made a wry grin and shook his grizzled head. "Looks like I'll have to take that pistol of yours and turn it in to the supply room."

"I suppose so," Mast said, feeling sick at his stomach. He put his hands to his rifle belt to unclasp it. He knew Sergeant Pender fairly well, although he had never run around with him or got drunk with him of course, any more than he had with any of the first-three-graders.

"Look, Sarge," he said suddenly. "Isn't there any way I can keep it? Anything I can do it keep it. It's—it's—important to me."

"Why?" Pender said.

"Well, it's—Well, I bought it, you know? And it—it makes me feel more like a soldier, sort of. You know? And it's a mighty good defense against those Samurai sabers you know."

"Yes, it is that," Pender said in his gentle way. "You mean you sort of feel it's insurance."

"Yes, I guess. Sort of."

"But not everybody has them," Pender said. "You know that. Riflemen don't carry them and machinegunners who have pistols don't carry rifles. Do you want to have a better break than the next man?" He peered at Mast shrewdly, his eyes glinting.

Mast didn't know what to answer, whether to tell him the truth or to lie. If he lied and said he didn't want a better break than the next guy, he would be forced by sheer logic to give up the pistol. And anyway, old Pender would know whether he was lying.

"Well, yes," he said finally. "Yes, I guess I do want a better break than the next man. Let me put it this way," he qualified, "let's say I want every break I can get for myself. Whether the next guy has them or not. But I don't want the next guy *not* to have them."

"Unless it's your pistol," Pender said.

Mast nodded. "Unless its my pistol."

Pender's eyes glinted again, even moreso, and he suddenly grinned, showing his stubby, broken, stained teeth. "Well, I guess that's only human, hunh, Mast?" he said. Mast's answer seemed to have pleased him in some way. For a moment he scratched his grizzled head. "Well, you know, I saw you with that pistol before. And I wondered where you got it. But I figured what I didn't know wouldn't hurt me any. So I didn't see it any more." Pender raised his eyebrows and shrugged ruefully. "But now that it's been brought to my official attention by Paoli, and everybody knows it, I don't see what else I can do but take it and turn it in."

"I don't think much of anybody knows it's been brought to your official attention, Sarge," Mast said. "Unless Paoli tells them."

"Paoli will tell them," Pender said.

"I suppose so. Then there isn't anything I can do to keep it?"

"I don't see what, Mast. Do you?"

Mast bobbed his head. "You've got one, Sarge. And you've got a rifle, too. The First has both a pistol and a rifle, too."

"I'm supposed to be issued a pistol."

Again Mast bobbed his head at it. "But everybody knows that that one's your own, and that you brought it with you into the company."

Pender looked down at his grimy thigh and slapped the holster on it. "This one? I've had this one since 1918 in the first World War."

"Please let me keep mine," Mast forced himself to say.

Again, Sergeant Pender scratched his grizzled head. "I tell you what, Mast. This is what I'll do. I'll just forget Paoli brought you up here and turned you in with it. How's that? I can't guarantee any more than that. If the lieutenant or somebody tells me I have to take it away from you, why I'll have to do it. But until then, I'll just forget Paoli brought you up here. How's that?"

"That's fine," Mast said, smiling all over. "That's swell." Then his face sobered. "But what about Paoli?"

"I'll handle Paoli. You send him back up here when you go down." Pender paused a moment. "Paoli's a genius with a machinegun," he added apropros of nothing, in an expressionless voice, and looked off at the road. Mast felt it was a partial explanation.

"You know this might really save my life someday, Sarge," he said gratefully. "Thanks. Thanks again."

"Yes, it might," Pender said. "It might do that."

Mast turned to go. "Sarge, how did you come by your pistol? In the last war."

"I stole it off a dead American," Sergeant Pender said expressionlessly.

"Oh," Mast said.

"But his bad luck was my good luck. He did me a big favor. Because it saved me twice," Sergeant Pender smiled. He scratched his beard, and his face sobered slowly. "And I don't *really* believe he had any more use for it. Do you?" he asked.

"No," Mast said, feeling suddenly strange. "How could he?"

"Well, I've wondered about it," Sergeant Pender said. "Sometimes." He coughed. "You send Paoli up."

"I will, Sarge," Mast said eagerly, smiling all over again.

The chunky Paoli did not change expression or say anything beyond an expressionless, clipped "Okay," when Mast came up to him still wearing the pistol and told him Sergeant Pender wanted to see him. And Mast stood and watched him go on off chunkily up the hill. Then he picked up his hammer, but he could not go back to work yet. For one thing his hand was trembling violently, and so were his legs, and the thought of his near-escape made him suddenly go weak all over. He sat down by himself on an outcropping, the hammer dangling from his hand.

Out of this had come the best of all possible things, the best position he had been in since first getting the pistol. He had Sergeant Pender on his side. If the lieutenant, who rarely seemed to notice anything, or some other officer, didn't notice it and make him give it up, he practically had it made. And why would an officer notice it? and if they did, how many of them would give a damn?

There would be other attempts to steal it, undoubtedly. Other bribes, attempting to gain Mast's salvation. Other tricks, other subterfuges. But Mast was sure he could handle all of them. And the thing which all along had troubled him most, since he had bought this pistol from that man in the 8th Field Artillery, the thing he feared the worst: that of being turned in with it: was no longer a problem. Mast felt safer now with his pistol, and with the chance of survival it gave him, the chance of being saved, than he had ever felt since he had had it. What could possibly happen to it now?

And as the weeks passed, he became more and more reenforced in this opinion.

(Chapter 10)

[The Return of Musso]

IT DAWNED CLEAR AND COLD that day, and as always just at dawn and at dusk, the never-ending, unceasing wind across Makapuu Head fell away to a sudden eery silence louder than any noise for perhaps fifteen minutes. Mast had come off post at the machineguns in hole number five at five o'clock, and since it was so near dawn he stayed up to see it. The thin, violet pencil-line of light along the horizon out at sea grew slowly, spreading upward toward the zenith, slowly turning itself red as it grew, tingeing the scattered clouds with red, then orange as it swelled and swelled, an inexorable lightening of the world, irresistible, not to be stopped. Mast always had loved watching the dawn come up when he was on post.

After the spectacle was over, and feeling refreshed as only dawn after a night awake can make one feel, Mast went down to his hutment to get his mess gear for morning chow. He had just spent two hours sitting in the pitch black of a pillbox, staring out intently past the snub barrel of the .30 caliber watercooled at even deeper blackness in which Japanese ships could not be seen had they been there, until his eyes had wanted to cross themselves or lock themselves open. As always the tension of staring, of expecting, had told on him, worn him out as it did all of them, and now he was hungry. But tired or not, hungry or not, he had his pistol to console him. It was a thought which always came to him at such moments, and he rested his hand on it as he stood in the chowline.

He waited half an hour for the kitchen truck, another ten

minutes for the line to move back to him, ate ravenously, cleaned his gear, and walked back to the hutment to get the book he was reading. So far it was just another day, a nice one. Work details were getting fewer and fewer at Makapoo and there was more time to load and read. He sat down on an outcropping with the book.

O'Brien was sitting not far from him on another outcropping, reading a comic book, which the traveling library thoughtfully provided also. Their association was still the same as it had been since that last day at Marconi Pass, because O'Brien had not given up on the pistol. It was in effect an armed truce. They spoke to each other abruptly and stiffly and that was all.

Now, as Mast sat down, O'Brien looked up from his comic book, his pale green eyes cold and hard, and nodded stiffly. Mast nodded back.

Just another day, like any day.

He had been reading perhaps an hour, and it was just about nine o'clock, when another weapons carrier came roaring down the road and turned in at the position. It was too soon to be the noon chow truck, obviously, and the breakfast one had already gone. Mast, like everybody else around, looked up to see what it could be. Weapons carriers from the CP were always big occasions. The sentry opened the wire gate for it and it came on in, and then Mast saw that it was Musso who was in it.

Perhaps it was at that moment that he had his first premonition. At any rate, it was then that his heart surged and then began to pound loudly in his throat. As he watched—with a sense of seeing inexorable, inevitable movement which made everything seem to slow down to an unbearable slowness—the little weapons carrier stopped, Musso unwound his long legs out of the seat well and got out, came walking over toward him. He was unbuttoning his shirt pocket as he came. And Mast merely sat and watched him come.

It was all very simple, really nothing at all. It took but a moment to complete. Mast didn't actually *feel* anything, except the pounding of his heart. All that would come later. But at the moment there was really nothing to it. Perhaps the most horrifying thing was that Musso had no idea at all of what he was doing, none at all. He was simply doing a job, and a trivial job at that. He was not angry at Mast, he was not even grinning at how Mast had almost 'put one over', he was simply picking up a lost pistol.

He was, if Mast had been forced to voice it, assuming Mast was able, which Mast was not, simply and inexorably Authority. The personification of absolute, inexorable, impersonal Authority.

"I've been looking for that damn pistol for over a month," Musso said indifferently. "Couldn't figure out where it disappeared to. I knew I was one short, but I couldn't figure where. Never thought to look up that old peacetime guard issue."

He had already pulled out the old requisition Mast had signed so long ago, so many eons ago that it was even back before the war. It took but a moment for Mast to unhook the pistol and hand it over, another minute to go inside the hutment and bring out the lanyard, brassard and web pistol belt.

"Okay, kid; thanks," Musso said and turned and left, other more important jobs obviously on his mind.

Mast was still standing, looking after him. Near him O'Brien had gotten up and was standing too, his face totally blank with disbelief and horror. Slowly he moved closer to Mast, his arms dangling disbelievingly, impotently. Mast hardly noticed him. He was thinking that the worst thing was the question which kept running through his head: Had it all been for nothing? all the worries? all that effort? the fight? all that concentration? really all for nothing? He had actually forgotten somewhere along the line that he had ever really signed a requisition for that pistol. Wasn't that silly? He really had believed he'd bought it.

Down below them Musso climbed back into the carrier, and the sentry opened the gate, and Mast simply stood. As O'Brien was simply standing, beside him. As the weapons carrier crawled out slowly through the gate, O'Brien began biting his lower lip furiously, as if the full import had finally reached him. Tears of rage, or frustration, had come into those pale green eyes of his, and his face was dark with anger.

Then, as the little weapons carrier with Musso in it shot off down the road and began to dwindle into the distance, O'Brien suddenly flung up a big fist and commenced to shake it after the dwindling carrier.

"You got no right!" he shouted. "You got no right! It ain't fair! You got no right to do that to us!"

In the violence of his emotion he threw his head back and yelled it at the top of his lungs, so that in an odd way, while he was shaking his fist after the carrier, O'Brien himself, his teeth bared, was staring fiercely upward at the sky, as he went on shouting.

"It ain't fair!" O'Brien shouted upward. "You got no right! It ain't fair!"

And beside him Mast stood staring at the picture of his Japanese major, who would someday come for him.

(from Chapter 11)

The Thin Red Line

(1962)

Written in Paris, *The Thin Red Line* is the second volume of Jones's army trilogy. Published by Scribner's, the best-selling novel received overwhelmingly favorable critical reviews and was compared to Stephen Crane's *The Red Badge of Courage*. Jones's work recounts in grim and uncompromising detail the Guadalcanal campaign. It is arguably the best combat novel ever written by an American. Its unique power derives from Jones's stark presentation of random and impersonal death in modern technological warfare, and from his success in depicting C-for-Charlie Company as a composite character. He accomplishes this while demonstrating, as Orville Prescott of *The New York Times* put it, "impressive skill in characterizing a variety of young and poorly educated men."

The novel begins with the American landings on the Japanese-occupied island and ends with its capture by U.S. troops. The selections have been chosen to reflect the novel's recurring themes and motifs—the absurdity of anonymous death in combat, the ineffectuality and corruption of the officer class, and the brutalizing effects of warfare on the most decent of men. Jones's vision of combat is not one-dimensional, however. As one reviewer (*New York Post*) noted, "The exultancy and antic spirit in combat that Jones captures so brilliantly are one step away from sheer, howling madness." Of special interest is the selection describing Bead's killing of the Japanese soldier in hand-to-hand combat, a scene based closely on an incident in Jones's own experience on Guadalcanal, one that haunted him for the rest of his life.

In the novel's last sentence Jones comments ironically on the selectivity of vision and remembrance of all who have ever been involved in combat. It should be considered in light of the novel's dedication: "This book is cheerfully dedicated to those greatest and most heroic of all human endeavors, WAR and WARFARE; may they never cease to give us the pleasure, excitement and adrenal stimulation that we need, or provide us with the heroes, the presidents and leaders, the monuments and museums which we erect to them in the name of PEACE."

[The Battle of the Bombers and the Fighters]

CORPORAL FIFE had, of course, been in the barge which brought off the company headquarters. Their barge pilot had told them substantially the same thing Doll's had: "Your outfit's lucky. The Jap's on his way." The transports must have been spotted, he said. But they were getting off just ahead of time, he said, so they'd be safe. The main thought uppermost in Fife's mind was that everything was so organized, and handled with such matter-of-fact dispatch. Like a business. Like a regular business. And yet at the bottom of it was blood: blood, mutilation, death. It seemed weird, wacky, to Fife. The air strip had got the news, by radio from a plane apparently, and had transmitted it to the beach, where the barge pilots were all informed—or else informed themselves and each other—and presumably the crews as well as the army commanders, if not the troops themselves, on board the ships were told, too. And yet there was nothing anybody could do about it, apparently. Except wait. Wait and see what happened. Fife had looked around at the faces in the barge covertly. Bugger Stein betrayed his nervousness by continually adjusting his glasses, over and over, with the thumb and fingers of his right hand on the frame. Lieutenant Band betrayed his by repeatedly licking his lips.

Storm's face was too impassively set. The second cook Dale's eyes were snapping bright, and he blinked them over and over. Welsh's eyes, through the narrow slits to which they were closed in the bright sun, betrayed nothing of anything. Neither amusement nor anything else, this time; not even cynicism. Fife hoped his own face looked all right, but he felt as though his eyebrows might be too high up on his forehead. Once they got ashore, and the guide had led them to their assigned spot in the edge of the coconut trees which came right down to the beach itself, Fife kept saying over and over to himself what the barge pilot had told them on the way in: "Your outfit's lucky. You're getting off ahead of time."

And in a way, it was quite right too. When the planes came, they were after the ships, not the shore. As a result, Fife, and all the rest of C-for-Charlie had a perfectly safe grandstand, ringside seat for the whole show. Actually Fife at least, who loved humanity, was going to find that he wished he hadn't had a seat at all, after it was over. But he had to admit it fascinated him, with a morbid fascination.

Apparently the news had not affected the beach very much at all. The LCIs and a welter of other types of barges still came roaring, jamming in to unload their cargoes of men or supplies, while others were in process of pulling back out to rejoin the shuttle. The beach was literally alive with men, all moving somewhere, and seemed to undulate with a life of its own under their mass as beaches sometimes appear to do when invaded by armies of fiddler crabs. Lines, strings and streams of men crossed and recrossed it with hot-footed and apparently unregulated alacrity. They were in all stages of dress and undress, sleeveless shirts, legless pants, no shirts at all, and in some few cases, particularly those working in or near the water, they worked totally stark naked or in their white government issue underpants through which the dark hairiness of their genitals showed plainly. There were no women anywhere around here at all anyway, and there were not likely to be any either for quite some little time. They wore all sorts of fantastic headgear, issue, civilian, and homemade, so that one might see a man working in the water totally naked with nothing adorning his person except his identity tags around his neck and a little red beany, turned-up fatigue hat, or a hat of banana leaves on his head. The supply barges were unloaded by gangs of men immediately, right at the water's edge, so that the barge could go back for more.

Then lines of other men carried these boxes, cases, cans back up the beach into the trees, or formed chains and passed them from hand to hand, trying to clear the space at the water's edge. Further away down the beach the heavier matériel, trucks, anti-tank guns, artillery, were being unloaded, driven by their own drivers, or hauled up by Marine tractors. And still further away, this whole operation was being conducted a second time for the second transport, anchored quite a few hundred yards behind the first.

All of this activity had been going on at this same pace since very early morning apparently, and the news of the impending air raid did not appear to affect it one way or the other. But as the minutes crept by one after the other, there was a noticeable change in the emotional quality and excitement of the beach. C-for-Charlie, from its vantage point at the edge of the trees, could sense the tautening of the emotional tenor. They watched a number of men who had been calmly bathing waistdeep in the sea in the midst of all this hectic activity, look at their watches and then get out and walk naked up to their clothes in the edge of the trees. Then, just a few moments after this, someone at the water's edge flung up an arm and cried out, "There they are!" and the cry was taken up all up and down the beach.

High up in the sunbright sky a number of little specks sailed serenely along toward the channel where the two ships lay. After a couple of minutes when they were closer, a number of other specks, fighter planes, could be seen above them engaging each other. Below on the beach the men with jobs and the working parties had already gone back to their work; but as the others, including C-for-Charlie company, watched, about half the engaged fighter planes broke off and turned back to the north, apparently having reached the limit of their fuel range. Only a couple of the remaining fighters started out to chase them, and they almost at once gave it up and turned back, and with the others began to attack the bombers. On they all came, slowly getting larger. The tiny mosquitoes dipped and swirled and dived in a mad, whirling dance around the heavier, stolid horseflies, who nevertheless kept serenely and sedately on. Now the bombers began to fall, first one here, trailing a great plume of smoke soon dissipated by the winds of the upper air, then another one there, trailing no smoke at all and fluttering down. No parachutes issued from them. Still the bombers kept on. Then one of the little mosquitoes fell, and a moment later, in another place, another. Parachutes appeared from both, floating in the sunbright air. Still the mosquitoes darted and swirled. Another injured horsefly fell. But it was surprising, at least to C-for-Charlie and the other newcomers, how many did not fall. Considering the vehemence and numbers of the attack, it appeared that they must all go down. But they didn't, and the whole concerted mass moved slowly on toward the ships in the channel, the changing tones of the motors as the fighters dived or climbed clearly discernible now.

Below on the beach the minutes, and then the seconds, continued to tick by. There were no cheers when a bomber fell. When the first one had fallen, another new company nearby to C-for-Charlie had made an attempt at a feeble cheer, in which a few men from C-for-Charlie had joined. But it soon died from lack of nourishment, and after that it was not again attempted. Everybody watched in silence, rapt, fascinated. And the men down on the beach continued to work, though more excitedly now.

To Corporal Fife, standing tensely in the midst of the silent company headquarters, the lack of cheering only heightened his previous impression of its all being like a business. A regular business venture, not war at all. The idea was horrifying to Fife. It was weird and wacky and somehow insane. It was even immoral. It was as though a clerical, mathematical equation had been worked out, as a calculated risk: Here were two large, expensive ships and, say, twenty-five large aircraft had been sent out after them. These had been given protection as long as possible by smaller aircraft, which were less expensive than they, and then sent on alone on the theory that all or part of twenty-five large aircraft was worth all or part of two large ships. The defending fighters, working on the same principle, strove to keep the price as high as possible, their ultimate hope being to get all twenty-five large aircraft without paying all or any of either ship. And that there were men in these expensive machines which were contending with each other, was unimportant—except for the fact that they were needed to manipulate the machines. The very idea itself, and what it implied, struck a cold blade of terror into Fife's essentially defenseless vitals, a terror both of unimportance, his unimportance, and of powerlessness: his powerlessness. He had no control or sayso in any of it. Not even where it concerned himself, who was also a part of it. It was terrifying. He did not mind dying in a war, a real war,—at least, he didn't think he did—but he did not want to die in a regulated business venture.

Slowly and inexorably the contending mass high up in the air came on. On the beach the work did not stop. Neither did the LCIs and other barges. When the planes had almost reached the ships, one more bomber fell, crashing and exploding in smoke and flames in the channel in full view of everybody. Then they began to pass over the ships. A gentle sighing became audible through the air. Then a geyser of water, followed by another, then another, popped high up out of the sea. Seconds later the sounds of the explosions which had caused them swept across the beach and on past them into the coconut trees, rustling them. The gentle sighing noise grew louder, carrying a fluttery overtone, and other geysers began to pop up all over the sea around the first ship, and then a few seconds later, around the second. It was no longer possible to distinguish the individual sticks of bombs, but they all saw the individual stick of three bombs which made the hit. Like probing fingers, the first lit some distance in front of the first ship, the second coming closer. The third fell almost directly alongside. An LCI was just putting off from the ship, it couldn't have been many yards away, and the third bomb apparently landed directly on it. From that distance, probably a thousand yards or more, one faint, but clearly discernible scream, high and shrill, and which actually did not reach them until after the geyser had already gone up, was heard by the men on shore, cut off and followed immediately by the sound wave of the explosion: some one nameless man's single instinctual and useless protest against the taking of his life and his own bad luck at being where he was instead of somewhere else, ridiculous, pointless, but not without a certain dignity, although, ironically, it was not heard, and appreciated, until after he himself no longer existed. His last scream had lived longer than he had.

When the spout of water had subsided so that they could see, there was nothing left of the LCI to be seen. At the spot where it had been a few figures bobbed in the water, and these rapidly became fewer. The two barges nearest them came about and made for the spot, reaching them before the little rescue boat that was standing by could get there. Losing way, they wallowed in the trough while infantrymen stripped off equipment and dived in to help both the injured and uninjured who had had no time to strip equipment and were being dragged under by it. The less seriously wounded and the uninjured were helped aboard the barges on little rope ladders thrown over the side by the pilots; the more seriously hurt were simply kept afloat until the rescue boat, which carried slings and baskets and was already on its way, could get there.

On shore, the watching men—the lucky ones, as the barge pilots had said, because they were out of it—tried to divide their attention between this operation and the planes still overhead. The bombers, having made their run, turned out toward the channel and headed back north. They made no attempt at strafing, they were too busy protecting themselves from the fighters, and the antiaircraft crews on the ships and shore could not fire either for fear of hitting their own fighters. The whole operation, except for the dropped bombs themselves, had taken place up there, high up in the air. Slowly, sedately, the bombers headed back into the north to where a protective blanket of their own fighters would be waiting for them, growing slowly and steadily smaller, as before they had grown slowly and steadily larger. The fighters still buzzed angrily around them, and before they were lost to sight a few more fell. All during the action the defending fighters had been hampered by having to break off and streak back to the air strip to renew fuel or ammunition. Replenished, they would return. But the number of fighters actually engaged was never as large as it might have been. Apparently the bombers were allowing for this factor. At any rate, slowly they dwindled to specks again, then to invisibility. Then finally, the fighters began to return. It was over. On the beach the work of unloading, which had never ceased during the attack, went right on.

(from Chapter 1)

[Queen and the Mass Grave]

THE POSITION was unmistakably Japanese. It was also clear that it was a lost position. They had had a line here along the edge of the jungle at some time or other, and C-for-Charlie's men had come upon it just where it turned in from the edge to wind its way tortuously back into the depths of the jungle. It was in acute disrepair. Mounds and humps and ditches and holes which once had been dugouts, trenches and parapets twisted in and out in a continuous band of raw earth between huge tree boles and clumps of undergrowth until they lost themselves in the dim light of the jungle interior. Total silence hung over it everywhere except for the occasional loud cries of birds. Eagerly in the dim light, more than glad to forget the shirt, the men hurried over and began to clamber up onto the mounds to inspect—with a sort of painful, almost lascivious masochism—what they one day soon would be up against themselves. It was beyond these mounds, where it had remained hidden from their view because of them, that the mass grave lay.

From the top of the mounds a look at the terrain was enough to show that the Marines and, as evidenced by the shirt, elements of the American Division had attacked or else counterattacked this line. Slowly (that much was apparent) and perhaps several times, they had come across the same ground which C-for-Charlie's men had themselves just traversed. Stumps of saplings, torn undergrowth, cut vines, pitholes all showed the volume of mortar and machinegun fire to which the ground in front of the position had been subjected. Already, new growth had effectively hidden most of these signs and they had to be searched for, but they were there. Only the scarred, bullet-hacked forest giants, standing impassively like rooted columns, seemed to have survived this new type of tropical storm without crippling effects.

Like a band of energetic ants the men spread out, poking here, peering there, looking at everything. Souvenirs had now become their preoccupation. But no matter how greedily they hunted, there was almost nothing left for them to find. Quartermaster Salvage units had been over the ground with fine-tooth combs. Not a piece of equipment, not a single strand of barbed wire, not even an empty Japanese cartridge casing or old shoe remained to be picked up by scavengers like themselves. Once they had disappointedly assured themselves of this, as if by a common accord they turned their rapt, still somewhat awed attention to the long mass grave.

It was here that the delayed emotional reaction to the death shirt caught up with them in the form of a sort of wild horseplay of bravado. Big Queen was the leader of it. The grave itself ran for perhaps forty yards along the very edge of the jungle, just inside the tight skin of leaves. It had been made by widening the former Japanese trench. Either it was very shallow or there was more than one layer of bodies, because here and there undecayed appendages or smaller angular portions such as knees and elbows stuck up out of the loose dirt that had been shoveled back over them.

Obviously it had been a sanitary arrangement more than anything else. Which was quite understandable, if one contemplated the acrid, bronzegreen odor that hung over the position and became slowly stronger the closer one came to the edge of the ditch. It must have been hellish before they buried them. They were of course all Japanese. An ex-undertaker, after examining a greenishcolored, half-clenched hand found sticking up near the edge, gave it as his opinion that the bodies were a month old.

It was up to the edge of this ditch, not far from where a stocky, uniformed Japanese leg thrust up out of it at an angle, that Big Queen advanced and stopped. Several men before him already had somewhat incautiously stepped out onto the grave itself in their eagerness to see, only to find themselves slowly sinking kneedeep into the dirt and dead. For men whose feet were still sinking and not resting on anything solid they all had leaped back out with astonishing nimbleness. Cursing savagely and smelling strongly they provided, to the guffaws of the others, a sterling object lesson. So Queen ventured no further.

Standing with the toes of his combat boots exactly at the edge of the solid ground, sweating a little, grinning a strangely taut, full-width grin which made his large teeth resemble a dazzling minature piano keyboard in the green light, Queen looked back at the rest challengingly. His face seemed to say that he had suffered enough personal indignities for one day and by God now he was going to get even.

"Looks like this one was a healthy spec'men. Ought to be somethin worth takin home on some of them," he said by way of preamble, and leaning forward seized the shod foot and jiggled it around tentatively to see how well it was attached, then gave it a solid heave.

The surface of the ditch quivered scismically, and along it tranquil flies rose buzzing in alarm, only to settle back in the quiet that followed. In the late afternoon jungle light everyone watched.

Queen still held the leg. The leg itself still remained in the ditch. After a time-dead second in which nothing moved or breathed, Queen gave the foot another, even more tremendous heave; and again the flies buzzed up in panic. The leg still held.

Not to be outdone another man standing by the ex-undertaker stepped forward and took hold of the greenishcolored halfclenched hand. This was Pfc Hoff, an Indiana countryboy from the second platoon. Clasping the hand as if in a handshake, as though he were wishing its former owner a bon voyage on his journey, Hoff took the wrist with his other hand and pulled too, grinning stupidly. In his case too nothing happened.

As though taking these two actions as their key, the rest began to spread out around the grave edge. They seemed seized by a strange arrogance. They pushed or poked at this or that exposed member, knocked with riflebutts this or that Japanese knee or elbow. They swaggered impudently. A curious Rabelaisian mood swept over them leaving them immoderately ribald and laughing extravagantly. They boisteriously desecrated the Japanese parts, laughing loudly, each trying to outbravado the other.

It was just then that the first souvenir, a rusting Japanese bayonet and scabbard, was found. It was found by Pfc Doll. Feeling something hard under his foot, he reached down to see what it was. Doll had taken a quiet backseat at the finding of the bloodstained shirt, and had not said a word. He did not know exactly what it made him feel, but whatever it was was not good. He had been left feeling so depressed that he had not even bothered to hunt for souvenirs among the mounds with the rest. The trenchful of dead Japanese made him feel even worse but he felt he must not show this so he had joined in with the others; but his heart wasn't in it, and neither was his stomach. Finding the bayonet by sheer luck like that restored his spirits somewhat. Cleaned up and shortened it would make him a better belt knife than the cheap one he had. Feeling considerably better Doll held it up to be seen and called out his find.

Further up the ditch on the other side Queen was still staring fixedly at his Japanese leg. He really had had no intention of disinterring the leg or the body at the other end of it. He was only showing off. He only wanted to show them, and himself, that dead bodies—even Japanese ones afflicted with God knew what horribly dirty Oriental diseases—held no terror for him. But with Hoff getting into the act, and trying to top him like that—And now that punk Doll had to go and find a Jap bayonet—

Tightening his mind and his grip on the foot, clamping his jaws even tighter in their piano-keyboard grin, Queen jiggled his leg around tentatively once more, issuing to it as it were the final definitive personal challenge. Then, grinding his exposed and grinning teeth together, he began to pull on it with every ounce of his great strength.

Standing back on the perimeter of all of this, taking no part, Bell was nevertheless watching it all with a horrified fascination. Bell still could not free himself from that earlier illusion that he was in the midst of a nightmare dream, that he would soon wake up home in bed with Marty and push his face between the softnesses of her breasts to forget it. He would slide his face down her to inhale the lifecreating, lifescented womanperfume of her which always reassured and soothed him. At the same time Bell knew he was not going to wake up; and once again his mind tricked him with that weird transcendental image of Marty's presence somewhere nearby watching this. But this time instead of seeing him as the leg in the grave, as before she had seen him wearing the shirt, she now stood somewhere up behind him watching the scene with him. *Brutes! Brutes! Animal brutes!* he could hear her cry. *Why dont you do something? Brutes! Dont just stand there! Stop them! Is there no human dignity? Bru-u-u tes!* It rang in his head, fading away eerily in the high gloom of the trees, as he continued to stand, watching.

Big Queen was now in the midst of making his main effort. His face was beet-red. Great veins stood out on his neck under his helmet. His big teeth, totally exposed now, dazzled whitely in his face. A high, semi-audible keening sound resembling one of those silent dog whistles came from his throat as he strained his strength beyond even his capacity.

It was clear enough to Bell that the leg was not going to pull off its body. Therefore, only two possibilities remained. Bell understood, not without sympathy, that Queen had publicly committed himself. He must now either pull the corpse out of the grave bodily, or admit he wasn't strong enough to do it. Fascinated by a great deal more than just simply what he was seeing, Bell watched quiescently while Queen fought to win his selfimposed test.

What could I have done, Marty? Anyway, you're a woman. You want to make life. You dont understand men. Even in himself there were elements of pride and hope involved; he didn't want to see Queen lose. Numb and sick as he was. Come on, Queen! Bell suddenly wanted to yell wildly. Come on, boy! *I'm* for you!

Across the ditch Doll was having an entirely different reaction. With all his heart and soul, furiously, jealously, vindictively, he was hoping Queen would *not* win. His new bayonet dangled from his hand forgotten and he held his breath, his belly muscles tensed with the effort of helping the corpse resist Queen's strength. Damn him, Doll thought with clenched teeth, damn him. Okay, so he's stronger than us; so what?

Queen couldn't have cared less about either reaction. He stared down with bulging eyes, teeth bared, his breath whistling through his nose as he strained. He was furiously convinced that the leg was stretching. Heavily muscled in the calf, wrapped in its wool leggin, bandylegged and cocky even in death, it seemed as selfconfident of its supreme Japanese superiority as its former owner must have been in life. Queen was dimly aware that the others had stopped what they were doing and were watching. But he had already used all his strength. In desperation he called upon a reserve beyond his capacity. He couldn't quit now, not with them all watching. Once on a fatigue detail he had lifted a whole tree down off its freshly cut stump on his back. He concentrated on remembering that. And miraculously, the leg began to move.

Slowly, dreamily, mercifully mudcovered, the body drifted up out of the grave. It was like some mad, comically impure travesty of the Resurrection. First came the rest of the leg; then the second leg, flung out at a grotesque angle; then the torso; finally the shoulders and stiff, spreadeagled arms which looked as though the man were trying to hold on to the dirt and keep himself from being dragged out; and lastly the mudcovered head. Queen released his grip on the foot with a great gasp and stepped back—and almost fell over. Then he simply stood, looking down at his handiwork. The helmeted head was so covered with mud it was impossible to distinguish its facial features as such. Indeed, the whole body was so mud-smeared that it was impossible to tell whether it wore any equipment in addition to its uniform or not. And Queen had no inclination to get closer. He continued to look at it, breathing heavily.

"Well, I guess I was mistaken," he said finally. "I guess there's nothin worth keepin on this one after all."

As if released from their rapt state by his words a sudden spontaneous, if feeble, cheer-for-Queen broke out from among the watchers. Overhead, birds fluttered, squawked in panic and fled. Attacked by modesty, Queen smiled back shyly, sweating heavily. But the cheer, as well as any subsequent action, was suddenly choked off by a new development. From the grave a new smell, as distinct from the former greenishcolored one as if they derived from different sources, rolled up like an oily fog from around the muddy body and began to spread. With dismayed curses and astonished, pained exclamations of consternation the men began to back off, then finally just simply turned and fled, jettisoning their dignity and everything else. Anything with a nose must retreat in rout from that odor.

Bell, escaping with the others and laughing as senselessly as they, ran breathlessly. He felt curiously surrealistic, and found a new popular-song title was running through his head over and over.

"Dont Monkey Around With Death"

It ran over and over in his mind to the tune of some real song whose title he could not remember, as he made up words for it.

> *"Dont monkey around with death,*
> *It will only get you dirty;*
> *Dont futz around with the Reaper,*
> *He will only make you smell.*
> *Have you got B O?*
> *Then do not go*
> *Fiddling with that Scythe-man;*
>
> (optional break:)
> *Because . . . .* (upbeat; pause)
> *Your best friend will not tell you:*
>
> *Dont monkey around with death;*
> *You will only wind up soiled."*

Bell reached the top of the mounds with the others, whistling his little melody between his teeth soundlessly and staring off blankly, then turned around to look back. The mudcovered Japanese man still sprawled stiffly and all spraddled out atop the ditch beside the pit his enforced disinterment had opened down into the depths of the grave there in the jungle gloom. Nearby Bell saw Doll still holding his souvenir bayonet and looking back also, with an odd faraway look on his face.

Doll was trying very hard not to throw up. That was the reason for the faraway look; it was one of intense concentration. There was a strong urge in his throat to swallow repeatedly, and Doll was trying to control it. It was not enough to refrain from vomiting; if he kept swallowing, someone would be sure to notice it whether he threw up or not. And that was unthinkable. He couldn't allow it. Especially with Queen standing not far from him.

When Queen first had stepped back from his labor, his heel had struck something metallic behind him. Wild hopes had risen in him that he might find a Japanese .31 caliber heavy machinegun or some such item, buried in the mud. He discovered instead that it was a mud-daubed helmet. He had seized it and retreated to the top of the mounds with the others.

But he got no chance to inspect his find there. It became apparent quite quickly that the top of the fortifications was not going to be far enough. By the time the last fleeing man reached the mounds, the smell like some invisible cloud had arrived too, right on his heels. There was no choice but to retreat again.

There was no fighting that smell. It was as different in kind and texture and taste from the earlier one as two smells could be. The earlier had been mild, was greenishbronze in color, acrid, dry, only slightly unpleasant. The second smell was wet and yellowwhite. It was not mild. No man who was sane and at liberty to leave was going to stay around to smell it.

They did not go back to the place of the shirt, but headed out toward the edge. Everybody had had enough exploring. At the tight skin of leaves they paused, still laughing senselessly, and looking back like Hallowe'en pranksters who have just upset the outdoor toilet of a farm. It was there that Queen finally got time to inspect the helmet.

It made a pretty poor souvenir. They all had heard that Japanese officers had stars of gold or silver on their helmets. Real gold, or real silver. If that was so, this was the helmet of a junior private. Its star was iron—and very thin iron at that, and badly bent. The outside of the helmet was covered with mud, but inside though badly sweatstained it was curiously clean.

Looking at it, this gave Queen a sudden inspiration. He had had a curious sense of oppression after dragging that poor damned muddy Jap corpse out of its final resting place—as though he knew he had done something bad and would be found out and punished for it. The oppression had abated somewhat during the stumbling, laughing, breathless trek back out to the jungle edge. And, instinctively in a way he could not have formulated, Big Queen sensed he had at hand the means of vanquishing it completely. By making himself laughable and ridiculous he could both atone and at the same time avoid admitting he needed to. Removing his own GI helmet Queen put the Japanese one on his head and struck a pose, throwing out his great chest with a silly grin.

There was a burst of uproarious laughter from the others. Queen's head was too big even for an American helmet, which rode high up on his head like a hat. The Japanese one, made to be worn by small men, did not come down over his head at all; it sat up flat on top of it. The chinstrap did not even come down to his nose, but hung in front of his eyes. From behind it Queen peered out at them. He began to caper.

Even Doll laughed. Bell was the only one who didn't. He grinned, and gave a short bark, but then his face sobered and he eyed Queen shrewdly. For a second they looked into each other's eyes. But Queen would not meet his gaze and looked away and unwilling to meet Bell's eyes after that, went on with his farce for the others.

It had stopped raining while they were in the jungle. But they had not known it. The falling moisture, trapped high above and retarded in its descent, had continued to drip down—and would continue to long after—just as if it still rained outside. With surprise they stepped out to find the sky was blue again, and the washed air clear. Almost instantaneously, as though Storm had been watching with binoculars for them to reappear through the green wall, the chow whistle sounded clear and shrill across the open ground from within the grove. It was an intensely familiar, curiously heartwringing sound to hear here, studded with memories of secure evenings. It rose and then fell away to silence in the late clear island air which carried a feel of the sea. And it shocked the explorers. They stared at each other, realizing that those dead Japanese men were really dead Japanese men. From the hills the mortarfire and small-arms fire of some struggle came down to them clearly, faintly, reinforcing the opinion.

They returned to the bivouac with Queen in the lead, clumping along and capering in his tiny enemy helmet. Doll dangled his new bayonet, showing it first to one then another. The others trooped along, and laughed and talked again after their shock. They were anxious now to tell their adventure to the rest of the company who had missed it. Before morning Big Queen's forcible disinterment of the dead Japanese man had been added to the company's annals of myth and legend, as well as to Queen's own.

(from Chapter 2)

[Witt and Cannon Company]

THIS MAN WITT was a small, thin, Breathitt County Kentucky boy, an old Regular, a former Regimental boxer. He had been in C-for-Charlie several years. His transfer had been a fine object lesson to Fife, an interesting study of the ways in which armies worked.

Shortly before its troops were hurled bodily into what was officially called Final Training Phase, a new company had been created in the Regiment. Existing first on paper as a directive from the War Department, and dreamed up for reasons largely technical and uninteresting to anyone not a student of tactics, this new unit was called the Cannon Company. There already was an Anti-Tank Company. But in addition to using its new type guns as antitank defense, Cannon Company was to be able to elevate them for use as artillery, and was to serve as a tiny artillery force within the Regiment, capable of putting heavy fire down quickly onto targets of platoon- or company-size.

Admirably conceived on paper, and existing only on paper, men were still needed to make Cannon Company an actuality. This was accomplished within the Regiment, by a strange process which might well have been named "shunting the crud." Fife observed how it worked. A Regimental memorandum was sent out ordering each company commander to donate a certain number of men. The commanders complied and the worst drunkards, worst homosexuals, and worst troublemakers all gathered together under one roof to form Cannon Company. This command was then given to the officer in the Regiment whom the Regimental Commander liked least. Witt was one of the men donated by C-for-Charlie.

Witt, though a drunkard (like most), was not one of the worst drunkards, and neither was he a homosexual. He could perhaps, by a loose application, be classed as a troublemaker—since he had been busted several times and twice had gone to the stockade on a Summary Court Martial. All this made him something of a romantic hero to Fife (though perhaps not on a level with Bell) but it did not endear him to Stein or Welsh. Still, he was not unique, and other men who were not sent to Cannon Company had had similar careers. Witt's trouble was that he had earned the personal enmity of Welsh by arguing back, because he did not like Welsh. Welsh did not like him, either. In fact, each thought the other stank, totally and abominably, without relief or reservation.

Though he refused to go and ask to stay, Witt was unhappy at being transferred. All his friends were in C-for-Charlie, and he liked the reputation he had there. As Witt saw it, everybody knew he loved C-for-Charlie and for Welsh to transfer him out while knowing this only proved his total contempt for Welsh correct, thus making it even more impossible for him to ask to stay. So he was transferred in silence, along with several real drunkards, and two homosexuals. And now he had come back for a visit.

Cannon Company along with other elements of the Regiment had arrived almost a month earlier with the first echelon of the Division. They had had a good deal more time to become "acclimatized," and Witt now had malaria. He looked wan and there was a yellowish tinge to his skin. Never heavy, he was now even thinner. He had kept his ears open for news of the old company and whenever a transport arrived with troops had tried to find them. He must have repeated this process twenty times. Finally he had been rewarded. He had been on the beach with a work detail the day they arrived, but had missed them because he was up at the other end unloading the other ship. So he had started out to find them. It was harder than it sounded. The island was jammed to boiling with men and matériel. After persistent inquiry he finally found someone who knew where they were bivouacked— only to find when he arrived (after slipping off and going AWOL and making the long walk up the island) that they had moved. He had had to start the whole thing over again. The feat was indicative of Witt's stubborn patience. It was a quality Fife wished he had more of himself.

Fife was overjoyed to see him, especially after the downhill route his friendship with Bell had taken lately. Also, Fife was not unaware that—for another reason—Witt admired him as much as he admired Witt. Fife admired and heroized Witt for all of the manly, tough, brave qualities he had; but Witt secretly admired Fife for his education. Fife was not above playing to this flattery.

(from Chapter 2)

[C-for-Charlie Company Man the Line]

NOTHING THEY HEARD or saw on the way up prepared them for the pandemonium they entered when they came over the crest. Climbing with the wind behind them they had heard no battle noises; then, rounding the last bend and coming out onto the open hilltop suddenly, they found themselves immersed in infernal noise and tumult. Like a river running into a swamp and dissipating its current, the line of files trudged over the crest and disappeared in a mob of running or standing, shouting and talking men who struggled to make themselves heard above the din.

Invisible but not far off, 81mm mortars fired off rounds with their peculiar gonglike sound. From further off came the monumental crashes of artillery firing sporadic salvos. Further off still .50 cal machineguns, chattering in bass voices, punctuated the intervals. And much fainter, but coming clearly across the rolling unjungled terrain in front, there were the sounds of small-arms fire and grenades, and the explosions of the mortar shells and artillery rounds landing. All of this, compounded by the excitement, shouting and rushing about, created a demented riotous uproar whose total effect could only be mad confusion. C-for-Charlie had arrived on the field, at just a few minutes after eleven.

They were on a high knoll overlooking a series of grassy hills and draws rising out of the surrounding sea of jungle. To their front the slope fell to a smaller knoll upon which the jungle encroached more closely, forming in effect a narrow neck of untreed land leading to the wider areas beyond. On this knoll, too, stood or ran groups of Americans in their green combat fatigues, a lesser number than up here, thirty perhaps. Beyond the second knoll the slope dropped again, not so steeply but much further, to a broken ravine covered with sparse grass; and beyond this low point the land rose again, steeply this time, to a high ridge which dominated the area and made invisible anything beyond it. On this slope, perhaps a thousand yards away and higher even than the original vantage point, infantrymen were fighting.

To a few men like Bell who were informed about The Dancing Elephant's terrain, it was clear that the knoll they occupied was The Elephant's hind foot. The lower knoll in front, which was obviulsy 2d Battalion's command post, thus became The Elephant's knee leading to the wider areas ahead which formed the torso. And the high ridge where the infantrymen now fought was the Elephant's Shoulder, the strong point labeled Hill 209.

A fire fight was obviously in progress. Several groups of squad or platoon size, tiny at this distance but plainly visible, were trying to get close to the crest and take it. The Americans, too far down the slope to lob grenades up to the crest, had to content themselves with riflefire. The Japanese, also clearly visible from time to time among the trees which rose above the crest from the jungled reverse slope, were under no such handicap; they could simply drop them down, and the black explosions from the Japanese grenades kept bursting out here and there, from the hillside. One American, receiving such a grenade near him, was seen to turn and simply jump out from the side of the hill like a man jumping off a ladder. He hit and rolled, the grenade exploded black behind him, and after a moment he rose and began to work his way back up to his group.

C-for-Charlie had arrived just at the climax. As they stood in the milling mob on the knoll trying to see and taking all of this in for the first time, the several groups on the slope rose into a concerted line and rushed the crest, lobbing grenades ahead of them and firing. They got to within perhaps fifteen yards of the top before they were repulsed. The machinegun fire, clearly heard on the knoll, was too much for them. They broke and began leaping and scrambling back down the hill where they went to ground as before, having left a number of their men, perhaps ten percent, behind them on the uphill slope. There were exclamations of dismay and a number of angry groans on the hilltop around C-for-Charlie.

The chorus of groans was not the only action on the knoll as a result of the repulse. Runners and junior staff officers began to push their way out through the crowd and go various places. The center of all this activity was a small group of seven men standing together in grand isolation on the knoll's peak. They were almost the only men present wearing any insignia, and all of them wore stars or eagles on the collars of their green fatigues. They were further distinguished from the others by their cleanliness. All of them were older men. From time to time they looked through binoculars or pointed at the terrain, talked to each other or into one of three telephones which they held. Occasionally one would also talk into a wireless radio packed on a much younger man's back. C-for-Charlie was able to recognize among them their battalion commander, their regimental commander and, from their photographs, their division and corps commanders.

One of these men now yelled irately into one of the sound power phones. Below on the second knoll the 2d Battalion's Colonel shouted back at him into its mate. The one above, tall and spare, listened intently, nodding his helmeted head. Then he turned to the wireless radio, looking angry and unsatisfied. Completing his call, he began to speak apologetically to three of the others who wore stars. He wore eagles. Below, the 2d Battalion's Colonel was now speaking into still another phone in his other hand.

Across the valley eight hundred yards in front of him the company CP of the repulsed platoons was located behind the crest of a subsidiary ridge growing out of the side of the main ridge. Off to one side of this small group two smaller clusters of men went through motions which could only mean that they were the company's mortar section plying the tubes of their 60mm mortars, invisible from here. As the Colonel talked, a figure detached itself from the CP group and dropped over the crest and went forward in rushes toward the groups which had been repulsed and which now were sporadically firing uphill at the Japanese. Before he reached them, he tumbled, shot. Immediately another dropped over the crest in his place. The moment this one reached them the groups began to withdraw along the ridge, again in rushes, firing in groups to cover each other, all the way back to the command post, where they lost no time in diving back over the crest of the subsidiary ridge. In the high-ranking group of older men on the hill, one was now waving his arms angrily and pounding himself furiously on the leg. Below, the 2d Battalion's Colonel was doing the same thing. Seconds later artillery shells began to fall in great mushrooming clusters on the Japanese-held ridge.

Whatever other manifestations occurred on the hilltop in connection with this operation, C-for-Charlie did not see them. They now were too involved in themselves and their own forthcoming part in the drama to care about watching the internationally famous command group. During the action Bugger Stein had gone over to report to his battalion commander, who was more a student observer there than an integral part of the group. Stein now returned to them. 1st Battalion less D-for-Dog was ordered as regimental reserve to occupy and hold the main ridge behind and to the left of the F-for-Fox CP which they had just been watching. The main ridge here, lower than Hill 209 on the right, had been labeled Hill 208 and formed, so to speak, The Elephant's middle and lower spine. The Japanese had never occupied it, but there was fear of a flanking counterattack. A-for-Able and C-for-Charlie were to man the line with B-for-Baker in reserve in the ravine, Colonel Tall's orders. Since Able and Baker were already moving down right now, this meant that C-for-Charlie would have to pass through Baker—always a difficult maneuver, and they should watch it. There was a crinkly look of painful preoccupation around Bugger's eyes behind his glasses as he spoke. His own dispositons were: 1st and 2d platoons on the line, 3d in reserve; Culp would set up his two MGs at optional points of choice along the line, the mortars to be set up near the company CP. Order of march would be 1st Platoon, 2d Platoon, Company HQ, Weapons Platoon, 3d Platoon. They were to move out right away.

In the fact, as they formed up by platoons, it was discovered that they could not move right away. Their front was being crossed by E-for-Easy, the 2d Battalion reserve. Easy was being committed to the right wing of 2d Battalion's attack where G-for-George, invisible from here around the corner of jungle, had also bogged down. C-for-Charlie knew many Easy Company people, and some of them called greetings. But Easy Company, going to certain attack instead of to a safe defensive position, preferred to ignore them and stared at them with a mixture of nervousness and hateful envy. Slowly they plodded across and disappeared down the righthand slope of the hill into the woods. It took them fifteen minutes to cross. Then C-for-Charlie began to move down the slope, 1st Platoon in the lead.

It was during this fifteen minute wait that First Sergeant Welsh suddenly came to the fore. Up to now Welsh had been very carefully taking a back seat. He had no intention of becoming conspicuous or committing himself until he knew where he stood. He had tried to prepare himself, and two of the three canteens on his belt were filled with gin. In addition, he had his Listerine bottle. He could not say exactly what the experiences of today made him feel. All Welsh knew was that he was scared shitless, and at the same time was afflicted with a choking gorge of anger that any social coercion existed in the world which could force him to be here. In addition the tremendously intense excitement on the hilltop affected him powerfully. It was not unlike the feeling in a stadium generated by a crowd rooting at an important college football game. It was this outrageous comparison which gave him the idea to do what he did.

Standing with Stein and the Company HQ while E-for-Easy jogged past their front, Welsh spied a whole stack of unopened hand grenade cases on the edge of the hill, and simultaneously realized somebody had fucked up somewhere along the line in not issuing grenades to C-for-Charlie. Grinning his sly, mad grin, he decided to issue them himself. But in such a way that the cheeringsection emotional tenor of the day should be properly honored. Without so much as a word to anyone, he suddenly crouched with his palms on his knees and at the top of his command voice bellowed: "Hup! Twenty-six, thirty-two, forty-three; *hike!*", whirled like a halfback, and ran over to the stack of cases drawing his bayonet and began splitting the soft pine cases open through the middle. The grenades inside were in black cardboard cylinders, their halves held together with yellow tape. Welsh began to draw them out and to bellow.

"Eggs! Fresh eggs! Nice fresh yard eggs! Who wants eggs!"

The enormous, booming command voice was easily heard despite the racket and tumult. The men of his company began to turn and look. Then hands began to shoot up out of the crowd. And Welsh, still bellowing, and still grinning crazily, began to forwardpass the canned grenades into the crowd.

"Eggs! Eggs! Footballs! Footballs! Sammy Baugh! Sid Luckman! Rah rah rah! Who wants footballs! Bronco Nagurski!"

His bellow rang magnificently over the entire hilltop. While men everywhere turned and stared as if he were insane, Welsh bellowed on and continued to forwardpass grenades to his company, a perfect caricature of the classic football passer's stance: left arm out, right arm cocked, right leg bent, left leg forward.

In the grandly isolated command group one of the seven older men heard him. He turned to look, then slowly grinned his approval. With his elbow he punched a companion to look, too. Soon the entire group were watching Welsh and grinning. This was the type of American soldier these generals liked to see. And across fifteen yards of hilltop crammed with American soldiers and matériel Welsh grinned back at them murderously, his insolent eyes crinkled slyly, and continued to bellow and to throw.

Perhaps only one man really understood it, if anyone did, and this was Storm. An ironic grin began to spread across Storm's cynical, broken-nosed face and drawing his own bayonet he ran over and began hacking open the cases and feeding Welsh the cylinders.

"Sammy Baugh! Sid Luckman! Jack Manders! Sammy Baugh!" they bellowed in unison. "Rah rah rah!"

They went through the entire stack of cases in very little time. By this time E-for-Easy had passed. Taking the last two each for themselves, and laughing idiotically in a moment of rare understanding, they rejoined the Company HQ. With the men stripping off the yellow tapes and opening the cylinders, spreading the cotter pins and buttoning the pull rings down under their pocket flaps as they'd seen the Marines do, C-for-Charlie moved off down the slope.

(from Chapter 3)

[Bead Kills a Japanese Soldier]

BUT SOME TIME BEFORE any of this had happened, young Pfc Bead had killed his first Japanese, the first Japanese to be killed by his company, or for that matter by his battalion.

It was, Bead reflected about it later, when indeed he was able to think about it at all, which was not for some time, typical of his entire life; of his stupid incompetence, his foolish idiocy, his gross mismanagement of everything he put his hands on; so that whatever he did, done so badly and in such ugly style, gave no satisfaction: action without honor, travail without grace. A man of a different temperament might have found it funny; Bead could not laugh.

At just about five o'clock he had had to take a crap. And he had not had a crap for two days. Everything had quieted down on the line by five and at the aid station below them the last of the wounded were being cared for and sent back. Bead had seen other men taking craps along the slope, and he knew the procedure. After two days on these slopes the procedure was practically standardized. Because every available bit of level space was occupied, jammed with men and equipment, crapping was relegated to the steeper slopes. Here the process was to take along an entrenching shovel and dig a little hole, then turn your backside to the winds of the open air and squat, balancing yourself precariously on your toes, supporting yourself on the dirt or rocks in front of you with your hands. The effect, because of the men below in the basin, was rather like hanging your ass out of a tenth floor window above a crowded street. It was an embarrassing position to say the least, and the men below were not above taking advantage of it with catcalls, whistles or loud soulful sighs.

Bead was shy. He could have done it that way if he'd had to, but because he was shy, and because now everything had quieted down to an unbelievable evening peace after the terror, noise and danger of the afternoon, he decided to have himself a pleasant, quiet, private crap in keeping with the peacefulness. Without saying anything to anyone he dropped all of his equipment by his hole and taking only his GI roll of toilet paper, he started to climb the twenty yards to the crest. He did not even take an entrenching tool because on the other side there was no need to bury his stool. Beyond the crest he knew that the slope did not drop precipitously as it did further to the left, but fell slowly for perhaps fifty yards through the trees before it plunged in a bluff straight down to the river. This was where D Company had caught the Japanese patrol earlier in the day.

"Hey, bud, where you going?" somebody from the 2d Platoon called to him as he passed through.

"To take a shit," Bead called back without looking around and disappeared over the crest.

The trees began three yards below the actual crest. Because the jungle was thinner with less undergrowth here at its outer edge, it looked more like the columnar, smooth-floored woods of home and made Bead think of when he was a boy. Reminded of times when as a Boy Scout he had camped out and crapped with peaceful pleasure in the summer woods of Iowa, he placed the roll of paper comfortably near, dropped his pants and squatted. Half way through with relieving himself, he looked up and saw a Japanese man with a bayoneted rifle moving stealthily through the trees ten yards away.

As if feeling his gaze, the Japanese man turned his head and saw him in almost the same instant but not before, through the electrifying, heart stabbing thrill of apprehension, danger, disbelief, denial, Bead got a clear, burned in the brain impression of him.

He was a small man, and thin; very thin. His mud-slicked, mustard-khaki uniform with its ridiculous wrap leggins hung from him in jungledamp, greasy folds. Not only did he not wear any of the elaborate camouflage Bead had been taught by movies to expect, he did not even wear a helmet. He wore a greasy, wrinkled, bent up forage cap. Beneath it his yellowbrown face was so thin the high cheekbones seemed about to come out through his skin. He was badly unshaven, perhaps two weeks, but his greasy looking beard was as straggly as Bead's nineteen-year-old one. As to age, Bead could not form any clear impression; he might have been twenty, or forty.

All of this visual perception occurred in an eyewink of time, an eyewink which seemed to coast on and on and on, then the Japanese

man saw him too and turning, all in one movement, began to run at
him, but moving cautiously, the bayonet on the end of his rifle
extended.

Bead, still squatting with his pants down, his behind still dirty,
gathered his weight under him. He was going to have to try to
jump one way or another, but which? Which side to jump to? Am I
going to die? Am I really going to die now? He did not even have
his knife with him. Terror and disbelief, denial, fought each other
in him. Why the Japanese did not simply fire the rifle he did not
know. Perhaps he was afraid of being heard in the American lines.
Instead he came on, obviously meaning to bayonet Bead where he
sat. His eyes were intent with purpose. His lips were drawn back
from his teeth, which were large, but were well formed and not at
all protruding as in the posters. Was it really true?

In desperation, still not knowing which way to try to jump, all
in one movement Bead pulled up his pants over his dirty behind to
free his legs and dove forward in a low, shoestring football tackle
when the Japanese man was almost to him, taking him around the
ankles, his feet driving hard in the soft ground. Surprised, the
Japanese man brought the rifle down sharply, but Bead was already
in under the bayonet. The stacking swivel banged him painfully on
the collarbone. By clasping the mudcaked shins against his chest
and using his head for a fulcrum, still driving hard with his feet,
the Japanese man had no way to fall except backward, and Bead
was already clawing up his length before he hit the ground. In the
fall he dropped the rifle and had the wind knocked out of him. This
gave Bead time to hitch up his pants again and spring upward once
more until, kneeling on his upper arms and sitting back on his
chest, he began to punch and claw him in the face and neck. The
Japanese man could only pluck feebly at his legs and forearms.

Bead heard a high, keening scream and thought it was the
Japanese begging for mercy until finally he slowly became aware
that the Japanese man was now unconscious. Then he realized it
was himself making that animal scream. He could not, however,
stop it. The Japanese man's face was now running blood from the
clawing, and several of his teeth had been broken back into his
throat from the punches. But Bead could not stop. Sobbing and
wailing, he continued to belabor the unconscious Japanese with
fingernail and fist. He wanted to tear his face off with his bare
hands, but found this difficult. Then he seized his throat and tried

to break his head by beating it on the soft ground but only succeeded in digging a small hole with it. Exhausted finally, he collapsed forward on hands and knees above the bleeding, unconscious man, only to feel the Japanese immediately twitch with life beneath him.

Outraged at such a display of vitality, alternately sobbing and wailing, Bead rolled aside, seized the enemy rifle and on his knees raised it above his head and drove the long bayonet almost full length into the Japanese chest. The Japanese man's body convulsed in a single spasm. His eyes opened, staring horribly at nothing, and his hands flipped up from the elbows and seized the blade through his chest.

Staring with horror at the fingers which were cutting themselves on the blade trying to draw it out, Bead leaped to his feet and his pants fell down. Hiking his pants up and standing spraddlelegged to keep them from falling, he seized the rifle and tried to pull it out in order to plunge it in again. But the bayonet would not come loose. Remembering dimly something he had been taught in bayonet practice, he grabbed the small of the stock and pulled the trigger. Nothing happened. The gun was on safety. Fumbling with the unfamiliar, foreign safety, he released it and pulled again. There was a flesh-muffled explosion and the bayonet came free. But the fool of a Japanese with his open eyes went on grasping at his chest with his bleeding fingers as if he could not get it through his thick head that the bayonet was out. My god, how much killing did the damned fool require? Bead had beaten him, kicked him, choked him, clawed him, bayoneted him, shot him. He had a sudden frantic vision of himself, by rights the victor, doomed forever to kill perpetually the same single Japanese.

This time, not intending to be caught in the same trap twice, instead of sticking him he reversed the rifle in his hands and drove the butt down full force into his face, smashing it. Standing above him spraddlelegged to keep his pants up, he drove the rifle butt again and again into the Japanese man's face, until all of the face and most of the head were mingled with the muddy ground. Then he threw the rifle from him and fell down on his hands and knees and began to vomit.

Bead did not lose consciousness, but he completely lost his sense of time. When he came to himself, still on hands and knees, gasping, he shook his hanging head and opened his eyes and discovered his left hand was resting in a friendly way on the Japanese man's still, mustard-khaki knee. Bead snatched it away as though he had discovered it lying across a burning stove. He had an obscure feeling that if he did not look at the corpse of the man he had killed or touch it, he would not be held responsible. With this in mind he crawled feebly away through the trees, breathing in long painful groans.

The woods were very quiet. Bead could not remember ever having heard such quiet. Then faintly, penetrating the immensity of this quiet, he heard voices, American voices, and the casual sound of a shovel scraped against a rock. It seemed impossible that they could be that close. He got shakily to his feet holding up his pants. It also seemed impossible that anything could ever again sound as casual as that shovel had. He knew he had to get back inside the lines. But first he would have to try to clean himself up. He was a mess. He had no desire to finish his crap.

First of all, he had to go back to the vicinity of the dead man to get his roll of toilet paper. He hated that but there wasn't any choice. His pants and his dirty behind were what bothered him most. Horror of that was inbred in him; but also he was terrified someone might think he had crapped his pants from fear. He used most of his roll of toilet paper on that, and in the end even sacrificed one of his three clean handkerchiefs which he was saving back for his glasses, moistening it with spittle. In addition he was spattered with blood and vomit. He could not remove every stain, but he tried to get enough so that nobody would notice. Because he had already decided he was not going to mention this to anybody.

Also, he had lost his glasses. He found them, miraculously unbroken, beside the dead man. Searching for his glasses, he had to go right up to the body, and to look at it closely. The faceless—almost headless—corpse with its bloody, cut fingers and the mangled hole in its chest, so short a time ago a living, breathing man, made him so dizzy in the stomach that he thought he might faint. On the other hand, he could not forget the intent look of deliberate purpose on the man's face as he came in with the bayonet. There didn't seem to be any reasonable answer.

The feet were the saddest thing. In their hobnailed infantry boots they splayed outward, relaxed, like the feet of a man asleep. With a kind of perverse fascination Bead could not resist giving one

of them a little kick. It lolloped up, then flopped back. Bead wanted
to turn and run. He could not escape a feeling that, especially now,
after he'd both looked and touched, some agent of retribution
would try to hold him responsible. He wanted to beg the man's
forgiveness in the hope of forestalling responsibility. He had not felt
such oppressive guilt over anything since the last time his mother
had caught and whipped him for masturbating.

If he'd had to kill him, and apparently he had, at least he could
have done it more efficiently and gracefully, and with less pain and
anguish for the poor man. If he had not lost his head, had not gone
crazy with fear, perhaps he might even have taken him prisoner and
obtained valuable information from him. But he had been frantic to
get the killing over with, as if afraid that as long as the man could
breathe he might suddenly stand up and accuse him. Suddenly
Bead had a mental picture of them both with positions reversed: of
himself lying there and feeling that blade plunge through his chest;
of himself watching that riflebutt descend upon his face, with the
final fire-exploding end. It made him so weak that he had to sit
down. What if the other man had got the bayonet down quicker?
What if he himself had tackled a little higher? Instead of merely a
bruise on his collarbone, Bead saw himself spitted through the soft
of the shoulder, head on, that crude blade descending into the soft
dark of his chest cavity. He could not believe it.

Settling his glasses on his face, taking a couple of deep breaths
and a last look at his ruined enemy, he got up and started clumping
up out of the trees toward the crest. Bead was ashamed and
embarrassed by the whole thing, that was the truth, and that was
why he didn't want to mention it to anybody.

He got back through the line all right, without questions. "Have
a good shit?" the man from the 2d Platoon called to him. "Yeah," he
mumbled and clomped on, down the slope toward the CP. But on
his way he was joined by Pfc Doll, on his way down from 1st
Platoon with a message to ask again about water. Doll fell in step
with him, and immediately noticed his damaged hands and the
blood spatters.

"Christ! What happened to your knuckles? You have a fight with
somebody?"

Bead's heart sank. It would have to be Doll. "No. I slipped and
fell and skinned myself," he said. He was as stiff and sore all over as

if he *had* had a fistfight with somebody. Horror welled in him again, suddenly, ballooningly. He took several very deep breaths into a sore rib cage.

Doll grinned with frank but amiable skepticism. "And I spose all them little blood splatters came from your knuckles?"

"Leave me alone, Doll!" Bead blazed up. "I dont feel like talking! So just leave me alone, hunh? Will you?" He tried to put into his eyes all the fierce toughness of a man just returned from killing an enemy. He hoped maybe that would shut him up, and it did. At least for a while. They walked on down in silence, Bead aware with a kind of horrified disgust that already he was fitting the killing of the Japanese man into the playing of a role; a role without anything, no reality, of himself or anything else. It hadn't been like that at all.

Doll did not stay shut up, though. Doll had been a little taken aback by Bead's vehemence, a forcefulness he was not used to expecting from Bead. He could smell something when he saw it. And after he had delivered his message, receiving the answer he expected which was that Stein was doing everything he could to get them water, he brought it up again, this time by calling it to the attention of Welsh. Welsh and Storm were sitting on the sides of their holes matching pennies for cigarettes, which were already beginning to be precious. They would match four best out of seven, to lengthen the game and cut down the expense in cigarettes, then both pull out their plastic pack holders which everyone had bought to keep their butts dry and carefully pass the one tube between them. Doll went over to them grinning with his eyebrow raised. He did not feel, at least not at the time, that what he was doing had anything to do with ratting on someone or stooling.

"What the fuck happen to your boy there? Who the hell he beat up with them skinned knuckles and all them blood splatters on him? Did I miss somethin?"

Welsh looked up at him with that level gaze of his which, when he wasn't pretending to be crazy, could be so penetrating. Already, Doll felt he had made a mistake, and guilty. Without answering Welsh turned to look at Bead, who sat hunched up by himself on a small rock. He had put back on his equipment.

"Bead, come over here!"

Bead got up and came, still hunched, his face drawn. Doll grinned at him with his raised eyebrow. Welsh looked him up and down.

"What happened to you?"

"Who? Me?"

Welsh waited in silence.

"Well, I slipped and fell down and skinned myself, that's all."

Welsh eyed him in silence, thoughtfully. Obviously he was not even bothering with that story. "Where'd you go a while ago? When you were gone for a while? Where were you?"

"I went off to take a crap by myself."

"Wait!" Doll put in, grinning. "When I seen him, he was comin down from the 2d Platoon's section of line on the ridge."

Welsh swung his gaze to Doll and his eyes blazed murderously. Doll subsided. Welsh looked back at Bead. Stein, who had been standing nearby, had come closer now and was listening. So had Band and Fife and some of the others.

"Lissen, kid," Welsh said. "I got more problems than I know what to do with in this screwy outfit. Or how to handle. I got no time to fuck around with kid games. I want to know what happened to you, and I want the truth. Look at yourself. Now, what happened, and where were you?"

Welsh apparently, at least to Bead's eyes, was much closer to guessing the truth than the unimaginative Doll, or the others. Bead drew a long quavering breath.

"Well, I went across the ridge outside the line in the trees to take a crap in private. A Jap guy came up while I was there and he tried to bayonet me. And—and I killed him." Bead exhaled a long, fluttering breath, then inhaled sharply and gulped.

Everyone was staring at him disbelievingly, but nevertheless dumbstruck. "Goddam it, kid!" Welsh bellowed after a moment. "I told you I wanted the goddam fucking *truth!* And not no kid games!"

It had never occured to Bead that he would not be believed. Now he was faced with a choice of shutting up and being taken for a liar, or telling them where and having them see what a shameful botched-up job he'd done. Even in his upset and distress it did not take him long to choose.

"Then god damn you go and *look!*" he cried at Welsh. "Dont take my word, go and look for your goddam fucking *self!*"

"I'll go!" Doll put in immediately.

Welsh turned to glare at him. "You'll go nowhere, stooly," he said. He turned back to Bead. "I'll go myself."

Doll had subsided into a stunned, shocked, whitefaced silence. It had never occurred to Doll that his joking about Bead would be taken as stoolpigeoning. But then he had never imagined the result would turn out to be what it apparently had. Bead killing a Jap! He was not guilty of stooling, and furiously he made up his mind that he was going along; if he had to crawl.

"And if you're lyin, kid, God help your fucking soul." Welsh picked up his Thompsongun and put on his helmet. "All right. Where is it? Come on, show me."

"I'm not going up there again!" Bead cried. "You want to go, go by yourself! But I'm aint going! And nothin's gonna make me!"

Welsh stared at him narrowly a moment. Then he looked at Storm. Storm nodded and got up. "Okay," Welsh said. "Where is it, then?"

"A few yards in the trees beyond the crest, at the middle of the 2d Platoon. Just about in front of Krim's hole." Bead turned and walked away.

Storm had put on his helmet and picked up his own Thompson. And suddenly, with the withdrawal of Bead and his emotion from the scene, the whole thing became another larking, kidding excursion of the "Tommygun Club" which had held the infiltrator hunt that morning. Stein, who had been listening in silence nearby all the time, dampened it by refusing to allow any of the officers to leave the CP; but MacTae could go, and it was the three sergeants and Dale who prepared to climb to the crest. Bead could not resist calling a bitter comment from his rock: "You won't need all the goddamned artillery, Welsh! There's nobody up there now but *him!*" But he was ignored.

It was just before they departed that Doll, his eyes uneasy but nonetheless steady, presented himself manfully in front of the First Sergeant and gazed at him squarely.

"Top, you wouldn't keep me from goin, would you?" he asked. It was not begging nor was it a try at being threatening, just a simple, level, straightforward question.

Welsh stared at him a moment, then without change of expression turned away silently. It was obviously a reprimand. Doll chose to take it as silent acquiescence. And with himself in the rear the five of them started the climb to the line. Welsh did not send him back.

While they were gone no one bothered Bead. He sat by himself on his rock, head down, now and then squeezing his hands or feeling his knuckles. Everyone avoided looking at him, as if to give him privacy. The truth was nobody really knew what to think. As for Bead himself, all he could think about was how shamefully he and his hysterical, graceless killing were going to be exposed. His memory of it, and of that resolute face coming at him, made him shudder and want to gag. More times than not he wished he had kept his mouth shut and let them all think him a crazy liar. It might have been much better.

When the little scouting party returned, their faces all wore a peculiar look. "He's there," Welsh said. "He sure is," MacTae said. All of them looked curiously subdued. That was all that was said. At least, it was all that was said in front of Bead. What they said away from him, Bead could not know. But he did not find in their faces any of the disgust or horror of him that he had expected. If anything, he found a little of the reverse: admiration. As they separated to go to their various holes, each made some gesture.

Doll had hunted up the Japanese rifle and brought it back for Bead. He had scrubbed most of the blood and matter from the butt plate with leaves and had cleaned up the bayonet. He brought it over and presented it as if presenting an apology offering.

"Here, this is yours."

Bead looked at it without feeling anything. "I don't want it."

"But you won it. And won it the hard way."

"I dont want it anyway. What good's it to me."

"Maybe you can trade it for whiskey." Doll laid it down. "And here's his wallet. Welsh said to give it to you. There's a picture of his wife in it."

"Jesus Christ, Doll."

Doll smiled. "There's pictures of other broads, too," he hurried on. "Filipino, it looks like. Maybe he was in the Philippines. That's Filipino writing on the back, Welsh says."

"I dont want it anyway. You keep it." But he took the proffered wallet anyway, his curiosity piqued in spite of himself. "Well—" He looked at it. It was dark, greasy from much sweating. "I dont feel good about it, Doll," he said looking up, wanting suddenly to talk about it to someone. "I feel guilty."

"Guilty! What the hell for? It was him or you, wasn't it? How many our guys you think maybe he stuck that bayonet in in the Philippines? On the Death March. How about those two guys yesterday?"

"I know all that. But I can't help it. I feel guilty."

"But why?"

"Why! Why! How the fuck do I know why!" Bead cried. "Maybe my mother beat me up too many times for jerking off when I was a kid!" he cried plaintively, with a sudden half-flashing of miserable insight. "How do I know why!"

Doll stared at him uncomprehendingly.

"Never mind," Bead said.

"Listen," Doll said. "If you really dont want that wallet."

Bead felt a sudden clutching greed. He put the wallet in his pocket quickly. "No. No, I'll keep it. No, I might as well keep it."

"Well," Doll said sorrowfully, "I got to get back up to the platoon."

"Thanks anyway, Doll," he said.

"Yeah. Sure." Doll stood up. "I'll say one thing. When you set out to kill him, you really killed him," he said admiringly.

Bead jerked his head up, his eyes searching. "You think so?" he said. Slowly he began to grin a little.

Doll was nodding, his face boyish with his admiration. "I aint the only one." He turned and left, heading up the slope.

Bead stared after him, still not knowing what he really felt. And Doll had said he wasn't the only one. If they did not find it such a disgraceful, botched-up job, then at least he need not feel so bad about that. Tentatively he grinned a little wider, a little more expansively, aware that his face felt stiff doing it.

(from Chapter 3)

[Bell's Realization and Keck's Death]

BELL LAY with his face against the rock facing Witt. Witt lay looking back. Quietly in the insect-humming heat they lay and looked at each other. Bell was thinking that Witt had come through it all all right. Like himself. What power was it which decided one man should be hit, be killed, instead of another man? So Bugger's little feeling attack was over. If this were a movie, this would be the end of the show and something would be decided. In a movie or a novel they would dramatize and build to the climax of the attack. When the attack came in the film or novel, it would be satisfying. It would decide something. It would have a semblance of meaning and a semblance of an emotion. And immediately after, it would be over. The audience could go home and think about the semblance of the meaning and feel the semblance of the emotion. Even if the hero got killed, it would still make sense. Art, Bell decided, creative art—was shit.

Beside him Witt, who was apparently not bothered by any of these problems, raised himself to his knees and cautiously stuck his head up over the ledge. Bell went on with his thinking.

Here there was no semblance of meaning. And the emotions were so many and so mixed up that they were indecipherable, could not be untangled. Nothing had been decided, nobody had learned anything. But most important of all, nothing had ended. Even if they had captured this whole ridge, nothing would have ended. Because tomorrow, or the day after, or the day after that, they would be called upon to do the same thing again—maybe under even worse circumstances. The concept was so overpowering, so numbing, that it shook Bell. Island after island, hill after hill, beachhead after beachhead, year after year. It staggered him.

It would certainly end sometime, sure, and almost certainly—because of industrial production—end in victory. But that point in time had no connection with any individual man engaged now. *Some* men would survive, but no *one* individual man *could* survive. It was a discrepancy in methods of counting. The whole thing was too vast, too complicated, too technological for any one individual man to count in it. Only collections of men counted, only communities of men, only *numbers* of men.

The weight of such a proposition was deadening, almost too heavy to be borne, and Bell wanted to turn his mind away from it. Free individuals? Ha! Somewhere between the time the first Marines had landed here and this battle now today, American warfare had changed from individualist warfare to collectivist warfare—or perhaps that was only his illusion, perhaps it only seemed like that to him because he himself was now engaged. But free individuals? What a fucking myth! *Numbers* of free individuals, maybe; *collectives* of free individuals. And so the point of Bell's serious thinking finally emerged.

At some unspecified moment between this time yesterday and this time today the unsought realization had come to Bell that statistically, mathematically, arithmetically, any way you wanted to count it, he John Bell could not possibly live through this war. He could not possibly go home to his wife Marty Bell. So it did not really make any difference what Marty did, whether she stepped out on him or not, because he would not be there to accuse her.

The emotion which this revelation created in Bell was not one of sacrifice, resignation, acceptance, and peace. Instead, it was an irritating, chaffing emotion of helpless frustration which made him want to crawl around rubbing his flanks and back against rocks to ease the itch. He still had not moved his face from the rock.

Beside him Witt, still kneeling and peering out, yelled suddenly. Simultaneously Doll yelled too from down at the other end.

"Something's comin!"

"Something's comin! Somebody's comin at us!"

As one man the line behind the ledge swept up and forward, rifles ready. Forty yards away seven pot-headed, bandylegged, starved-looking Japanese men were running down at them across an ungrassed area carrying hand grenades in their right hands and bayoneted rifles in their left. Keck's Thompson, after his firing of almost all its ammo on the way up, had finally jammed, too. Neither gun could be unstuck. But the massed riflefire from the ledge disposed of the seven Japanese men quickly. Only one was able even to throw; and his grenade, a dud, landed short. At the same moment the dud grenade should have exploded, there was a loud, ringing, halfmuffled explosion behind them. In the excitement of the attack and defense they continued to fire into the seven bodies up the slope. When they ceased, only two bodies continued to move. Aiming deliberately in the sudden quiet, Witt the Kentuckian put a killing round into each of them. "You never can tell about them tricky suicidal bastards," he said. "Even when they're hit."

It was Bell who first remembered the explosion behind them and turned around to see what had caused it. What he saw was Sgt Keck lying on his back with his eyes closed, in a strangely grotesque position, still holding the ring and safety pin of a hand grenade in his right hand. Bell called out, and rushing to him, they rolled him over gently and saw that there was nothing they could do for him. His entire right buttock and part of his back had been blown away. Some of his internal organs were visible, pulsing busily away, apparently going about their business as if nothing had happened. Steadily, blood welled in the cavity. Gently they laid him back.

It was obvious what had happened. In the attack, perhaps because his Thompsongun was jammed, but at any rate not firing his rifle, Keck had reached in his hip pocket to pull out a grenade. And in the excitement he had gotten it by the pin. Bell, for one, experienced a dizzying, near-fainting terror momentarily, at the thought of Keck standing and looking at that pin in his hand. Keck had leaped back from the line and sat down against a little dirt hummock to protect the others. Then the grenade had gone off.

Keck made no protest when they moved him. He was conscious, but apparently did not want to talk and preferred to keep his eyes closed. Two of them sat with him and tried to talk to him and reassure him while the others went back to the line, but Keck did not answer and kept his eyes shut. The little muscles at the corners of his mouth twitched jerkily. He spoke only once. Without opening his eyes he said clearly, "What a fucking recruit trick to pull." Five minutes later he stopped breathing.

(from Chapter 4)

[Gaff's Assault Force]

GAFF DID NOT BOTHER to give them any peptalk. He had already explained the operation to them thoroughly, back at the position. Now all he said was, "You all know the job we've got to do, fellows. There's no point in my going over it all again. I'm convinced the toughest part of the approach will be the open space between the end of the trough here and the shoulder of the knob. Once past that I think it won't be so bad. Remember that we may run into smaller emplacements along the way. I'd rather bypass them if we can, but we may have to knock some of them out if they block our route and hold us up. Okay, that's all." He stopped and smiled at them looking each man in the eyes in turn: an excited, boyish, happy, adventuresome smile. It was only slightly incongruous with the tensed, crinkled look in his eyes.

"When we get up to them," Gaff said, "we ought to have some fun."

There were several weak smiles, very similar to his own if not as strong. Only Witt's and Big Un's seemed to be really deep. But they were all grateful to him. Since yesterday all of them, excepting Big Un, had come to like him very much. All last evening, during the night, and again during the predawn movements, he had stayed with them except during his actual conferences with Colonel Tall, spending his time with them. He kidded, cajoled and boosted them, cracking jokes, telling them cunt stories about his youth at the Point and after, and all the kooky type broads he had made— had in short treated them like equals. Even for Bell who had been one it was a little thrilling, quite flattering to be treated as an equal by an officer; for the others it was moreso. They would have followed Gaff anywhere. He had promised them the biggest drunk of their lives, everything on him, once they got through this mess and back down off the line. And they were grateful to him for that, too. He had not, when he promised, made any mention about 'survivors' or 'those who were left' having this drunk together, tacitly assuming that they would all be there to enjoy it. And they were grateful for that also. Now he looked around at them all once

more with his boyish, young adventurer's eager smile above the
tensed, crinkled eyes.

"I'll be leading from here on out," he said. "Because I want to
pick the route myself. If anything should happen to me, Sergeant
Bell will be in command, so I want him last. Sergeant Dale will be
second in command. They both know what to do.

"Okay, let's go." It was much more of a sigh than a hearty bellow.

Then they were out and crawling along the narrow, peculiarly
sensed dangerousness of the familiar trough, Gaff in the lead, each
man being particularly careful of the spot where the trough opened
out into the ledge and Lieutenant Gray the preacher had absent-
mindedly got himself killed. Big Un Cash, who was new to all this,
was especially careful. John Bell, waiting for the others to climb
out, caught Charlie Dale staring at him with a look of puzzled, but
nonetheless hateful enmity. Dale had been appointed Acting
Sergeant at least an hour before Bell, and therefore should have had
the seniority over him. Bell winked at him, and Dale looked away.
A moment later it was Dale's turn to go, and he climbed out into the
trough without a backward look. Only one man, Witt, remained
between them. Then it was Bell's own turn. For the—what was it?
third? fourth? fifth time? Bell had lost track—he climbed out over
the ledge and crawled past the thin screen of scrub brush. It was
beginning to look pretty bedraggled now from all the MG fire
which had whistled through it.

In the trough ahead with his head down Charlie Dale was
thinking furiously that that was what you could always expect from
all goddam fucking officers. They hung together like a pack of
horse thieves, busted out or not. He had broke his ass for them all
day yesterday. He had been appointed Acting Sergeant by an
officer, by Bugger Stein himself, not by no fucking platoon
sergeant like Keck. And about an hour before. And look who got
command? You couldn't trust them no further than you could
throw them by the ears, no more than you could trust the
govermint itself to do something for you. Furiously, outraged,
keeping his head well down, he stared at the motionless feet of Doll
in front of him as if he wanted to bite them off.

Up ahead Gaff had waited, looking back, until they were all
safely in the trough. Now there was no need to wait longer.
Turning his head to the right he looked off toward the strongpoint,

but without raising his head high enough to see anything above the grass. Were they waiting? Were they watching? Were they looking at this particular open spot? He could not know. But no need in spotting them a ball by exposing himself if they were. With one last look back directly behind him at Big Un Cash, who favored him with a hard, mean, gimleteyed grin that was not much help, he bounced up and took off with his rifle at high port, running agonizingly slowly and pulling his knees up high to clear the matted kunai grass like a football player running through stacks of old tires. It was ludicrous to say the least, not a dignified way to be shot, but not a shot was fired. He dived in behind the shoulder of the knob and lay there. After waiting a full minute he motioned the next man, Big Un, to come on. Big Un, who had moved up, as the others had moved up behind him, took right off at once running in the same way, his rifle pounding against his back, the shotgun in his hands, his helmet straps flapping. Just before he reached the shoulder a single machinegun opened up, but he too dived to safety. The machinegun stopped.

The third man, Doll, fell. He was only about five yards out when several MGs opened up. They were watching this time. It was only twenty or twenty-five yards across, the open space, but it seemed much longer. He was already breathing in ripping gasps. Then his foot caught in a hole in the mat of old grass and he was down. Oh, no! Oh, no! his mind screamed at him in panic. Not me! Not after all the rest that's happened to me! Not after all I've lasted through! I won't even get my medal! Blindly, spitting grass seeds and dust, he clambered up and staggered on. He only had ten yards more to go, and he made it. He fell in upon the other two and lay sobbing for breath and existence. The bright, washed sun had just come up over the hills in the east.

By now in the early morning sunshine and stark shadows all the MGs from the strongpoint were firing, hosing down the trough itself as well as the open space. Bullets tore over the heads of Charlie Dale, Witt and Bell in bunches which rattled and bruised the poor thin little bushes. It was now Dale's turn to go, and he was still furious at Bell. "Hey, wait!" Bell yelled from behind him. "Wait! Dont go yet! I got an idea!" Dale gave him one hate-filled contemptuous look and got to his feet. He departed without a word, chugging along solidly like a little engine, in the same way he had gone down and come back up the slope in front of the third fold yesterday. By now a sort of semi-path had been pushed through the grass, and this aided him some. He arrived behind the shoulder and sat down, apparently totally unmoved, but still secretly angry at Bell. Nothing had touched him.

"You must be out of your mind!" Captain Gaff shouted at him.

"Why?" Dale said. Maliciously, he settled himself to see what fucking Bell would do now. Heh heh. Not that he wanted him to get hurt, or anything.

Bell demonstrated his idea immediately. When he and Witt had crawled to the end of the trough, the MGs still firing just over their heads, Bell pulled the pin on a grenade and lobbed it at the strongpoint. But he did not throw it straight across; he threw it into the angle formed by the ledge and the trough, so that it landed in front of the bunker but further back much closer to the ledge. When the MGs all swung that way, as they did immediately, he and Witt crossed in safety before they could swing back. Clearly the three of them could have done it just as easily, and when he threw himself down grinning in the safety behind the shoulder, Bell winked at Charlie Dale again. Dale glowered back. "Very bright," Gaff laughed. Bell winked at Dale a third time. Fuck him. Who did he think he was? Then suddenly, after this third wink, like some kind of a sudden stop, Bell realized the fear he had felt this time had been much less, almost none at all, negligible. Even when those bullets were sizzing just over his head. Was he learning? Was that it? Or was he just becoming inured. More brutalized, like Dale. The thought lingered on in his head like an echoing gong while he sat staring at nothing, then slowly faded away. And so what? If answer is yes, or if question does not apply to you, pass on to next questionnaire. What the hell, he thought. Fuck it. If he only had a drink of water, he could do anything. The MGs from the strongpoint were still hosing and belaboring the empty trough and its poor straggly bushes as the party moved away.

Gaff had told them that he thought the rest of the route would be easier once they were past the open space, and he was right. The terrain mounted steeply around the knob which jutted out of the ridge and up here the mat of grass was not quite so thick, but now they were forced to crawl. It was next to impossible to see the camouflaged emplacements until they opened up, and they could not take any chances. As they moved along in this snail's way, sweating and panting in the sun from the exertion, Bell's heart—as well as everybody else's—began to beat with a heavier pulse, a mingled excitement and fear which was by no means entirely unpleasant. They all knew from yesterday that beyond the knob was a shallow saddle between the knob and the rock wall where the ledge ended, and it was along this saddle which they were to crawl to come down on the Japanese from above. They had all seen the saddle, but they had not seen behind the knob. Now they crawled along it, seeing it from within the Japanese territory. They were not fired upon, and they did not see any emplacements. Off to the left near the huge rock outcrop where the seven Japanese men had made their silly counterattack early yesterday, they could hear the tenor-voiced Japanese MGs firing at Baker Company at the ledge; but nothing opened up on them. When they reached the beginning of the saddle, sweating and half-dead from the lack of water, Gaff motioned them to stop.

He had to swallow his dry spittle several times before he could speak. It had been arranged with Colonel Tall that the commander of Baker's right platoon would move his men along the ledge to the trough and be ready to charge from there at Gaff's whistle signal, and because of this he unhooked his whistle from his pocket. The saddle was about twenty or twenty-five yards across, and he spaced them out across it. Because of the way it fell the strongpoint below was still invisible from here. "Remember, I want to get as close to them as we can before we put the grenades to them." To Bell's mind, overheated and overwrought, the Captain's phraseology sounded strangely sexual; but Bell knew it could not be. Then Gaff crawled out in front of them, and looked back.

"Well, fellows, this is where we separate the men from the boys," he told them, "the sheep from the goats. Let's crawl." He clamped his whistle in his teeth and cradling his rifle while holding a grenade in one hand, he commenced to do so.

Crawling along behind him, and in spite of his promise of a big beerbust, everything paid for by him, Gaff's volunteers did not take too kindly to his big line. Shit, I could have done better than that myself, Doll thought, spitting out yet another grass seed. Doll had already entirely forgotten his so near escape crossing the open space, and suddenly for no apparent reason he was transfixed by a rage which ranged all through him like some uncontrollable woods fire. Do not fire until you see the red of their assholes, Gridley. You may shit when ready, Gridley. Damn the torpedoes, full crawl ahead. Sighted Japs, grenaded same. There are no atheists in foxholes, Chaplain; *shit* on the *enemy*! He was—for no reason at all, except that he was afraid—so enraged at Gaff that he could have put a grenade to him himself right now, or shot him. On his left, his major competition Charlie Dale crawled along with narrowed eyes still hating all officers anyway and as far as he was concerned Gaff's final line only proved him right. Beyond Dale, Big Un Cash moved his big frame along contemptuously, his rifle still on his back, the fully loaded shotgun cradled in his arms; he had not come along on this thing to be given dumb slogans by no punk kid officers— sheeps and goats my ass, he thought and there was no doubt in his hard hackpusher's mind about which side he would be on when the count came. Witt, beyond Big Un and himself the extreme left flank, had merely spat and settled his thin neck down into his shoulders and set his jaw. He was not here for any crapped up West Point heroics, he was here because he was a brave man and a very good soldier and because his old outfit C-for-Charlie needed him— whether *they* knew it or not; and Gaff could spare him the conversation. Slowly, as they crawled, the extreme left of the strongpoint came into view fifty yards away and about twenty yards below them.

On the extreme right of the little line John Bell was not thinking about young Captain Gaff at all. As soon as Gaff had made his bid for an immortal line Bell had dismissed it as stupid. Bell was thinking, instead, about cuckoldry. Why that subject should come into his mind at a time like this Bell didn't know, but it had and he couldn't get rid of it. Thinking about it seriously, Bell discovered that under serious analysis he could only find four basic situations: sad little husband attacking big strong lover, big strong lover attacking sad little husband, sad little husband attacking big strong wife, big strong wife attacking sad little husband. But always it was a sad little husband. Something about the emotional content of the word automatically shrunk all cuckolded husbands to sad little husbands. Undoubtedly many big strong husbands had been cuckolded in their time. Yes, undoubtedly. But you could never place them in direct connection with the emotional content of the word. This was because the emotional content of the word was essentially funny. Bell imagined himself in all four basic situations. It was very painful, in an exquisitely unpleasant, but very sexual way. And suddenly Bell knew—as well and as surely as he knew he was crawling down this grassy saddle on Guadalcanal—that he was cuckold; that Marty was stepping out, was sleeping with, was fucking, somebody. Given *her* character and *his* absence, there was no other possibility. It was as though it were a thought which had been hanging around the borders of his mind a long time, but which he would never allow in until now. But with one man? or with several? Which did one prefer, the one man which meant a serious love affair? or the several which meant that she was promiscuous? What would he do when he got home? beat her up? kick her around? leave her? Put a goddamned grenade in her bed maybe. Ahead of him the entire strongpoint was visible by now, its nearer, right end only twenty-five yards away, and only a very few yards below their own height now.

And it was just then that they were discovered by the Japanese.

Five scrawny bedraggled Japanese men popped up out of the ground holding dark round objects which they lobbed up the hill at them. Fortunately only one of the five grenades exploded. It lit near Dale who rolled over twice away from it and then lay huddled as close to the ground as he could get, his face turned away. None of its fragments hit him, but it made his ears ring.

"Pull and throw! Pull and throw!" Gaff was yelling at them through the noise of the explosion, and almost as one man their six grenades arched at the strongpoint. The five Japanese men who had popped up out of the ground had by now popped back down into it. But as the grenades lit, two other, unlucky Japanese popped up to throw. One grenade lit between the feet of one of these and exploded up into him, blowing off one of his feet and putting him down. Fragments put the other one down. All of the American grenades exploded.

The Japanese with his foot off lay still a moment then struggled up to sit holding another grenade as the blood poured from his severed leg. Doll shot him. He fell back dropping the ignited grenade beside him. It did not go off.

"Once more! Once more!" Gaff was yelling at them, and again six grenades arched in the air. Again all of them exploded. Doll was a little late getting his away because of the shot, but he got it off just behind the others.

This time there were four Japanese standing when the grenades lit, one of them carrying a light MG. The exploding grenades put three of them down, including the man with the Nambu, and the fourth, thinking better of it, disappeared down a hole. There were now five Japanese down and out of action in the little hollow.

"Go in! Go in!" Gaff cried, and in a moment all of them were on their feet running. No longer did they have to fret and stew, or worry about being brave or being cowardly. Their systems pumped full of adrenaline to constrict the peripheral blood vessels, elevate the blood pressure, make the heart beat more rapidly, and aid coagulation, they were about as near to automatons without courage or cowardice as flesh and blood can get. Numbly, they did the necessary.

The Japanese had shrewdly taken advantage of the terrain to save themselves digging work. Behind the holes into the emplacements themselves was a natural little low area where they could come out and sit in cover when they were not actually being shelled, and it also served as a communication trench between the holes. Now in this hollow the scrawny, bedraggled Japanese rose with rifles, swords and pistols from their holes to meet Gaff and his crew. At least, some of them did. Others stayed in the holes. Three tried to run. Dale shot one and Bell shot another. The third was seen to disappear in a grand broadjump over the edge of the rockface where it fell clear, sixty or eighty feet to the jungle treetops below. He was never seen again and no one ever learned what happened to him. The others came on. And Gaff and his troops, the Captain blowing his whistle shrilly with each exhalation of breath, ran to meet them, in clear view of Baker Company at the ledge until they passed out of sight into the hollow.

Big Un killed five men almost at once. His shotgun blew the first nearly in two and tore enormous chunks out of the second and third. The fourth and fifth, because the gun was bucking itself higher each time he fired, had most of their heads taken off. Swinging the empty shotgun like a baseball bat, Big Un broke the face of a sixth Japanese man just emerging from a hole, then jerked a grenade from his belt, pulled the pin and tossed it down the hole after him into a medley of voices which ceased in the dull roaring boom of the constricted explosion. While he struggled to unsling the rifle from his back, he was attacked by a screaming officer with a sword. Gaff shot the officer in the belly from the hip, shot him again in the face to be positive after he was down. Bell had killed two men. Charlie Dale had killed two. Doll, who had drawn his pistol, was charged by another screaming officer who shouted

"Banzai!" over and over and who ran at him whirling his bright, gleaming sword around his head in the air. Doll shot him through the chest so that in a strange laughable way his legs kept right on running while the rest of him fell down behind them. Then the torso jerked the legs up too and the man hit the ground flat out with a tremendous whack. Doll shot him a second time in the head. Beyond him Witt had shot three men, one of them a huge fat sergeant wielding a black, prewar U.S. Army cavalry saber. Taking the overhead saber cut on the stock of his rifle, cutting it almost to the barrel, Witt had buttstroked him in the jaw. Now he shot him where he lay. Suddenly there was an enormous quiet except for the wailing chatter of three Japanese standing in a row who had dropped their weapons. There had been, they all realized, a great deal of shouting and screaming, but now there was only the moans of the dying and the hurt. Slowly they looked around at each other and discovered the miraculous fact that none of them was killed, or even seriously damaged. Gaff had a knot on his jaw from firing without cheeking his stock. Bell's helmet had been shot from his head, the round passing through the metal and up and around inside the shell between metal and fiber liner and coming out the back. Bell had an enormous headache. Witt discovered he had splinters in his hand from his busted riflestock, and his arms ached. Dale had a small gash in his shin from the bayonet of a downed and dying Japanese man who had struck at him and whom he subsequently shot. Numbly, they stared at each other. Each had believed devoutly that he would be the only one left alive.

It was clear to everyone that it was Big Un and his shotgun which had won the day, had broken the back of the Japanese fight, and later when they discussed and discussed it, that would remain the consensus. And now in the strange, numb silence—still breathing hard from the fight, as they all were—Big Un, who still had not yet got his rifle unslung, advanced snarling on the three standing Japanese. Taking two by their scrawny necks which his big hands went almost clear around, he shook them back and forth gaggling helplessly until their helmets fell off, then grinning savagely began beating their heads together. The cracking sound their skulls made as they broke was loud in the new, palpable quiet. "Fucking murderers," he told them coldly. "Fucking yellow Jap bastards. Killing helpless prisoners. Fucking murderers. Fucking prisoner killers." When he dropped them as the others simply stood breathing hard and watching, there was no doubt that they were dead, or dying. Blood ran from their noses and their eyes were rolled back white. "That'll teach them to kill prisoners," Big Un announced, glaring at his own guys. He turned to the third, who simply looked at him uncomprehendingly. But Gaff jumped in between them. "We need him. We need him," he said, still gasping and panting. Big Un turned and walked away without a word.

It was then they heard the first shouts from the other side, and remembered they were not the only living. Going to the grassy bank they looked out over and saw the same field they themselves had tried to cross last evening. Coming across it at a run, the platoon from Baker was charging the strongpoint. Back beyond them, in full view from here, the other two platoons of B had left the ledge and were charging uphill, according to Colonel Tall's plan. And below Gaff and his men the first Baker platoon charged on, straight at them, yelling.

Whatever their reason, they were a little late. The fight was already over. Or so everyone thought. Gaff had been blowing his whistle steadily from the moment they first had gone in right up to the end of the fight, and now here came the heroes. Preparing to wave and cheer ironically and hoot derision at their 'rescuers', Gaff's men were prevented by the sound of a machinegun. Directly below them in one of the apertures, a single MG opened up and began to fire at the Baker Company platoon. As Gaff's men watched incredulously, two Baker Company men went down. Charlie Dale, who was standing nearest to the door of the embrasure which was firing, leaped over with a shocked look on his face and threw a grenade down the hole. The grenade immediately came flying right back out. With strangled yells everyone hit the dirt. Fortunately, the grenade had been thrown too hard and it exploded just as it fell over the lip of the rockface, where the broadjumping Japanese had also disappeared, hurting nobody. The MG below continued to fire.

"Look out, you jerk!" Witt cried at Dale, and scrambled to his feet. Pulling the pin on a grenade and holding it with the lever depressed, he grabbed his rifle and ran over to the hole. Leaning around the right side of it, holding his rifle like a pistol in his left hand with the stock pressed against his leg, he began to fire the semi-automatic Garand into the hole. There was a yell from below. Still firing, Witt popped the grenade down the hole and ducked back. He continued to fire to confuse the occupants. Then the grenade blew up with a dull staggering roar, cutting off both the scrabble of yells and the MG, which had never stopped firing.

Immediately, others of the little force, without any necessity of orders from Gaff, began bombing out the other four holes using Witt's technique. They bombed them all, whether there was anyone in them or not. Then they called to the Baker Company platoon to come on. Later, four Japanese corpses were found huddled up or stretched out, according to their temperaments, in the small space Witt had bombed. Death had come for them and they had met it, if not particularly bravely, at least with a sense of the inevitable.

So the fight for the strongpoint was over. And without exception something new had happened to all of them. It was apparent in the smiling faces of the Baker Company platoon as they climbed up over the emplacement leaving five of their guys behind them in the kunai grass. It was apparent in the grinning face of Colonel Tall as he came striding along behind them, bamboo baton in hand. It showed in the savage happiness with which Gaff's group bombed out the empty bunkers using Witt's safety technique: one man firing while another tossed the grenades. Nobody really cared whether there was anyone in them or not. But they hoped there were hundreds. There was a joyous feeling in the safety of killing. They slapped each other on the back and grinned at each other murderously. They had finally, as Colonel Tall was later to tell newsmen and correspondents when they interviewed him, been blooded. They had, as Colonel Tall was later to say, tasted victory. They had become fighting men. They had learned that the enemy, like themselves, was killable; was defeatable.

It was on that same night that Private Witt paid them his angry, drunken visit. And so it was from Witt, whose Cannon Company outfit was bivouacked at Regimental Rear Echelon Headquarters, that C-for-Charlie learned for the first time that Captain Johnny Gaff had been recommended for the Medal of Honor, and that he had been evacuated to Esperito Santo for safekeeping. Witt naturally first looked up his old buddies from Gaff's 'assault force' for some drinking, and it was to them he told the story. But it soon spread like wildfire through the whole company, and there was a big laugh about it. Because, naturally, everybody knew that Gaff had never looked up his little 'assault force' to pay off that big drunk he had promised them, everything paid for by him. It was a bitter laugh. Witt himself waxed drunkenly eloquent about the treachery of any man who could use them as Gaff had and then shuck them off like a wornout fatigue blouse. Gaff had buggered them all in the ass, was Witt's opinion and he thought they all ought to admit it. But the rest of them tried to laugh it off, as the company in general had. Gaff was the final bitter sauce on the bitter meat all C-for-Charlie had been masticating without appetite for most of this past week. Neither, as far as Witt or anybody else could find out, had Gaff recommended Doll for the Distinguished Service Cross he had promised personally to recommend him for. Sergeant Doll— who now could remember clearly how he had shrewdly saved the group by deliberately drawing the Japanese fire knowing the ledge was ten yards off to the right—tried to laugh this off too, but he found it a little harder to do than the others did. As far as medals were concerned, from what any of them could find out, nobody from C-for-Charlie had been recommended for any medals at all so far. Except of course for Gaff.

(from Chapters 5 and 6)

[Train's Samurai Saber]

THE INSPECTION began at ten-thirty. This was because the Division Commander was spending the morning going over the battleground down the hill with his staff. But long before ten-thirty the Division Press Officer was up on the line going over the area, checking, arranging, changing, setting up camera angles— and searching. He was a big, bluff, open sort of man, a Major, who had been an All-America tackle during his years at The Point. He found what he was searching for in the person of Private Train, the stutterer, upon whose lap young Corporal Fife had fallen after being hit with his mortar shell.

There had been a number of 'Samurai Sabers' taken during the two days. Queen (now evacuated), Doll and Cash each had one. So did several others in both companies. But it was left by fate to Train (through no particular fault of his own, it must be said) to take the only real jewel-encrusted sword like the ones they had all read about in the papers for so long. Train, more from exhaustion and to catch a breather than anything else, had stumbled into one of the stick shanties along the crest for a moment, and had found it lying on the mud floor.

This particular sword had a sort of false hilt of dark wood chased with a lot of gold and ivory, in addition to its beautifully made leather hilt cover. It was not an especially secret mechanism, and later when Train took it off, he found jewels—a couple as large as his thumbnail—embedded in the steel tang. Rubies, emeralds, some small diamonds. The false wooden hilt had been cunningly carved inside to fit perfectly together over the protuberances of the stones. The whole sword was a beautiful piece of workmanship. It must have belonged to at least a general, Train's wide-eyed buddies told him when he showed it—though, however, they said, 2d Lieutenants were known to carry such swords when they were family heirlooms.

The sword caused a great deal of excitement in the Battalion, its value being variously estimated at everything from $500 up to $2000. And it was this sword which the Division Press Officer was seeking, in addition to doing the rest of his duties. He did not know it belonged to Train, but he knew it was somewhere in C-for-Charlie. Rumor of it had penetrated far to the rear, and the Press Officer had had a brilliant idea when he heard about it. He went straight to Lieutenant Band when he arrived. After thinking a moment, Band sent him to Train. He thought that must be the one. He hadn't seen it himself, or paid much attention. But that must be the one. It was.

"That is it!" the Press Officer cried excitedly when Train showed it to him. "This is the one! Son, you're a very lucky man! You know what you're going to do? You're going to present this sword to the General when he makes his inspection!"

"I-I a-am?" Train said.

"You sure are! Why, I'll have your face in every movie theater across the whole of the United States that shows newsreels! Think of that! What do you think of that? *Your* face!"

Train gulped beneath his sharp-edged, dangling, pickle nose. "W-Well, I-I k-kind of thought I'd l-like to k-keep it, M-Major, S-Sir," he said timidly.

"Keep it!" the Major roared. "Whatever for! What the hell for! What would you do with it!"

"W-Well, y-you know. N-Nothing r-really. J-Just k-keep it," Train tried to explain. "F-For a s-souvenir, l-like."

"Dont be silly!" the Major bellowed. "In the first place, you'd probably lose it before this war is over! Or sell it! The General has a marvelous collection of bizarre and antique weapons! A piece like this belongs in a collection like his!"

"W-Well—"

"And think what a newsreel shot it will make," the Major hollered. "The General comes up! You give him the sword! You draw it and you show him how to take the false hilt off! Then you give it back to him! He puts the hilt back on! He shakes your hand! General Bank shakes your hand! And we'll record your voice! You'll say, 'General Bank, I'd like you to have this Japanese sword I took!' Or something like that! Think of it! Think of that! You'll have *your* face, and *your* voice, in every movie theater across the nation! Maybe even your family will see you!"

"W-Well," Train said with timid regret, "if you r-really think it's the b-best th-thing to—"

"Think it!" the Major trumpeted. "Think it! I, personally—personally! can guarantee you that! It's something you'll never regret! Wait until your family writes you they have seen you!" He shook his hand. "Now, give me the sword! I want to look at it some more! Have to figure out the best angle to photograph it, you know! I'll give it back to you just before the General takes it! Thank you, —uh, —uh, Train?"

"Y-Yes, S-Sir," Train said. "Frank P."

"You go ahead with your work here, and I'll see you later on!" the Major shouted.

With the sword, the Press Officer came back down to the little CP where Welsh and Band were still working on their casualty listings. They all looked at it. But the Press Officer was scratching his head and didn't look very happy.

"What a face," he said. "I guess I never saw a more goddamned un-soldierly-looking face in my whole life. With that nose. And no chin. And he would have to stutter." He looked up. "You suppose I could get another, slightly better looking type to do the actual presentation?" He looked at both of them.

"I suppose not," the Press Officer said, answering himself. "But, God." Then he brightened. "I suppose in one way it'll really look even more democratic, won't it? A little rear-tank pipsqueak like that. Yeah, I guess it'll even be better, in a way."

It was, in fact, the highlight of the whole camera-recorded inspection tour, the movie cameras grinding, the General smiling, shaking Train's hand, Train smiling. The still cameras got it all the first time, but the movie cameras had to shoot their sequence over a second time because Train was so nervous at speaking to a General that he stuttered more than usual. But the second time he was better.

There was some muttered comment and bitter grumbling in the C-for-Charlie platoons, about Train letting himself be talked into giving his trophy away like that. Several of his friends told him he was stupid. Train tried to explain that it did not appear that he had had much choice. And anyway, if the General really wanted it that bad ... His friends shook their heads in disgust.

But nobody really cared very much. They were all too excited, and too relieved, to be getting a chance to go back off the line. As soon as the Division Commander had passed on to the B Company line, they began getting their stuff together to make the move.

The march back, over that terrain where they had lain so long in such fear and trembling the last two days, and which now was so peaceful, was strange to everyone. And they all felt a bit numb.

(from Chapter 5)

[Storm, Queen and the Prisoners]

STORM HAD KILLED four Japs up there today during the break-through to Tall and the mopping up afterward, and had enjoyed every one of them. Only one of the four had had even the remotest chance of killing him, and that was all right with Storm too. That was fine. But his four Japs, each one of whom he remembered distinctly, were the only things that he had enjoyed during the whole four days C-for-Charlie had spent at the front. He had been scared shitless all the rest of the time. And the pageant, the spectacle, the challenge, the adventure of war they could wipe their ass on. It might be all right for field officers and up, who got to run it and decide what to do or not do. But everybody else was a tool—a tool with its serial number of manufacture stamped right on it. And Storm didn't like being no tool. Not, especially, when it could get you killed; and fuck organization. Combat was for foot sloggers and rifle platoons, and he was a messergeant. He felt sorry, and perhaps even a little guilty, to have left the company and come back down here with his 'wounded' hand. But for a sensible man that was the only thing for it and that was all there was to it. If this hand didn't get him clean away from this fucking island, he would go back to being a messergeant. He would cook hot food for them and get it to them—if he could. But he would not carry it himself. That, the carriers could do. A lot of people were going to come out of this war alive, more than got killed, and Storm intended to be one of them if he possibly could. Why, even that trip down from up there—which he should have been very pleased over, should have enjoyed immensely—had been ruined by those Jap prisoners they had had to bring down with them.

He had come down with the next party to leave after the one Bugger Stein left with. Stein's party was the last of the stretcher parties, and most of the walking wounded cases had gone down long before. A few like himself and Big Queen had elected to stay till the mopping up was finished. There were seven of these, four from Baker Company three from C-for-Charlie, and with four unwounded men they were told off to act as guards to a party of eight prisoners—half of the total number taken. In this way Tall could free more unwounded men to remain up on the line for the anticipated night counterattack.

It was great to be leaving with a night counterattack expected (though Storm felt a momentary sharp thrust of guilt) and everything went off well at the start. Queen's flesh wound in his left upper arm was beginning to stiffen up, and he was not as chipper and energetic as he had been during the fighting at the bivouac. But just before leaving he roused himself to brightness again. "I'll be back!" he cried in his bull voice. "I'll be back! It'll take more than a little old flesh wound to keep me from comin back to old C-for-Charlie! I dont care where they send me! I'll be back if I have to stowaway on a replacement boat!" A few C-for-Charlie men who were watching the departure grinned and waved and cheered, and Brass Band who was there came over to shake hands with Queen—with unnecessary showiness, Storm felt. Storm had no idea why Big Queen had elected to stay behind for the mopping up when he could have gone down earlier. As for himself, he had stayed because he was already planning to parlay this hand wound into an evacuation, if he could, which would take him as far back from this Rock as he could milk out of it; and he wanted to leave a good impression on his old outfit when he left it perhaps forever.

The eight Japanese prisoners were a sorry, sicklooking lot. Feeble, stumbling, they shambled along appearing to be totally benumbed by their experiences, and looking as though they would not have had the energy or the will to escape even if they were guarded by just one GI. All of them were suffering from dysentery, jaundice and malaria. Two of them (just why, no one ever learned) were stark bareass naked, and it was one of these who finally collapsed and caused all the serious trouble. When Big Queen came over to kick him to his feet, he just lay vomiting and shitting at the same time, leaving two yellow trails of liquid behind him as each kick slid him sideways a few feet further down the path. Half-starved, his ribs and shoulder bones showing starkly through his sick-looking yellow skin, he looked more like some lower grade type of animal and really did not appear to be worth saving. Neither did the other seven, who now squatted on their haunches in patient numb resignation under the eyes of their guards. Some Lieutenant who spoke a little Japanese had learned from them that they had all been living off lizards and the bark off of trees for the past couple of weeks. On the other hand, the party was under the strictest personal orders from Colonel Tall to see that all of these men got back to Regimental Intelligence alive for questioning.

Queen, though stiffening badly and still bleeding, was still chipper enough to enjoy booting and clubbing his charges down the trail with hysterical joyousness whenever they fell behind, and the rest of the party had joined in the fun. Now Queen gave his considered opinion.

"I say shoot the fucker," he grinned, growling. "Look at him."

"You know Ol' Shorty ordered us to get them all back alive," someone else said.

"So we'll say he tried to escape," Queen said.

"Him?" someone said. "Look at him."

"So who'll see him?" Queen said.

"I'm with Queen," someone else said. "Remember what they did to our guys on the Bataan Death March."

"But Shorty gave us *personal* orders," the first man said. He was the corporal in charge of the four unwounded guards. "You know damn well he's gonna check up if one turns up missin. What if he has Intelligence ask these other guys what happened to their buddy? I dont want to get in no trouble, that's all."

"Well, it's either that or carry him," Queen said with finality. "I'm not about to carry no fuckin Jap all the way back to Hill 209. Are you? Anyway, I outrank you. I'm a sergeant. I say kill him. Look at him. Be doin the poor fuck a favor." He looked around at the others.

"The corprl's right," Storm said, putting in for the first time. He had been thinking it all over, pros and cons. "Shorty's sure to check up if one is missin. If we shoot him or lose him, he'll be on our ass like a bullwhip, spittin and bitin. Might even courtmarshal us." He did not add that he was a S/Sgt, and thus outranked Queen.

Queen stared down at the Japanese man, then shrugged and grinned ruefully. "Okay. I guess you're right," he said good-naturedly. "It looks like we carry him." He slapped his great palms together. "All right then! Come on! I'll take a leg! Who wants the rest of him?"

Storm, who wisely had already considered this problem, too, and decided he preferred vomit to fesces, moved over to him and took an arm. Two of the other wounded got hold of the other arm and leg, and with Queen comically in command and calling the movements for them like a coxswain of a crew shell hollering "Stroke!", the party moved off down the trail again.

Queen's goodnatured surrender to wisdom, plus his comical commands about portaging the sick Japanese, had put them all back into the high humor of their departure. Whooping and hollering they descended the steep hillside in a sort of nonsensical hysteria of cruel fun, slipping and sliding, one or another of them falling from time to time, and all of them except the four portagers who had all they could take care of, booting or shoving their seven walking prisoners to make them keep up. "Hey, Jap," one of them cried once. "Come on, Jap! Tell the truth! Aint you glad you dont have to fight no more now? Hunh? Aint you?" The Japanese he had addressed, who obviously did not understand a word, bobbed and bowed and nodded his head smiling numbly. "See there!" cried the guard. "I told you! They dont want to fight no more than we do! What's all this Emperor shit?" "Just you dont give him your loaded rifle," laughed another, "and then see how much he want to fight." Queen soon caught on to the fact that he had made a mistake by taking a leg to carry. Both of the men on the sick man's legs had difficulty keeping out of the way of the jets of yellow liquid the nude Japanese kept squirting as they bobbed him along down the steep hillside, and Queen goodnaturedly chided Storm for being smart enough to take an arm without letting him in on the idea. Then he had an idea of his own. "Let's bump him a little," he said as they came to a rock. "Maybe we can *knock* the shit out of him, hunh? Or, at least, enough of it to make him stop till we get him down." Swinging him in unison, they bumped his behind against the rock and made him squirt, all of them laughing uproariously. The other Japanese bobbed and grinned, because they too had gotten the idea by now. Nevertheless, the bumping did little good. He kept right on squirting as they continued to carry him down. Conscious enough to blink his open eyes from time to time, he was too far gone, too near out, to control his bowels, and when his head hit the ground from time to time it did not even make him flinch. They would bump him against every rock they came to as they went on down, and then go on. When they delivered him to Regimental Hq, a doctor was called and went to work on him immediately. It was interesting to note that Big Queen passed out two minutes later on his way down the reverse slope and rolled the rest of the way down into the Battalion aid station, causing great consternation.

(from Chapter 6)

[Numbness]

ONE MORE THING, gift of a grateful nation, came to them before they left, and this was the medals. Cynically, they had forgotten all about them when they hadn't come through, but now here they came, complete with the citations. There was a presentation. Every member of Captain Gaff's little assault force on The Dancing Elephant received a Bronze Star or better. Big Un Cash's, of course, was posthumous. John Bell's was sent on to him. Skinny Culn, recommended for a Bronze Star by Bugger Stein, got one. Don Doll, recommended for a Distinguished Service Cross by Captain Gaff, received a Silver Star instead. Charlie Dale, recommended for a Distinguished Service Cross by both Stein and Glory Hunter Band for all his braveries during The Dancing Elephant, got a Distinguished Service Cross, the only one in the Battalion. There was some bitching about this, but—as some wit immediately said— it would look good with his collection of gold teeth. Everyone pretended medals didn't mean anything, but everyone who got one was secretly proud.

One last word of the legendary Captain Gaff reached them also, just two days before they left. A fairly recent copy of *Yank* Magazine somehow fell into the hands of a C-for-Charlie man, and in it was a full page photo of the former Battalion Exec. Dressed in his tailored dress ODs (it was winter back home), wearing his Medal of Honor on its ribbon around his neck, the Captain had been photographed for *Yank* while making a speech at a bond selling rally. The caption below the photo said that his by now world famous statement to his trusty little band of exhausted but unbeaten volunteer Infantrymen on Guadalcanal (*This is where we separate the sheep from the goats and the men from the boys!*) had become a national slogan and was being flown on bunting in letters a foot high all across the country, while two song publishers had brought out patriotic war songs using it for a title, one of which was succeeding and was now on the Hit Parade.

They of course had to march to the beach, as no trucks happened to be available for them at the moment. Their route led them past the new cemetery. Plodding along gasping in the airless humidity and tripping over mud rolls and grass hummocks as they were, the cemetery looked very green and cool. The area had been well drained, and bluegrass had been planted on it. Big sprinklers sent their long gossamer jets swirling through the air above the crosses, and the white crosses were very beautiful in their long even rows. Quartermaster men moved here and there on its long expanse keeping it up and tending it.

Half a mile further on, passing a rusting wrecked Japanese barge, they met a man eating an apple. Perched high up on the prow of the wreck, he could look directly down on them as he leisurely munched his apple. One apple. Somehow, by some incredible mistake in bills of lading and shipping tickets in quintuplicate, a gross oversight by some nameless but usually efficient functionary, one fresh red apple had gotten sandwiched in amongst all the cans and crates and boxes and cases of precooked, dried and dehydrated foods, and hidden away in some unsearched corner had stowed away overseas. By some unbelievably marvelous stroke of luck this man had gotten it and could sit on the high prow of a wrecked barge eating it while they passed. Had he known them, this stranger, he could have ticked off their names as they passed below him in macabre review, their faces twisted up at him to stare hungrily at his apple: Captain Bosche, his officers, 1st/Sgt Eddie Welsh, Platoon Sergeants Thorne, Milly Beck, Charlie Dale, S/Sgt Don Doll, Corporal Weld, Sgt Carrie Arbre, Pfc Train, Pvt Crown, Pvts Tills and Mazzi, each looking back and upward at him as they passed. But, of course, he couldn't do this, since to him they were all strangers.

Mad Welsh, marching on behind the sturdy little figure of Captain Bosche, didn't give a fuck for apples. He had his two canteens of gin. Which was all he could carry this time, and he felt for them furtively. In his mind he was muttering over and over his old phrase of understanding: "Property. Property. All for property," which he had once said in rudimentary innocence arriving on this island. Well, this was a pretty good sized chunk of real estate, wasn't it? this island? He had known the combat numbness now—for the first time, at Boola Boola—and it was his calculated hope and belief that if pursued long enough and often enough, it might really become a permanent and mercifully blissful state. It was all he asked.

Ahead of them the LCIs waited to take them aboard, and slowly they began to file into them to be taken out to climb the cargo nets up into the big ships. One day one of their number would write a book about all this, but none of them would believe it, because none of them would remember it that way.

(from Chapter 8)

Whistle

(1978)

In his comfortable attic study in the old farmhouse ("Chateau Spud") on Long Island that he and Gloria bought and restored to a warm, welcoming home, a dying James Jones struggled valiantly to complete *Whistle*, the last volume of the army trilogy. Tragically, he died on May 9, 1977, before he could finish it. In a labor of love and pain, Willie Morris, with considerable help from Jones's daughter Kaylie, completed the novel by transcribing Jones's notes and tapes for the last three and a half chapters. It was published posthumously by Delacorte. While the novel's critical reception was mixed, several influential writers and critics praised it highly. In the *Chicago Tribune*, Philip Caputo wrote: "If the universal figure of this age is the soldier, Jones ought to be taken very seriously because no one has written about the soldier and his world more accurately and eloquently."

Focusing on the "de-evolution of a soldier," *Whistle* develops Jones's vision of the embittered American soldier returning "home" from combat overseas only to experience a new kind of alienation in a suddenly affluent and overwhelmingly materialistic "new America." The homefront had no place for the camaraderie that the returning wounded American soldiers had come to depend on for physical survival. In addition, the sense of being "already dead" (something many soldiers had been forced to accept for psychological survival), was incomprehensible to a civilian population devoted to family, jobs, homes, and the other material benefits of victory. More than a quarter of a century earlier, Jones had first developed the theme of the alienated returning soldier in his unpublished first novel, *They Shall Inherit the Laughter. Some Came Running* is also devoted, in great part, to this theme.

The first selection describes, from a brilliantly evoked "we" perspective, the distress of C-for-Charlie Company's wounded as they convalesce in a military hospital in Tennessee. They receive the news that "the four" who had represented "the heart of the old company"—Prell, Winch, Strange, and Marion Landers, a sensitive young man struggling to accept his own anonymity—have been wounded and are being returned to the States. The remaining selections illustrate various stages in the de-evolution of the soldier. Most compelling are the accounts of Prell's doomed patrol, one of the best single pieces in all of James Jones's work, and the description of Strange's suicide by drowning. The experience of death by congestive heart failure, the disease that killed Jones (Winch also has it), has been compared to drowning. Strange's suicide was virtually the last thing Jones dictated on his tape recorder.

[The Heart of the Old Company]

WE GOT THE WORD that the four of them were coming a month before they arrived. Scattered all across the country in the different hospitals as we were, it was amazing how fast word of any change in the company got back to us. When it did, we passed it back and forth among ourselves by letter or post card. We had our own private network of communications flung all across the map of the nation.

There were only the four of them this time. But what an important four. Winch. Strange. Prell. And Landers. About the four most important men the company had had.

We did not know then, when the first word of them came, that all four would be coming back to the exact same place. That is, to us, in Luxor.

Usually, it was us in the Luxor hospital who heard news soonest. That was because we were the largest individual group. At one point there were twelve of us there. It made us the main nerve center of the network. We accepted this responsibility without complaint, and dutifully wrote the letters and post cards that would keep the others informed.

News of the company still out there in those jungles was the most important thing to us. It was more important, more real than anything we saw, or anything that happened to us ourselves.

Winch had been our 1st/sgt out there. John Strange had been the mess/sgt. Landers had been company clerk. Bobby Prell, though busted twice from sgt and only a cpl, had been the company's toughest and foolhardiest sparkplug.

It was strange how closely we returnees clung together. We were like a family of orphaned children, split by an epidemic and sent to different care centers. That feeling of an epidemic disease persisted. The people treated us nicely, and cared for us tenderly, and then hurried to wash their hands after touching us. We were somehow unclean. We were tainted. And we ourselves accepted this. We felt it too ourselves. We understood why the civilian people preferred not to look at our injuries.

We hospitalized knew we did not belong there in the clean, healthy areas. We belonged back out in the raging, infected disaster areas; where we could succumb, die, disappear, vanish forever along with what seemed to us now the only family we had ever had. That was what being wounded was. We were like a group of useless unmanned eunuchs, after our swinging pendants had been removed, eating sweetmeats from the contemptuous fingers of the females in the garden, and waiting for news from the seneschals in the field.

There was arrogance in us, though. We came from the disaster areas, where these others had never been. We did not let anyone forget it. We came from the infected zones, had been exposed to the disease, and carried the disease in us to prove it. Carrying it was our pride.

For our own kind, an insane loyalty flamed in us. We were ready to fight all corners and sometimes, drunk and out in the town, did fight them. We would fight anybody who had not been out there with us. We wore our Combat Infantryman badges to distinguish us, and nothing else. Campaign ribbons and decorations were considered contemptible display. All that was propaganda for the nice, soft people.

And the company had been our family, our only home. Real parents, wives, fiancées did not really exist for us. Not before the fanatical devotion of that loyalty. Crippled, raging, enfeebled, unmanned in a very real sense and hating, hating both sides of our own coin and of every coin, we clung to each other no matter where or how far the hospital, and waited for the smallest morsel of news of the others to filter back to us, and faithfully wrote and mailed the messages that would carry it on to the other brothers.

Into this weird half-world of ours the first news we had of the four of them came on a grimy, mud-smeared post card from some lucky-unlucky man still out there.

The card said the four of them had been shipped out to the same evacuation hospital, almost at the same time. That was all it said. The next news we got was that all four had been shipped back home on the same hospital ship. This came from the base hospital, in a short letter from some unlucky, or lucky, man who had been wounded but had not made the boat. Later, we received a letter from the company's tech/sgt, giving more details.

Winch was being shipped back for some kind of unspecified ailment that nobody seemed to know much about. Winch himself would not talk about it. He had bitten through one thermometer and broken another, chased a hospital corpsman out of the compound, and gone back to his orderly tent where he was found slumped over his Morning Report book in a dead faint on his makeshift desk.

John Strange had been struck in the hand by a piece of mortar fragment which had not exited. The hand had healed badly, the wound becoming progressively more crippling. He was being sent back for delicate bone and ligament surgery and removal of the fragment.

Landers the clerk had had his right ankle smashed by a heavy-mortar fragment and needed orthopedic surgery. Bobby Prell had taken a burst of heavy-machinegun fire across both thighs in a firefight, sustaining multiple compound fractures, and heavy tissue damage.

This was the kind of personal news we ached to hear. Could it be that we were secretly pleased? That we were glad to see others join us in our half-unmanned state? We certainly would have denied it, would have attacked and fought anyone who suggested it. Especially about the four of them.

There were quite a few of us sitting in the shiny, spotless, ugly hospital snack bar, having coffee after morning rounds, when Corello came running in waving the letter. Corello was an excitable Italian from McMinnville, Tennessee. No one knew why he had not been sent to the hospital in Nashville, instead of to Luxor, just as no one knew how his Italian forebears happened to wind up in McMinnville, where they ran a restaurant. Corello had been home once since his arrival in Luxor, and had stayed less than a day. Couldn't stand it, he said. Now he pushed his way through to us among the hospital-white tables, holding the letter high.

There was a momentary hush in the room. Then the conversations went right on. The old hands had seen this scene too many times. The two cracker waitresses looked up from their chores, alarmed until they saw the letter, then went back to their coffee-drawing.

Rays of Southern sun were streaming through the tall plate glass from high up, down into all that white. In sunny corners lone men sat at tables writing letters, preferring the clatter and people here to the quiet of the library. There were five of us from the company at one table and Corello stopped there.

At once, men of ours sitting at other tables got up and came over. In seconds all of us in the snack bar had clustered around. We were already passing the letter back and forth. The patients from other outfits looked back down at their coffee and conversation and left us alone.

"Read it out loud," someone said.

"Yeah, read it. Read it out loud," several others said.

The man who had it looked up and blushed. Shaking his head about reading out loud, he passed the letter to someone else.

The man who took it smoothed it out, then cleared his throat. He looked it over, then began to read in the stilted voice of a student in a declamation class.

As he read the news, a couple of men whistled softly.

When he finished, he put it down among the coffee mugs. Then he saw it might get stained, and picked it up and handed it to Corello.

"All four of them at the same time," a man who was standing behind him said hollowly.

"Yeah. The same day practically," another said.

We all knew none of us would ever go back to the old company. Not now, not once we had been sent back to the United States, we wouldn't. Once you came back to the States, you were reassigned. But all of us needed to believe the company would continue on as we knew it, go right on through and come out the other end, intact.

"It's as if—It's almost like—"

Whichever one of us it was who spoke did not go on, but we all knew what he meant.

A kind of superstitious fear had descended over us. In our profession, we pretty much lived by superstition. We had to. When all of knowledge and of past experience had been utilized, the outcome of a firefight, or a defense or an attack, depended largely on luck. Awe of and reverence for the inexplicable, that heart of the dedicated gambler's obsession, was the only religion that fit our case. We followed a God which coldly incorporated luck within Itself, as one of Its major tools. For a commander, give us the commander who had luck. Let the others have the educated, prepared commanders.

We were like the dim early human who watched his mud hut destroyed by lightning and created God to explain it. Our God could be likened to a Great Roulette Wheel, more than anything.

We had thought the God looked warmly on us, or at least our company. Now it seemed the Wheel was rolling the other way.

There was nothing to do about it. As superstitious men, we understood that. That was part of the rules.

We could only not step on the crack, not walk under the ladder, try not to let the black cat cross our line of advance in front.

But it was difficult to accept, without fear. That the old company could change so completely. Become the home, the family, the company of some other group. It was about the last thing we had left.

"Well—" one of us said, and cleared his throat massively. It sounded like a shotgun fired in a barrel. We all knew what this man meant, too. He did not want to pursue it. Otherwise, might not some of the bad luck rub off?

"But all four of them at once," someone said.

"Do you think one of them might get shipped here?" someone else said.

"If we could get Winch here," one said.

"Yeah, it would be like old times," another said.

"Anyway, we could get some inside scoop firsthand," someone said. "Instead of letters."

"Speaking of letters," another said, and got up. "Speaking of letters, I guess we might as well get on with our chores. Huh?"

At once, two or three men got up with him and moved away toward a couple of clean tables. Almost at once, two other men followed and joined them. Paper, pens, and pencils appeared, and post cards, envelopes, and stamps.

In the sweet, reassuring, late-summer slant of Southern sun which exploded in a dazzle below against all that white, they began to write the letters that would pass the news on to the other hospitals across the country. Some wrote with their tongues sticking out of their mouth corners.

The rest of us went on sitting. There was curiously little talk for a while. Then there was a sudden wave of signals for more coffee. Then we went on sitting. Most of us stared at the white walls or the white ceiling.

We were all thinking about the four of them. The four of them could legitimately be said to be almost the heart of the old company. Now those four were making the same strange trip home. We had all of us made it. It was a weird, strange, unreal voyage. We had made it either on the big fast planes, or on the slow white ships with the huge red crosses on their sides, as these four were doing.

We sat there in our demiworld of white, thinking about the four men making it as we ourselves had done. We wondered if those four were feeling the same peculiar sense of dislocation, the same sense of total disassociation and nonparticipation we ourselves had had.

(Chapter 1)

[Landers on the Hillside]

SOMETHING HAD HAPPENED to Landers with his wounding in the New Georgia islands. But it was hard to say exactly what it was. It had been an easy enough wounding. Commonplace, even. A big-sized mortar round had landed close by him and blown him up and knocked him out. It must have happened to thousands. That part had not been bad at all. There was no pain, nothing hurt him, there was no time to be afraid. The noise-fire blossomed so swiftly to engulf him that he had hardly heard it. Then swift comforting blackness, buzzing up. If anything at all, there was only a half-beginning of a surprised thought: Why, this isn't so bad—

He assumed, later, he meant dying. The thought seemed to include the idea that he would never come to. Then he did come to, his nose bleeding, his head heavy and unable to think. His head was bleeding and his helmet had disappeared. Contrary to all the rules of first aid, somebody was rolling him around and slapping his face. There was the usual comic moment of panic when he felt all over his crotch to make sure he had everything. Then he walked out. At the aid station the medical lieutenant had told him he had a mild concussion and said he would send him back to rest a couple of days. It was not till then, when he tried to get back on his feet, that they discovered his smashed ankle. He had walked out on it.

It was during the time he was waiting to be jeeped out that the peculiar thing, the something, happened to him. They had cut off his shoe, which turned out to be full of blood, and had bandaged his ankle. Four men had placed him on a stretcher and carried him over and put him down where there were others waiting. He sat on the stretcher on the crest of the ridge and with some of the other wounded placidly, contentedly almost, watched the battle in progress below them.

At this point Landers' job designation was Battalion Communications Sergeant. Wandering around with his company, where as company clerk he was not even supposed to be, he had been picked up four days before by the lt colonel commanding the battalion and impressed as his communications sergeant, to replace the original who had been killed. He had been up forward to deliver a message from the colonel to one of the platoon commanders when the mortar round knocked him off.

Being a replacement as well as a clerk, this was only Landers' second time up in fighting country. The first time he had roamed around with his outfit a few days, been part of a small firefight, watched several men wounded, then been unconditionally ordered back to the regimental rear area to his job by the company commander, at Top/Sgt Winch's instigation. The second time, he had armed himself with three three-day passes from the head of G-1 who thought his request marvelous. Charming, if not actually quixotic. Landers himself thought it bizarre, a good story to tell some day, how he had to get a pass to go *toward* the fighting. But under that was the nagging feeling which always gnawed at him, that he was back in the relative safety while they were up there in the smoke and fire. But after one day with them he had been caught and shanghaied by the battalion's colonel. The truth was, he at once became the pet enlisted aide of the colonel, who had looked up his dossier and found he had a twenty-one-year-old with three and a half years of college. All of this had infuriated Winch, whose clerk he'd been. But the result was he spent most of his time intellectualizing the war with the battalion officers and doing organizational things fairly far back. And probably, if he had not been wounded, he would have been transferred to the colonel, with a raise in grade. But at least he could have said he was doing his share.

But on the ridge all that changed. At some unspecified point, Landers watched as below him in the shallow bowl men roared and shouted and hollered and yelled, ran forward carrying things, ran back carrying things (as often as not other men), fired guns, threw things, struggled and fought. Landers thought only one thought. They were all silly idiots. What did they think they were doing? They were ridiculous. He did not know then that most of them felt the same way when they were wounded.

On his ridge Landers watched with perfect equanimity as they bopped and banged and shot and exploded and stabbed each other. Good. Good for them. They deserved it. They deserved whatever happened to them. He felt completely acquiescent. But he was outside of it. But being outside went further than just being on the ridge. It extended to his special pet colonel, to his old outfit, to the whole Army, to his entire nation, to the enemy nation—to the whole human race, finally. He was not part of it.

He realized this did not particularly affect anything. They could still give him orders. They could put him in jail. And he would go to jail. He could be bayoneted and he would scream. They could even give him a medal and he would salute and say Thank you. Or they could kill him, and he would die. But that was all. Because all the rest was bullshit. Just plain bullshit.

It was not because they were insane. He had suspected that before, from the beginning. It was not that modern war itself was insane. He had known that, too. It was not even that in ten years these same men battling down there, those who survived, would be making trade agreements with each other, signing mutual business deals for mutual profit, while the dumb luckless dead ones moldered in some hole. Landers had been cynically aware of all that, long before. It was that, seeing it, it was all so foolish, so abysmally stupid and ridiculous and savage, he could not consider himself a part of it.

Suddenly, sitting there on the hillside, he began to weep.

(from Chapter 3)

[Strange's Hand Wound]

COMPARED TO THAT, Strange felt his own wounding had been little more than a dirty cosmic joke.

His had happened back on Guadalcanal. Way back. In January. It was just at the time when the company had successfully terminated its first big combat and first big attack against the Japs. Strange and a couple of his cook force had walked up with a resupply to visit the company. They were bivouacked on top of a hill they had taken two days before. Some staff colonel had named it the Sea Horse. They sat around on the slope talking, the guys filling Strange and his cooks in on all that had happened, and

Strange had noticed how they were all somehow changed. He did not know exactly how they were changed. They just were different. Then suddenly there was the soft, almost soundless shu-shu-shu of mortars coming in, and someone squawked, and everyone hit the dirt. Strange threw himself flat. There was a yell from somewhere, during the explosions. When he sat back up, he noticed the palm of his hand was burning hot. A sharp, hot, toothy little piece of fragment half the size of your little fingernail had hit him in his palm between the knuckles of his middle fingers but hadn't come out the other side. There it was, sticking in his palm, just above the center. While the wounded man who had yelled was being taken care of, Strange started showing his hand around. He had been briefly terrified, his heart somewhere up between his ears, but when he found himself to be all right, and the man who was wounded was found to be okay, neither maimed nor killed, he began to laugh. And soon they were all laughing. It was a great joke, his hand. Mother Strange had come up to visit the company and had got himself a Purple Heart. There was no blood on his hand. The hot metal apparently had itself cauterized the wound. Carefully they pulled the piece of fragment out, and Strange put it in his pocket. No blood followed it out. There was only this longitudinal little blue slit. Like a miniature pussy, someone said. They took him around to the command post, everybody laughing, and showed it to the company commander to make sure of the Purple Heart and then a medic put a Band-Aid on it. A little later, still laughing, he and his two cooks left and walked back with another, returning resupply.

Later on, though, he hadn't laughed. When he thought about it, it was with a sense of irritated anger. What he remembered was the sense of fear, and the momentary feeling of total helplessness. He hadn't liked either worth a damn.

Along the ship's promenade, Strange spotted a window that was empty and went over and stood and watched the American coastline himself for a while.

It was summer here back home, mid-August, and the glass was open. He pulled up the sleeves of his bathrobe and leaned on the glass and let the light breeze of passage along the glass riffle the hairs on his forearms.

It was enough to bring the fear back to him, just for him to think that if it had been a little harder, it would have gone right on through his hand; and if it had hit hard enough to do that, and had hit him in the head, he would be dead. And none of it meant a damn thing. Not to anyone but Johnny Stranger. It just hadn't happened to hit him in a vital spot, and that was all it meant. It was at that point that the irritated anger always rose up on him.

Each time he clenched and unclenched the hand it hurt him and inside his head he could hear it grate. The doc had said there was still a tiny piece of metal in it. And that a tendon was rolling over the piece of metal, or over a bone growth. But getting the metal out was the least of it. The trauma and continued use had caused a degenerative arthritis to set in in the hand, in the six months since he got it.

(from Chapter 4)

[Prell's Sasaki Patrol]

WHENEVER PRELL thought of his squad and the patrol, a kind of fluttering qualm of apprehension rose in his stomach. It was not a qualm of conscience. It was a spasm of responsibility, dread and helplessness—a simple reflex to cry out No! no! It verged on panic. He always wanted to cry No! no!—and always, crying No! no! did not help or was too late. Their individual portraits flashed across the front of his mind like in-motion close-ups on a movie screen. A head turning sideways to grin. A shoulder rising beside a smiling face in a gesture. Then the anguished but clearly focused mental pictures he had of the hurt ones, each man of them, would follow. Dead, or dying, or wounded. He would never lose those. That horrible, Godawful clank that had given them away. A canteen, it had sounded like.

They were not even Prell's own squad. Prell had been moved to them when the original squad leader was shipped home sick. But he found little to improve on or change. They worked well together without him.

The mission was to patrol out and seek contact. A large Jap force had moved away from the center of the line in front of Munda and couldn't be found. Specifically, they were to find out if the Japs had reoccupied a small steep valley on the right that they had previously abandoned but now, intelligence thought, might have moved back into.

It was an almost routine job. If you counted it ordinary and routine to be walking miles in enemy territory along jungle trails that might at any moment be trip-wired or foot-mined in a jungle too dense to travel off the trails. It was impossible to describe the fatigue and exhaustion of that kind of walking. The narrow foot trails slicked over with mud. The valley they were to inspect they found empty.

On the way back, on a hunch, Prell decided to take them on a little detour up a side trail, to look at a small side valley, The trail veered off to the left uphill two hundred yards through the jungle to a low ridge. And the trail had been heavily used lately. Both Prell and his point man sensed something was going on over there beyond the ridge.

Halfway to the top he halted the squad and he and his point man crawled on up to have a look. The valley was alive with Jap infantry. The opposite valley wall was a semicliff and there were some small caves and overhangs on it and Japs were crawling all over it. They obviously were preparing an attack.

Both of them recognized Sasaki immediately. It wasn't hard to recognize a Jap general. Whenever he said anything, everybody else jumped. Sasaki was a heavy-chested man, well-fed, with a thick graying British-officer-type mustache. His picture had been posted around the Division, and a reward of $1000 was being offered to the man who killed him. Prell and the others knew about him only that Imamura and Admiral Kusaka, joint commanders of the Jap Southeast Area, had sent General Noboru Sasaki to command all of New Georgia after the American invasion. It gave Prell a sudden thrill to know that he held the life of an important man in his hands, and had carte blanche to kill him. He knew how political assassins must feel. Sasaki was with a group of other men, obviously officers, and they were studying two maps. In addition, Sasaki was smoking a big fat, very un-Oriental cigar. He walked back and forth gesticulating with the cigar as he declaimed to the others. Prell put the binoculars he had been issued for the mission on him, anyway, to be sure. It was him, all right.

A lot of things were going through Prell's mind at that moment. He was already getting down into prone position and loop sling to fire. First was the idea Sasaki might get away, walk off somewhere out of sight or into one of the caves, the way he was moving about. Second was the thought that he himself, Prell, was the best shot in the squad, in any case. Third, the New Georgia campaign and the possible effect on it if he succeeded. Only fourth, if at all, was the splintered fast flash of thought of the personal fame and that $1000 he might get by knocking off the Jap commander in New Georgia. Prell was absolutely certain about the thought sequence.

As he got into his sling, he was already whispering to his point man. To go back. Get them ready to move out. No, get them moving now. But quietly. No noise. When he heard the first shot, he should start them running.

Prell was not worried about how he himself would get out. He would get out, all right. If only to claim that reward. But it had already occurred to him it was odd that with a general like Sasaki present there were no outposts around.

Thank God the two of them had gotten off the trail into the undergrowth, before they peeked over the crest. Prell had never felt more fully and more joyously alive than at that moment.

With the point man moving, he rolled down to get his sight. He was satisfied he had done everything correctly. He had his men already moving out. Everything was proper. He had forgotten nothing. Now all he had to do was shoot. Hoo, man. He had not scored High Expert and high regimental rifle four years running for nothing. But he wished he had a 1903 Springfield for this shot, with its folding leaf sight, instead of a Garand. He should have kept the point man here with him as a witness to the kill.

Below him the general was still walking and gesticulating. He must remember to allow for shooting downhill. He moved the rifle ahead of the general, to where the officers with the maps were. The general would stop, just there, just when he came up to the map . . .

It was then that he heard the single, loud clank of American equipment somewhere on the trail behind him, and wanted to curse.

It stopped him. And he lost his sight picture. The general was moving away from the maps again. Well, he would catch him at the other end of his pacing, when he stopped to turn. Prell moved the rifle ahead of him again.

Then he heard—or sensed—the jungle plants move behind him, and a Jap soldier leaped on him screaming and firing his rifle.

It was amazing the Jap did not hit him, at that short range. It did not say much for their rifle training. Warned a fraction of a second ahead of time, Prell was already rolling, and fired three fast rounds into the man's chest as it touched his rifle barrel. Then he was on his feet ready to run. But nobody else was there. More firing and screaming was coming from back down the trail. It had the sound of catastrophe.

Prell cast one last, anguished glance behind him. There was no hope. The general was moving swiftly, into one of the caves, surrounded tightly by the bodies of the other officers, to protect him. There was nothing to do. Prell ran.

They were lucky. A big, well-prepared patrol would have killed them all, at once. Apparently the group that heard them was a small one of only five men, and had no help nearby. When he came running down, his men were just finishing killing the fifth. One of his men was slightly wounded. A nick. His own single Jap trooper apparently had been all alone.

Prell slowed long enough to yell at them to move. The ones in front were already running down the trail, and needed no urging. The others began to follow. "Move, move," he screamed at them. The Jap troops often called mortars down in on themselves, and Prell had anticipated it.

Mortar shells began to whump in around them. One man a little in front of Prell went down from a near direct hit. Prell and the man immediately in front of Prell, hardly pausing, scooped him up by the armpits and half-carried him. A man up ahead dropped back and took over Prell's half of him to free Prell. Prell paused, to make sure they were all in front of him and running, then turned around to fire rear guard, running backward. But no enemy were visible behind them on the trail. Another man went down from a mortar round but got up and ran on by himself. Then the patrol was apparently through the mortar screen. That was when the .50 caliber took them from the flank.

The Jap was firing from an obtuse angle to the line of the trail. Fortunately, they had run nearly through his field of fire by the time he could get his gun going. Fortunately, most of them were already through. Only the men at the tail end caught the fire.

Prell, of course, was the last man. A burst caught him across the thighs, and cut him off from his legs and feeling them just as if a big scythe had swept through a field, and Prell knew he had had it, or if he hadn't, his legs certainly had. The impact seemed to fling him forward. As he started to fall, he watched the same burst, drifting higher, take the two men running downhill in front of him across the lower back and lungs, inches higher on the third man than on the second. There was no question they were killed. The third man was his point man, Crozier. Both bodies went on running several yards before they fell. Prell, his teeth clenched, by sheer force of will, helped along by the push of the heavy bullets, managed to run past them on his non-legs before he too folded up like thin cardboard and fell straight down on his face, headlong, sprawling. He had the curious impression that he was continuing still to run, horizontally, even as he struck. But as he fell his mind told him none of it really mattered anyway, because his mind told him he was finished.

He yelled and a couple of his squad ran back for him, in tandem, like a pair of matched, finely trained horses, and got him by his armpits. But in the same moment, miraculously, all firing stopped. The jungle quiet, always ominous, and never really quiet, which seemed to drip from the trees like moisture, fell on them.

They turned him over on his back. His number two crawled over. Their faces looked scared. "Well, let's see! Let's see!" Prell demanded irately. "Damn it!" He needed passionately to know. See for himself how bad it was. "Don't just sit there!" His number two and another man unbuckled his belt and began to pull his pants down. Prell, beginning to sweat as they moved him, sent two men back up the trail for the two dead. Crozier, and Sims. He was damned if he was going to leave them here, for the Japs to piss on, or eat, or whatever it was they did with their captured dead.

The legs were a mess, when they got his pants down. Like hamburger. It made his belly go cold inside, looking at them. The skin across his thighs was already turning blue from bruise. It was impossible to tell how many of the heavy .50 caliber bullets had hit him. He was bleeding badly. But there didn't seem to be any arterial bleeding. The first hopeful sign. His number two sprinkled sulfa powder on them and began tying on tight compresses.

While he did, Prell briefed him, through clenched teeth, on what he had seen and on the presence of Sasaki, "In case anything should happen to me."

Prell knew he had to get them out of there. And do it swiftly. There wasn't anything he could do for Crozier and Sims, but he could still do something for the others. The other two wounded could walk, after a fashion. He himself couldn't walk, and he could feel the bones grate together in his legs. Two other men were already improvising a stretcher out of their buttoned-up fatigue blouses and two rifles. When they got him on it and hoisted him, Prell thought for a moment he would pass out. Then he got them moving and out of there.

As they moved away, mortar rounds began to drop singly around the trail junction, searching for them with tree bursts. By a matter of minutes he had anticipated them again.

As they moved along, the thought of the state of his legs made Prell's belly go cold again inside. You never considered how important your legs were to you until you didn't have them and couldn't call on them. There was no way you could move much at all, when you didn't have legs. It was then that he made up his mind that if he lost them, he wouldn't stay.

They knew they only had half a mile to go. But on the mud-slicked trail the going was difficult. For the walking wounded, the men carrying the dead and the men carrying Prell. Up to then Prell had not felt much pain, just a dull toothache in his legs that warned him the pain would be coming and he could depend on it. On the march, it came. With each step of the men carrying him he could feel the splintered ends of his femurs moving around in the already tortured flesh of his thighs like sharp instruments, further lacerating the already torn meat. He was worried one of them might cut its femoral artery, and tried to hold as still as possible. But it was impossible to be still. For Prell it was the beginning of an odyssey of movement and pain that would continue for two months and carry him halfway around the world to the Army hospital in Luxor. And the pain part wouldn't end then. He had put one of his BAR men back as rear guard and the other out front, to try to fend off any Jap patrols hunting for them. Luckily they did not meet any head-on. As they got nearer to their own lines, the trail branched out into a series of parallel trails and transverses that the Japs had built to supply their now-abandoned line. Here he could maneuver a little and give them the slip. Twice they hid, as talking Jap squads moved along nearby parallel trails looking for them. But the fatigue-blouse stretcher under Prell's legs was beginning to be soaked with his heavy bleeding. He went halfway out and came back several times. When they got within hailing distance of their own line, they decided they had better take a chance and yell for help.

A reinforced patrol with a medic in it came out to cover them while the medic worked on Prell and strung a plasma bottle on him, and then escorted them in, to everybody's vast relief and delight. At the battalion aid station the battalion surgeon looked at the legs and shook his head. Dolefully. He crudely splinted the legs to keep the femurs from working any more and had Prell strapped on a regular, real stretcher to be jeeped out. For Prell this was the end of it, and he knew it, at least with this outfit. He would probably never see this outfit again. There had been times when he had hated it, and every person in it, but now he hated to leave it. As they hung him on the body-loaded jeep, he kept his face set. He was flown out the next afternoon. The battalion commander gave the whole squad the morning off, to come down and see him. That did not sound as if anybody suspected him of misconduct.

It had not been a lucky patrol. All the same, Prell knew he had done everything right and correctly. He had done everything both according to the rules themselves, and according to the unwritten law that, unspoken, went along with the rules. The unwritten law was that you never risked your men. Unless the gain was worth it. Double worth it. In Prell's case the gain had been worth more than that. Even if it had never got realized.

(from Chapter 5)

[Winch's Speech]

BY THE NEXT AFTERNOON he had made a public speech in Washington Square, nearly gotten picked up by the MPs for it, and his cold had developed into a serious bronchitis.

Arlette had gone out up to Chinatown to get them a Chinese dinner to bring back to the hotel. Winch decided to go out and do a little bar-crawling on his own. It was coming back to the hotel past the Square, after three or four bars and three or four drinks, that he got the idea to make the speech.

It was all the old duffers on their soapboxes, droning out their worn-out, ancient, old-fashioned political speeches that gave him the idea. Socialism. Unionism. Communalism. And Winch thought with a snort, Why not? Although he had siphoned a huge amount of it off into Arlette, there was still a thin, ashy residue of outrage left in him. He walked over to one of the old duffers and gave him a five-dollar bill to borrow his soapbox.

The concept for it was one he had had quite a while. It had occurred to him first on Guadalcanal, last year, lying up under a mortar barrage. He had developed and expanded it later, playing with it at times when he sat alone drinking, or watched from a ridge with the company commander as their overheated, mud-breathing platoons tried to advance. He had summarized the whole concept in the slogan he worked out for it. *"Soldiers of the world, unite! You have nothing to lose but your guns!"* That was what he began to shout from the soapbox.

A crowd of amused servicemen formed fairly quickly. At first they were laughing, and cheering him on, but some began to get disturbed as he went on. "Hey, you," he singled out a private. "What are you making a month? Thirty-eight bucks, right? What do you think you'd be making if we were organized, hah? No, don't laugh. Think about it. What couldn't we do, if we were organized? Every country needs us, right? Everybody else has unions, why not us? Jap soldiers, German soldiers, English soldiers, US soldiers. Russians, French, Australians. All united. We'd corner the market. Hell, we could take the explosive charges out of the mortar shells and artillery! Put white flour in them instead! How would that be?" A couple of derogatory whistles came from the back of the crowd. "You don't like that? Why not? No more casualties!" Winch bellowed in his command voice. "You simply walk to the rear. We could have arbitration committees to decide where the battles would be held." He spread his arms. "No more jungles, right? Who'd pick a jungle?"

"What are you? A Communist?" a voice yelled from the rear. "They're our enemies."

"Me? Hell, no. Look at me. I'm a first sergeant. Look at my stripes," Winch yelled. (Arlette had wanted to sew them on, and he had let her; she was so proud of them.) "But I'm more like a Jap first sergeant or a German first sergeant than I am like these civilian sons of bitches." That brought cheers. "And you! You know what I make a month? You could be making that as a private, if we were organized."

He saw the MPs coming through the crowd, pushing their way up toward him, and drew himself up to full height. "Soldiers of the world! Unite! I'll be back. Same time tomorrow." And jumped down off the box and fled.

Whistles and good-natured cheers and a lot of handclapping followed him.

It was only fifty yards to get into the narrow streets where he could hide and sneak off, but by the time he had run it he was astonished to find he was gasping for breath and had to stop. In an alley. He simply could not go on. A violent fit of coughing seized him. Fortunately, a number of the GIs had gotten themselves in front of the MPs, and impeded their progress. In his alley Winch was coughing up strings of foamy white mucus. But after a few minutes he was able to make it around a corner and into a bar and order a drink. The drink seemed to help.

He made it back to the hotel. But then he thought he wasn't going to make it up the three flights of stairs to their third-floor room. He had to stop and gasp at every landing.

When he got to the door, Arlette was there looking horrified, and the Chinese food was in cardboard containers on the table. All piping hot and waiting.

"Good God, I could hear you all the way up the stairs. What's happened to you?"

"Nothing," Winch said hollowly, and leaned on the door and stared at her. "A little touch of bronchitis. Nothing a good Chinese dinner, a few drinks and a fine fuck won't cure. Don't worry about it."

And, indeed, after he sat in a chair and rested awhile, he felt much better. They ate the Chinese dinner, had the drinks, and accomplished the sexual assignation. Winch felt fine. The whole attack, which seemed to have been brought on by the fifty-yard run out of the Square, seemed to have disappeared. But then in the night another coughing fit seized him, and he woke up unable to breathe. No matter how hard he pulled, he could not seem to get air down into his lungs. When he coughed, he brought up the same foamy white froth. A couple of drinks were the only thing that seemed to help it. But then when he lay down to sleep, he found he could not breathe lying down. He wound up spending most of the night sleeping sitting straight up in a chair.

Arlette, when she wasn't sleeping, or drinking or screwing Winch, worried about it, and about him. But whatever it was, the bronchitis did not seem to impair his ability to screw. But then in the morning, when they went out for breakfast, he almost did not make it back up the three flights of stairs. He wouldn't have made it, if Arlette hadn't helped him. After that, he did not go out, and let Arlette go out by herself when she wanted to go out.

He stuck it out like that for two days, but in the middle of the third night he knew he had had it. He had spent most of it leaning on his elbow on two corner towel racks in the bathroom unable to breathe, coughing up the frothy white stuff.

"I'm going to have to go back to the hospital," he told her hollowly. "There's nothing else for it. Will you help me? I hate to ask you, but I don't think I can make it by myself."

"Of course I'll help you," Arlette said, frowning at him. "You're bad sick, you know. Anyway, I have to be getting back to my job myself."

"Then go down and call a cab."

They said little in the cab. Once Arlette took hold of his hand and held it, and leaned over and kissed him. "I put my address and phone number in your shirt pocket," she said.

"Expect me when you see me," Winch said hollowly. "They're going to be shipping me out of here someplace east."

At the hospital entrance he turned back to look at her a last time and wave. Standing by the cab, she waved back, and got in and shut the door. Winch watched her white face at the dark cab window as it pulled away.

There was a look about the set of her head on her neck which said she was glad to be going, and made Winch grin.

"Well, what have we here?" the young doc on duty said, when the orderly brought him into the emergency.

"I dunno," Winch said hollowly. "Bronchitis. You better put me in bed for a day or two. But I've got to see W/O Hoggenbeck. I'm supposed to be shipping out of here for Luxor, Tennessee."

The young doctor checked his pulse and then looked up sharply.

"My orders are already cut," Winch said. "I'm going to Luxor, Tennessee."

The doctor put his stethoscope under his shirt and listened to his heart, and then to his lungs. "Bronchitis, hell," he said. "You're in acute congestive heart failure, man. You're not going anywhere."

"Heart failure?"

"Your lungs are full of fluid," the doctor said. "Water. You're drowning."

"I'm going to Tennessee," Winch said tiredly, but stubbornly. "Luxor. Hoggenbeck knows all about it."

"I'm putting you to bedrest," the doctor said. "And a diet of diuretics. Your heart must be as big as a football. You're not going anywhere for quite a while."

Winch could only shut his eyes. He was too exhausted to argue.

(from Chapter 7)

[Pay, Pay, Pay]

THE FOUR OF THEM had gone down for a quiet, peaceful dinner in the main dining room downstairs. The old-fashioned main dining room off the lobby, with its wall paneling and quiet old colored gentlemen waiters, had in general been kept back out of the way of the huge influx of wild-eyed, fire-breathing servicemen, and was the place for that kind of dinner. Old Luxor families still took their older and younger generations there for family dinner outings. And Strange and Landers were after a quiet dinner, in keeping with the mood they had had upstairs.

Afterward, they had gone across the lobby to the bar for a drink, Strange picking up a bottle at the package store in the corridor.

They could have gone back upstairs. And none of them knew why they went to the bar. The truth was, they were feeling affectionate and, if not in love, felt warm and close. Like lovers, they wanted other people around for contrast.

Needed the audience, Landers thought sourly, later.

The contrast they got in the bar was immediate and cataclysmic. The whole place was packed. And the noise level was commensurate. They got a table for four, luckily, because a party of four got up to leave as they came in. Right behind them crammed against the wall was a long table filled on the three open sides with these Navy people, ranging upward in rank and topped off with two chiefs, one of them an old duffer in his dress whites.

Strange got up to go out to the john, after they were seated and he had poured a drink. And at the same time, behind him, another sailor came in to the long table. It was then the old duffer in dress whites reached over a huge hand and grabbed Strange's seat away from the table. The white uniform had lots of unfamiliar WW I ribbons above the left breast, and he had gold hash marks literally all the way up his left sleeve from the wrist to his insignia.

Something blazed up in Landers' mind like a fire ball. Though the two girls hardly seemed to notice the theft. Keeping his voice carefully empty of rage, Lander stepped over to the long table.

"That seat's taken."

"There was nobody in it," the old chief said.

"Yes there was. My friend just went out to the pisser." Still politely. But the red fire ball had already exploded.

"Didn't you hear him?" the second chief, who was younger and in blues, said contemptuously. "If it was an empty seat, it was free."

"Yeah. You want it, take it," the old chief said, and grinned down the table at his mob.

"Okay. I will," Landers said evenly. The rage in him was threatening to overflow.

But he held it in. And waited. He waited, until he saw Strange come in through the outside door. A full minute, or minute and a half. Strange of course marked them right away. When he saw Strange had seen them, he signaled him with his eyebrows. Meanwhile, the Navy personnel all just stood or sat, however they had been before, looking at him, waiting too. Waiting for him.

"Well?" the younger chief said, smiling with contempt. "You going to take it?"

They really don't know, Landers thought. Who we are. While Strange came on, he studied them. The old chief in white on his left was still seated. The younger chief was on his right, standing. Landers was between them. Beyond the younger chief was the new man, his hand still on the stolen chair. The others were all seated.

Behind him Landers heard Strange say softly, "Go ahead. Bust him."

He swung with his right hand first at the old chief. It went in accurately alongside the nose just under the right eye, cutting deep. Without bothering to look at the effect, he swung with his left at the chief in blues, rolling his body, like a whip, a punch that was half hook, half uppercut. It caught the young chief two inches back from the point of his chin. Landers heard his teeth clap together. He went down.

Landers swung his body to take care of the third man coming in, but Strange had already accounted for him. Swinging his good, left hand in a hook to the belly that swung the moving man back toward himself, Strange clapped him alongside the head and jaw with the plaster plate bound to the open palm of his right hand. The third man went down.

Meanwhile, Landers's second chief was coming back up, valiantly but slowly. Landers hit him with both hands, hook and short rights, in the belly and in the face. One, two; one, two; one two three four. Faster than the eye could count. And as he landed each punch Landers shouted insanely.

"Pay!" he yelled. "Pay! Pay, goddam you! Pay, pay, pay!"

The chief in blues sagged down.

Beyond him Strange grabbed a water pitcher by its handle from a table, ready to crack it in half on a table edge and turn it into a weapon. His right hand was held ready to slap again. "Just come on," he warned in a hiss, as insanely. "Just come on."

The four seated Navy men looked up at the two insane men, astonishment spread over their faces. None was inclined to get up, and wisely they sat still. It had happened with murderous speed and a blinding violence.

Behind Landers a tall, kindly-looking soldier got awkwardly to his feet, and put one arm half around Landers. Landers spun, ready to hit again.

"No, no. Don't swing. Don't swing," the kindly-looking soldier said. He looked worried. "Don't swing. You guys better get out of here. Right now. The MPs will be here in seconds. I've seen them."

Landers swung back to the table. He had one satisfying look at the old chief sprawled against the wall, his chair overturned, bright blood red from below his eye down over the dress whites. "Pay!" he screamed at all of them. "Pay, you cocksuckers! Goddam you, pay!"

Strange had heard the kindly-looking soldier, too, and carefully put his uncracked water pitcher back on its table. He started backing toward the door, his good hand gripping Landers' arm and pulling him.

"You girls go on, you leave," he called to the table. "Meet us upstairs."

Landers followed him. "Don't forget my cane," he called, "don't forget my cane."

At the door a huge MP already blocked the way, his hand on his black holster, and stopped them. He looked in at the now-quiet bar, inspecting the carnage, then looked at the two of them.

"God damn," he said wearily. "You guys. All right, go on. Git. Out that way." He pointed on down the corridor, away from the lobby. "It goes to the street. Move it, damn it."

"We got a room in the hotel," Strange said breathlessly. "A suite, we got."

"Then go around the block, and come back the other way," the MP said. "My partner'll be here in a minute, damn it. He aint as sympathetic."

Strange was already moving, pulling along with his good hand Landers who was limping without his cane, Strange breathlessly already beginning to laugh. Landers was not laughing.

"Appreciate it," Strange called.

"Go fuck," the MP called back, and stepped inside.

"Those dirty fuckers," Landers was muttering, "those dirty fuckers."

"Come on," Strange said, laughing. "We got to move it."

"Let them see something," Landers muttered. "Let them see something."

It was difficult, going clear around the block with Landers limping so badly. He had pulled or turned something in his ankle, and the pain was bothering him. So Strange led them through an alley beyond the hotel, which went around it and came back out on Union.

Thus as they slipped in through the revolving door and across the lobby, they were able to see the MPs and some medics leading the battered Navy group out from the bar. The old chief in his bloody dress whites was on a stretcher, out.

"You don't think I really hurt him, do you?" Landers whispered anxiously in the crowded elevator.

"No," Strange said. "He was just knocked out." Strange was still laughing, and still breathless. Suddenly his eyes glinted meanly. "And what if you did?"

"He was the one who took the chair," Landers whispered. "Just like that. Without so much as a by your leave. But I wouldn't want to hurt him."

Fortunately Strange had already given Annie a key and the girls were in the suite waiting. And immediately there were all the breathless, laughing recapitulations of battle. Everybody had a viewpoint and story of his own to expound.

Landers came out as the unquestioned hero, but Landers was not taking part. He sat off by himself quietly, nursing his ankle, ministered to by Mary Lou who brought him drinks. He kept popping his knuckles and said nothing. "Let them learn something," he would mutter to no one every so often, "let them learn something." The knuckles of his right hand had been seriously barked but he would not let anybody doctor them. "You must have hit teeth somewhere," Strange said happily.

Very shortly after, the four other old-company men and their girls came back in, and the stories had to be told again.

"I tell you," Annie Waterfield said, "I never saw anything like it. It was all so fast. After you left, that tall soldier? Who warned you against the MPs? He went over to them where they were pickin' up that poor chief petty officer in blues, and tryin' to bring the old one to, slappin' his face, and he told them who you all were."

"What do you mean, told them who we were?" Strange said. "He didn't know us."

"He figured it out because of Marion's cane and your hand plaster. You don't want to mess with them, he told those sailors. Those are overseas men from the hospital, who've been wounded. Don't ever fuck with them. They're all crazy. That's exactly what he said. Someone asked him how he knew, and he made this awful grin and said, 'Because I'm one of them.' Then he pulled up his pants leg, and showed them his artificial leg.

"It was just awful. Terrible."

"Maybe he's seen us around the hospital," Strange said. "But I've never seen him. Have you?" he asked Landers.

Landers only shook his head. "No."

"What did you mean?" Annie Waterfield asked him, "when you kept hollerin' Pay?"

"Hollering Pay?" Landers said. "Pay?'

"Yes, Every time you hit somebody you kept hollerin' Pay! Every time, Pay! 'Pay, you sons of bitches! Pay, pay, pay!'"

"I don't know," Landers said hollowly. "I don't remember saying that. I don't know what I meant." He accepted another drink from Mary Lou.

But he thought he did know. It was easy to say it was because of the booze they had put away. That they were drunk. But Landers knew there was something more. Something inside him. Aching to get out. There was something in him aching to get out, but in a way that only a serious fight or series of serious fights would let it get out. Anguish. Love. And hate. And a kind of fragile, short-lived happiness. Which had to be short-lived, if he was going out of this fucking hospital and back into the fucking war. It had just built up in him.

There was no way on earth to explain it to anybody, though. Not without sounding shitty. There was no way to say it.

It had been building up in him ever since that episode on the train with the Air Force sergeant, on his trip home. It was in his fight with his father over the medals. In that time he had tried to talk to Carol Firebaugh and failed so abominably. It had grown and built in him at an even quicker pace, since his awful boo-boo he had made with Prell.

Landers thought that, probably, it had been building in him even longer. Growing. Ever since he was sitting on that damned evil hilltop in New Georgia, with all those other weeping men with the white streaks down their dirty faces, watching the men below in the valley whanging and beating and shooting and killing each other, with such stern, disruptive, concentrated effort.

Anguish. Love. And hate. And happiness. The anguish was for himself. And every poor slob like him, who had ever suffered fear, and terror, and injury at the hands of other men. The love, he didn't know who the love was for. For himself and everybody. For all the sad members of this flawed, misbegotten, miscreated race of valuable creatures, which was trying and failing with such ruptured effort to haul itself up out of the mud and dross and drouth of its crippled heritage. And the hate, implacable, unyielding, was for himself and every other who had ever, in the name of whatever good, maimed or injured or killed another man. The happiness? The happiness was the least, and best, and most important, because the most ironic. The happiness was from those few moments in the fight, when the bars were down, when the weight of responsibility lifted, and he and every man could go in, and destroy and be destroyed, without fear of consequences, with no thought of debt. In short, do all the things they shouldn't and couldn't want to do, or want others to do, when they were responsible.

What a melange. All tossed up in the air and churned around until one element was indistinguishable from another, and the steam from the whole boiling stew seethed and billowed until its pressure forced a safety crack in even the strongest self-control.

Landers suspected something like that was pushing Strange on, too, from the thin explosive laugh he had heard behind him, as Strange had called in a soft but ringing voice, "Go ahead. Bust him."

It was somewhat the feeling that if all of these awful things had been done to so many of them, somebody was going to have to pay, pay, pay, including himself, themselves. What better way was there for all to pay, pay than in a fight, in which he himself, they themselves, were taking lumps and damage, and getting smashed around, too.

It didn't make any sense. None whatsoever. That was why you couldn't tell it to anybody. You couldn't tell that, even to Strange. Landers was about resigned to never being able to tell it.

Did it mean the two of them had a future of such episodes to look forward to? Landers knew somewhere inside of him that he hadn't had enough of it, even yet. And he didn't think Johnny Stranger had either. It seemed to promise ill for any future.

When everything in the suite had quieted down, though he had
to wait quite a long time, he took Mary Lou (Salgraves, was it?) and
hobbled to bed and locked the door and fucked her and made love to
her until her tongue was hanging out and even Mary Lou didn't
want any more. He was pretty sure Johnny Stranger was doing the
same thing on the other side of the suite, behind the other locked
door.

That great sage who had said so wittily that a man didn't want
sex after he had had a fight, didn't know what he was talking about.

On the way home in the cab at five in the morning, drunk like
the others and riding with all four of them, Landers felt Strange
lean against his shoulder and put his mouth against his ear.

"She wanted it, too," Strange coughed a drunken hiccup.

"I didn't do it," Strange whispered, drunkenly, so the other
drunks couldn't hear. "I didn't do it. I almost did. But I just
couldn't quite bring myself to do it."

(from Chapter 19)

[Landers's Suicide]

IT WAS SO SIMILAR to the previous time at Kilrainey that Landers
had a weird, eery sense of déjà vu. There was the same dark,
formalized room. There was the same group of five civilian-looking
men wearing lots of hardware on their collars, behind the same long
table. It had the somber smell of a criminal courtroom. And
Landers suddenly knew he desperately wanted out of the Army.

It had the distinct feel of a repeat performance. Except that now
as Landers went up against this kindly, middle-class, bourgeois
enemy, it was with all the pessimism and experience he had not had
at his fingertips the first time out. Landers knew now that all the
fine promises they made would have nothing to do with him once
he was out in the field again, in the real world. They might not

know that, but Landers did; now. He was prepared at any moment to tell them he wanted to stay in the Army.

But the moment would not come. That was apparently what they were trying to get him to say. But everything they said to him, every question they asked him, seemed to drive him away from the point of wanting to say it.

All the questions they asked him about his abilities and intentions were the same questions the five men at Kilrainey had asked him. All the statements they made about wanting to use his talents, his experience, were the same statements made at Kilrainey.

Finally the round-faced, jowly man in the middle wearing glasses, a full colonel among three other full colonels in the five but plainly the chief, asked him in a perplexed, slightly amused voice, "Well, Sergeant, what kind of job in the Army would you like?"

Drawing himself up, his voice fluting with the rage he was trying to hold down, Landers gave the only answer he felt he could give them. "Sir, there's no job in the Army I want," he said stolidly.

"All right, that's all. You may go," the bespectacled colonel said.

The word was around the ward almost before he could get back to it. Landers was out. The board had voted, unanimously, to discharge him. So many other prisoners, who saw this as a major triumph, rushed over to him to congratulate him and slap him on the back that the morose Landers finally insulted them and ran them all off, cursing.

After that, he was even more of a marked man. Not only was he out while all of them were still in, but they did not like it because he had rejected their well-meant congratulations. All of them left him strictly alone.

It didn't really matter. The winding-down, the mechanics, took only five days. Five days, from the meeting of the board till Landers was out on the street, a free man. The wheels ground slowly, but once they got started, they rolled very fast. And much of the last three of the five days was spent out of the ward, signing releases in first one office then another. Landers wasn't in the ward that much to suffer his new rejection. Anyway, he didn't care what they thought. He wasn't like them.

He went to the Finance office, to sign his last payroll. He went to the QM office, to turn in the last of his gear. To the Insurance office, to keep or cancel his GI insurance. Landers decided to cancel his. If he was going out, he did not want any more to do with the Army than was obligatory. Most of the rest was done in offices in the hospital HQ section itself.

As was required by the regulations, everywhere he went an armed guard had to go with him. He was still a prisoner. But it was indicative of his status that the pistol-wearing MP joked with him and hardly bothered to watch him. No guy who was going out in two days was going to run off from a guard.

In retrospect it seemed like a wild, fantastic rush, the last five days. Then on the morning of the sixth he was signing his last paper, which was the receipt for his engraved, pure, white Honorable Discharge which was tendered to him. That took place in the hospital clerical office itself.

Then, totally unprepared for it, he was suddenly out in the street in front of the hospital, in uniform, with an old blue barracks bag half full of personal gear, a free man able to go anywhere he pleased to go.

He walked the three blocks down to the bus stop, and waited there. After a moment, he set the bag on the frozen ground. A bus for Luxor should be along in a little bit. It was a dry day, but cold, and a little snowy on the ground.

Landers huddled down into his GI greatcoat. In front of him on the asphalt main street a long column of men in fatigues and field jackets marched by, wearing the Divisional patch of the new infantry Division, their faces gaunt and haunted and worn-down looking. It took them a long time to pass, and Landers watched them.

It had been running through his mind all the places he was now free to go. Places these guys couldn't go. He would probably wind up going home, to Indiana, in the end. To his lousy family. The thought of going home filled him with anguish. But he didn't have to do that yet.

Normally he would have gone into Luxor to the Peabody to see Johnny Stranger. But Strange had told him during his visit that in two or three days' time, from then, he would be coming back to duty himself. Somewhere here on the post at O'Bruyerre. That meant Landers would have to go up to see Winch at the Command building and say good-by to him, in order to find out where Strange was. And Landers didn't have the stomach for that at the moment. Of course, he could always go in to the Peabody by himself. Though Strange was giving up the suite, Strange had said, having run out of money.

In front of him the last of the troop column had made their right turn off of the main road, and were dwindling away down one of the hole-pocked gravel side roads. Behind them on the main road, coming fast, was a civilian car, but with post plates. Driven by a woman. Women were so important.

Landers watched the last of the troops dwindle, getting smaller and smaller, their breaths throwing out the same plumes as before, but now at this distance the plumes seemed bigger than they were. Landers was devoutly glad he wasn't one of them. On the other hand, he had no desire really to go in to the Peabody all by himself. Even if he could get a room, this late.

Landers watched the woman coming on in the car. She was very good-looking, even at a distance. Probably some officer's wife. But she was really going too fast. Landers bent with the tie rope of the barracks bag he was holding, and rolled it meticulously down and around onto the top of the bag, and then stood teetering on his heels and watching her.

Just as she was about to come level with him on the road, Landers stepped out off the curb in front of her.

As he stepped out, he realized he would not have done it if she had been a man, driving a jeep or a GI truck. But she really was so beautiful. Her coat was thrown back open in the heat of the car, and in the sweater under it her breasts swelled out thrusting their weight against the lapels deliciously. So delicious. And her hair fell to the collar of the coat with an equally delicious feminine grace.

Landers heard the wild squeal of the brakes. And perhaps a cry. And then the crash of glass and tear of headlight metal. And a loud thumping thud.

He saw or thought he saw the look of horror that came across her face in back of the windshield. Because she thought she was doing something wrong, and he wanted to laugh. The mouth a wildly spread O of lipstick. Eyebrows arched up. Eyes staring. He hated to do all that to her. But, by God, at least she knew she had hit something. Then the helicopter moved away from the ship.

The big red crosses were still on its white flank. And the sea still moved backward along its waterline. Everything was still silence.

Far off, the great blue continent still stood. Uninhabited. Green with the silent, unpeopled forests and soft grasses. The breakers clashing on the white, unpeopled sands. And the silence of home.

(from Chapter 28)

[The Death of Prell]

WHEN WE LAST LEFT Prell in Chapter 29, he was on his bond-selling tour in Kansas City, Lincoln, and Denver. Strange had telephoned him from Luxor in the Muehlebach Hotel in Kansas City to tell him of Marion Landers' death. Prell was feeling guilty about his own lack of reaction, during his talk with Strange, to Landers' apparent suicide. As with the others, he was being beset with nightmares involving the squad again, the patrol on New Georgia, and in his dreams Landers was now one of the dead. He was guilty also about his own position, the Medal of Honor hero, which he did not believe he deserved. He felt he was making speeches for a living—that he had become an entertainer, part of a vaudeville team.

His reaction when he returned briefly to Luxor from this first bond-selling tour was to avoid getting in touch with either Strange or Winch. He did not want to see them; he did not want to expose himself to the ridicule he imagined he would provoke in them because of what he considered his false role as a public relations man.

All he had left now, Prell felt, was his son-and-father relationship with former colonel, now Brigadier General Stevens, the commander of the hospital, a kindly relationship which began with Stevens' first visit to Prell in the hospital when the doctors were threatening to amputate his leg, and deepened as the months passed.

But in a scene with Brigadier Stevens in his office in the hospital in Luxor, Prell found to his sorrow that Stevens did not truly understand his feelings of guilt and inadequacy, and that in fact Stevens never had understood him. Prell did not feel up to explaining to Stevens what he believed to be his hypocritical role as a salesman and a fake hero.

Prell left his session with Stevens more desolate than ever, realizing that perhaps Strange and Winch were the only two people who genuinely did sympathize with what was happening to him. But he was still unwilling to call either one of them.

Warrant Officer Jack Alexander informed Winch that Prell had returned to the Luxor hospital for a few days. As far as Alexander could see, in his uncomprehending attitude, Prell was all right. Winch had hoped that Prell would come and see him and Strange, but his talk with Alexander nonetheless reassured him.

Prell was then ordered more or less permanently to Los Angeles with Major Kurntz and the same public relations crew with which he had made his first bond-selling trip. Since he had had a highly unsatisfactory reunion with his pregnant wife, Della Mae, and his ambitious mother-in-law in Luxor, he took an apartment in Los Angeles and did not give them his telephone number or address.

In Los Angeles Prell made a couple of appearances with several movie stars and starlets. But after his first speech there, which was a huge success, he got drunk and went out that night in the limousine which had been put at his disposal with its Army driver, a sergeant. He ran around down in the low-bar areas of Los Angeles and ended up in a seedy bar filled with drunk servicemen. The driver waited for him outside.

With all the accumulated rage burning in him, he tried to pick a fight. But with his bad legs he was practically incapable of self-defense. Just as the irate soldiers whom he had insulted and challenged were about to beat him up, perhaps even kill him, one of them suddenly recognized the Medal of Honor ribbon he was wearing on his blouse, and then remembered him from his pictures in the Los Angeles papers. The soldier said: "Good God, we're about to beat up on a Medal of Honor winner!" and stopped the fight.

The soldiers found out that there was a sergeant waiting for Prell in the limousine outside the bar. They went and got him. The soldier who had recognized Prell warned the sergeant, "He shouldn't be in a place like this." The sergeant took Prell home. He did not inform Major Kurntz of what had happened, thinking that he was protecting Prell, and doing so with his natural soldier's instinct not ever to tell the authorities anything they did not already know.

The next speech was in Bakersfield. The entire bond-selling group drove out in limousines for the evening "performance." After his speech, Prell repeated the same pattern with a different driver. He got very drunk and asked the driver to let him off at another tough bar.

He got out of the limousine and hobbled into the bar on his ruined legs. There was an expression on his face of hard desperate determination. He walked into the bar. It was a green place, smoke-filled, with the rattling of pool balls, and mean drunken soldiers at the tables and on the bar stools, and a couple of poker games in the corner. After two or three drinks he began to bait some of the servicemen around him, and picked another fight. This time he was not recognized by the soldiers. The result was a bloody brawl, with Prell at the center, in which he seriously hurt someone. In the smoky haze one of the soldiers picked up a pool cue. He hit Prell over the head with it and killed him.

The sergeant driver, having heard the noise, rushed into the bar and saw Prell bleeding on the floor. He felt his pulse. He told the men what they had done, told them whom they had killed. The soldiers were horrified, but left the impression that Prell had brought it all on himself, as in fact he had done, deliberately picking the fight with them.

(Chapter 32)

[Winch and the Wurlitzers]

THIS BRIEF CHAPTER is from Winch's viewpoint after learning of the death of Prell. In this chapter we see the progressive deterioration of Winch. He goes crazy.

We have already seen the signs of Winch's imminent crackup: the night he saw the image of one of the platoon's dead infantrymen on the windshield of his car and skidded off the road; his urge to pinch the Gray Lady at Prell's wedding; his wild poker game at the

Claridge and later his burning Jack Alexander's IOU; his bad dreams of the Japanese charging with the bayonet during the mortar fire and of the soldier in no man's land being wounded over and over again with no hope of rescue; the fart in the Peabody restaurant; his hatred for the two Wurlitzer jukeboxes in the main PX, which he viewed as the world of the future—"chrome, and pipe, and plastic, and whirling iridescent lights, and jarred, canned music"; his pent-up grief over the death of Landers. All of this mental stress was compounded by the increasing symptoms of congestive heart failure. When Strange left Winch in the Camp O'Bruyerre PX at the end of Chapter 30, he "did not think Winch looked good at all."

"Prell and Landers and Strange were what was left to him of his real life," the author wrote in Chapter 22. And now Winch hears of the death of Prell.

Beginning with Winch's dwelling on the fate of Prell, the action in this chapter took place in May, 1944, not long before the D-Day invasion.

Winch was still seeing Carol, buy they were beginning to make their farewells. He had not yet broken up with her—she was not leaving Luxor until June—but he had in fact pushed her toward leaving and encouraged her to marry her new boyfriend from Ohio. When she finally departed, it was the end of their affair.

During the time he was making his farewells to Carol, and advising her to marry the second lover rather than the boy from Luxor, Winch had been wandering down to the grenade range of Camp O'Bruyerre in the afternoons. Being a top sergeant and now a junior warrant officer, he was on friendly terms with the grenade officer and grenade warrant officer, and there was a lot of amiable banter among them as they watched the raw draftees learn about hand grenades. While he was there one afternoon, when no one was looking he casually picked up a couple of grenades and slipped one into each pocket of his coat, then walked away unnoticed. Later, in his room, he unscrewed them with a pair of pliers and poured the powder into a jar, which he hid. For two or three nights he slept with the defused grenades under his pillow.

Then late one night, after he had been in the main PX drinking wine against the contradictory blasts of the two Wurlitzer jukeboxes, he returned to his room and put the powder back in the grenades. He waited for the base to quieten down. At 3:00 A.M. he put the grenades into his pockets and snuck across the deserted grounds to the PX.

Winch broke the window of the PX with the butt of one of the grenades. Then, very slowly and deliberately, he pulled out the pins and tossed the grenades one at a time through the broken windows into the empty room, so that they rolled across the floor and landed under the Wurlitzer machines.

Winch moved away and ducked. A terrific explosion followed, blowing up not only the Wurlitzers but most of the PX as well. Smoke and debris were everywhere.

Winch allowed the wreckage to settle and then peered in through the broken window at the results of his raid. He began to laugh maniacally. In not time at all the MPs descended on the area in jeeps. They spotted Winch hiding in the shrubbery. He tried to run from them, still laughing wildly, but because of his heart condition he could not get away from them, he bent over with breathlessness, and the MPs captured him and took him away. He wound up in the hospital prison ward.

(Chapter 33)

[Strange's Suicide]

IN THIS, the final chapter of Book 5—"The End of It"—and the novel, the viewpoint is Johnny Strange's, the last one of the old company.

The time shift from Winch's incarceration in the mental ward to the concluding chapter is roughly a month and a half, late June after the D-Day invasion. Strange was now happily set in with the infantry Division to which he had persuaded Winch to transfer him. With the destruction of the old company, he had given all his loyalties, affections, and emotions to his new company and Division. But curiously enough, having left the communications outfit in exactly the way he wanted, he now found he was so attached to the new men in the infantry unit that it was almost impossible for him, with his foreknowledge of what they were about to go through (they did not have this foreknowledge, and would be going into combat innocently), to relive the whole experience. This was to be the climax of Strange's story and the book.

In this last chapter, Strange and his new outfit were en route to England and Europe in a large troop convoy. It was generally known among the men that they would be thrown into the fighting in western France as cannon fodder as soon as possible.

The troop convoy was several days out from New York in the Atlantic. It was late on a foggy night and Strange was wandering around the ship alone. A series of flashback scenes took place in Strange's mind as he moved about. He pondered the fate of the old company.

He thought first of Winch. He remembered the early morning at Camp O'Bruyerre when someone at headquarters told him about Winch's mad raid on the PX. There was very little he could do to help Winch that morning, although he got a pass and loitered around outside the hospital prison ward for a long time.

Then Strange remembered going to the hospital ward the next day to visit Winch. As he walked down the corridor, Strange heard Winch crying out from his room that same old phrase from the day on Hill 27 on Guadalcanal: *"Get them out! Get them out of there! Can't you see the mortars got them bracketed!"* Strange acknowledged then to his sorrow that there was no point in visiting Winch, and he went back to his new outfit, which was getting ready to ship out to dry dock in New York. Just before he left Camp O'Bruyerre, another soldier told him he had seen Winch looking out the barred window of the mental ward shouting the same words.

Now, as he was roaming about the troop ship in the North Atlantic, Strange's thoughts turned to his wife, Linda, whom he realized he still loved, although he knew she could not care less. Then he thought of Marion Landers, and finally of his terrible grief when he had learned of the death of Bobby Prell in the bar fight in California.

As Strange looked out on the ocean and on the other darkened ships in the convoy moving eastward to Europe, there was an echo in his memory of their hospital ship from the Pacific as it finally approached the American landfall, "the great blue continent," almost a year before. Just as with Landers when he was struck by the car at Camp O'Bruyerre, Strange remembered as in a dream the slow white ship with the huge red crosses on its sides, his visits to Prell in the old main lounge where the serious casualties were segregated—"the repository, the collection-place and bank, of all human evil," his gazing out the window port on the California shore in the calm moonless night.

From these thoughts of the hospital ship those months before, Strange returned to reality, to the troop convoy:

At this point comes the final scene, the final climax, the final everything of the book...

As Strange gets out of the crowded hold with all the stinks and smells of overcrowded men, he goes up on deck in the drizzly, foggy night—an unpleasant night, quite chilly, although it is June—and leans against the boat davit.

He faces finally the fact that he simply cannot go through the whole process again. He simply can't go into England and into Europe with this new outfit knowing what he knows from the Pacific, and sit back in his relatively safe position as a mess sergeant and watch the young men be killed and maimed and lost. He can't stand being a witness again to all the anguish and mayhem and blood and suffering.

And when he reaches this realization he sees what a trap he has placed himself in by insisting that he should go to Europe, and that he should go in an outfit, an infantry Division, that he likes rather then the old Signal Corps unit he had a great deal of power in and didn't really care that much about.

With all this in his head, somewhat on the spur of the moment, wearing his overcoat, his helmet, his boots, and in the chill night his woolen gloves, he grabs the railing by the boat davit and just slips over the side, quietly without anyone around. No one hears, no one notices.

As he hits the water he himself is shocked by what he has done. It was such a sudden thing that he didn't know he was going to do it.

He treads water in the sea as the ship moves away and out of sight in the fog and the night. He doesn't try to attract attention... As he watches the ship go away he's not distressed really. And in his full uniform he treads water alone, the ship slowly moving out of sight in the fog.

He thinks now that he is never going to know the answer to those peculiar dreams of Roman justice or injustice he had both times coming out of the anesthetic during his hand operations. All that Strange thinks with a certain regret is that he will never find out now.

And then as he's treading water with his woolen GI gloves, he can feel the cold beginning to swell his hands. And from this, in a sort of semihallucination, all of him begins to seem to swell and he gets bigger and bigger, until he can see the ship moving away or thinks he can. And then he goes on getting bigger and bigger and swelling and swelling until he's bigger than the ocean, bigger than the planet, bigger than the solar system, bigger than the galaxy out in the universe.

And as he swells and grows this picture of a fully clothed soldier with his helmet, his boots, and his GI woolen gloves seems to be taking into himself all of the pain and anguish and sorrow and misery that is the lot of all soldiers, taking it into himself and into the universe as well.

And then still in the hallucination he begins to shrink back to normal, and shrinks down through the other stages—the galaxy, the solar system, the planet, the ocean—back to Strange in the water. And then continues shrinking until he seems to be only the size of a seahorse, and then an amoeba, then finally an atom.

He did not know whether he would drown first or freeze.

(Chapter 34)

WWII

(1975)

In 1974, Jones returned from Paris. He first taught creative writing at Florida International University; then he and Gloria purchased the farmhouse in Sagaponack, New York, that they shared with their children Kaylie and Jamie. About the same time, Jones agreed to collaborate on a book about "World War II graphic art" with Art Weithas, the former head art director of *Yank* magazine. Weithas was in charge of the reproduction of the art in the volume, while Jones wrote the accompanying commentary. The result of this fortunate collaboration was one of the best and most instructive of Jones's books, *WWII*, published by Grosset & Dunlap. Weithas's reproductions, ranging from the realistic to the humorous and satiric, are superb; and Jones's commentary on them is rich and incisive. Especially memorable is his analysis of the combat illustrations of Howard Brodie ("Brodie somehow had permanently captured on paper the filth and misery and fatigue we had lived through... somebody *had* understood. We *did* exist, after all"); Tom Lea (Lea captured the essence of "combat numbness," the state of willed mental self-annihilation necessary for enduring battle); and Kerr Eby (more than any other artist, Jones says, Eby drew the grim "anonymity" of combat—the condition that Jones had so effectively captured in prose in *The Thin Red Line*).

In *WWII*, Jones analyzes the war from an enlisted man's point of view. At one point, he asserts that "as in most wars, in the United States in World War II... most of the commanding was done by the upper classes, and most of the fighting was done by the lower."

Inevitably, Jones says, the upper-class historian writes from a viewpoint of idealism and economic security. As a result, the vision of this upper-class historian is distorted and limited: "and this is not to say that the ideals are not eminently admirable. But they have almost no effect on your proletarian infantry soldier...."

Besides Jones's art commentary and proletarian war analysis, there is another, even more instructive, strand in *WWII*. It is in this book that Jones most fully develops his concept of "the evolution of the soldier," which is the unifying idea of the army trilogy. The selections that follow have been chosen primarily to show the crucial stages in this process. The third selection briefly outlines Jones's own experience in the "pretty primitive" Guadalcanal campaign. The selection entitled "The Big War" describes the desperate hedonism on the homefront. "Hospital" describes Jones's convalescence during 1943 in a military hospital in Memphis, Tennessee—the inspiration for the fictional Luxor, Tennessee, of *Whistle*.

THE EVOLUTION OF A SOLDIER

Almost all war art is by definition propaganda. No government is going to commission its nation's artists to go out in the field and paint and draw the awful animal indecencies to which war subjects its citizens. Any government will want to make its cause and its action look as palatable as possible. Thus, there is a tendency to depict and perpetuate the good and let the bad get conveniently lost, which became increasingly apparent in the collections we looked at. If one is to believe the complete collections of *Yank* and *Stars and Stripes*, there *were* no bitter American soldiers in the whole of World War II. Even the death shown (and one must show a little death, if one is doing a war) is generally "good" death, meaningful death, clean death. All of this has given rise today to the idea, particularly among the veterans of the Vietnam War, that World War II should be thought of as a good war, a "pure" war. (So strong still is our American's firm and steadfast Puritan need for a "purity" in everything of value.)

And yet every now and then, poring through the collections, one sees a given artist, as though pressed beyond his official commitment by his own emotions, suddenly breaking out momentarily from this more or less unstated conspiracy to tell the folks back home only the "meaningful"; and then the work can rise to the level of greatness in art, which in the end can probably be defined simplistically as telling the whole truth beautifully, to create catharsis.

But there is an even greater power than government at work here. Physiologically we are so constructed that it is impossible for us to remember pain. We can remember the experience of having had pain but we cannot recall the pain itself. Try it sometime. In your next meditation session, reflect on your last dental appointment. In the same way our psychic memory is constantly at work winnowing out the bad and the unpleasant from our remembered experience, to leave and file away only the good parts and the pleasant. A summer day from childhood is remembered for the way the sun fell like greenish gold through the leaves of the maple trees and for the hot still quiet of anticipation in the air, not for the way one's mother cried out harshly across the back yard to get back to work weeding the tomatoes. It would seem the internal Universe as well as the external is built on the principle of letting the dead past bury its dead.

Thus we old men can in all good conscience sit over our beers at the American Legion on Friday nights and recall with affection moments of terror thirty years before. Thus we are are able to tell the youngsters that it wasn't all really so bad. Perhaps fortunately for us all, there appears to be a psychic process one might label THE DE-EVOLUTION OF A SOLDIER, as well as the process I call THE EVOLUTION OF A SOLDIER.

And perhaps because of it, perhaps the hardest thing is to try to recreate it as it really was.

IN THE BEGINNING

There was never any question about the beginning of World War II for the United States. Pearl Harbor began it crisply and decisively and without discussion.

Absolutely nobody was prepared for it. At Schofield Barracks in the infantry quadrangles, those of us who were up were at breakfast. On Sunday mornings in those days there was a bonus ration of a half-pint of milk, to go with your eggs or pancakes and syrup, also Sunday specials. Most of us were more concerned with getting and holding onto our half-pints of milk than with listening to the explosions that began rumbling up toward us from Wheeler Field two miles away. "They doing some blasting?" some old-timer said through a mouthful of pancakes. It was not till the first low-flying fighter came skidding, whammering low overhead with his MGs going that we ran outside, still clutching our half-pints of milk to keep them from being stolen, aware with a sudden sense of awe that we were seeing and acting in a genuine moment of history.

As we stood outside in the street huddled back against the dayroom wall, another fighter with the red suns on its wings came up the boulevard, preceded by two lines of holes that kept popping up eighty yards in front on the asphalt. As he came abreast of us, he gave us a typically toothy grin and waved, and I shall never forget his face behind the goggles. A white silk scarf streamed out behind his neck and he wore a white ribbon around his helmet just above the goggles, with a red spot in the center of his forehead. I would learn later that this ribbon was a *hachimaki*, the headband worn by medieval samurai when going into battle, usually with some religious slogan of Shinto or Emperor worship inked on it.

One of the first rules Weithas and I made for this book was that we would use no art work that was not done at the time by the original combat artists, and here I am breaking my own rule right at the beginning. But the painting shown here, done by Robert T. McCall in 1971, was so like my Jap pilot over Schofield on December 7 that I simply had to include it.

There weren't many American artists standing around waiting to paint Pearl Harbor, since the Japanese had not informed us of their plans. Lieutenant Commander Coale's panorama shows clearly the destruction the Japanese achieved. On the left the battleship *Nevada* is steaming away with three near-misses geysering around her. Behind the capsized minelayer *Oglala* the *California* has already settled. On the right the *Oklahoma* has capsized hull up, the *Maryland* burning behind her. Far right the *Arizona* (now the monument), afire and under explosive attack, is settling. Lieutenant Commander G. B. Coale did this painting in 1944. Coale was in a large measure responsible for creating the whole navy art program, which is one of the most beautiful of all the collections, if perhaps a bit depersonalized. You have to try and imagine yourself standing on one of those flaming decks with explosions going up all around you and the water ablaze with burning fuel.

Battleship Row was turned into a living inferno and men there, precipitated into full-scale war without previous experience and with no preparation, performed feats of incredible heroism and rescue that seemed unbelievable later. Men dove overboard from red-hot decks to try to swim a hundred yards underwater beneath the oil and gasoline fires that spread over the surface. Some made it, God knows how. One sailor told of seeing a bomb land beside a buddy who was just starting to climb an exterior ship's ladder. When the fumes cleared, he saw the concussion had blown the buddy completely through the ladder and into neatly rectangular chunks the size of the ladder openings. "But I don't think he ever knew what hit him," the sailor said with a shaky smile.

Looking at Coale's painting, it seems to me that he minimized the vast amount of smoke from the fires. Later that Sunday in mid-afternoon, when in the confusion and shock my unit, along with several hundred others, finally pulled out of Schofield for our defensive beach positions, we passed Pearl Harbor. We could see the huge rising smoke columns high in the clear sunny Hawaiian air for miles before we ever got near Pearl. I shall never forget the sight as we passed over the lip of the central plateau and began the long drop down to Pearl City.

Down toward the towering smoke columns as far as the eye could see, the long line of army trucks, each with its splash of "OD"—the olive-drab field uniform shirts—wound serpentlike up and down the draws of red dirt through the green of cane and pineapple. Machine guns (MGs) were mounted on the cab roofs of every truck possible. I remember thinking with a sense of the profoundest awe that none of our lives would ever be the same, that a social, even a cultural watershed had been crossed which we could never go back over, and I wondered how many of us would survive to see the end results. I wondered if I would. I had just turned twenty, the month before.

I expect most of us felt about the same, if many were less able to verbalize it. It was one of the first, tiniest steps in what I've labeled THE EVOLUTION OF A SOLDIER. Many had taken multiple giant strides along the path that day. And many had gone right on out the other end of the tunnel, without taking any steps at all.

GUADALCANAL

Guadalcanal was the first American offensive anywhere, and as such got perhaps more than its fair share of notoriety, both in history and in the media of the time; more than later, perhaps tougher fights such as Tarawa and Peleliu. Fought at an earlier period of the war, when the numbers and matériel engaged were smaller, less trained and less organized, there was an air of adventure and sense of individual exploit about it (at least in the press) where small units of platoon and company strength still maintained importance, more than in the later battles of massed armadas, masses of newer equipment, and massed units of men in division and corps strength. It was still pretty primitive, Guadalcanal.

Everybody now knows, at least everybody of my generation, how the marines landed virtually unopposed on the 'Canal itself, after heavy fights on two smaller islands, Tulagi and Gavutu; how the Japanese, for reasons of their own deciding not to accept their first defeat, kept pouring men and equipment into the island; how Major General Vandegrift's tough First Marine Division, learning as they went along, fought them to a standstill, while the navy sank their loaded transports of reinforcements behind them—until in the end they were finally forced to evacuate it anyway. Not many, even of my generation, know that from about mid-November, 1942, on, U.S. infantry was doing much of the fighting on Guadalcanal, and from mid-December were doing it all. The doughty First Marine Division, dead beat, ill and tired, decimated by wounds and tropical diseases, but evolved into soldiers at last, had been relieved and evacuated.

The first elements of the American Division had landed in mid-October. The first elements of my outfit landed in late November, the rest in early December. No living soul looking at us, seeing us come hustling ashore to stare in awe at the hollow-eyed, vacant-faced, mean-looking First Marines, could have believed that in three months from that day we would be known as the famed Twenty-fifth Infantry Tropic Lightning Division, bearing the shoulder patch of the old Hawaiian Division Poi Leaf, with a streak of lightning running vertically through it. In the interim we had taken over from the First Marines, prosecuted the final offensive on the 'Canal, chased the Japanese to Tassafaronga in the whirlwind windup which gave us our name, and begun to move up to New Georgia for the next fight of our campaign. By then we would have had a fair amount of casualties and sick, and as a division and as individuals have made our own EVOLUTION OF A SOLDIER.

My own part in all of this was relatively undistinguished. I fought as an infantry corporal in a rifle company in a regiment of the Twenty-fifth, part of the time as an assistant squad leader, part of the time attached to the company headquarters. I went where I was told to go, and did what I was told to do, but no more. I was scared shitless just about all of the time. On the third day of a fight for a complex of hills called "The Galloping Horse" I was wounded in the head through no volition of my own, by a random mortar shell, spent a week in the hospital, and came back to my unit after the fight and joined them for the relatively little that was left of the campaign. I came out of it with a Purple Heart and a Bronze Star for "heroic or meritorious achievement" (not the V-for-Valor one), which was given to me apparently by a process as random as that of the random mortar shell that hit me. At least, I don't know anything I ever did to earn it. I was shipped out after the campaign for an injured ankle that had to be operated on.

It's funny, the things that get to you. One day a man near me was hit in the throat, as he stood up, by a bullet from a burst of MG fire. He cried out, "Oh, my God!" in an awful, grimly comic, burbling kind of voice that made me think of the signature of the old Shep Fields' Rippling Rhythm band. There was awareness in it, and a tone of having expected it, then he fell down, to all intents and purposes dead. I say "to all intents and purposes" because his vital functions may have continued for a while. But he appeared unconscious, and of course there was nothing to do for him with his throat artery torn out. Thinking about him, it seemed to me that his yell had been for all of us lying there, and I felt like crying.

Another time I heard a man yell out "I'm killed!" as he was, although he didn't die for about fifteen minutes. But he might have yelled the same thing and not been killed.

One of the most poignant stories about our outfit was one I didn't see myself, but only heard about later. I was in the hospital when it happened. One of our platoon sergeants, during a relatively light Japanese attack on his position, reached into his pocket for a grenade he'd stuck there, and got it by the pin. The pin came out but the grenade didn't. No one really knows what he thought about during those split seconds. What he did was turn away and put his back against a bank to smother the grenade away from the rest of his men. He lived maybe five or ten minutes afterward, and the only thing he said, in a kind of awed, scared, very disgusted voice, was, "What a fucking recruit trick to pull."

A lot of the posthumous Medals of Honor that are given are given because men smothered grenades or shells with their bodies to protect the men around them. Nobody ever recommended our platoon sergeant for a Medal of Honor that I know of. Perhaps it was because he activated the grenade himself.

I think I screamed, myself, when I was hit. I thought I could vaguely remember somebody yelling. I blacked out for several seconds, and had a dim impression of someone stumbling to his feet with his hands to his face. It wasn't me. Then I came to myself several yards down the slope, bleeding like a stuck pig and blood running all over my face. It must have been a dramatic scene. As soon as I found I wasn't dead or dying, I was pleased to get out of there as fast as I could. According to the rules, my responsibility to stay ceased as soon as I was hurt. It really wasn't so bad, and hadn't hurt at all. The thing I was most proud of was that I remembered to toss my full canteen of water to one of the men from the company headquarters lying there.

SOLDIER'S EVOLUTION

What was it, really, this EVOLUTION OF A SOLDIER? What is it still? I've been talking about it all through this book, but I'm not sure I can explain or define it. I think that when all the nationalistic or ideological propaganda and patriotic slogans are put aside, all the straining to convince a soldier that he is dying *for* something, it is the individual soldier's final full acceptance of the fact that his name is already written down in the rolls of the already dead.

Every combat soldier, if he follows far enough along the path that began with his induction, must, I think, be led inexorably to that awareness. He must make a compact with himself or with Fate that he is lost. Only then can he function as he ought to function, under fire. He knows and accepts beforehand that he's dead, although he may still be walking around for a while. That soldier you have walking around there with this awareness in him is the final end product of the EVOLUTION OF A SOLDIER.

Between those two spectator episodes I described earlier, that first air raid we watched and cheered albeit guiltily, and the naval night battle we watched and cheered with callous pleasure, something had happened to us. Between those two points in time, somewhere during our first long tour up on the line, we changed. Consciously or unconsciously we accepted the fact that we couldn't survive. So we could watch the naval battle from the safety of the hills with undisguised fun.

There is no denying we were pleased to see somebody else getting his. Even though there were men dying. Being blown apart, concussed, drowning. Didn't matter. We had been getting ours, let them get theirs. It wasn't that we were being sadistic. It was just that we had nothing further to worry about. We were dead.

Now, not every man can accept this. A few men accept it immediately and at once, with a kind of feverish, self-destructive joy. The great majority of men don't want to accept it. They can accept it, though. And do accept it, if their outfit keeps going back up there long enough. The only alternative is to ask to be relieved and admit you are a coward, and that of course is against the law. They put you in prison.

And yet, strangely, for everyone, the acceptance and the giving up of hope create and reinstill hope in a kind of reverse-process mental photo-negative function. Little things become significant. The next meal, the next bottle of booze, the next kiss, the next sunrise, the next full moon. The next bath. Or as the Bible might have said, but didn't quite, Sufficient unto the day is the existence thereof.

This is a hard philosophy. But then the soldier's profession is a hard profession, in wartime. A lot of men like it, though, and even civilian soldiers have been known to stay on and make it their life's work. It has its excitements and compensations. One of them is that, since you have none yourself, you are relieved of any responsibility for a future. And everything tastes better.

It is absolutely true, for example, that when you think, when you *know*, you are going off to die somewhere soon, every day has a special, bright, delicious, poignant taste to it that normal days in normal times do not have. Another perversity of the human mechanism?

Some men like to live like that all the time. Some are actually sorry to come home and see it end. Even those of us who hated it found it exciting, sometimes. That is what the civilian people never understand about their returned soldiers, in any war, Vietnam as well. They cannot understand how we could hate it, and still like it; and they do not realize they have a lot of dead men around them, dead men who are walking around and breathing. Some men find it hard to come back from their EVOLUTION OF A SOLDIER. Some never come back at all, not completely. That's where the DE-EVOLUTION OF A SOLDIER comes in. Sometimes it takes at least as long to accomplish as its reverse process did.

Everything the civilian soldier learned and was taught from the moment of his induction was one more delicate step along this path of the soldier evolving toward acceptance of his death. The idea that his death, under certain circumstances, is correct and right. The training, the discipline, the daily humiliations, the privileges of "brutish" sergeants, the living en masse like schools of fish, are all directed toward breaking down the sense of the sanctity of the physical person, and toward hardening the awareness that a soldier is the chattel (hopefully a proud chattel, but a chattel all the same) of the society he serves and was born a member of. And is therefore as dispensable as the ships and guns and tanks and ammo he himself serves and dispenses. Those are the terms of the contract he has made—or, rather, that the state has handed him to sign.

Most men in a war are never required to pay up in full on the contract for the life the state has loaned them. For every combat soldier there are about fifteen or twenty men required to maintain and service him who are never in much danger, if any. But everybody pays interest on the loan, and the closer to the front he gets the higher the interest rate. If he survives at all, it can take him a long time to get over the fact he isn't going to have to pay.

GREEN AND OBSCENE

The worst thing about being a seasoned soldier was they wouldn't let you go home. Your experience was needed, sorely needed, they told you, you yourself—that is, your body and its recently acquired skills—were at least ten times as valuable as when you were a green hand. So that the better you became, the less chance you had. About the only hope left was a serious wound.

It was probably simple vanity and pride which made Eisenhower, Marshall and company believe untested U.S. soldiers could go headlong straight on into the France of Hitler's "Fortress Europe" and win. The U.S. officer corps of those far-off days before the war lived in a sort of sealed-off plastic shell of their own making which could support such unrealistic dreams. The Great Depression years hurt them less than most citizens. Low-salaried though they were, their creature comforts were well seen to, by even lower-salaried enlisted slaves: and they could live well on their well-gardened, manicured posts and forts with booze and food at PX prices, and conduct their obsolete little training exercises with the same flair that they used to conduct the Saturday night Officers' Club dances. Polo was a great sport among them, for example, in those days when the use of horseless armor was just being understood. But they were brave men, and dedicated, and intelligent, great men a few of them, and with a Churchill and a Roosevelt to guide them, and some time in the field in a war to humble them a little, they could and would do great things to preserve the nation.

In the meantime, while the army leaders and the heads of state and their entourages gathered to debate the movement and the use of masses of lesser mortals and the millions of long tons of supplies needed to maintain them (gathered to decide, in fact, the actuarial statistics of death for tens and scores of thousands), the civilian soldier objects of this loving attention (and it was loving) themselves slogged on ahead, fighting and fearing one day, sleeping wet in

mud the next. Gasping on the desert and in the hills (or puking and
shaking with malaria in the jungles), his total horizon limited to
from one to about five hundred yards in front of him, the private,
noncom or junior officer knew little about what was going on or the
grand design for his life for the next year. Or two years. Or three
years.

There was no way for him to know. Strategic aims and planning,
for simple reasons of security, could not be handed down to the
rank and file. Even if he knew them, they wouldn't change his life
much, or what he had to do. They might very well change his
death date, but why tell him that. Anyway, he knew that (or
suspected it) already.

The worst thing about being green was that he didn't know what
to look for or listen for, or smell for. No amount of training behind
his own lines could teach him what it was like to move out beyond
them where there might be enemy. Where, eventually, there was
sure to be enemy. But where? How did he look for them? What did
he listen for? Those men seriously meant to kill him. Beyond the
lines, a strange still breathlessness seemed to come down and settle
on things: trees, roads, grass. Handling his fear was another
problem. Learning to live with it, and to go ahead in spite of it,
took practice and a certain overlay of bitter panache it took time to
acquire. There were damned few fearless men. I knew, I think, two
personally. But they were both crazy, almost certifiably so. That
made them good soldiers.

But the human body, the animal human body, is incredibly
adaptable. Did you ever begin using a new set of house and
apartment keys? How you have to stop, and search, and look down
till you find the right key for the right door? And how after several
weeks or a couple of months, without any conscious participation
on your part, you find that your hand itself is finding and selecting
the right key by itself as the ring comes out of your pocket, without
your even having to look? It was the same process which worked in
the combat infantryman, almost entirely without conscious awareness, if he survived long enough to acquire it. (And the vast
majority did survive: that was another thing he learned.) But there
was no way to learn it except by actual practice on the actual
ground under the actual fire. Meantime, he exhausted himself
daily.

It's a pity the old men can't fight the wars. From the way they talk to the young we all know that they would love to do it. And they probably would be a lot more willing. At least, they have lived out a good part of their lives, and have some living chalked up behind them. But the truth is that physically they couldn't stand the gaff. I know from myself, now at fifty-three, that I couldn't possibly have stood the physical stresses I had to go through back then. And, secretly, I'm glad. But, of course, I won't admit it and will deny it with my last breath.

So there he stood—our once green, now obscene infantryman or tanker. Filthy, grimy, bearded, greasy with his own body oils (body oils aided by a thin film of dirt could make a uniform nearly completely waterproof, if it was worn long enough), dedicated to his own survival if at all possible, and willing to make it as costly as he could if it wasn't possible. He knew by the sound of incoming shells whether they would land near enough to be dangerous. He knew by the arc of falling aerial bombs if they would light nearby or farther out. He had learned that when fire was delivered, being thirty yards away could mean safety, and that fifty or a hundred yards could be pure heaven. He had learned that when the other guy was getting it a couple of hundred yards away, it had nothing to do with him: and that conversely when he was getting it, the other guy two hundred yards away wanted nothing to do with him, either. He had learned, maybe the most important of all for survival, that danger only existed at the exact place and moment of danger, and not before and not after.

He was about the foulest-mouthed individual who ever existed on earth. Every other word was fucking this or fucking that. And internally, his soul was about as foul and cynical as his mouth. He trusted nobody but his immediate outfit, and often not them. But everybody else, other outfits, he would cheerfully direct straight into hell. He had pared his dreams and ambitions down to no more than relief and a few days away from the line, and a bottle of booze, a woman and a bath.

But the green man had all this to go through yet. He had yet to serve his apprenticeship, to be accepted. Smart replacements soon learned that they got the dirtiest most-exposed jobs in the squad or platoon or section. They prayed for newer replacements to come in behind them, so that they might be, if not accepted, at least less noticed. The lucky, the tough, and the smart survived, and the rest were forgotten, shipped home, or buried. For the green hand the worst quality was the uncertainty and the total unfamiliarity with everything. And only time and lucky survival would change it to skill. On to Sicily! On to New Georgia!

THE BIG WAR

In March of 1943 the biggest single convoy battle of the Battle of the Atlantic ended with twenty-one Allied ships lost, sunk by U-boats operating in packs. If people read about that in their papers (if, in fact, it was even in the papers), nobody paid much attention or cared much.

In June of that year, in Memphis, Tennessee, where I was in the hospital, I rode home on a street bus and heard one tired plant-worker say to another, "If this son-a-bitching fucking war only lasts two more years, I'll have it made for life."

I couldn't get angry at him for it. I understood him. He didn't really mean he wanted the war to continue. He meant he was another working stiff who remembered the Depression. As for the rest, it was too big for a single mind to try to encompass. Ordinary citizens were lost in the almost incomprehensible boom and mass movement, trying to pick their way uphill through the crush to some island of security, in a new world that seemed to have gone crazy with both destruction and a lavish prosperity.

This wrenching social upheaval and realignment, as much as the fact of the war itself, accounted for an almost total breakdown of the moral standard of prewar U.S. living. And nothing would ever quite be the same again.

In Miami Beach, where I spent a brief furlough with my brother after getting home from overseas in the hospital, platoons and companies of young-looking OCS cadets marched through the golf courses and ritzy shopping areas shouting out old army rhymes to the command "Count off!" In marching rhythm and at the top of their lungs they sang songs like "I've Been Working on the Railroad" and "Roll a Silver Dollar" and "For Me and My Gal." The government had taken over most of the hotels along the beach for the use of depleted and nerve-shattered flyers who had completed their fifty missions over Europe. Two Red Cross women (working under my brother) served each commandeered hotel: organizing "singe binges" (wiener roasts) and beer busts on the beach, and getting up fishing parties. My sister, having run away from home, worked as a barmaid and elevator operator at the Roney Plaza, lived with a zapped-out flyer for a while, was married to him for four months, and never saw him again. Once, driving down to Key West on the overseas highway in a borrowed car, he had to pull over to the side and stop and let her drive the rest of the way because the whumps the tires made on the concrete joints of the roadbed sounded so like the flak explosions he remembered over Germany. Men and women everywhere—a lot of the women with husbands overseas—took what love they could get from each other on a day-to-day basis, and then moved on. A person took what fun he could find. Because no one person counted for anything anymore in the sweeping calculations and ramifications of this big war that was moving them all along.

CASUALTIES

Something strange seems to happen when a man is hit. There is an almost alchemic change in him, and in others' relationship to him. Assuming he isn't killed outright, and is only wounded, it is as though he has passed through some veil isolating him, and has entered some realm where the others, the unwounded, cannot follow. He has become a different person, and the others treat him differently.

The dead, of course, really *have* entered a different realm, and there is a sort of superstitious mystique of dread and magic about the dead. Where do people really go when they die? Do they go anywhere? Nobody has ever gone through death and lived to tell the tale. So it can only remain a question. There is a sort of instinctive dislike of touching them, as though what has happened to them has contaminated them and might contaminate the toucher.

Perhaps part of this feeling passes over to the wounded as well. Perhaps we think some of their bad luck might rub off, too. In any case, while they are treated as tenderly as humanly possible, and everything to make them comfortable as possible is done for them that can be, they are looked at with a sort of commingled distaste, guilt and irritation, and when they are finally moved out of the area everybody heaves a sort of silent sigh of relief without looking anybody else in the eyes.

The wounded themselves seem to acquiesce in this attitude, as though they are half-ashamed for having been hurt in the first place, and feel that now they can only be a drag and a weight on their outfit. Nor do the wounded seem to be less isolated from each other. Being in the same fix does not make them closer, but even farther apart than they are from the well.

The first wounded I ever saw were the remnants, picked up by the rescue boat, of the bombed-out barge that was hit in the air raid the day we arrived at Guadalcanal. Of course we were all totally green hands at the time, so perhaps we watched with more awe than we would have done later. But only a short time before, some of us had been talking to some of these men on the ship. With practical comments as to the extent of the various injuries in our ears from nearby old-timers who had been there longer, we watched as the survivors were landed and led or carried up from the beach to where a field dressing station had been set up at dawn. A few of them could walk by themselves. But all of them were suffering from shock as well as from blast, and the consummate tenderness with which they were handled by the corpsmen was a matter of complete indifference to them. Bloodstained, staggering, their eyeballs rolling, they faltered up the slope to lie or sit, dazed and indifferent, and allow themselves to be worked on by the doctors. They had crossed this strange line and everybody realized, including themselves dimly, that now they were different. All they had done was climb into a barge and sit there as they had been told. And then this had been done to them, without warning, without explanation, perhaps damaging them irreparably; and now explanation was impossible. They had been initiated into a strange, insane, twilight fraternity where explanation would be forever impossible. Everybody understood this. It did not need to be mentioned. They understood it themselves. Everybody was sorry, and so were they themselves. But there was nothing to be done about it. Tenderness was all that could be given, and like most of our self-labeled human emotions, it meant nothing when put alongside the intensity of their experience.

With the Jap planes still in sight above the channel, the doctors began trying to patch up what they could of what the planes had done to them. Some of them would yet die, that much was obvious, and it was useless to waste time on these which might be spent on others who might live. Those who would die accepted this professional judgment of the doctors silently, as they accepted the tender pat on the shoulder the doctors gave them when passing them by, staring up mutely from liquid eyes at the doctors' guilty faces. We watched all this with rapt attention. The wounded men, both those who would die and those who would not, were as indifferent to being stared at as they were to the tenderness with which they were treated. They stared back at us with lackluster eyes, which though lackluster were made curiously limpid by the dilation of deep shock. As a result, we all felt it, too—what the others, with more experience, already knew—these men had crossed a line, and it was useless to try to reach them. The strange, wild-eyed, bearded, crazily dressed marines and soldiers who had been fighting there since August didn't even try, and stood around discussing professionally which wounds they thought might be fatal, and which might not.

Even the army itself understood this about them, the wounded, and had made special dispensations about their newly acquired honorary status. Those who did not die would be entered upon the elaborate shuttling movement back out from this furthermost point of advance, as only a short time back they had been entered upon the shuttle forward into it. Back out, further and further back, toward that amorphous point of assumed total safety: home. Depending upon the seriousness of their conditions, they would descend part way, or all way, to the bottom of the lifeline home. The lucky ones, those hurt badly enough, would go all the way to the bottom, and everybody's secret goal: discharge....

ANONYMITY

In writing about the work of Kerr Eby, I found myself using the words anonymous and anonymity over and over, in describing his paintings. And I think that same anonymity is one of the last big obstacles the EVOLUTION OF A SOLDIER has to encounter and step over. To accept anonymity, along with all the rest he has to accept, is perhaps the toughest step of all for the combat soldier.

Anonymity has always been a problem of soldiers. It is one of the hardest things about a soldier's life. Old-time regular soldiers (like Negroes, women and other slaves through history) learn ways to cherish their servitude and ingest it and turn it into nourishment for power over the very establishment figures who administer it for the establishment which creates it. The old-timer first sergeant is analogous to the Negro mammy slave who ran the master's big plantation house and family with a hand of iron, or the modern housewife who carefully rules her lord and master's life with dexterity from behind the scenes.

But to do that the soldier, like the slave and the housewife, must first learn duplicity. He must immerse himself in and accept wholeheartedly the camouflage position of his servitude—in his case, the unnamed, anonymous rank and file of identical uniforms stretching away into infinity, all of them sporting identical head-gear (caps or helmets) to hide the individual faces, which them-selves, even, must remain forever fixed and set in expressionless expressions to match all the other expressions. He must work within the mass of anonymity to find his freedom of expression, and this is probably the hardest thing of all for the wartime civilian soldiers to pick up and learn. Most never did learn it.

But to accept anonymity in death is even harder. It is hard enough to accept dying. But to accept dying unknown and unsung except in some mass accolade, with no one to know the particulars how and when except in some mass communiqué, to be buried in some foreign land like a sack of rotten evil-smelling potatoes in a tin box for possible later disinterment and shipment home, requires a kind of bravery and acceptance so unspeakable that nobody has ever given a particular name to it.

Of course the catch is always there: you may live through it. But the drain on the psyche just contemplating it is so great that forever after—or at least for a very long time—you are a different person just from having contemplated it.

I don't think I ever learned this one of the last steps in the EVOLUTION OF A SOLDIER, and I think it was just there that my EVOLUTION OF A SOLDIER stopped short of the full development. I remember lying on my belly more than once, and looking at the other sweating faces all around me and wondering which of us lying there who died that week would ever be remembered in the particulars of his death by any of the others who survived. And of course nobody else would know, or much care. I simply did not want to die and not be remembered for it. Or not be remembered at all.

I think it was then I learned that the idea of the Unknown

Soldier was a con job and did not work. Not for the dead. It worked for the living. Like funerals, it was a ceremony of ritual obeisance made by the living for the living, to ease their pains, guilts and superstitious fears. But not for the dead, because the Unknown Soldier wasn't them, he was only one.

I once served on a Grave Registration detail on Guadalcanal, after the fighting was all over, to go up in the hills and dig up the bodies of the dead lost in some attack. The dead were from another regiment, so men from my outfit were picked to dig them up. That was how awful the detail was. And they did not want to make it worse by having men dig up the dead of their own. Unfortunately, a man in my outfit on the detail had a brother in the other outfit, and we dug up the man's brother that day.

It was a pretty awful scene. In any case. Even without the man's brother. The GRC lieutenant in charge had us get shovels out of the back of one of the trucks, and pointed out the area we were to cover, and explained to us how we were to take one dogtag off them before we put them in the bags. He explained that some of the bodies were pretty ripe because the fight had been two weeks before. When we began to dig, each time we opened a hole a little explosion of smell would burst up out of it, until finally the whole saddle where we were working was covered with it up to about knee deep. Above the knees it wasn't so bad, but when you had to bend down to search for the dogtag (we took turns doing this job) it was like diving down into another element, like water, or glue. We found about four bodies without dogtags that day.

"What will happen to those, sir?" I asked the lieutenant. Although he must have done this job before, he had a tight, screwed-up look of distaste on his face.

"They will remain anonymous," he said.

"What about the ones with dogtags?" I asked.

"Well," he said, "they will be recorded."

HOSPITAL

In the Army General Hospital in Memphis, where I was sent from San Francisco, we had two full wards of foot and lower-leg amputations from frozen feet in the invasion of Attu in the Aleutians, where some forgetful planner had sent the troops in in leather boots. This was in full accord with the general grim air and iron-cold mood the hospital had. Men there did not laugh and smile about their wounds, as they always seemed to do in the pictures in *Yank* and the civilian magazines.

Of course, not everybody there came from overseas. The others, broken legs, broken heads, service-connected Stateside illnesses, were still in the majority. We overseas returnees comprised about one quarter of the patients in mid-1943. The percentages would rise later as the war broadened abroad. We were among the first big influx.

There was a noticeable difference between the overseas combat men and the others. The combat men were clannish, and stayed pretty much by themselves, and there was this grim sort of iron-cold silence about them, except when they were in town and had a bottle in their hand. They made everybody else uncomfortable, and did not seem to care if they did or not. Almost without exception, they were uncheerful about their wounds. Alongside them, the others seemed much younger, and very much more cheerful about everything.

I myself was somewhere in the middle of all this. I wasn't there because of a wound—but I had been wounded, and had been overseas, and so was automatically a member of the clan, and I tended to associate mentally with the overseas men, and could understand what they were feeling, because I was feeling it myself. I suppose the best way to describe it—or the kindest way to describe it—is that they felt a certain well-controlled angry irascibility because everyone but themselves took everything so much for granted.

Whenever I looked at them I was reminded of a little scene I'd witnessed the day I was hit. I had arrived at the regimental aid station with my face all covered in blood from what turned out to be a minor head wound, no doubt looking very dramatic, and the first person I saw was our old regimental surgeon with a cigar butt in his teeth, cutting strips of skin and flesh out of a wound in the back of a boy sitting on the table. I had known old Doc, at least to speak to, for at least two years and when he quit working on the other boy and examined me, he said, "Hello, Jonesie. Getting more material for that book of yours you're gonna write?"

I laughed, a little hysterically probably. "More than I want, Doc." Though he was a light colonel, we always called him Doc.

When he found I had no hole in my head, only an unseparated crack, he went back to working on the boy. The wound in his back was inside and down from the shoulderblade and about the size of three silver dollars laid edge to edge, and was just a hole, a red angry wet hole, from which blood kept welling up and spilling in a red rill down his back, which Doc had to keep wiping up. That little rill of blood that wouldn't quit kept fascinating me. "How bad is he?" I asked. "He going to be all right?"

"I think so. Too soon to tell for sure. Doesn't seem to have internal bleeding," Doc said, and picked out another shred with his tweezers and cut it off with his scalpel. "But there may be some small pieces down in there." I nodded, not knowing what else to say. The boy, whom I didn't know, turned his head, favoring his bad side, and gave us both such a silent cold unforgiving look that I have never forgotten it. "There you are, son," old Doc said around his cigar butt, and patted his good shoulder. "No, don't get up. Lie down here and they'll come get you."

That look the wounded boy gave Doc and me was the same cold silent unforgiving stare the overseas men at the hospital gave to everybody who was not one of them. It was not so much that they were specifically blaming anyone for anything, as that everybody remained unforgiven. I felt the same way myself.

They had other peculiarities. For some reason I could never find the source of, none of the combat men at the hospital would ever wear their decoration ribbons or campaign ribbons when they went into town in uniform on pass. The only decoration they would allow themselves to wear, at least for the infantrymen, was the blue and silver Combat Infantryman's Badge, with the silver wreath around it. There was an awards ceremony at the hospital about every two or three weeks, and after I had been there about a month I was awarded my Purple Heart and my mysterious Bronze Star. But I never wore either of the ribbons. I knew without being told by anyone that we just didn't wear them. So instead I bought myself a Combat Infantryman's Badge (which I had not been officially awarded yet) and wore that.

Nobody ever mentioned aloud that you shouldn't wear your decorations. It was not some kind of private conspiracy. But everybody got the message just the same. As far as I know, no one ever asked if they were *not* supposed to wear their ribbons. Once a couple of men I knew, as a sort of ironic joke, started wearing the

Good Conduct ribbon—a decoration which just about every man in the army received who had not been convicted of murder. Nobody ever said to them that they should not wear it, but at the same time nobody laughed, either. After a few days they stopped.

Our hangout in Memphis was a hotel called the Peabody in downtown Memphis on Union Street. It was just about everybody else's hangout, too. In addition to flocks of ground troops and administrative troops in the area, there was a Naval Air Training Station in Memphis, as well as an Army Air Force field. It was a regular stop and center for the Air Transport Command also. Apparently before the war the Peabody had been the chic place in Memphis, and it sported a Starlight Roof with dancing music and dinner. But the great influx of servicemen had taken it over from the local gentry, and at just about any time of day or night there were always between half a dozen and a dozen wide-open drinking parties going in the rooms and suites, where it was easy to get invited simply by walking down the corridors on the various floors until you heard the noise.

Money was not much of a problem. Nor were women. There was always plenty of booze from somebody, and there were also unattached women at the hotel floor parties. You could always go up to the Starlight Roof and find yourself a nice girl and dance with her a while and bring her down. Everybody screwed. Sometimes, it did not even matter if there were other people in the room or not, at the swirling kalcidoscopic parties. Couples would ensconce themselves in the bathrooms of the suites and lock the doors.

Most of the overseas men received pretty substantial payments in back pay. I received, in one lovely lump sum, eleven months' back pay at a corporal's rate, when I finally got paid. This plus an allotment I'd been sending home to a bank for years to go to college on when I got out, gave me something over four thousand dollars. Two other overseas men and I kept a living room, two-bedroom suite, paying daily rates, for something like just under two months. If none of us happened to be going to town from the hospital on any given day, we would loan one of the keys to someone else. Our suite became one of the chief centers of what passed for gaiety at the Peabody Hotel in 1943. And we liked that.

No nation in history ever laid out such enormous sums and went to such great lengths to patch up, repair and take care of its wounded and its injured as the United States did in World War II.

Other nations watched and wondered at the United States's richness and largesse to its damaged. It was only in the functioning and in the administration of it that there was slippage, and graft. But the government couldn't be blamed for that. Any more than the government could be blamed for the grafting congressmen and senators the people chose to elect to office. Most of us overseas men knew that we would probably be returned to duty in some limited form or other, and that would probably mean heading out for General Eisenhower's Europe.

Except for a lucky few who were too crippled up to be of even partial use, we were essentially in the same boat as the others who had never been over and were finishing up their training and heading out every few days. Except for the sole fact that we had already been there, and knew what to expect. It was a pretty big sole fact.

There is a regulation in army hospitals that no man can be sent back into duty until he is physically fully ready for Full Duty, or physically fully ready for Limited Duty. There are only the two categories. And it could be no other way, since in the army there is no convalescent period at home. All told, I spent the last seven months of 1943 in the Memphis hospital. I was in love at least six times. I learned a lot about living on the home front. When I was shipped back out marked fit for Limited Duty, my four thousand dollars was gone and all I had to show for it were two tailored tropical worsted officer's uniforms with shoulder straps that I couldn't wear on the post. That, and a lot of memories. Memories I didn't want, particularly. It was during a period when nobody wanted to remember things.

I was shipped to what was then Camp Campbell (now Fort Campbell), Kentucky, in late December, 1943, a Limited Duty soldier.

THE FINAL EVOLUTION

I suppose the best way to describe it would be to say it was the miserable reawakening of hope. This was the worst despair of all, and somehow it had to be handled. Probably the best way to handle it was to become like the British soldier and the German soldier: a "professional." We already had nuclei of these in some of the older outfits like the First Division. And we were getting more nuclei of them in the greener units since D-Day. Probably the man in question had to already be three-quarters of a "professional," before he could go ahead that last half-step and become wholly one. So it took the new men a while longer.

I put the term professional into quote marks above because I did not intend it to mean the true professional of the officer corps or the permanent party NCO corps, whose sole career was the army. Rather, just the reverse. I meant the draftee or volunteer soldier who by dint of having served his apprenticeship and survived, came gradually to be an expert in his work and to love it and to take great pride in his performance of it.

The problem itself—this miserable, shitty reawakening of a hope long since laid to rest—stemmed from the realization that he was now fighting in a war which was already won. A won war, but a won war whose fighting was going to continue for a while, and in which he might still be killed just the same: one of the last KIAs of a waning war. Not an enviable position. Perhaps the *only* recourse was to take refuge in his professionalism.

Up to now, he has already accepted the correctness and rightness of his own death, and has even gone so far as to write himself off the rolls. He has gone the subtle step further and faced and accepted the anonymity of his death, and its lack of recognition—except in the grossest numbers. Accepted that he will be more unknown, and therefore deader, than the Unknown Soldier. He has gone through all that, all these successive abandonments of hope: and has come out on the other side into that other bath-to-bath, bottle-to-bottle hope that is the only hope the combat men can have. (Woman-to-woman, that third element in his litany, was too far above his restricted possibilities except very occasionally.) He had done all that, and here suddenly the old-fashioned human kind of hope had pushed itself back up into his thoughts because the war was won. Any fool could see that, in the closing days of 1944. And if the war was a won war, then there must be some point in time in the foreseeable future when it would cease. There was suddenly a possibility he might survive its end. Such thoughts awakened all the pain he had learned so laboriously over the months, in many cases years, to amputate at the root.

It was the last metamorphosis that would be asked of him. And if he could weather that one, he would be about as fully a soldier as a nonprofessional could be, a "professional" among the Professionals.

AN END TO IT

How did you come back from counting yourself as dead?

The plans called for nine million Americans to be demobilized between June, 1945, and June, 1946. The slow demobilization was necessary. Not only were large numbers required for the armies of occupation until they could be replaced, but the sheer physical logistics of transport made it necessary to string out the return. And what would happen to the happily humming economy, buzzing along, if you suddenly dumped nine million men on the job market? Already the "veterans" were a problem, even before they got to be "veterans." Many home-front assembly-line workers feared for their jobs, as the huge numbers of "vets" flooded back into the country.

If the "vets" were a problem to the economy and to the society as a whole, they neither minded nor cared. All they wanted was to get there: home. The combat men—the new "professionals"—of course got priority, or were supposed to. Out of the nine million very few had ever put their lives on the line, and fewer still had ever heard a shot fired in seriousness. There was a lot of payola under a lot of tables, but in general the plans were followed pretty closely. If out of nine million men a few tens of thousands got home earlier than they should have, who was going to worry about it, except the men they had got themselves squeezed in front of? And among such huge numbers, who would hear or listen to such a small number of voices? In Europe they started coming home even before it was finished in the Pacific.

Housing was a problem. President Truman begged the public to find living space for the veterans. Getting your old job back, or getting a new one, was less of a problem. And the civilian world went merrily on in its happy, dizzy whirl of prosperity in a booming economy. Articles appeared in women's magazines with titles like "What You Can Do to Help the Returning Veteran" and "Will He Be Changed?" *Good Housekeeping* said, "After *two or three weeks* [my italics] he should be finished with talking, with oppressive remembering. If he still goes over the same stories, reveals the same emotions, you had best consult a psychiatrist. This condition is neurotic." *House Beautiful* recommended that "home must be the greatest rehabilitation center of them all" and showed an apartment fixed up for some homecoming general. *Ladies' Home Journal* asked, in 1945, "Has your husband come home to the right woman?"

The answer, of course, was no. How could any woman be the right woman for a man who had just spent one year or two years as essentially a dead man, waiting, anticipating having his head blown off or his guts torn out? Even if she was the same woman he left (and most were not; how could they be?) she was not the right woman for such a man.

Instead of talking about it, most men didn't talk about it. It was not that they didn't want to talk about it, it was that when they did, nobody understood it. It was such a different way of living, and of looking at life even, that there was no common ground for communication in it.

It was like a Ranger staff sergeant I met in St. Louis years ago told me, "One day at Anzio we got eight new replacements into my platoon. We were supposed to make a little feeling attack that same day. Well, by next day, all eight of them replacements were dead, buddy. But none of us old guys were. We weren't going to send our own guys out on point in a damnfool situation like that. We knew nothing would happen. We were sewed up tight. And we'd been together through Africa, and Sicily, and Salerno. We sent the replacements out ahead." He gave me a sad smile, "But how am I going to explain something like that to my wife? She'd think it was horrible. But it was right, man, right. How were we going to send our own guys out into that?" We had some more drinks, got pretty drunk in fact, then he went home to his wife. Who, I am sure, was angry at him for getting drunk.

Another time an infantry sergeant who had fought in the Bulge told me how his platoon had taken some prisoners west of St. Vith. "There were eight of them, and they were tough old-timers, buddy. Been through the mill from the beginning. It was about the fourth or fifth day, and we needed some information. But they weren't talking, not those tough old birds. You had to admire them. So we took the first one off to the side, where they could see him, and shot him through the head. Then they all talked. They were eager to talk. Once they knew we were serious. Horrible? Evil? We knew all about Malmédy, man, and Stavelot. We needed that information. Our lives depended on it. We didn't think it was evil. Neither did they. But how am I going to tell my wife about something like that? Or my mother? They don't understand the problems." We went on getting drunk, and talking, until he felt he was ready to go home.

Slowly, bit by bit, it began to taper off. Men still woke up in the middle of the night, thrashing around and trying to get their hands on their wives' throats. Men still rolled out from a dead sleep, and hit the dirt with a crash on the bedroom floor, huddling against the bed to evade the aerial bomb or the artillery shells they had dreamed they heard coming. While their wives sat straight up in bed in their new frilly nightgowns bought for the homecoming, wide-eyed and staring, horrified. An old buddy would have roared with laughter. There is no telling what the divorce rate was then, in the early year or two. Certainly a lot higher than was ever admitted.

A number of men I knew slept with loaded pistols or unsheathed bayonets under their pillows for a number of months. Just made them feel more comfortable, they said shamefacedly, but it sure scared the shit out of their wives. And their wives' psychiatrists.

The DE-EVOLUTION OF A SOLDIER. It was longer in coming in some than in others. Some never did lose it, and some—a few— went off to the booby hatch. But not the vast majority. The majority, as they had survived the process of evolving into soldiers, now began to survive the process of devolving.

There was nothing the good old government could do about that. As with Uncle Sugar's expensive, astonishingly rich, lavish care which was being expended on the wounded and maimed, so with Uncle Sugar trying to fix things up for the returnee. Omar Bradley was put in charge of Veterans' Affairs, to modernize it and clean up its graft. Not only was the government sending everybody who wanted back to college, but it was sending anybody at all to college, anybody who asked, on their GI Bill of Rights. So much so that girls and civilian men who wanted to go had to score enormously high on the preschool exams, in order to get in. There simply wasn't room for them. But the government had never set up any DE-EVOLUTION OF A SOLDIER center, to match its induction centers. When you went in, they had the techniques and would ride you all the way to becoming a soldier. They had no comparable system when you came out. That you had to do on your own.

And with the de-evolving, as with the evolving, the first sign of change was the coming of the pain. As the old combat numbness disappeared, and the frozen feet of the soul began to thaw, the pain of the cure became evident. The sick-making thoughts of all the buddies who had died. The awful bad luck of the maimed. The next thing to go was the professionalism. How could you be a professional when there was no more profession? The only way was to stay in The Profession. And some, quite a few, did.

About the last thing to go was the old sense of *esprit*. That was the hardest thing to let go of, because there was nothing in civilian life that could replace it. The love and understanding of men for men in dangerous times, and places, and situations. Just as there was nothing in civilian life that could replace the heavy, turgid, day-to-day excitement of danger. Families and other civilian types would never understand that sense of *esprit*, any more than they would understand the excitement of the danger. Some old-timers, a lot of them, tried to hold onto the *esprit* by joining division associations and regimental associations. But the feeling wasn't the same, and never would be the same, because the motivation—the danger—was gone. Too many people lived too far away, and had other jobs and other interests, and anyway the drive was no longer there, and the most honest in their hearts had to admit it.

After all, the war was over.

When the veterans began to spend two nights a week down at the local American Legion, the families and parents and wives could heave a sigh of relief. Because they knew then that, after all, it—the war—was truly over.

PASS IN REVIEW!

How many times they had heard the old, long-drawn-out, faint field command pass down the long length of vast parade grounds, fading, as the guidons moved out front.

So slowly it faded, leaving behind it a whole generation of men who would walk into history looking backwards, with their backs to the sun, peering forever over their shoulders behind them, at their own lengthening shadows trailing across the earth. None of them would ever really get over it.

The Ice-Cream Headache and Other Stories

(1968)

The Ice-Cream Headache is probably Jones's most underrated book. It is made up of thirteen short stories, the best of which are either tales of childhood in a small town in Illinois or war stories. Along with *The Pistol*, the collection illustrates Jones's too rarely appreciated mastery of the techniques of short fiction. Because of the emphasis of *The James Jones Reader*, only war stories are included here, though anyone desiring a full appreciation of Jones's art should look at the Midwestern childhood stories as well. For the publication of *The Ice-Cream Headache*, Jones wrote short introductions to each story, which cumulatively reveal his informal and sometimes playful nature. In addition, he wrote an entertaining and informative introduction to the collection in which he says that

> In planning this book of stories I decided against any rewriting or revising. So these are presented to you just as they were when they were first finished no matter how long ago and then published, or in the case of two, not published at all.... The truth is, I don't think I could revise them, because I am no longer the man who wrote them. As a matter of fact, the man who wrote each story probably ceased

to exist after the story was written and finished, by the mere fact of having written it.

He adds that anyone interested in "the progression" of his writing will get a sense of it by reading the thirteen stories in the order in which they appear in the collection.

"The Temper of Steel" and "The Way It Is," Jones says, "were written in the summer of 1947 just after I had sent in to Maxwell Perkins the first two hundred pages of the first draft of *From Here to Eternity*." "The Temper of Steel" was, in fact, Jones's first publication. "Greater Love," according to the author, was written in a Memphis, Tennessee, trailer park in the summer of 1949 and was his "first real attempt at writing seriously about combat." The story, Jones adds, grew out of long conversations with a fellow veteran of Guadalcanal who moved into the trailer park. All three stories were products of Jones's literary apprenticeship with his first mentor, Lowney Handy of Robinson, Illinois. She eventually became the young writer's lover as well.

The Ice-Cream Headache and Other Stories was published by Delacorte while Jones was living in Paris. It was well-received by critics, but, as with most short story collections, soon fell into neglect. Jones ends his introduction with a wry observation:

> In 1951 when *From Here to Eternity* was published I had five unpublished stories on hand. Within four months I sold four of the five, and sold them in every case to a magazine which had previously turned all five stories down at least twice. I don't know what this statistic signifies. But I'm damn sure not going to knock myself off over it like [Jack London's fictional hero] Martin Eden did.

The Temper of Steel

Edward Weeks chose this story from among the first five to print as an "Atlantic First" in the March 1948 issue of *Atlantic Monthly*. It seems young to me today, but I think it makes a good and serious point. The point however is well concealed. See if you can find it. In case you can't, I'll explain it after the story. It's possible I didn't point it up enough, but at the time I believed with Hemingway that one should not point one's story points up.

(Jones's note)

"KNIVES," the tall man said, looking down at the gate-leg table. "They are truly ingenious things, are they not?"

Johnny moved his cocktail glass and followed the tall man's gaze down.

Their hostess smiled brightly. "Yes, aren't they? So gruesome." She spared the table one polite glance from her quick peerings about the room at her other guests. Her short hair, feathered about her ears and forehead, heightened the effect of a sparrow looking for bread. "Oh," she said. "I see someone I must speak to. You two know each other? You won't mind?"

"No," Johnny said. He looked at his drink and decided he needed it.

"My dear lady," the tall man said. "We met here in your home, at dinner. Don't you remember?" He eyed Johnny. "Did we not?"

"Yes, Lon," Johnny said. "Yes, we did."

"But of course." Their hostess smiled brightly. She put her frail hand on Johnny's arm. "I want you to relax and just make yourself at home here. Another cocktail? These affairs are really nothing." She brought the cocktail and flickered away after new crumbs.

The tall man picked up one of the knives and his eyes burned down into Johnny's face. He tugged abruptly. The sheath embraced the knife, surrendered it only under pressure and with a squeak of protest. He held the knife with its tip pointed at Johnny's chest and looked at him with that bright hard stare.

"Truly," he said, "they are ingenious. Now you take these: there are none of the too heavy, too chrome, too fine-lined characteristics of mass production about these."

Johnny looked at him and did not say anything. There were two knives in their embossed sheaths on the small table. Both knives had come from Africa in the hill country. The tall man had picked up the smaller one. The frantic buzz of conversation by which people earned their way at cocktail parties was incessant, fearing a letdown.

"These are individual pieces of work." The tall man spoke

authoritatively and gestured toward Johnny with the knife in his hand. "The savage who made this tried in his dim ignorant way to express himself, to put some of his knowledge of life and living into the making of it. To him, probably, it was truly beautiful. In fact, it is beautiful, because of its very crudeness, in the sense of being directly the opposite of our smoothly machined knives. Don't you think so?"

"Yes, Lon," Johnny said. "I guess that's right." It was his own fault for coming to cocktail parties. He had only met Lon twice. Lon had lived an adventurous life. That was all right, he liked Lon, but he did not want to talk knives.

Lon tossed the knife into the air and caught it deftly by the blade as it flickered down. His eyes glittered an answer to the knife's flicker of light.

"Yes," he said caressingly, "this is a nice knife."

Lon swung the knife up and down lovingly, as if tentatively measuring the weight for throwing. He looked almost as if he would throw it through the cocktail party to stick it quivering in the wooden door. His hatchet face turned toward Johnny, stabbing at him like a knife itself, like the killing knives Lon knew, and used, and loved.

Johnny could hear the unending slur of voices around the large room playing Lon's accompaniment. All of them knew of Lon's achievements. He knew them too, and he wished that Lon would drop it.

"The wide part of the blade," Lon explained technically, "that is for cutting. You can slash a man to ribbons with this one—in spite of its crude workmanship. Knowing where our host got it, I don't doubt that the lifeblood of a number of men has flowed along this blade, right where my finger is. Does that not evoke a peculiar emotion?"

"Yes."

Johnny could tell what he was doing but he was not angry, he was only tired. He wondered abstractedly if Lon knew why he avoided knives, or if Lon knew that there was a memory struggling to crawl up from the bottom of his mind.

"The point is also very sharp," said Lon. "Not much power would be needed to push this knife through the thick outer epidermis of a man."

"That's right," Johnny said wearily. "But the trouble with a long thin point like that is if it hits a bone, it's liable to break or bend and then your beautiful knife is ruined."

Lon nodded approvingly. He squinted down the thin length of the blade, holding the point with his thumb in the old practiced manner.

"That is true. Still, this is a fine knife. Better than the other, which is too long. One wants a short knife. Knife fighting is a lost art, just as the making of fine knives is a lost art."

"You must have had an adventurous life," Johnny said. He could feel the memory climbing the ladder of his spine into his brain.

Lon looked at him quickly. "Well," he said. He pinged the point with his thumbnail. "Most of my knife experience came after the *first* war. In Spain and in northern Africa when I was wandering around. Of course, I had already learned my technique in Mexico, but the Mexican has not the finesse of the Spaniard, in knife fighting or anything else.

"Alley fights were the best. You have to learn to be quick and clean, or you do not get to use your technique very long. *N'est-ce pas?*" His hatchet face grinned. His bright eyes commanded Johnny as he jammed the knife back into its sheath. His bright eyes commanded everybody.

Johnny stood quietly wondering when he would finally shut up. Perhaps he did not know left hooks as he knew knives? He drew a deep breath and let it out slowly but the other would not go out with it. It was like a cat on the ladder and would not come down.

"I think I will go and find our host," Lon said. "It is about time I was leaving."

He stuck out his hand. Johnny shifted his glass to his left hand and took it. There was a heavy, smooth, clean pressure in Lon's handclasp.

"I hope I have not upset you by my bloody talk," Lon said.

"No. It didn't bother me." The knife was lying sheathed upon the table as before.

When Lon left him, he sat down in the nearest chair. He could feel the memory rising, as a gas-filled corpse rises to the surface of the sea. He tried listening to the conversation near him. His jaws tightened in the struggle.

2

They had conversed little and softly, lying in a slit trench three feet by seven feet by two feet. Most people did not know the difference between a slit trench and a foxhole since the famous chaplain said there were no atheists in foxholes. You could not lie down in a foxhole and they were harder to dig and they were only for special cases. Even after digging a slit trench a man would be exhausted and drenched with sweat. And that when they were not even under fire.

On the line they never dug them any closer than five and it was often ten or fifteen or even twenty yards, when the line was too great for the number of them as it so often was in the early days of the 'Canal.

It was so different, this war, from the other, it was not like you read. Archie Binns did a good job of showing what it would come to be, next time, with his Japanese and Russians in Siberia in *The Laurels Are Cut Down*. Chivalry Was Dead, he said. Long live chivalry, I said, it all was dead. That trick of crawling in between the slit trenches at night, then jumping in from behind. Probably some point of *Bushido* honor: come back with a souvenir of a kill. Apparently honor also is subject to the Law of Relativity. But then they did not mind dying. Or maybe it was just that they were so hungry and they did it to get the luxurious cans of C ration each Yankee carried. You never knew, not any more.

He was terribly sleepy. After a certain point you were always terribly sleepy. Even if the guy in the next slit trench had the watch you did not sleep. How could you sleep? It was an all-out war, they said, twenty-four hours a day, seven days a week, no time off for good behavior. Paydays used to be a half holiday, back in peacetime. This was it, they said, this was really the war to end war, this time we mean it, no crap, this is the one that counts, think of your sons. Probably the Russians said the same thing. But apart from that your ears and your nerves were always wide awake anyway, for a sound or a feel, always reaching, reaching out.

He heard no sound. Or felt anything either. He just knew it was there, suddenly. The hairs on the back of his neck rose up and prickled. Somewhat the same feeling you get when you suddenly know somebody is staring at you from behind and you turn around and sure enough there is somebody staring at you. Only this, of course, was greatly enhanced. When it hit him it shot clear through like an electric shock and he was wide awake. Yet he heard nothing.

He was lying on his belly with the brim of his helmet dug into the dirt to keep his face out of the mud. This slit trench was not really wet. It was only muddy with that thin film clay gets when the dew is mashed into it. Oh, it was a slick war all right, they said, it was a slick war.

He always lay on his belly with his back up. Really comical how hard it is to lay on your back. You can't do it. Whenever you heard one coming you always lay on your belly while you waited. Maybe you dug your fingernails into the slick too, but then that was different. They will always flop over on their belly when they hear one coming if they are on their back. You just can't help it. Like a fish or a porcupine.

He turned his head to the left very slowly to look back. He could see nothing. The sky was clouded and there were no stars to outline a figure. He strained his eyes until he felt their muscles would crack and curl up like springs. Nothing.

Stil, he knew it was there. He could tell. The instinct told him. It was invariably right. He had developed it over a period of weeks. It was what they did not teach you in the field manuals.

It was very quiet and his eyes rolled in his head. Somewhere in the silence a grenade popped, fizzed, went off, sending a shower of little screamings outward. This was too close for a grenade and you could not fire without the muzzle blast betraying you. At night it was always the knife. This was his first.

The thought of it there sent a spasm of refined terror through him. A terror of hopelessness that made him want to shrug and turn his head back and close his eyes and simply wait. Waiting for it dejectedly, yet hoping all the time the instinct was wrong, and knowing at the same time the instinct was never wrong. He felt, then, it was not worth the trouble. There were a lot of things worse than dying. Slowly disintegrating day by day was worse than dying.

He did not know, you never knew any more. When you looked back and you saw how it all came about, it was so logical. How, in the beginning, it was not at all necessary. Just simply cause and effect that, in the beginning, was not at all necessary. It was not that people did not see it, everybody saw it. Everybody always saw it. That was why it was so hard to know. It was like the being always terribly sleepy. Just to relax, to sit quietly and not be sleepy, maybe then you could know. Just to relax was all. It was really very simple. It was not a question of being paralyzed with fear, it was simply having to decide. He was wide awake and terribly sleepy and he could not decide.

While he lay in the mud-slick fatigues, unable to decide, his hand with the rolls of dirt under the cracked and crusted nails decided. It slid down over the cloth made waterproof by weeks of soaking up his body oil. Quite silently it unfastened the snap and freed the knife from the sheath strapped to his leg. Then it relaxed full length along his side, cunning as animals are cunning. Perhaps in the end that was all it was.

Over the luxurious feeling of resignation was something else apparently, a flame over the sour damp ashes; a flame, now, that never came alive until there was no other thing, burning strongly in a wind of death. The hand and this primitive flame worked together leaving him out of it.

He was astonished to realize it was not five seconds since the hair first rose. He felt like he had just carried three thousand pounds a couple of miles.

The hand jerked sideways when the nothing jumped, flopping him over on his back and raising the knife in an arc until it was sticking straight up. The knife in the hand made of the arm the sharpened spike of the elephant trap. The nothing impaled itself by the weight of the body. The falling body jarred through his arm releasing the hand from its responsibility, pushed his arm down till the knob on the knife hilt ground against his pelvic bone.

The Jap's knife struck his helmet slitheringly and stuck itself into the clay without power. The Jap hardly made a sound, only a sharp "unh" as the knife went into him. Such a silent war this one was.

There was a little struggle when he grabbed the Jap's wrist with his left hand. But not much. The Jap's hand came away from the hilt of his knife fairly easily. The knife had gone into him just under the breastbone. Sort of a solar plexus punch you might say, and it took his wind.

Blood ran distastefully over his hand and he pushed the Jap's leaden weight away from him and pulled his knife out. He could see him now, the inscrutable almond eyes and the funny bell-

shaped helmet, like a woman's 1920s hat. The Jap put both hands
over his belly where the knife had been. The Jap lay on his back,
eyes watching, chin pulled down against his chest, breathing with
a kind of grunt.

Johnny heard the breathing above the explosions of his own heart
and knew he had nothing more to fear from this one.

They looked at each other for a little while, both breathing
softly. Then Johnny put his hand over the Jap's face, the heel of his
palm on his chin. The Jap did not shut his eyes and opened his
mouth and bit at one of the fingers. Johnny moved the finger and
thrust it up the Jap's nose, the Jap still trying to bite it. Then he
pulled his knife across the Jap's bent throat, downward and away.
The Jap quit trying to bite. He had not moved his hands from his
belly.

Johnny grabbed him and rolled him out of the slit trench on the
downhill side. His right hand had escaped, but he had not jerked
his left hand quick enough and the geyser pumped against his arm.
He wiped his hand vigorously and then lay in the slit trench, trying
to keep out of the blood, waiting for morning to come. Somewhere
in the silence a grenade popped, fizzed, went off, sending a shower
of little screamings outward. A Nambu MG chattered in its falsetto
foreign tongue. And him wishing to relax, just to relax, lying slow
and easy, maybe under a tree, on a creek.

3

Johnny took a sip from his fresh martini. The olive oscillated
slightly and a few drops sloshed over his fingers. People nearby
were laughing at some quip of a Succesful Author. He had missed
it. The woman next to him offered to explain it, so that he could
laugh too. He thanked her, seeing Lon coming toward him across
the room with their hostess. Lon was wearing his rakish trenchcoat
and carrying his slouch hat.

Lon shook his hand again. "Do not let my talk of knives get on
your nerves. It is only that knives fascinate me."

"No," he said. "Forget it, Lon. Do you remember the scene in *All
Quiet* where Paul kills the Frenchman in the hole and then begs his
forgiveness?"

Lon looked at him curiously. "Yes. That scene. Highly sentimen-
tal stuff."

"That's what I mean. It's outdated, isn't it? You couldn't write it that way now, could you?"

"No," Lon said. "You couldn't write it like that now. Pointlessly hysterical. What they call a chaotic reaction."

Johnny nodded. "Chaotic reaction. Psychological? That's good. In other words, they had not developed the high art of proper indoctrination in those days."

"Yes. That's it."

"But this war was different, wasn't it, Lon?"

"Yes," Lon said. "This war was different. I must go." He shook Johnny's hand again. "I hope I did not upset you with my bloody talk."

"Forget it, Lon. I've got a couple knives you might like to see. I took one of them off a dead Jap."

Lon was interested. "What kind of knife is it?"

"American-made. The Jap probably took it off a dead American."

"Oh," Lon said. "I thought it might have a story behind it. . . . Well, good-bye."

"So long." He watched Lon stride to the door, the trenchcoat ballooning about his legs, the high collar covering his ears.

"I must see him out," their hostess whispered. "Isn't he fascinating? He has been everywhere and done everything."

"He must have led a truly adventurous life."

"Oh, you can't know. Truly incredible. Do you want another cocktail? You are enjoying yourself? You veterans, you who have done so much, you need to relax.

"Excuse me, my dear. I must really see Lon out. I was very lucky to get him. He abhors cocktail parties, you know. Truly an amazing personality."

"Yes," Johnny said. "I can see that. Truly he is."

AUTHOR'S NOTE:
The point is in the reference to Archie Binns and the quote about chivalry being dead, and in the boy's comparison of his own coldblooded killing of the Japanese to the comparable scene in *All Quiet*. This is what modern warfare has come to be, with all of our blessings, and God help us for it.

The Way It Is

Frederick L. Allen printed this one in the June 1949 *Harper's*. We argued so much over it that Allen sent me back free the ms of the other story he bought, "Just Like The Girl," saying he wasn't up to it a second time. We argued over things like the fact that Allen wrote into my story a paragraph explaining it was Hawaii and Pearl Harbor. I refused to allow this. We argued over things like the abbreviation of lieutenant. I didn't want a period after it. Allen wanted a period after it. We compromised by spelling it out.

(Jones's note)

I SAW THE CAR coming down the grade and got up from the culvert. I had to push hard with my legs to keep the wind from sitting me back down. I stepped out into the road to stop him, turning my back to the wind, still holding the mess kit I had been scouring. Some of the slop of sand and grease dripped out of it onto my leg.

Then I saw Mazzioli was on the running board and had his pistol out and aimed at the driver's head. I tossed the mess kit, still full, over against the culvert and got my own pistol out.

I couldn't see the driver. It was hard to see the car in the red air of the dusk against the black of the cliff and with the cold wind pouring against my eyes. It was a foreign make, a runabout with strange lines and the steering wheel on the right-hand side. When it stopped Mazzioli jumped off the running board and motioned with his pistol.

"All right," he said in that thick voice. "Get out of there, you."

I knew the man when he climbed out. He used the road every day. He could have passed for a typical Prussian with his scraped jowls and cropped bullethead. He wore a fine tweed jacket and plus-fours, and his stockings were of ribbed wool and very fine. I looked down at my legging and kicked off the gob of sand and grease. It didn't help much. I hadn't even had my field jacket off for three weeks, since the bombing.

"What's up, Greek?" I said, peering through the deepening dusk. I had to yell to make it heard above the wind.

"I hopped a ride down the hill with this guy," he said woodenly. "All the way down he was asting me questions about the position. How many men? How many guns? Was there a demolition? What was the road-guard for? I mean to find out what's the story." He looked offended.

I walked over to him so I could hear above the wind. He was a little Wop but very meaty. His father ran a grocery store in Brooklyn.

"What do you figure on doing?" I asked. I thought I had seen the Junker before someplace, and I tried hard to make my mind work.

Mazzioli waved his pistol at the standing man. "Git over there, you, and put your back to the cliff," he said ominously. The beefy Junker walked to it slowly, his steps jerky from rage, his arms dangling impotently. He stood against the black, porous cliff and Mazzioli followed him. "Where's the men?" Mazzioli shouted to me above the wind. "I want a man to stand guard over this guy. You git a man and have him . . ."

"There's nobody here but me," I called back. "I let them go up to the top of the hill. Two of them didn't get any chow tonight. They went up to number one hole to listen to the guitar a while." I walked over to him.

I could see him stiffen. "Goddam you. You know there's always supposed to be three men and one noncom here all the time. That's the orders. You're supposed to be second in command. How do you expect to handle these men when you don't follow the orders?"

I stared at him, feeling my jaws tighten. "All right," I shrugged. "I let them go. So what?"

"I'm turning this in to Lieutenant Allison. The orders are the orders. If you want to be on this road-guard to do your duty, okay. If you want to be on this road-guard to stop Coca-Cola trucks you can go back upstairs to the position. This road-guard is vital, and as long as I'm in charge of it everybody does like the orders says."

I didn't say anything.

"You're a rotten soldier, Slade," Mazzioli said. "Now look what's happened. I wanted you to help me search this guy's car. Now there's nobody here to guard this guy."

"Okay," I said. "So I'm a rotten soldier. My trouble is I got too many brains." He was making me mad and that always got him. Ever since I went six months to the University downtown in Honolulu.

"Don't start giving me that stuff," he snarled.

The Junker against the cliff stepped forward. "See here," he said. "I demand you stop this bickering and release me. You're being an idiot. I am..."

"Shut up, you," Mazzioli snarled. "Shut up! I warned you, now shut up!" He stepped to meet him and jabbed the muzzle of his pistol into the Junker's big belly. The man recoiled and stood back against the cliff, his beefy face choleric.

I stood with my hands in the pockets of my field jacket, my shoulder hunched down against the rawness of the wind and watched the scene. I had put my pistol away.

"All right," Mazzioli said to me. "The question is what're we gonna do now? If there's nobody here but you and me?"

"You're in command," I said.

"I know it. Keep quiet. I'm thinking."

"Well," I said. "You could have the guy drive you up the hill to the lieutenant. You could keep him covered till you turned him over to the lieutenant. Then you would be absolved," I said. Big words always got him.

"No," he said dubiously. "He might try something."

"Or," I said, "you could search the car and have me watch the guy."

"Yeh," he admitted. "I could do that... Yet....No, I don't want to do that. We may need more men."

It was dark now, as black as the cliff face, and I grinned. "Okay," I said, telling him what I had in my mind all along, "then I could call Alcorn down from up on the cliff and he could watch the guy."

"Yes. That's it. Why didn't I think of that before?"

"I don't know. Maybe you're tired."

"You call Alcorn down," he commanded me.

I walked toward the cliff wall that reared its set black face up and up in the darkness several hundred feet. The wind beat on me with both fists in the blackness.

"Wait a minute," Mazzioli called. "Maybe we shouldn't call Alcorn down. There's supposed to be a man up there all the time."

"Look," I said. "I'll tell you what I think. Before you go ahead, you better get the lieutenant's permission to do anything with this guy. You better find out who this guy is."

"I'm in charge of this road-guard," he yelled into the wind, "and I can handle it. Without running to no lieutenant. And I don't want back-talk. When I give you an order, you do it. Call Alcorn down here like I said."

"Okay," I said. I leaned on the culvert and called loudly, my face turned up to the cliff. There was no answer. I flashed my light covered with blue paper. Still no answer.

For a second I couldn't help wondering if something had got him. The Japanese invasion of Hawaii had been expected every day since Pearl was bombed. It was expected here at Kaneohe Bay on the windward side where the reef was low and there was good beach. Nobody doubted they would get ashore.

"What's the matter?" asked Mazzioli sharply from the darkness. "Is Alcorn asleep?"

"No," I said. "It's the wind; it carries off the sound. The light will get him." I picked up a handful of pebbles and threw them up the cliff with all my strength, trying to make no noise the Greek could hear.

Sixty feet up was a natural niche and the BAR man was stationed there twenty-four hours a day. It was a hidden spot that covered the road and the road-guard. In case of surprise it would prove invaluable. That was Lieutenant Allison's own idea. The road-guard was Hawaiian Department's idea.

Alcorn had stayed up there alone for the first four days after the bombing. In the four days he had one meal before somebody remembered him. Now he and the other man pulled twelve hours apiece.

The road-guard was part of the whole defense plan. It was figured out in November when the beach positions were constructed. The defense was to mine the Pali Road and Kamehameha Highway where it ran up over this cliff at Makapuu Point. It was planned to blow both roads and bottle them up in Kaneohe Valley and force them north, away from Honolulu. They were great demolitions and it was all top secret. Of course, in December they found maps of the whole thing in the captured planes. Still, it was very vital and very top secret.

A rock the size of my fist thumped into the sand at my feet. I grinned. "You missed me," I called up the cliff. "Come down from there, you lazy bastard." I barely caught a faraway, wind-tossed phrase that sounded like "truck, too." Then silence, and the wind.

The machinegun apertures in the pillboxes up the hill all faced out to sea. Whoever planned the position had forgotten about the road, and all that faced the road was the tunnels into the pillboxes. To cover the road the MGs would have to be carried up into the open, and it was a shame because there was a perfect enfilade where the road curved up the cliff. But they couldn't rebuild the pillboxes we had cut into solid rock, so instead they created the road-guard.

The road-guard was to be five men and a BAR from up above. That was us. We were to protect the demolition when the Jap landed. It was not expected to keep him from getting ashore. We were to hold him off, with our BAR, till the demolition could be blown behind us. After that we were on our own. It was excellent strategy, for a makeshift, with the invasion expected truly every day. And the road-guard was vital, it was the key.

Every man at Makapuu volunteered for the road-guard. The five of us were lucky to get it. The job was to stop and search all vehicles for anything that might be used to blow the demolition. The Coca-Cola trucks and banana trucks and grocery trucks and fruit trucks used this road every day to get to market. We stopped them all, especially the Coca-Cola trucks.

In a couple of minutes I heard a scrambling and scraping and a bouncing fall of pebbles and Alcorn came slouching along the sand at the road edge, blowing on his hands.

"The Greek wants you, Fatso," I said.

He laughed, low and rich and sloppy. "I think I'm deaf from this wind, by god," he said and scratched inside his field jacket. "What's he want now?"

"Come over here," Mazzioli ordered. We walked over through the blackness and the wind and I felt I was swimming under water against a strong current. The Greek swung his blue light from the Junker onto us. Alcorn's clothes hung from him like rags and on the back of his head was a fatigue hat with the brim turned up that defied the wind. He must have sewed an elastic band on it. Beside him I looked like I was all bucked up for a short-timer parade.

"Where's your helmet?" Mazzioli said. "You're supposed to wear your helmet at all times. That's the orders."

"Aw now, sarge," Alcorn whined. "You know the steel band of them things gives a man a headache. I cain't wear one."

I grinned and gave the brim of my own inverted soup-plate helmet a tug. Alcorn was a character.

"When are you men going to learn to obey orders?" the Greek

said. "An army runs by discipline. If you men don't start acting like soldiers, I'll turn you in."

"Off with his head," I said.

"What did you say?"

"I said, coffee and bed. That's what we need. There's not a man on this position who's had three good hours sleep since this bloody war started. Putting up barbed wire all day and pulling guard all night. And then putting up the same wire next day because the tide washed it out."

Alcorn snickered and Mazzioli said nothing. The Greek had had charge of a wire detail that worked one whole night to put up three hundred yards of double apron wire on the sand beach below the road. In the morning it was gone. Not a single picket left.

"Alcorn," Mazzioli ordered, "get a rifle and keep a bayonet against this guy's belly till I tell you not to."

"I don't know where the rifles are down here," Alcorn said.

"I'll get it," I said.

I walked to the culvert and climbed down around it. The wall made a protection from the wind and I felt I had dropped into a world without breath. The absence of the wind made me dizzy and I leaned my face against the concrete. I felt the way you feel when you look out the window at a blowing rainstorm. All our blankets and stuff were down here. Against the wall of the culvert lay four rifles with bayonets on them, wrapped in a shelter-half. I pulled one out and made myself climb up into the wind again.

Alcorn took the rifle and kept the bayonet against the Junker's paunch. Every time the Junker moved or tried to speak Alcorn jabbed him playfully in the belly. The Junker was getting madder and madder, but Alcorn was having a fine time.

I knew the lewd nakedness of that scraped face someplace before. I went over in my mind all the people I had seen at the University.

The Greek was doing a bang-up job of searching the car, he even looked under the hood. I sat on the culvert and got my mess kit and put a handful of fresh sand in it from beside the road and rubbed it around and around. The dishwater that got out to us from the CP at Hanauma Bay gave us all the dysentery until we started using the sand.

I tried to think where I'd seen him. It wasn't the face of a teacher, it had too much power. I dumped the greasy mess from the mess kit and poured in a little water from my canteen. I sloshed it around to rinse the sand out, listening vacantly to the Greek cursing and fidgeting with the car.

Just three days ago a two-man sub ran aground off Kaneohe and the second officer swam ashore, preferring capture. It was expected the sub was scouting the invasion that was coming truly any day.

They said he was the first prisoner of the war. I got to see him when they brought him in. He was a husky little guy and grinning humbly. His name was Kazuo Sakamaki. I knew a girl at the University named Harue Tanaka. I almost married her.

It seemed like the wind had blown my mind empty of all past. It had sucked out everything but Makapuu and the black rocks and blue lights and the sand-choked grass. The University with its clear, airy look from the street, its crisp freeness all hidden away in a wind-free little valley at the foot of rocky wooded Tantalus, it was from another life, a life protected from the wind, a life where there were white clouds in the sun but no wind, just gently moving air.

I wiped the mess kit with the GI face towel I kept in it and clamped it together and stuck it back in my pack that lay by the culvert, wanting to go down behind the culvert and light a cigarette.

Maybe the Junker was one of the big boys on the University board. The big boys always sent their kids to Harvard or some school on the mainland, but they were the board. The only white faces you saw were the instructors and the haoles who didn't have the dough to send their kids to the mainland—and an occasional soldier in civvies, looking out of place. Only these and the board. And the tourists.

Then I remembered the scraped face, coming out of the main building on a hot still August day, wiping the sweat from the face with a big silk handkerchief.

"Couldn't find a thing," Mazzioli said, coming up from the car. "I don't know what to do. This guy looks like a German. He even talks like a German."

"Listen," I said. "No German who looks like a German and talks like a German is going to be a spy. Use your head. This guy is some kind of big shot. I seen him at the University."

"To hell with you and your University."

"No," I said. "Listen."

"Why would he ask me questions about the number of men and guns and pillboxes?"

"Hell, I don't know. Maybe he wanted to write an editorial for the *Advertiser.*"

"I can't let him go," he said.

"All right. Send Alcorn up for the lieutenant and let him handle it. You worry too much, Greek."

"Yeh, I could do that." But he was dubious. He walked back to the car for a moment and then went over to Alcorn. "Alcorn, you go up and get the lieutenant down here. Tell him we got a suspicious character down here." He turned to me. "Slade, you watch this guy and don't take any chances with him. I'm going over this car again."

Alcorn handed me the rifle and started off up the road. Through the darkness Mazzioli hollered after him. "Double time and jerk the lead," he shouted. The wind carried it away. The wind carried everything away.

To me Mazzioli said, "If he tries anything, shoot the bastard."

"Okay," I said. I set the rifle butt on the ground and leaned on it. "Take it easy, mister," I said. "Remember there's a war on. The lieutenant's coming down, and you'll be on your way home in a little bit."

"I am not accustomed to such treatment," he said, staring at me with flat eyes, "and I intend to see somebody pays for this indignity."

"We're only doing our duty," I said. "We got orders to stop all suspicious persons. This is important to the defense plan."

"I am not a suspicious person," he said, "and you men..."

I interrupted; it was probably the only chance I'd ever get to interrupt a big shot. "Well," I said, "you were asking suspicious questions about our position."

"...and you men should have something better to do than hold up citizens."

Mazzioli, looking harassed, came over from the car. "What's that?" he snarled. "What's your name?"

The Junker stared at him. "My name is Knight," he said, and waited for it to sink in. When Mazzioli's face was blank he added, "Of Knight & Crosby, Limited." His voice was cold with rage and hate.

Above the wind we heard the voices of Lieutenant Allison and Alcorn on the road.

I looked at the Greek but he showed nothing. Nobody could live in Hawaii without knowing Knight & Crosby, Ltd. The Big Five were as well known as Diamond Head.

Lieutenant Allison put one hand on Mazzioli's shoulder and the other on mine. "Now," he said paternally. "What's the trouble?"

Mazzioli told him the whole tale. I went back to the culvert and listened to the wind playing background music to the double tale of woe. After both stories were told, Lieutenant Allison escorted Mr. Knight to his runabout with extreme courtesy.

"You can appreciate, Mr. Knight, our position." Lieutenant Allison put his foot on the running board and rested his hands on the door. "You can understand my sergeant was only doing his duty, a duty conceived to protect you, Mr. Knight."

Mr. Knight did not speak. He sat with his hands gripping the wheel, staring straight ahead.

"I'm sorry you feel that way, Mr. Knight," Lieutenant Allison said. "These men were carrying out orders we have received from Hawaiian Department Headquarters."

Mr. Knight made no sign he had heard. He gave the impression he was suffering this association under duress and was fretting to have done and be gone.

"A soldier's duty is to follow out his orders," Lieutenant Allison said.

"All right," the lieutenant said. He took his foot off the running board and dropped his hands. "You may go, Mr. Knight. You can rest assured such a thing won't happen again, now that my men know who you are."

"It certainly won't," Mr. Knight said. "Bah!" He started his runabout with a roar and he did not look back.

I watched from the culvert and grinned contentedly. "Now there'll be hell to pay," I told Mazzioli.

After Knight was gone, Mazzioli called the lieutenant over to the other side of the road and spoke earnestly. I watched the excited movement of his blue light and grinned more widely.

Lieutenant Allison came over to me with the Greek following close behind. "Alcorn," he called. Alcorn shuffled over from the base of the cliff.

"I've been having bad reports about you two men," Lieutenant Allison began. "Where's your helmet, Alcorn?"

Alcorn shuffled his feet. "It's up the cliff. I cain't wear one of them things more'n a half hour, Lootenant," he said. "I get a turrible headache if I do. When Corporal Slade called me down, I clean forgot all about it."

"You're all through down here," Lieutenant Allison said, "Get back up there and get that helmet on. I'll be coming around inspecting and I don't want to catch you without a helmet. If I do there'll be some damned heavy details around here, and if that don't stop your headache, by god, maybe a court-martial will.

"You're no different than anybody else. If I can wear a helmet all the time, then you can do it. I don't like it any better than you do.

"Now get the hell back up there."

Alcorn saluted and started for the base of the cliff.

"Alcorn!" Lieutenant Allison called after him in the darkness.

"Yessir?"

"You don't ever go to sleep up there, do you?"

"Oh, no sir."

"You'd better watch it. I'll be inspecting tonight."

I could hear the scrambling and falling of pebbles and I thought it was a very lonely sound.

"Come over here, Slade," Lieutenant Allison said. He walked away from Mazzioli and I followed him, pleased the calling-down would be in private instead of in front of the Greek. It was a luxury.

"I'm going back up the hill," Lieutenant Allison said. "You walk part of the way with me. I want to talk to you." The two of us started up the road. "I'm going to send those men back down here when I get to the top," Lieutenant Allison said. "You won't need to go up."

"Thank you, sir," I said.

"Why did you let those men go up the hill tonight, Slade?"

"They didn't get any chow tonight, sir," I said. "I felt sorry for them."

"You're not supposed to feel sorry for anybody. You're a soldier. You enlisted in the Army, didn't you?"

"Yes, sir," I said. "But it was because I couldn't get a job."

"A soldier's job is to feel sorry for nobody."

"I can't help it, sir," I said. "Maybe my environment was wrong. Or maybe I haven't had the proper indoctrinization. I always put myself in the other guy's place. I even felt sorry for Mr. Knight. And he sure didn't need it."

"What happened with Mr. Knight was the proper action to take.

It turned out badly, but he could have been a saboteur with a carload of TNT to blow the demolition."

"What will happen about Knight, sir?" I said.

"Mr. Knight is a big man in Hawaii. The Big Five run the whole territory. There may be some bad effects. I may even get an ass-eating. Nevertheless, Mazzioli acted correctly. In the long run, it will all turn out all right because we did what was right. The Army will take that into account."

"You believe that?" I said.

"Yes," he said. "I believe it. You don't realize how important that road-guard is to the whole war. What if the enemy had made a landing at Kaneohe tonight? They'd have a patrol on you before you knew it. The very thing you did out of kindness might be what lost the war for us. It's not far-fetched: if they took this road and cliff, they'd have this island in a month. From there it'd be the west coast. And we'd be fighting the war in the Rocky Mountains."

"All for the want of a horseshoe nail," I said.

"That's it," he said. "That's why every tiniest thing is so important. You're one of the smartest men in the Company, Slade. There's no reason for me to explain these things to you. There's no reason why you shouldn't make OCS, except for your attitude. I've told you that before. What would you have done? Alone there with the men on the hill?"

"I knew who he was," I said.

Lieutenant Allison turned on me. "Why in the name of Christ didn't you tell Mazzioli!" He was mad.

"I did," I said. "But he didn't listen. Orders is orders," I said.

Lieutenant Allison stopped. We were halfway up the hill. He looked out over the parapet and down at the sea, vaguely white where it broke on the rocks.

"What's the matter with you, Slade? You don't want to be cynical about this war."

"I'm not cynical about this war," I said. "I may die in this war. I'm cynical about the Army. It's a helluva lot easier to be an idealist if you're an officer. The higher the officer, the higher the ideals." To hell with it, I thought, to hell with all of it.

"Slade," he said, "I'd like for you to buckle down. I wasn't kidding when I said you could make OCS. I'd like to see you go to OCS because you're smart. You could do it if you'd only buckle down."

"I've been an EM too long," I said. "I'm too cynical."

"You know, you could be shot for talking like this in the German Army."

"I know it," I said. "That's why I don't like the German Army, or the Japanese Army, or the British Army, or the Russian Army. I could get ten years in the American Army if you wanted to turn me in."

Lieutenant Allison was leaning on the parapet. "If I didn't like you, by god I would."

"Trouble with me," I said, "I'm too honest. They didn't have indoctrinization courses yet when I enlisted," I said.

"It's not a question of briefing," he said. "It's a question of belief."

"Yes," I said. "And also of who manufactures it."

"We have to be cruel now so we can be kind later, after the war."

"That's the theory of the Communist Internationale," I said. "I hear their indoctrinization courses are wonderful."

"They're our allies," he said. "When the enemy is defeated, why, it will all be set."

"I could never be an officer," I said. "I've not been indoctrinated well enough."

He laughed. "Okay, Slade. But you think over what I said, and if you want me to, I'll recommend you. You know, an intelligent man who refuses to use his intelligence to help win the war is a bottleneck. He's really a menace. In Germany he would be shot if he didn't use his intelligence to help win."

"Japan too," I said. "And in Italy and in Russia," I said. "Our country we only lock them up as conchies, as yet."

"Do you think I like being an officer?"

"Yes," I said. "I would like it. At least you get a bath and hot chow."

He laughed again. "Okay. But you think it over."

"I'll think about it," I said. "I'll think about all of it. But I never find an answer. Sometimes I wonder if there is an answer. The Greek is the man you ought to recommend."

"Are you kidding?" he grinned. "Mazzioli is a good sergeant."

"He believes the end justifies the means," I said. "He's been properly indoctrinated. I couldn't turn a man in if I had to."

Lieutenant Allison stood up from the parapet. "Think it over, Slade," he said.

"All right, sir," I said. "But I can tell you one thing. It's damn fine I can talk to you. But I always remember you're not all officers and I'm not all the EM," I said.

"Thanks, Slade," he said.

I walked on back down the road. I stopped every now and then to listen to the sea's attack against the cliff. It would be nice to be an officer. The sea and the wind were like two radio stations on the same dial mark. You could even have a bed-roll and a dog-robber. The old Revolutionists in Russia, I thought, they really had it all figured out; they really had the world saved this time. I kicked a pebble ahead of me down the road.

I must have gone very slow because the three men from the top were on my heels when I reached the bottom.

"Hey, Slade," one of them said. He came up. "I'm sorry we got you in trouble tonight. Nobody guessed this would happen."

"Forget it," I said. "All I got was a ass-eating."

Mazzioli was sitting on the culvert. "I'm going to roll up," he said belligerently.

"Okay, Greek," I said. I sat on the culvert a while, facing the wind. I liked to sit there at night alone, defying the wind. But a man could only do it so long. After a while a man got stupid from its eternal pummelling. A man got punch-drunk from it. Once before it made me so dizzy I fell down on my knees when I got up.

It was a wild place, the roaring sea, the ceaseless wind, the restless sand, the omniscient cliff.

I said good night to the men on post and rolled up myself. When I went under the wall it took my breath again. I lay in my blankets and listened to it howl just over my head.

It was three o'clock when the messenger from up on the hill woke me.

"What?" I said. "What is it? What?"

"Where's the Greek?" he said.

"He's here."

"You gotta wake him up."

"What's up?"

"You're moving back up the hill. Lieutenant's orders."

"Whose orders?" I said. "What about the demolition? What about the road-guard?"

"Lieutenant's orders. The road-guard is being disbanded. Altogether."

"What's the story?" I asked.

"I dunno. We got a call from the Company CP; the cap'n was maddern hell. He just got a call from Department HQ; they was maddern hell. Told the cap'n to disband the road-guard immediately. The orders'll be down in a couple days."

I laughed. "Orders is orders," I said.

"What?"

"Nothing," I said. "Is the lieutenant still up?"

"Yeh. He's in hole number one, with the telephone. Why?"

"I got to see him about something," I said.

"I'm going back," he said. "This wind is freezin' me. You sure you're awake?"

"Yes," I said. "You take off." I got up and woke the rest of the detail. "Get your stuff together, you guys. We're moving out. One of you call Alcorn down."

The Greek sat up, rubbing his eyes. "What is it? what's up? what's wrong?"

"We're moving out," I said. "Back up the hill. The road-guard is disbanded." When I stood up the wind hit me hard. I got my pack and kicked my blankets up into a pile. I slung my rifle and pack and picked up the blankets.

"You mean the *road-guard*?" Mazzioli's voice asked through the darkness and the wind. "For *good*?"

I climbed up around the wall and the wind caught at my blankets and I almost lost them.

"That's the way it is," I said.

Greater Love

I've already given most of the interesting bits on this one in the Introduction. I remember it was the summer when they were filming *Intruder in the Dust* down in Oxford. A friend of mine studying to be a photographer on the GI bill wanted me to go down there with him and introduce ourselves to Faulkner, but I didn't want to. Almost anybody can recognize Sgts. Warden and Welsh in

"The First." I once served on a Graves Registration Corps detail where a man helped to dig up his own brother. That memory set me to thinking.

Published in *Collier's*, Summer, 1951.

(*Jones's note*)

"HERE'S that detail roster," Corporal Quentine Thatcher said.

"Thanks," the first sergeant said. He did not look up, or stop working.

"Would you do me a favor?"

"Probably not," the First said. He went on working.

"I wish you wouldn't send Shelb down to the beach on this unloading detail. They've been bombing the Slot three or four times every day since the new convoy got in."

"Pfc Shelby Thatcher," the First said distinctly, without stopping working, "just because he's the kid brother of the compny clerk, does not rate no special privileges in my outfit. The 2nd Platoon is due for detail by the roster; you typed it out. Pfc Shelby Thatcher is in the 2nd Platoon."

"So is Houghlan in the 2nd Platoon. But I notice he never pulls any these details."

"Houghlan is the Compny Commander's dog robber."

"I know it."

"See the chaplain, kid," the First said, looking up for the first time. His wild eyes burned the skin of Quentin Thatcher's face. "That ain't my department."

"I thought maybe you would do it as a favor."

"What are you going to do when we really get into *com*bat, kid? up there on the *line*?"

"I'm going to be in the 2nd Platoon," Quentin said. "Where I can look out for my brother Shelb."

"Not unless I say so, you ain't." The First grinned at him evilly. "And I ain't saying so." He stared at Quentin a moment with those wild old soldier's eyes. Then he jerked his head toward the typing table across the mud floor of the tent. "Now get the hell back to work and don't bother me. I'm busy."

"Damn you," Quentin said deliberately. "Damn you to hell. You don't even know what it is, to love somebody."

"For two cents I'd send you back to straight duty today," the First said calmly, "and see how you like it. Only I'm afraid it would kill you."

"That suits me fine," Quentin said. He reached in his pocket and tossed two pennies onto the field desk. "I quit."

"You can't quit," the First grinned malevolently. "I won't let you. You're an ass, Thatcher, but you can type and I need a clerk."

"Find another one."

"After I spent all this time training you? Anyway, there ain't a platoon sergeant in the compny would have you. And I still got hopes maybe someday you'll make a soldier. Though I wouldn't know the hell why. Now get the hell out of here and take them papers over to the supply room like I told you, before I throw you over there with them bodily."

"I'm going. But you don't scare me a bit. And the last thing on this earth I'd ever want to be is a soldier."

The First laughed. Quentin took his own sweet time collecting the papers. The two pennies, lying on the field desk, he ignored.

The pennies were still there the next morning when Quentin came out of the orderly tent for a break. He watched the First legging it off down the road toward Regiment, then he walked across to where the four men were sitting on water cans in the tracky mud in front of the supply tent like four sad crows on a fence. They had only got back from the detail an hour before.

"Any news yet?" his brother Shelb asked him.

"Not a bit," Quentin said. "Nothing."

The waiting was beginning to get into all of them. The division had been here a month now, and both the 35th and 161st had gone up to relieve Marine outfits on the hills two weeks ago.

"Where was the first sergeant going, Quentin?" Al Zwermann asked hopefully. "He looked like he was in a hurry." Al Zwermann's brother Vic was in C Company of the 35th.

"Just to Regiment," Quentin said. "See about some kind of a detail."

"Not another detail!" Gorman growled.

"Sure. Ain't you heard?" Joe Martuscelli said sourly. "They done transferred the whole Regiment into the Quartermaster."

"You don't think it might be the order to move, then?" Zwermann asked.

"Not from what I heard over the phone. From what he said over the phone it was just another detail of some kind."

"A fine clerk," Gorman growled. "Why the hell dint you ask him what kind of a detail, you jerk?"

"Go to hell," Quentin said. "Why the hell didn't you ask him? You don't ask that man things."

"How'd the unloading go?"

"The unloading went fine," Shelb grinned. "They only bombed twice, and I stole a full fifth of bourbon off an officer's orderly on one of the transports."

"Yeah," Martuscelli said sourly. "A full fifth. And he has to save it all for his precious big brother."

"You think you'll have time to help drink it, Quent?" Shelb said, getting up, "before the First gets back?"

"Sometimes I don't think we'll any of us ever get to see any action," Gorman growled.

"To hell with the First," Quentin said.

"I'll go get it then," Shelb grinned.

"A hell of a fine way to treat your own squad," Martuscelli said sourly, watching him leave.

"I took a bust from corpul to transfer into this outfit," Gorman growled. "Because it was shipping out. They put me in Cannon Compny and I took another bust from pfc to get in a rifle compny. All because I wanted to see action."

"We all enlisted," Martuscelli said sourly.

"All I ask is they give me a rifle," Gorman growled. "None of your 155s for this soldier. Just a rifle, a bayonet and a knife. That's all. Gimme that and I'm ready." He thought a second, then added inconclusively, "Maybe couple grenades."

"You talk like my brother Vic," Zwermann said.

Somebody grunted. On the road that had not been a road a month ago a couple of jeeps hammered by, fighting the mud that came clear up to their belly plates. From where the men sat, the rows of coconut trees wheeled away in every direction like spokes from a hub. The sun was bright and clear in the sea air under the tall trees of the grove. It was a fine summery morning. Whenever the wind veered you could hear the sound of the firing from back in the hills.

"Vic's up there now," Zwermann said wonderingly.

"Well, when we do go up," Quentin said suddenly, committing himself, "I'm putting in for straight duty. With the 2nd Platoon. Soon's we got our orders to move."

"What the hell for?" Gorman asked, startled.

"Because I want to," Quentin said.

"If you do, you're nuts," Martuscelli said sourly.

"Ha," Gorman growled. "He won't. You know where he'll be when we go in, don't you? He'll be sitting under a hill on the first sarnt's lap punching his typewriter. That's where."

"You think so?" Quentin said.

"I know so. You don't think the First is going to let his protégé get where it's dangerous, do you?"

"I'm putting in to the Company Commander," Quentin said. "Not to the first sergeant."

"So what, clerk? you think that'll make any difference?"

"Don't worry about the clerks," Quentin said. "There's a lot of things you don't know about soldiering, too."

"What do you want to do it for, Quentin?" Zwermann said.

"Oh, a lot of things," Quentin said vaguely, "but mainly so I'll be able to look after Shelb."

"I'm glad my brother's in Africa," Martuscelli said sourly.

"I'm gladder yet," Gorman growled, "I ain't got one."

"Vic can take care of himself," Zwermann said. "Better than me." He was looking away from them.

"In a war," Groman growled, "*every* man's got to take care of himself. That's my philosophy."

"That's a hell of a thing to say!" Quentin said. Then he began to laugh, feeling a wild need to do something—he didn't know what—and there was nothing to do.

"What're you laughing at, clerk?" Gorman said stiffly.

"Because," Quentin said, stopping himself. "I'm laughing because here comes Shelb with the bottle, and here comes the First back from Regiment just in time to spoil everything."

"What'll I do with it?" Shelb said.

"Well, don't just stand there," Martuscelli said savagely. "Hide the damn thing." He grabbed the bottle desperately and stuck it down between two of the stacked water cans.

"If he finds it," Gorman said bitterly, "I know where it'll go."

"Thatcher!" the First bellowed. He was raging.

"Yes, sir," Shelb said resignedly.

"Not you," the First raged, "damn it."

"What do you want?" Quentin said.

"Go down and get Sergeant Merdith. Tell him to get his men together and report to me. The 2nd Platoon is going out on a detail."

There was a dull pause of adjustment.

"But hell, First," Martuscelli protested, "we just got back from one."

The First said, "And you're just now going out on another one. Ain't you heard? There's a war on. The 1st and 3rd Platoons and the Weapons Platoon already out. Who you think I'm going to send? the cook force?"

"What kind of a detail is it, Sergeant?" Zwermann asked.

"How the hell do I know! You think they tell me anything? All they tell me is how many men. And how soon." He ran his fingernails through his hair a moment. "You're going up in the hills," he said, "with a shavetail from the Graves Registration Corps. You're going up to dig up casualties and carry them down to the graveyard so the Quartermaster Salvage can come in and clean up."

"That's great," Martuscelli said.

"Well," the First raged, "what the hell're you waiting for, Thatcher? Get a move on. The truck's on its way."

"Sergeant," Quentin said, "I'd like to have permission to go along on this detail."

"What do you think this is, Thatcher? A vacation resort? There's work to be done."

"I've done everything you had laid out for me."

The First looked at him shrewdly. "Okay," he said. "Go. *Now get the hell down there and get Sergeant Merdith.*"

"Right," Quentin said, and took off.

Behind him, he heard the First say, "The rest of you men can wait here. But first Martuscelli, I want that bottle. Maybe it'll teach you not to be so slow the next time. You men know better than to have whisky in camp. It's against Army Regulations."

There were four trucks with the GRC second lieutenant. The detail rode in the first two. They wound away down through the endless coconut grove, breasting the mud like swimmers, the two empty trucks lumbering along behind.

"I always wondered how they got them down to the cemetery," Martuscelli said.

"Well, now you know," Gorman growled.

It took them an hour to get through the belt of jungle in low gear. Then they came up out of it into the hills like submarines surfacing and ground on for another hour up the hills before they stopped at one that had a crumbling line of slit trenches along the rearward slope.

"Okay, everybody out," the GRC lieutenant said briskly, climbing out of the cab of the first truck. "Each man get a shovel."

The drivers dropped the tail gates and the detail clambered down and went immediately to the lip of the hill. Beyond the crest was a wide saddle that led up to the next hill. The saddle was littered with all kinds of equipment—packs, entrenching tools, helmets, rifles, bayonets, abandoned stretchers, even stray shoes and empty C ration cans. It gave the impression that everyone had suddenly dropped everything in a mad rush to cover ground.

"If any of you are interested in tactics," the GRC lieutenant said, pointing to a faint haze of smoke three miles to the east, "that's the present line of the 35th Infantry over there. Three days ago the 35th was here, and jumped off across this saddle."

The men looked at the distant hills, then at the far-off line of smoke from which sporadic sounds of firing came faintly, then at the saddle below them. There were a few half-muttered comments.

"Okay, fellows," the GRC lieutenant said briskly. "First, I want to warn you about duds and unexploded grenades. Don't touch them. There's nothing to worry about as long as nobody gets wise, but the Ordnance hasn't been in here yet.

"Now," he said, "I want you to spread out. We're only covering the saddle today. Make a line and whenever you see a grave, stop. Some of them, as you see, are marked with bayoneted rifles stuck in the ground. Others are marked with just helmets on sticks. Still others aren't marked at all, so be watchful. We don't want to miss any.

"If there are dog tags on them, make sure one is fastened securely to them and give the other to me. If there's only one, leave it on them, and come get me and I'll note the information. If there's no dog tags, just forget it.

"It's best to work in threes or fours. Two men can't handle one very well, as advanced as the decomposition is by now. And there's no rush, men. We've got all day to cover the area and we want to do a good job. Someday after the war they'll be shipped home to their families.

"There are shelter-halfs to roll them in in the last two trucks. The best way is to work shovels in under the head, the knees and the buttocks; that's why it's best for three to work together on one; and then roll them up out of the hole with one concerted movement onto the shelter-half which you have already placed alongside. That way you don't get any on you, and you also keep them from coming apart as much as possible.

"Now. Any questions?" the GRC lieutenant said briskly. "No? Okay then, let's go to work," he said, and sat down on the running board of the first truck and lit a cigarette.

The line spread out and moved forward down the crest out onto the saddle and began breaking up into little huddles of moving shovels from which there began to come strained exclamations followed by weak laughter and curses.

As each mound was opened, the smell, strange and alien as the smell of the jungle, burst up out of it like a miniature explosion and then fell heavily back to spread like mercury until it met and joined the explosions from other mounds to form a thick carpet over the whole saddle that finally overflowed and began to drip down into the jungled valleys.

"Just like a treasure hunt back home in the Y.M.C.A.," Martuscelli muttered sourly, sweating heavily.

"You don't reckon I'll ever look like that, do you?" Gorman growled, grinning.

"If you do," Shelb said, "I won't speak to you."

"What his best friends wouldn't tell him," Quentin laughed wildly.

"Well, I hope you're happy now, clerk," Gorman growled. "You finally got to come along and find out what straight duty in a rifle company's like. You still putting in for it?"

"Sure," Quentin said. "Wouldn't miss it."

Al Zwermann, of them all, was the only one who did not say anything, but nobody noticed. They were all too busy trying to carry off the collective fantasy that they were unmoved.

It was Quentin's turn to feel for the tags at the sixth mound, and when he brought them out and cut one off and read it he was somehow not surprised at all. The tag read:

ZWERMANN VICTOR L
12120653 T43 B

and Quentin put it in the handkerchief with the other five and straightened up and wiped his hand off and heard his voice saying toughly, "Well, let's get him out."

"Let me see that tag, will you, Quentin?" Zwermann said.

"What tag?" he heard his voice say. "This one?"

"I've seen all the others. Let me see that one."

"I don't even know which one it was, now, Al."

"Quentin, let me see that tag!"

Shelb, Martuscelli and Gorman were still standing at the head, knees and buttocks with their shovels. They had all known Vic back at Schofield, and Vic's battalion of the 35th had come over on the same transport with them. Quentin noticed that there was an odd, distant look on all their faces except Zwermann's and it made him think of those slugs in the garden with their eyes on the ends of two horns and when they got scared or worried they pulled in the horns.

"Well," Martuscelli said with a voice that had been pulled in along with the horns, "we might as well get him out of there."

"Don't touch him," Zwermann said, still holding the tag.

"But, Al," Quentin said, "We got to get him out of there, Al. We can't leave him there," he said reasonably. "That's against orders."

"I said don't touch him, damn you!" Zwermann yelled. He picked up one of the shovels and started for Martuscelli and Gorman and Shelb, who were still holding theirs and standing all together like three hens in the rain. "You're not going to put any shovels on *him*, damn you!"

They let go of their shovels and stepped back guiltily, still all together like three hens in the rain. Zwermann stopped and brandished the shovel at them and then flung it over the edge of the saddle into the jungle.

"Nobody's going to touch *him* with shovels!" he yelled.

The four of them backed off slowly, back up the saddle toward the hill where the GRC lieutenant and Sergeant Merdith were watching. The men working at the other mounds near them began to back off, placatingly in the same way, still holding their shovels, collecting the men at the further mounds as they moved, until the whole line that had descended into the saddle was slowly backing up out of the saddle.

"Nobody's going to touch *him*! I'll shoot the first man that touches *him*! Nobody's going to see *him*!"

The line went on backing placatingly out of the saddle, and Zwermann stood holding them off as if at gun point and cursing, his bald head shining in the afternoon sun.

"My Lord," the GRC lieutenant said dismally, when they were hidden behind the number one truck. "I wouldn't've had this happen for anything. What do you suppose he's going to do?"

They stood, milling a little like nervous sheep, listening to Zwermann moving around down on the saddle. Then they heard him staggering up the slope to the number two truck, where he dropped something heavily onto the iron floor and then clambered in. Then there was silence. It was Sergeant Merdith who finally peered over the hood.

Zwermann was sitting on the bench of the truck, glaring out at them. He had gotten his brother out of the hole by himself and wrapped him up in the shelter-half and carried him up and put him instinctively, without thinking, in the same truck he himself had ridden out in.

"Let's just leave him alone," the GRC lieutenant said. "He'll be all right now."

Sheepishly they straggled back down onto the saddle and went back to work. When they had the rest of the corpses wrapped and stacked in the two empty trucks, as many men as could squeezed into the first truck. Only an unlucky handful rode home in the second truck. Zwermann sat on the bench, holding a shovel, and glared at them forbiddingly all the way down.

At the cemetery on the Point there was a moment of unpleasant suspense when the handful of GRC men, who had taken over with the swift efficiency of long practice, prepared to unload the number two truck. But Zwermann only glared at them with a kind of inarticulate fury and seemed to feel he had relieved himself of some obscure obligation and did not protest. He climbed down and started off to walk the mile and a half back to the bivouac.

"Somebody better go with him," the GRC lieutenant said apprehensively. "He's liable to wander off in the jungle or something. I'm still responsible for you men till I deliver you back to your outfit."

"We'll go," Quentin said, "the four of us. We're sort of his buddies."

"Then you're responsible for him, Corporal," the GRC lieutenant said after them. "You and these other men."

When they caught up to him, Zwermann glared at them with the ferocious suspicion of a man who has learned not to trust strangers. But he did not protest their walking behind him.

That night, instead of waiting till they got marching orders, Quentin Thatcher put in to the Company Commander personally to go back to straight duty with the 2nd Platoon immediately. His request was immediately rejected, emphatically and with finality.

Five days later the Regiment moved out, and Quentin marched with the Company Headquarters at the head of the company column beside the First, who carried a Listerine bottle full of whisky and took frequent gargles for his sore throat without offering Quentin any for his. The 2nd Platoon was somewhere in the rear.

Their battalion hiked seven miles the first day and bivouacked that night in the jungle, dead beat. The next day they crossed an Engineers' bridge and started up a steep hill that rose abruptly up out of the jungle from the riverbank. The noise of the firing did not sound any closer than it had back down on the beach.

Then they came up over the crest of the hill and found themselves in combat. The noise that had sounded faint in the jungle beat about their ears and fell upon them with both drumming fists. It seemed a little unfair for no one to have warned them.

The hilltop was alive with men, but none of them noticed the new arrivals except to curse them for being in the way. The men cursed one another ferociously and ran back and forth, with boxes of ammo and C rations. Over on the next hill the men in Quentin's battalion could see the little black figures of the 3rd Battalion toiling doggedly up the slope toward other little black figures at the top.

Their first reaction was to tiptoe back down the hill and get the hell out of the way before they disturbed somebody or were run over; or at least to go back down and come up properly this time, in squad column with scouts out. They stood around awkwardly, trying to see, waiting for someone to tell them what they were supposed to do, feeling like poor relations at the family reunion.

Quentin found himself standing beside Fred Beeson, the supply sergeant, who had insisted on coming to see the fun.

"I thought they'd have a better system of supply than this in combat," Beeson said excitedly. "Didn't you?"

"Yeah," Quentin said, wondering what had become of the First. He looked around to see if he could see Shelb. His eyes found the First, over on the right. The big man was kneeling over some cases of grenades and hacking at them with his bayonet as if he were using a machete, deftly splitting box after box open around the middle.

"Hey, hey! let's go!" the First, who still had his Listerine bottle, whooped, drunkenly happy. "Let's go, let's go. Here's grenades. Who wants grenades?" he hollered, pulling the black containers out of the racked boxes and forward-passing them like footballs at arms raised out of the crowd.

"Let's go, you men!" he roared at them. "What the hell you guys waiting for?"

"Yeah," somebody said indecisively, "what we waiting for?"

They started fixing bayonets, as if each man had thought of it first, individually by himself, and then they were walking down the hill with the Company Commander in the lead, as if that were the most nearly normal thing to do, under the circumstances.

"Get your eggs here!" the First howled at them happily as they passed. "Nice fresh yard eggs!"

Quentin found himself in motion between the mess sergeant and two of the cooks. They had also come along to see the fun. Wondering again where Shelb was, he looked around and discovered he was surrounded by fun-seeking members of the cook force.

"This is better'n slingin' hash any day," one of them grinned at him excitedly.

"Yeah," Quentin said. *We're in combat*, he thought; and then repeated it: *we're in combat*. Was this all there was to it?

Ahead of them the hill sloped down, long and gradual and quite bare, to a brushy creek at the bottom. Ahead was the steep hill where the black figures of the 3rd Battalion were still toiling doggedly, but closer to the top now.

As Quentin watched them, he saw one marionette at the top throw something down at another marionette below him. The second marionette turned without hesitation and jumped out from the side of the hill as a man jumps out from a ladder. He fell maybe seven yards before he hit again and began to roll. From where he had jumped something burst black like a cannon cracker. The second marionette stopped rolling and got up and began to toil doggedly back up toward the top again. The first marionette disappeared over the crest.

Then Quentin's company was at the bottom, fighting through the brush and starting up the slope, and Quentin could not see the men at the top any more.

Mortar shells were beginning to drop down here and there around Quentin's company, and that was when Quentin noticed that the explosions did not make any noise. Men around him were beginning to shuck out of their combat packs and leave them where they fell.

Quentin shucked out of his own pack, wishing momentarily that he knew where Shelb was. He looked around.

He could not see Shelb, but way off to the left he saw Gorman a second, climbing doggedly. Then somebody came between. Gorman had no pack. Gorman's face looked peculiar, as if somebody had poulticed it with plastic wood. The heel.

The silent mortar shell explosions were getting thicker, and the 3rd Battalion was puffing hard and digging holes along the military crest, in the shelter of the real crest of the hill. As the uneven line passed through between the holes on toward the real crest, the diggers glared up at them furiously without stopping digging. Then Quentin's company was over the crest and going down the second hill toward the jungle that came halfway up, only this time there was nobody in front of them and everything changed weirdly and seemed to shift its gears. Quentin felt as if a light bulb had been turned off in his mind. He was all alone in the silence of the dark locked closet.

He was also getting very tired.

Two strangers who were walking beside him on his left suddenly quit and lay down to rest. Quentin closed over automatically, wishing he had guts enough to quit and lay down to rest. That Gorman. Quentin's legs ached, and a dull rage began to grow in him at this obvious laziness that would only leave more dirty work for him and Shelb to do.

A mortar shell burst silently in front of him and he saw three more strange men he did not know lie down to rest. Quentin felt like kicking them, but he closed over further left and went around. Smoke burned his eyes. One of the strangers yelled something at him. The other two strangers were asleep already. Quentin went on. There sure were a lot of strangers with the company today.

It was when he closed over that he saw Shelb for the first time since at breakfast. Shelb was walking with Joe Martuscelli and Al Zwermann and Gorman, off to Quentin's left. Quentin had difficulty telling them apart; they all four seemed to be wearing the same poulticed face. As he opened his mouth to yell at them through the silence, a mortar shell geysered silently in front of them and three of them jerked, and lay down to rest. Only Shelb went on walking.

Quentin was outraged. *Who do they think they are? They're no better than I am. Or Shelb is. Is everybody going to quit but me and Shelb?*

Joe Martuscelli sat back up and looked at Quentin dully. Shakily, he got to his feet with his rifle, holding his left arm close in to his side, and started on.

Sure, Quentin thought furiously, *that damn Martuscelli, he always was a goldbrick. Looks like me and Shelb will have to do it all.*

Then Shelby, who had moved perhaps ten yards, dropped his rifle and put his hands to his face and fell down.

Why, damn him! Quentin thought outragedly. *I thought at least he would stick with me. What do they want me to do? win this war all by myself?*

Shelb did not move and Martuscelli stumbled past him and went on. Shelb lay as he had fallen, face down and shoulders limp, his lax hands still up by his face.

Well, I'm damned, Quentin thought disgustedly, *if he hasn't fainted dead away*. Embarrassment for his brother made him suddenly hate him for failing in the clutch. *Gone yellow. Can't take it. Ought to go and kick him up*.

"Hey!" the man on his right said. "There's one. I see one."

"Where?" Quentin said.

"There," the man said. "Right there. See him?"

"No," Quentin said. The man was a big man and right beside him but his voice came from a long way off.

"Well, I see him," the big man said. He raised his rifle and fired the whole clip into the jungle. "Must of missed him," he said. "Come on."

"Okay," Quentin said. Then he stopped. Fifteen yards away on the edge of the jungle was a dark blob of wood on the side of a tree. Somehow his eyes had fastened themselves upon it and recognized it for a helmet. He was astounded.

"What is it?" the man beside him said.

"Shh," Quentin said craftily. He dropped down to a kneeling position. No shooting from the offhand this time; he was taking no chances. The big man beside him stopped, trying to see what it was, and Quentin chuckled to himself.

As he took up the slack and started the squeeze, the helmet moved. Slowly and carefully it raised itself and a face appeared over the sights. Quentin was astonished. He touched her off and in firing was even more astonished to see the same plastic-wood poultice on this face, too.

Ha, he's afraid, he thought savagely; and all the hate and fear of the past two hours compressed itself into his forefinger vindictively.

The recoil slammed his shoulder and he kept both eyes open like he had been taught and saw the face open redly like a thrown tomato. A piece of bridgework popped out of the mouth.

"I got him!" Quentin yelled. "I got him!"

"Good work," the big man said. "Congratulations."

"Come on!" Quentin said. He jumped up to run to the tree. A mortar shell, a ninety, burst close by and slammed him right back down. He lay there stunned by the concussion, reminded that there were other Japanese. He had forgotten the war.

"Come on," the big man beside him said "Get up. You ain't hurt. Get up!" A big hand grabbed Quentin by the shoulder and hoisted him back up.

His chin was bleeding from a cut where it had hit a rock but it did not seem important. He wiped it off and started to walk on toward the jungle. The big man stayed close beside him. All around them groups of men were entering the jungle.

The dead Japanese lay sprawled out on his back. The bullet had gone in just below his nose and smashed the teeth. Thick glue-like blood had filled the mouth and run out at both corners to hang in strips down to the ground.

"He looks awful dead," Quentin said, looking at the other man. Slowly, he recognized him; it was the First. But his face looked different.

"Your face looks different," Quentin said.

"So does yours," the First said.

"It does?" Quentin said. He felt of his face. "I need a shave," he said. He picked up the piece of bridgework that had popped out of the Jap's mouth and stuck it between his helmet and the liner strap and struck a pose for the First.

"The immortal infantryman," the First said. "How about his wallet?"

"I forgot!"

Quentin fished it out of the grimy shirt pocket. There was a picture. It showed a Japanese woman holding a baby and smiling toothily. There was Japanese writing in up-and-down lines on the back. There was no money.

"Tough luck," the First grinned.

"Mine by right of conquest," Quentin said. "I guess you won't be so damn wise about clerks now, will you?"

"Nope," the First said. "I guess not."

"You and Gorman."

"Want a little drink?" the First said.

"Sure," Quentin said. The rifle fire was getting heavier down below in the jungle. He wiped his mouth. "Hear that? Come on." He turned down toward the firing, then turned back. "Did you see that damn Shelb poop out back there on the hill?"

"No," the First said. "I didn't see him."

"He was right beside us."

"I didn't see him," the First said, impassively.

"You don't have to kid me," Quentin said. "I know you saw him. Wait'll I get my hands on him! I'll beat his damned head in!" He moved away between the trees down the hill toward the firing, looking for more Japs to kill.

"He'll never make a soldier. Come on, First, let's go," he said eagerly to the man moving slowly behind him. "Come on, damn it, let's go."

"I'm coming," the First said, watching up in the trees. "Go ahead. I'm right beside you. Go ahead, you're doing fine."

"He ought to be shot," Quentin said.

"Watch the trees," the First said. "You're doing fine."

Some Came Running

(1958)

Jones's second published novel focuses on a returning GI, Dave Hirsch, and his failed attempts to come to terms with a postwar society (1946–49) moving into commercial overdrive. It is set in the small town of Parkman, Illinois, which is based on Jones's hometown of Robinson, and, to some extent, Marshall, Illinois. The latter was the home of the Handy Writers' Colony, which Jones helped found and support with royalties from *From Here to Eternity*. The novel was written at the colony.

Critics were unkind to *Some Came Running*, complaining about, among other things, its length and eccentric punctuation (Jones dropped the apostrophes in common contractions, e.g., "dont"), but Jones remained fond of the novel. In 1973, he called it "the best single book I have written." *Running*, published by Scribner's, became a best-seller and a popular (abridged) paperback which drew praise for its sharp rendering of small-town narrow-mindedness and hypocrisy. In Robinson, there was consternation over Jone's use of events and people from his own past.

Jones conceived of the novel as a "romantic tragedy," a bitter revelation of the folly of romantic love. But its action unfolds beneath the long overhang of World War II; its prologue and epilogue, reprinted here, are scenes of warfare. *Some Came Running* opens by looking back on Dave during the Battle of the Bulge— Jones's only fictional depiction of the European theater. Its conclusion looks forward, after Dave has been killed by a deranged

Marine hero, to Korea where Dave's friend, Wally French, encounters a new kind of warfare.

[The Battle of the Bulge]

They came running through the fog across the snow, lumbering, the long rifles held up awkwardly high, the pot helmets they were all so proud of and never seemed to camouflage gleaming dully, running fast, but appearing to come slowly, lifting their feet high in the big thick boots, foreign, alien, brain-chilling. They came that way again and again, and then again, and when you thought there could not be any more of them left on earth to come, they came still again, and still again. Dave knelt behind the wall at the end of the field, his knees soggy wet and numb cold in the snow, and fired carefully and mechnically at them with the carbine he had taken (like the Torch! ha ha) from the dead man whose face he would always see but never be able to recognize as human because the open mouth and the nostrils and eye sockets and ears were all filled with snow. Sometimes when he fired one of them would fall but there was no way of knowing whether it was himself who hit him or one of the other men behind the wall kneeling in the snow that the sun had not melted and firing too. The other men of the 3615th QM Gas Supply Company. At least, he was quite sure, some of them must be.

At other times they came with the tanks, riding, or running along behind them, and it was no longer the wall but a road ditch where there was no snow, and where the land sloped down and away from him, that he fired from behind, and then behind him he could hear the armor and the TDs firing too. Most of the tanks would stop and disgorge their unhuman contents smoking and running, and finally the others would turn back. Even so, sometimes the running figures would still come on, lumbering through the fog across the snow, the long rifles held up awkwardly high, the pot helmets they were all so proud of and never seemed to camouflage gleaming menacingly, dangerously, and lifting their feet high in the big thick boots. Sometimes it was snow they came across, and sometimes it was only mud, and at other places it was through the woods, and at one place it was broken buildings that he stood behind and fired at them from, the white Red Cross brassard (because he was the medic of the 3615th QM Gas Supply Company) still on his arm forgotten, though he had meant to take it off. Dave was never just quite sure how he got from one of these places to another. Four days, eight days, ten days, twelve days. And in all this time they never stopped coming. They might have been mechanical, electric robots; or they might have been little bandy-legged Japanese men; or they might have been strange, alien man-creatures disgorged and dropped by the thousands and the millions with all their ammunition and vehicles and equipment from giant cigar-shaped space ships hovering in the stratosphere to conquer this foreign planet for their race, their civilization and their leaders. The broken rubble of buildings he stood behind as he fired at them was, somebody said, called Malmédy; or was it Stavelot? He was at both, at different times. Most of the time he did not know the faces of any of the men he was with. But sometimes, at other times, usually when he least expected it, he would see the face of a man he recognized from the 3615th QM Gas Supply Company . . .

. . . The lonely, solitary, unexpected MP carrying a slung rifle had stopped the convoy at the crossroads, standing in the road his gloved hand held up high, and directed them to turn back north away from St Vith toward Spa. Dave was riding in the cab of the second truck, behind Lt Perry.

"Theyre comin in all through around here," the MP yelled over the motors. "Nobody knows all just where. Everythings to circle back north. If you get to Spa youll probably be all right. I dont know if you can make it."

It was the first that any of them had ever heard about the Battle of the Bulge. Which, in fact, was not even called that yet, then.

"But we're supposed to deliver this gas in St Vith," Lt Perry yelled back. "We've got twelve bays of cans here. They may need it in St Vith."

"Then you better burn it. There probably wont be anybody in St Vith when you get there except Jerry. My orders are to send everything back north to report to V Corps."

"Well, maybe we can get it through to the dump at Spa," Lt Perry yelled.

"You better burn it. Youre more liable to get cut off from Spa than not before you get there. And for that matter there may not be no dumps left in Spa by the time you get there. Just try and get it off the road to burn it, thats all I ask."

So they had left him there, solitary, alone, and—to Dave's eyes at least— incredibly valiant, a lone MP set down from some passing truck to direct traffic at a nameless crossroads during the end of the world, and a mile

*further on they pulled the carrier trucks off into a patch of field and pulled
the distributor caps and sloshed the gasoline around and set fire to it, and
then went on in the two personnel trucks. They never did get to Spa. At
Stavelot they were shuttled along into the line by a frantic irate Major.*

"What outfit?" he yelled.

"3615th QM Gas Supply Company," Lt Perry answered.

*"What?!" the Major yelled incredulously. "The 3615th QM Ga—Well,
go along north and east and report to the first line colonel you see."*

"We havent got any rifles, except two or three."

*"Pick some up off the dead casualties," the Major had yelled disgustedly.
"Theres plenty around. Dont stand on ceremonies. And dont forget to get
the bandoliers!" he had bellowed after them as they had moved away....*

*...It was that same afternoon, they learned later, that Battery B of the
283rd Field Artillery Observation Battalion, together with the MP who
was directing traffic at the crossroads where they stopped, were ambushed
and most of them massacred, three miles south of Malmédy....*

*...The strange thing was that you did not really feel anything much at
all, after the first two hours. The first two hours of being scared. When the
bullet that clipped the big arm muscle below his left shoulder knocked him
down and he got back up and found he could still move the arm, he went
right on firing the dead man's carbine without thinking much about it one
way or the other and before very long forgot all about it. At least it took care
of that Red Cross brassard. It wasn't that he was brave, it was just that
there wasnt anywhere really to go it seemed, or anyone to go to. No place in
the world was there anyplace, or anyone, to go to. No one to appeal to. No
Supreme Court anymore. No President, no Congress, no FBI, no police who
had used to pick him up for vagrancy to protect the citizenry. No nothing.
And it was important to keep firing at them as they came, and kept on
coming, and did not stop coming, running big-footed in the big thick boots,
the pot helmets gleaming cruelly and inhumanly through the fog. They
hadnt wanted him for an Infantryman when they drafted him because he
was fat and over thirty. But now he was an Infantryman anyway in spite
of them. Once he saw Lt Perry, somewhere, with blood running all down
one side of his head, his big thick glasses lost and broken somewhere evidently,
and looking very disbelieving at finding himself a Lieutenant of Infantry at
last finally, as someone led him away.*

*It was a strange way to live—without lawyers, and without judges, and
without Courts of Appeal any more. Without mealtimes, and without
bedtimes, without a morning crap somewhere, without running water.
Strange, very strange. And still they seemed to keep on coming. Where did*

they all come from? They had told you that there werent even that many of them left everywhere, *any more. That they were all on the run, back to Berlin. That everything was practically over, the war was practically over.*

Sometimes when they came they got real close. Close enough you could see that they were men after all, with the same strained numb disbelieving hopefully-cruel faces as the faces all around you up and down the ditch, and then it was great fun and a real satisfaction to shoot them and see their faces as they fell twist with pain you were glad they felt, and know that it was you who definitely hit them.

Four days, eight days, ten days, twelve days. And he had eleven definites and two or three very probables, of which he kept careful track. One time, coming with and behind a tank that was not stopped, they got so close that with the tank some of them overran the wall and then someone finally got the tank stopped and a man near him tripped up one of them and Dave jumped and smashed his face in with the butt of the dead man's carbine which had no bayonet, but that was the only time he ever really touched one of them. All the other definites were carbine shots—at twenty feet, at ten yards, at twenty yards. And still they seemed to keep on coming. Like ants or spiders. That when you tramped a mess of them, the others only ran on up over your shoe top and up inside your pants leg on your leg itself.

Four days, eight days, ten days, twelve days. And it appeared as thought it was never going to stop. Then, finally, he knew definitely it was never going to stop.

It was the new way of life—without lawyers, without judges, without Courts of Appeal. No Supreme Court, no President, no Congress, no FBI. It was the new way of life, and he knew, definitely, at last, that it would never stop.

[Korea]

They came running through the paddy fields across the snow, dogtrotting, their rifles held at a rigid precise Port Arms, in their quilted uniforms or large long overcoats and the quilted boots, the conspicuous white bandoliers crossing their chests, and you shot them down. Sometimes, later,—on those occasions when the Company held—you could count upwards of a hundred bodies lying on the slope up which they came in front of the position. Other times—on those occasions when the Company did not hold; and these were in the majority—you did not know how many the all of you might have killed. But then it didnt seem to matter, really. There were so many of them that no matter how many hundreds of them you might kill, it was never enough. They swarmed around like ants or termites, everywhere, coming from every direction, all around you, all over you. And on those times the Company would finally, under the constant never-wavering overpowering pressure, have to fall back as best they could to another hilltop and regroup and reform and set up another perimeter.

They did not always run. Sometimes they walked. In long thin evenly spaced lines, those rifles held at that rigid Port like on parade, right up the slope at you. At other times they would come ramming down a draw, all running in unison and in step in their quilted boots, rifles at rigid Port, in a regular column of fours, close packed. Trying to outflank, of course. And usually they did. Those were the best for shooting. But—much more often than not, of course—it would be at night.

In the evening, as dusk came on, if the wind was right, you could sometimes hear them on the next hill: that strange weird out-of-tune chant; they were death-singing: getting ready to die. Ought to do some death-singing ourselves, somebody would say. Then, with the dark, the bugles and the shepherd's pipes and the whistles and the cymbals and the rattles would start making their weird ungodly noises, and the attack would begin again. And if the night was light enough, or if some house or something was burning somewhere, you could see those widely spaced lines of widely spaced men—strange, alien, totally foreign and un-understandable—coming down their own hill, crossing the frozen paddy fields, beginning to mount your hill below you. They seemed to always prefer the gentlest slope—for their main attack, at least. Sometimes,—if the BARs and LMGs didnt jam, or freeze, or just simply burn out—the fire would be too much for them and they would go to ground among the rocks. Then the grenading and countergrenading and the firefight would begin, while they tried to work up close enough to rush. They had a trick of—when they thought they were close enough—three men rushing in a V—point first—the two men behind firing to cover the one in front. Lots of times, small knots would break inside the perimeter in their rushes. But they fought funny. Once they were inside, most of them didnt seem to know what to do and just sort of ran around aimlessly until somebody cut them down. Although all of them didnt do that though. So far the Company had kept its unity, as Regiment withdrew slowly westward back onto Division. They had never quite been caught bad enough to be broken up entirely. But if they had kept their unity, attrition was thinning them out swiftly and dangerously.

The pattern was set—had been set for some days now. After the first big battle at the Chongchon—which we had lost, so badly; and which the Company had only got a very little of—it was withdraw and fight, withdraw and fight. Luckily, moving back on their own Division to the west, they had not had to run "The Gauntlet". But they were catching hell of their own kind, just the same. The trouble was, in these damned hills that nearly overlapped each other and this damned weather, nobody knew where anybody else was most of the time. They might be behind you in a big column, they might be ahead, they might be on either side. You just had to set up as tight a perimeter as you could, and fight. Then when they drew off next day to eat and bury their dead, as they always seemed to do, take the road and withdraw. That was the pattern. There wasnt much question any more of trying to attack.

Wally Dennis: Wallace French Dennis: former holder of the Parkman College Fellowship for the novel: could, as he cleaned his piece and saw that his squad was altogether, think back wryly to his former life in Parkman Illinois—so many thousands of miles and thousands of years away. That just hadnt been him, that was all: it had been another guy. When he thought of Gwen French, and of Dave Hirsh, and of 'Bama Dillert, and of old Bob— they just werent real. They were only a dream, and this, here, now, was all that was real. Funny, had he once been in love with some girl named Dawn? he would think wryly; some girl who had been the cause of him enlisting in the goddamned Army? Funny. How funny people were. Howlingly funny. But the only people he knew existed anywhere were, and in that order: one, his squad that he had to take care of all the time and check them to see they changed their socks; and two, the Company and the Captain—Captain Hewitt—whom they all of them loved desperately, and who was the main instrument that up to now had kept the Company together—he wasnt scared of anything that lived, Captain Hewitt wasnt; and three, a long line of unknown men behind him up through Regiment and Division whom he had never seen and would never know, but who were governing with their strategy the continued existence of his life. And that was all. His bad ear had been running for some time now, with him unable to take proper care of it. But little things like that just didnt matter any more. Not now. Wally had been at the Pusan Perimeter—was the only one left in his squad who had, in fact—but the Pusan Perimeter had never been anything like this. He had long ago—on November 25th, to be exact, when he saw all the antlike hordes pouring in—given up the idea of ever getting out of this alive.

"Here they come," someone would say, and he would get his little pile of M1 clips ready and at hand. Nobody had any helmets any more; you just couldn't wear them in this cold without freezing off your ears; and it was always a funny feeling to stick your head up over the edge of the hole in the big pile cap. But you had to do it. It was just something that had to be done.

He still had his Randall #1, and in fact had carried it all through—from Pusan Perimeter on through. He had rigged a prong-hook on the sheath so he could wear it on his ammo belt like a canteen, and he kept it bright and shining clean. Every time he cleaned his piece—which in this freezing weather had to be frequently—he also got out the Randall #1 and cleaned it too and wiped it carefully with the oily rag he carried in his shirt. Oil, of course, could not be put on the gun at all, in this weather: it would thicken and lock it in a minute. But the Randall #1 had no working parts—unless you wanted to count his own right arm—and the oil was good for it: it still looked as bright and shining clean as when it used to lie on his dresser at home. And he loved it. It had saved his life on more than one occasion. He bet he had sold a couple of hundred knives for that W.D. Randall. Guys were always coming up to look at and handle it. Most all of them said they were going to order one;—and back before all this bugout started, a lot of them probably had. Well, if he had helped sell a bunch of Randall knives, he was glad: because more than anything else, more than any other thing anywhere, his Randall #1 gave him a sense of comfort and luck. It was funny, in times of stress, what things men cadged onto to believe in and superstitiously hang their hopes on as luckypieces. Wally's was his knife: If he could just keep his knife with him, and keep it clean and in good shape, he felt he might still yet get out—be one of those who wouldnt have to be hauled out like cordwood in the trucks, dead. Besides, it was beautiful: a lethally beautiful work of art: the only piece of beauty he had been able to hang on to—except for some snatch pictures he had picked up in Japan. He had killed eight Gooks with it.

Funny, even now that fact was still almost unbelievable. It took a lot more force to drive a sharp knife into a man's body than he had anticipated. The shock in your arm was about the same as punching a guy in the head. It didnt take much effort to slash their throats—if you could get at them—but even then there was more pull against the knife than he had ever thought there would be. The flesh clung to it. And he had killed eight with it. Unbelievable. Eight Gooks. Eight ants. Only, they werent ants; they were men.

They were so different from us, these Asiatics. They had no idea of the individual importance of the separate human life. And in that, they were like ants. It was like fighting the terrifying Mongol hordes of Genghis Khan. Apparently they had no thought at all about killing one man, or five, like we did. They were terribly poor equipped. Their quilted uniforms were almost completely inadequate to the cold. The rice bags they lived off of would not have sustained our men at all. Their Russian rifles were evidently not of the best grade, either. —Of course, now, lots and lots of them were equipped with captured American equipment: our own M1s and grenades, being used against us.— But the others: some of them even attacked uphill without any weapons at all. And yet none of them seemed to mind all this much at all, not one twentieth that we would. You couldnt help feeling sorry for the poor bastards sometimes—or would have, if there were not so many of them all around you—trying so hard to kill you.

"Here they come," *somebody would say, and he would stick his head up over the edge of his hole—with that extraordinary feeling of complete nakedness it gave you—and then would, as soon as he could pick out targets, begin to fire.*

They want what we got, was the phrase that always jumped into Wally's head as he squinted through the sights at targets. They want what we got. Our bread, our food, our guns, our ammo, our grenades, our warm clothes. And more than that they want all of that that weve got behind us back home: the luxuries theyve never dreamed of: the richness of America: they want what we got, he would think, and fire. And we want to keep it, and thats why we're here: we mean to keep it. We built it, we made and invented it, why shouldnt we want to keep it? Squint and fire. Squint and fire. Pick your targets. Dont waste ammo. Squint and fire.

And still they kept on coming, dogtrotting up the slopes at the perimeter. Or walking, in the slow thin widely spaced lines. You could go on killing them forever, Wally sometimes thought, with all the ammunition of the whole world, and you just couldnt kill them all: and they would still keep on running, dogtrotting uphill in their funny quilted uniforms, silently, stubbornly, endlessly. It was like some new kind of way of life, he would think. Without justice for either side; no law; no courts; no police forces; and only The Company existed truly. *They want what we got. They want what I got. But I intend to keep it. If I can.*

"Theyre going back," *somebody would say, and the firefight would slack off and once again you could hear the bugles in the night, and the funny shepherd's pipes blowing, and the cymbals and weird rattles that sounded like Hallowe'en.*

"They're going back!"
Or—
"Bug out! They're gettin in! we got to pull out. Fall back, fall back. Bug out, bug out." And shepherding his squad, what was left of it, they would try to work their way back, and reform again, on some other hill. Almost every time they would lose at least a man or two in the platoon; sometimes more.

Dead tired. Dead asleep. Almost all the time, except when the firefight started. They want what we got. And mean to take it. And we got to keep it. Squint and fire. Squint and fire. Keep them out. And still they kept on coming. They werent like people, not like people we know anyway, they were more like animals.

The ROKs were the ones he felt sorry for the most. The Chinese did not hesitate to shoot them, without compunction, most of the times when they took ROKs prisoners. They didnt shoot nearly so many of the Americans, though they did shoot some; a lot. But the ROKs also shot the Chinese when they took them prisoner—unless forcibly detained by some American—shot them even when prisoners were wanted for information. And yet they were your close friends. But they were like children. They just werent like us, that was all. They were Asiatics, of the most primitive sort. One man just wasnt important. Wally had read Harold Lamb's Genghis Khan and The March of the Barbarians—*long ago, in some other life*—and they chilled his spine then. And they chilled his spine now, these inheritors of Genghis Khan

"They're turning back!"
Or—
"Pull out, pull out! Fall back, fall back! Bug out!"
What was it Napoleon had once said? when asked of China? "There lies a sleeping dragon, let it sleep." Maybe someday, in some faroff future, the Russians themselves would be turned upon and destroyed by this Frankenstein they had created so cavalierly. That would be nice, he thought drowsily. Squint and fire.
—*"They're turning back!"*—
—*"Pull out, pull out!"*—
The last time, the time he had somehow always known was coming, he shepherded his dwindling squad—four men now, besides himself—ahead of him toward the rearward crest and off the hill, and it was then that the burp gun firing from somewhere near took him through the ass and legs with a prolonged burst and he fell. Am I dead? No, not dead. But he couldnt move his legs much, and when he did it hurt so much he had to quit.

Must have got him through the hips. The remnants of his carefully shepherded squad—good boys; good boys—were a good little ways ahead of him, running hard. Maybe they would notice he was gone, and somebody would try to come back for him. But maybe they wouldnt, either. And maybe they wouldnt even notice, in the confusion, until later. Much later.

Working hard with his arms and sweating with pain in the cold, Wally squirmed himself around until he was facing the other way; toward the enemy: the "enemy." Such a funny word. He had dropped his rifle when he fell running, and it had bounced away somewhere; he couldnt see it, and he could not go and look for it. He had no pistol. All he had left now was his knife.

He got it out, then held it comfortingly in his hand against his side. There was no describing the enormous comfort that it gave him, holding it. And it was still razor-shaving-sharp, too. The little stone in its pocket on the sheath assured that. Grinning, wryly, briefly, Wally thought suddenly of the time he had slashed his finger with it, and the scar. The scar he had been so proud of.

Was anybody coming back? Had they found out he was gone yet?—Well, maybe they wouldnt come this way. The Chinks. Maybe theyd go on around the other side of the position. They might. They might bypass him completely. That had happened to guys lots of times, and they were collected later.

Then he heard the jabbering voices, talking in their funny droning firecracker talk, dead ahead of him. Raising his head, he saw several Chinese appear over the crest, their heads showing first, then their quilted shoulders, then their waists. All but one of them were to his left. But that one saw him, and he stopped. He must have been eight or ten yards away. And for a moment they simply looked at each other, the Chink standing, him lying there on his belly with his head up, two foreigners, two total aliens, two men. Then the Chink approached him cautiously. He wasnt carrying any rifle. And Wally raised the knife and menaced him with it. The Chink stopped again.

He might have tried playing dead. But hell, they shot most of the dead ones again anyway, just to make sure. Maybe it was a mistake not to have tried it, but then the Chink had seen him looking right at him as his head came over the hill. Once again the Chink started to approach him, cautiously, curiously, and once again Wally menaced him with the knife and stopped. Then, fumbling with his uniform he took out a grenade—an American grenade—and pulled the pin and tossed it over at Wally. There was the loud, familiar pop, as the spoon flew loose, and then the fizz. Then he and the others with him who had been watching all this jumped back down over the crest grinning.

Wally lay, staring at the fizzing hand grenade fascinatedly. It was only just a few feet in front of him. But of course he couldnt reach it. Not in time. At least hed got the squad out.

Wally Dennis. Sgt Wally F Dennis, Infantryman. And he thought suddenly of the unfinished manuscript locked up in his bureau drawer back there at home. He did not even drop his head down or close his eyes, he just stared fascinatedly. Then the whole world blew up; blew up in his face.

The several Chinese came back up over the crest after the grenade exploded, and the one who had tossed it walked grinning and curiously over to the blackened figure. The American grenade had not torn the figure up much, but the whole head was blackened. The Chinese approached it cautiously and rolled it over with his foot, then he stepped on the wrist and pried the long beautiful knife out of the hand and looked at it curiously. Squatting on one knee, he pushed the chin back and drew the knife sharply across the throat, cutting the big artery which pumped blood out in a gush. Looking down at the body, the Chinese stood up grinning happily, and inspected his new knife. Then he unfastened the ammobelt around the waist with its sheath hanging on it and jerked it loose. Putting it round his own waist, he swaggered back to his companions jabbering excitedly, proudly flourishing the blood-covered knife he had taken as a prize. All of them looked at it enviously. The one man, more acquisitive than the others, reached out and made a grab for it. The new owner merely flicked his wrist, and the envious one drew back a badly cut hand. Except for him, everybody laughed. Then the proud new owner jammed the bloody knife down into its sheath without bothering, or having the slightest notion, to wipe it off; and the four of them walked on.

Viet Journal

(1974)

This nonfiction account of Jones's visit to Vietnam was the result of
a request from the *New York Times Magazine* for an article. The idea
was to give a novelist's viewpoint on the war-torn country just
before the U.S. forces pulled out. For one month in early 1973,
Jones travelled from the DMZ to the Delta and made notes on his
experiences. He completed work on the book in Paris just before
his return to the United States in 1974. It was published by
Delacorte.

Jones was against American intervention, but had scant sympathy for the Vietcong and North Vietnamese. He was, he said,
"cynical about both sides." Some reviewers criticized the book for
not being sufficiently critical of American involvement in Vietnam.
Today, its balance and penetration seem admirable. Jones said later
that *Viet Journal* was "in effect, an appeal to Americans to stop
hating ourselves so much."

Jones was not surprised to find that the U.S. Army and jungle
combat had not essentially changed. As always, he was most
interested in the soldiers and made friends everywhere he went.
Brigadier Gen. Mike Healy is easily the most memorable of these;
three excerpts about him follow.

The longest excerpt from *Viet Journal* included here is Jones's
finest nonfiction essay, which is the book's epilogue. "Hawaiian
Recall" recounts his stopover in Hawaii after leaving Vietnam.
Jones felt that by returning to Honolulu and Schofield Barracks,
after more than thirty years, he was somehow bearing witness. "I

could not not go," he said. One reviewer (*National Review*) noted, "Prewitt...would like this book."

The Call

I've been known to say over the years—usually when in my cups—that had I not opted to become a writer, I'd have stayed in the Army, acquired a commission, and been a career soldier.

Advancing middle age does strange things to men. In January of 1942 my father went around to the nearest recruiting station and tried to volunteer for a commission in the Infantry, as a lieutenant. He was 56 at the time, a known alcoholic, a mediocre vet of World War I, and a failure at his profession of dentist. The Army turned him down. Cold. They didn't even want him as a dentist. He wrote me a rather despairing letter about it. I read it, wondering how he could imagine the Army would want him for anything. At the time I was on a beach position in Honolulu, a corporal of Infantry myself. Before that spring was out, my father was to commit suicide by shooting himself in the head. Later I would speculate often whether that turndown by the Army had not been such a slap in the face that it helped awaken him to what he was, what he had become, and he could not stand to face it. I loved my father, and I hated to see it end like that. He deserved a better fate.

Over the long years of the Vietnam War I had always been against sending a large US Army there. Particularly a draftee Army, in which the soldier had no right to say "Yes" or "No." I would not have minded so much a recruited Army of volunteers, who knew what they were getting. I was against European or American colonialism in the area, but I had no great love for the North Vietnamese, either. I would not have liked to live in their society. Over the years I had been asked two or three times to go out there and write about the war, and had always declined. Mainly because I could not see getting my ass shot off, over Vietnam. Partly because I was cynical about both sides, including US involvement. So I went ahead with my life, and my work, trying to steer between the fanatics on both sides.

The first call came sometime in mid-January, 1973, from a Mrs. Lazar who was the *New York Times Magazine* stringer in Paris. If I was interested, I should call a Mr. Robert Wool in New York. I called Wool that afternoon. Wool laid it out for me. They wanted me to go out there and write up for them what it was like, after the cease-fire. "The sights, the sounds, the smells of Vietnam—after the end." That sounds funny now. "I'm not political," I said. They didn't want a political, they had hundreds of those to send. They wanted a "novelist's viewpoint." "A Novelist's Journal." I could feel my pulse speeding up. They would pay me X dollars a piece for one, or two pieces. They would pay expenses. It wasn't much money. But I could always get a book out of the trip, too, Wool said. They wanted me to go to both North Vietnam and South Vietnam. They would take care of the visas, and all that.

"To both?" I said.

Absolutely, both. They would handle the visas. I found the idea of going to both a lot more enticing.

Take a day or two to think it over, and call him back, Wool said.

I hesitated. I had just finished a "thriller" novel, which was coming out, and that was out of the way. But I was just starting back to work on a big novel, one I had put aside twice, to do something else. As I said, advancing middle age does strange things to men. I told Wool I would call him back, and put the phone down gently as if it might break in my hand, or bite me.

Doubts

They started coming right away.

First I had to find out what my wife thought. And, naturally, she was almost certainly going to be against it. She was. What could anybody my age, who was not a reporter, and who had not been around any dangerous shooting for thirty years, possibly want in Vietnam? But she was pretty good about it. I cast around, trying to analyze why I wanted to go. Finally, I said I wanted to go because I was fifty-two. She nodded at that. I would probably never get another chance at an adventure like this, I went on. In a few years, one more novel perhaps, and I would be too old for it. She nodded again. I don't know what was going on down in the deep bottom of her mind. But she said, go. I knew how hard it was for her to say it. We had only been separated a couple of times for a few days in fifteen years.

So her objections were out of the way. But other demurrers began to rise up, steadily, regularly, one by one. What could I possibly write about Vietnam that hadn't already been written?

All I knew about Vietnam was what I had more or less been forced to read in the daily papers. The whole thing was such a colossal fiasco for America—if I could believe what the papers said—that I had tried to avoid thinking about it.

After World War II I had detested politics, and politicians. That is not to say I imagined we could get along without them. But I had never seen a politician whose personal ambition did not come first, before his desire to help humanity. Politicians were people who either had too much money, or not enough. Either way, they went into politics because they lacked the talent or the guts to suceed in a decent profession. That they often wound up working harder in politics than they would have in a decent profession, was beside the point.

If this was perhaps a heartless view, I had seen nothing much in the intervening years to make me change my mind.

But that we were becoming the new fascists, in America? I could not believe that. A lot of the foreign press was calling us that. A lot of our own press, in a kind of moral hysteria, was taking up the same cry, without much discrimination.

We were still a nation of Puritans—still hungering after that same Plymouth purity that had never existed, except in some half-baked theory.

On the other hand, I knew of no other nation that would allow its press to come out in full attack against the good faith of its government. Certainly not North Vietnam. And not South Vietnam.

Granting that we were wrong in Vietnam, the problem was how far wrong were we. Granting that we had failed, how far had we failed? And why? Had we failed because we were fascist, were morally evil? A lot of people were trying to prove that. I had never seen a defeated US Army. Did I really want to?

Were we really in danger of becoming a military-industrial dictatorship? Was the Army really a collection of sadistic fascist redneck killers? It had changed a lot since my day. Had it changed that much? Did I really want to find out?

I was not sure I did. But I called Wool in New York next day and told him I would go. I did not even wait the two full days. Something else a lot more powerful than politics was working in me, that sense of encroaching age and a last adventure, telling me to go.

Trip to Pleiku

An Army car came for me. Healy's plane was a U-21, a little five-seater, two-motor, propeller job. It made me think more than anything of the old Beechcraft Executive, a plane I had ridden in a lot, years before. It was apparently the executive workhorse of Vietnam. There wasn't much to see through the small windows. We had an hour and 50 minute ride ahead of us. I caught flashes of tough green mountains and once beyond those, of jungled draws and valleys and mile after mile of open red-earth country not unlike the central red-dirt plateau of Oahu. I had expected more jungle. Healy had the old soldier's trick I had forgotten about, of catching a half hour's nap whenever he could, and as soon as we were airborne shut his eyes. But after he woke, we talked.

Healy did not look like I'd expected. From hearing his voice on the phone with Weyand, I had expected a younger man, maybe thirty-five, blond and slim and burr-cut. Healy was forty-six, heavily muscled like a weightlifter, getting a little thick around the middle, with dark curly Irish hair that was not burr-cut. His broad face was pockmarked, he wore glasses, and every now and then one eye fiercely seemed to not quite track for a moment. Even at rest, asleep, he exuded a phenomenal fiery physical energy that seemed to be infinite.

Healy told me the fighting was easing off at Kontum. The North Viets had tried mightily to take Kontum just before the cease-fire. As elsewhere, they had launched a major attack some thirty-six hours before the cutoff hour. When they failed, they had not stopped at the appointed hour. When they failed there, they had pulled back and sent troops around the city to the east, after the cease-fire, a week after the cease-fire, to cut Route 14 at a little pass between Kontum and Pleiku. That was what the month-long fighting had been over. If the NVA could show the ICCS they held

Route 14 below Kontum, Kontum would theoretically lie within their territory and they could claim it. The ARVN had counterattacked this position on the road, and immediately been accused of violating the cease-fire by Hanoi. Now they were mopping up the area after the NVA had withdrawn. Not many NVA had withdrawn. They had wanted that road bad. And the ARVN had to push them back 2000 yards, in order to clear the road of fire from their big mortars. It had been a real fight, Healy said and grinned. The members of his advisory staff had dubbed the little Chu Pao pass the Rock Pile.

I had been told he was a "fighter," Healy, and not only by General Weyand. And I was too much of an old soldier not to appreciate him. And I was glad, whatever my intellectual propensities about war might be, that the United States still had men like him. He also had that kind of explosive wild-Irishman's charm, which could talk the pennies off the eyes of a dead nun, as they say. Back in the waiting room of the dispatcher's office at Tan Son Nhut—where he was sending his aide, Lt Charlie Vasquez, off to Bangkok for a week's R & R—he had stridden in in his bluff way and in seconds charmed and dominated everyone in the place. He was also a superb, masterful, old-fashioned Irish storyteller. The structure of his Second Regional Assistance Command (SRAC), I gathered, with himself as advisor to the II Corps commander, apparently ran right on down through the Viet chain of command to his junior-officer advisors at the regiment and battalion level. On the spur of the moment I asked him if while I was around there, he could get me into Kontum, and maybe as well have me flown up to the Border Ranger post at Dak Pek. His face sobered and got a little distant, and he gave me a funny little look. As if he thought I might be using him. He could probably get me into Kontum all right, for a short while, he said. But Dak Pek was out of the question. It was fifty miles inside the enemy lines, with antiaircraft positions all the way up.

It suddenly occurred to me—I thought I sensed—that Healy might not be feeling too happy about his assignment from General Weyand of squiring a novelist around. That I was getting off on the wrong foot with him. I didn't want that to happen. So when he asked me how long I'd been in service, I told him the truth. I'd been in five and a half years. But—I added—I was discharged early, in 1944. Invalided out. He looked up. Actually, I continued, with a vague intuitive flash of some irrational inspiration, I had wangled myself a discharge. After first coming back from the Pacific wounded, and then spending some time in a couple of Army jails. Perhaps he knew the type? Healy grinned suddenly, and nodded. I said I felt I'd used up all my luck and if I was sent to Europe I would never get back. Healy nodded again. Anyway, at the time I was in a lousy Quartermaster Gas Supply outfit with a bunch of other cripples. Otherwise, I said, if I hadn't wanted to be a writer, I'd probably have stayed in for the full trip. And suddenly I found myself launched into the telling of the long involved story of my reassignment from an Army hospital to Camp Campbell, Kentucky, which formed one of the main themes of the third Army novel I was working on. The point was, I had both loved and hated the Army.

Healy was an excellent listener. When I finished, he was silent for a long moment. Mine was certainly no tale of blind, Gung-Ho devotion. Then he rubbed his nose, and said the Army was only a tool after all, for molding and shaping your life into something. And then launched into a story of his own. Of when he had first enlisted and was serving as a private in Fort Riley, Kansas. He had been on guard duty on New Year's Eve, at the Officers' Club. And freezing half to death had climbed up on a wall and rubbed the frost off the window and watched the officers inside with their ladies and their dates, warm and drunk and enjoying their ball. When he got off post, he went back to his freezing barracks with its windowpanes knocked out and looked at the latrine with its stopped-up johns and pieces of turd frozen onto the floor and stormed downstairs and told the CQ to call the company commander and tell him to come over there. The CQ of course thought he'd gone crazy. But he insisted. And when the CC finally came, Healy took him upstairs and showed him the latrine, and the broken windows in the barracks room, where the heat was off. How did the Army expect men to serve in and believe in an outfit that forced them to live like that? he stormed. Like pigs. Like swine. The CC of course thought he was crazy, too—on New Year's Eve. The next day he was called up before the post commander. He expected at least a Special court-martial. Instead he was invited to go to Officers' Candidate School.

Telling me the tale, Healy was silent for a moment. Certainly, with his Irish talent, he told his tale at least twice as well as I'd told mine. I had listened captivated, thinking that after all perhaps I had struck the right note, hit the right chord.

That post commander had been a very intuitive man, Healy added. Certainly that night in Fort Riley had been one of the major turning points of his life. If they'd court-martialed him, he might easily have turned into a criminal. If they'd reprimanded him, he would certainly have quit the Army. He grinned his Irish grin. Instead, here he was. If I had had that kind of commanding officer, I might still be in the Army today. But then—he grinned impudently—the world might have lost a damn fine writer. We both lapsed into silence for a while.

Where was I staying in Pleiku? Healy asked after a while. I said I didn't know. I understood there was a hotel. Healy made a face. It was no good. If I wanted I could stay with him at SRAC. He had a guest room free for a couple of nights at least.

When the aircraft came down over Pleiku, it looked as if it had been a pretty town once, with lots of trees. Now it was an armed camp. Fortifications and artillery positions outlined it to the north and west. Convoys of troop trucks moved along all the roads in and out. Healy apologized for the pall of dust and smoke. It was the end of the dry season. He told me that in the '72 offensive the North Viets had gotten a quarter of the way into the town, before they were thrown out. We came in to land over a big lake which had a tall statue of the Virgin on a pinnacle that ran out into it.

Breaking Point

After an hour of drinking and a cigar most of the officers had left the general's rather spartan, pedestrian quarters. that was when the young lt colonel from the Kontum trip came over and sat down by me. He was a little unsteady on his feet and his eyes were bright. He had been relieved of duty as of five o'clock that afternoon. He wanted to know what I, as a writer and student of human nature, thought about his theory about breaking points. Was he right? Or wasn't he? What did I think? I said I didn't know. Probably I thought he was right. But I thought a lot of it depended on the individual. Not on just his psychological state, but on his physical nervous system. On his just sheer animal physical nervous system and just how much it could take, and for how long, and at what intensity. He nodded repeatedly as I talked. But I doubt if he heard me. He kept right on that he believed every man had his breaking point, and after that point, he got so he just didn't care any more. And when he got like that, he had reached it, passed it. He had not reached his, but he had come very close a couple of times. Up at Tan Canh last year, during the '72 offensive, when we had lost Tan Canh, he had almost reached it. Tan Canh was the worst he had ever seen, two weeks of it. For two weeks they had thrown everything they had available at Tan Canh. He shook his head. Then he began to tell me about Firebase November and his friend Bob Moore. Bob had lost his whole command at Firebase November, just last December. Only three months ago. A shell, or a big mortar, had made a direct hit on the command post bunker. When Bob came to, they were all dead except two. A division commander, two regimental commanders, the communications colonel, all dead. Except two, and they were just going out the door. When old Bob could walk, he went outside and found that *everybody* had gone. He was all alone there in the middle of the night. Not one man left. Two tanks were just pulling out of the perimeter and he ran over and managed to get a ride on the outside of one of them. And I was right up there over him, the lt colonel said, trying to talk him in. I couldn't go down in all that fire without giving the position away. He had tried every frequency on the console panel, to try and reach those tanks. He could see Bob but Bob couldn't see him and of course the radio at the firebase was gone. Anyway, nobody there. Nothing he could do. Finally he got them, but there still was nothing he could do. They got out finally, but Bob had passed his breaking point that night. He, the young lt colonel, had had letters from him since and they didn't sound like the same man. And *he* believed Bob reached his breaking point. Every man has one, and when he reaches it, he reaches it. He hadn't reached his but what bothered him was how was he going to know when he was going to reach it? Nobody could tell. But every man had his breaking point, he was sure of that.

"That's a lot of crap," Healy bawled heatedly from across the room. "Nobody has a breaking point unless they think they do. You can go on forever, if you have to." I beg to differ with you, General, Sir, the young lt colonel said; but I know different. "That's no way to think," Healy called heatedly. The young colonel said he didn't care, he knew what he knew. Later Healy helped him place a long-distance Army call on Healy's official phone to the colonel's wife in Washington, so she could fly out to San Francisco to meet him. After he came out of the bedroom, where the phone was, he drew himself up and saluted us all formally, a merry salute, smiling. Then he went off to bed.

"I'm glad he's going out," Healy said to me, heavily. "Of course, he's right, you know. Probably every man does have a breaking point. But I've never reached mine. Anyway, it's bad to talk about it. I don't believe in breaking points." A little later I went to bed myself, but I couldn't sleep. I couldn't get out of my head the picture of that young lt colonel drawing himself up, and saluting us merrily, standing at attention in Healy's bedroom door.

Healy

There was always one thing with Healy. You knew his aggressive physical courage was monumental, and that his nerves were absolute steel. But with Healy there was an added quality of unstated sadness, an overblanket of sorrow, about things. Many men who don't have absolute physical courage have a deep irrational almost animal envy of men who do, and like to think of them as brutes. That is their defense. Other men look at them with boyish hero worship. But to a good professional soldier physical courage is like physical fitness, it is not a fetish but a foregone conclusion of the line of work, an accepted fact, a necessary tool of their trade, and they don't think about it much. But with Healy there was this additional quality of sorrow about life that was very appealing. Maybe his aging had something to do with it. Maybe it was just Irish. But you felt he had been born knowing that nothing could last forever. And he was quite willing to tell you that, if you asked him. But not unless you did.

Special Forces Soldier

Mike Healy was something of a legend, I learned. He wore a third dog tag that was famous in the Army. At someone's instigation he had shown it to me the night before. Hanging from his neck chain with the other two was a third identical plaque which, in the same GI stamped-in letters, said: IF YOU ARE RECOVERING MY BODY, FUCK YOU. It became so famous that once a visiting senator in

Vietnam asked Healy to see it. Unembarrassed, Healy whipped it out and showed it to him.

A lieutenant, then a captain, of Rangers in Korea, Healy had gone into the Special Forces almost from the start. He seemed made for them. Wounded in the abdomen in Korea, he survived only because of the helicopter ferry service shown so graphically in the movie *Mash*. In Special Forces he went to Vietnam early, and was the model for one of the fictional characters in Robin Moore's *The Green Berets*. Later as a lieutenant colonel he was sent out to Vietnam again to replace Colonel Rheault as commander of the Special Forces, after the big scandal in the press about the killing of the double agent, when Special Forces was at its lowest ebb of public image. This time, he had accepted to come back again, as a brigadier, to command the II Corps advisory command for General Weyand, during the phase-out. When he went home at the end of March, he would go to command the old 5th and 7th Special Forces Group at the John F. Kennedy Center in Fort Bragg.

Since Healy was an old dyed-in-the-wool hard-core Special Forces man to the bitter end, this pleased Healy more than anything. Although the beret was banned for wear now anywhere in Vietnam, with the American combat units gone, Healy's personal green beret reposed on top the wall cupboard behind his desk in his bedroom along with his two baseball-type field caps and his overseas cap. More than anything the North Viets wanted to get the Special Forces out of Vietnam, Healy grinned. "Nobody points it out now, but Special Forces learned a lot of their dirty tricks and tactics from the VC and NVA. They actually taught us how to fight a dirty war." Most of his staff, chosen by him for this current assignment, had served with him in Special Forces. One of his idiosyncrasies was his old sergeant major, whom he took with him on every job, and who had served with him in the field in Special Forces. When the sergeant major, a tough wise old bird of 42 as strong as an ox, came over for a drink and to gossip—which was almost every night—he and Healy would get out the tape of Barry Sadler's *The Ballad of the Green Berets* and play it. Sadler, a fairly famous country music recording artist, had served in Special Forces under Healy, and had written other Vietnam War songs. *Letter from Vietnam, Saigon, Badge of Courage, Salute to the Nurses, Ba-Mi-Ba* (the name of an excellent Vietnamese beer), *Garri-Trooper, Trooper's Lament*. Healy had them all, and he and the sergeant major played them all. This caused some looks to pass between some of the other non-Special Forces officers having a drink in his quarters. But they were careful that Healy did not see them. And in fact, I suspected that half the time Healy did it just to ragass them.

With March 28th coming up so fast and so little to do now that the Kontum road was open, Healy was edgy and had difficulty sleeping. So most of the nights I was there I sat up late talking with him after everyone else had gone to bed. He felt he was going to have a hard time adjusting to the quiet, regularized life back home. Like most of the former enlisted soldiers who had become higher-ranking officers, he had picked up a BA degree somewhere, I think the U of Colorado, by studying at night while stationed nearby. This was apparently a government policy, and lots of the non-West Point officers I met later had picked up BAs and even MAs during their tours of duty across the United States. I had mentioned one night that I thought Orientals felt very differently about an individual human life than we did in the West—as long, of course, as it was not their own life—but that my wife got furious at me for saying so and called me a fascist. Healy picked up on this and said he agreed, and said he felt the Orientals had a "wheel" religious philosophy about life while we in the West had a "ruler" religious philosophy. With the Oriental everything came back around, and then came back around again, and again. In our Christian thinking a life had a beginning point, and progressed toward a final end, and that was it. Naturally that would make us view an individual life differently, give it more value. The "wheel" versus the "ruler." He said he did not think the two could ever really get together and discuss anything in any way that made any sense because the terms of reference were so different.

We talked about the "New Army." And Healy stated the concept which I would hear later over and over from "New Army" officers: having a strong discipline was no longer enough, you had to explain to these youngsters why and for what you wanted them to do something, you had to make them see why they needed to go out there and take a chance with their lives. Healy felt very strongly about this, having been an EM in the old Army. It was a far cry from the old Army I had known before World War II, and even in the middle of World War II.

The last night I was there a big-shot Medical Corps officer from Saigon, a colonel, was Healy's guest at dinner, having come up to check the closing down of the Army hospital in Pleiku. After that, there would be only a dispensary, which Healy's own medical officer would run. In the general's quarters afterward, the talk got around to why men did stay in the Army. The MC colonel, a huge dark very broad-shouldered Texan, said there wasn't any question about it with him. He loved the life. He liked the pay, and the travel, and the excitement, and the companionship. It was fun. Of course, he added quickly, he wasn't any infantry officer. He had been called up for a year, and he liked it so much when he got out he had gone back home and sold his practice and come back in permanently. "Are you divorced?" I asked. The colonel made a face. Yes, he was. Matter of fact, it was that first year of service that had broken up his marriage. Here Healy chimed in and said it was hard on soldiers' wives, being the wives of soldiers. And it got harder to take assignments overseas, as the years went by. I had never heard him talk much about his family.

Later that night after everybody had left Healy and I sat on, and he talked about his family. It had been very hard on his wife, all the time he spent away. Naturally she didn't like it, and she liked it less and less as the years ran on. He felt he hadn't spent enough time with his kids. He had six sons. In one way, he felt he hardly knew them. This would probably be his last tour overseas, he figured. But the kids were all so grown up now it didn't matter. It was the bane of a soldier's life, this being away. Two of his boys had flubbed up pretty good. One of them had botched up his career at West Point and let himself get dropped, and was just drifting. Another was a longhair and wanted to be a writer. He grinned at me and said, "Maybe I'll send him to you in Paris." I said I'd love to have him. Mind you, he was no hippie dropout, and he was probably the most intelligent of the six. I said I had lots of friends' kids coming over from time to time, wanting to be writers, but none of them ever wanted to work hard enough. That was it, Healy said. This whole generation didn't want to work for anything. Anyway, this was probably his last tour overseas, he said again and bounced a big fist on a hard thigh. He hated to leave Vietnam. Quite a lot of his life had been spent here, with these people. Then he said something I would hear over and over again the rest of the time I spent in Vietnam. In about five years he wanted to come back, Healy said, and see how things were still developing. Even if it meant using his own leave time to do it. He stood up and blew out his lips in a sigh.

It must just be that he was getting old. He said he'd walk outside with me.

Fear

That night I lay in bed and thought about Meese going to bed night after night in Vi Thanh not knowing if he would wake up to a mortaring. And that got me to thinking about fear.

There had been a little drinking in the bar after dinner and one of the administrative officers talking to some of us had said to me with a smile, "I wouldn't have gone up there to Tri Ton like that." I looked around at the others and said sure he would, if it had been an order. Oh, yes; if it had been an order, he said. But I had not been ordered to go. I wanted to go. I had said so. I grinned and admitted that I had wanted to go. And then suddenly I shut up—because I did not want to admit out loud that I did not know why I wanted to go.

Anyway, I added, it was not the same thing as an infantryman who had to stay there day after day, week after week, watching his percentages chances diminish. Everybody agreed to that, and the subject changed.

I did not think it made Meese afraid to go to bed in Vi Thanh. And I did not think it would make me afraid. But it is hard to know what makes one man afraid, and not another. I had not been afraid when I went into Tri Ton with General Blazey. And I had not been afraid on the trip to Dak Pek with Mike Healy. I had honestly not been afraid when I vaguely saw and then heard the falling object clang against the helicopter and looked down to see if it was a grenade.

Usually fear came to me when I was alone, and there was nothing to do, like those last few moments before going to sleep at night; when I was going to do something the next day and imagined all the things that could happen to me, or when I had already done something and imagined all the things that *might have* happened to me. Then I could become terrified. I had been terribly afraid the night before I flew up to Dak Pek with Healy. And I had been terribly afraid the night after I had flown into Tri Ton with Blazey. So afraid I was ashamed of myself.

And yet that fear was oddly seductive. It was a strange thing, fear. It wasn't always so unpleasant. It could be as exciting as sex.

And in the same way. If all the factors were right, fear could be terribly exciting. So exciting you could get hooked on it like a drug. And want to do it again. Like sex.

I had been made terribly afraid the first day I was back in Saigon, when I first heard of the hand-grenading of the Buddhist temple. I had gone back to my room in the Continental Palace and stood for a long time looking down at the bustling, crowded square, wondering at how bestial men could be to each other and still enjoy it. I felt as if I had been personally raped by the VC hand-grenade tossers. And when I looked back up, I thought for a split second flash I had glimpsed again my hairy, jug-eared, bucktoothed little friend in the branches, among the leaves of the big tree outside, his tiny eyes glinting, his small body bouncing up and down excitedly.

I had seen my hairy little pal again the night before I went to Dak Pek. And I had glimpsed him again the night after I got back from Tri Ton. I still did not know why I wanted to go to Dak Pek and Tri Ton. And I did not know what my hairy little friend meant or stood for.

I could remember being terribly afraid under mortar barrages in World War II. Getting to shoot back at the enemy and hurt him had helped that fear a lot. Anyway, I was younger. Back then, I had been afraid of dying without having made my voice heard in the world, without having made the fact of my existence at least known. I did not want to be lumped namelessly together with a lot of dead heroes who got remembered only collectively. A perhaps legitimate vanity.

But I had not been terrified when I was wounded, or even much afraid. Afterward, I had been afraid I might get hit again, before I could get out of there, legitimately and honorably. I thought that would be the most unholy, Godless irony. And I had seen it happen to men.

But in those days I had never touched on this odd conspiratorial physiological alliance between fear and thc scnsc of scx. And I had never seen my apelike little friend.

The Simian Figure

It was only a literary device, of course.

I hadn't really seen him. I hadn't even glimpsed him from my eye corner. I wasn't even sure I had imagined him, and made him up, on the scene in Vietnam at the actual time, as I wrote I had. Perhaps I had invented him later, at the time of the writing.

But all of that didn't really matter. He was just as real.

Whether I actually saw him as a hallucination in my real eye, or imagined him at the time of the experience, or whether I invented him later when writing about the experience, he was just as authentic. From somewhere down there, in some subsurface part of me, he had drifted up in that dreamlike way, worming his way past the grid-filter I used to keep out the trash or the too-terrifying. An unreadable metaphor. Indecipherable, because being unreadable was part of his very function. I didn't know what he stood for, and I couldn't know. If I ever did know, certainly the answer would be trite, and his emotional usefulness would cease.

Surely, he wasn't death. Or, at least, not only just death. Death certainly carried with it some of the ridiculous ugliness, as well as the animal wisdom, that he had. And surely he wasn't fear. Though he carried about his person some of the hairy, squawky, smelly, shrewd selfishness of fear. Certainly he was sly. And certainly he was a clown. And certainly he was scary. I had the awful feeling that he was laughing at me, at us.

He could pass as a caricature, a cartoon of all humanity. And with his pea-brained sense of humor, that seemed to be just what he was doing. Could he be a symbol of the race, and our needs for fury and danger and fear and their excitements? Maybe he was a mirror image of myself? Myself before I shaved all over and put on airs and clothes, and pretended to be different? Maybe it was him I was trying to encounter face to face when I went to Dak Pek and Tri Ton.

Whatever he was, I had him. And now that I had him, probably I would have to go on exploring him, and trying to figure out what he stood for, forever. Like one of those lovable dear awful old friends who are always turning up when you least want to see them. The ones you can bet will always appear when you are trying most to impress somebody else. The ones you are always happy to see and hate to have run into.

The Beggar Woman

I had seen her on the Sunday, when I was walking back to the hotel from lunch. It being Sunday, there was almost nobody on the street. That made her more noticeable. I was as inured to beggars as the next man. In fact, I had just turned down two ladies with credentials, begging for some Catholic orphanage. If you did not get hardened to the beggars, you would have no money left at all—and you still would not have made a dent in them. But this one was not begging. She was standing, leaning against a shuttered Sunday storefront. I was across the street from her.

Something about her posture caught me. I thought I had never seen anyone look so beat. She stood with her head against the grillwork of the closed store, her face in the corner angle the grill made with the masonry. She didn't move.

She seemed vaguely familiar, as if I might have seen her up the street near the hotel or the *Times* office, where the beggars congregated. She was dressed like any Viet woman, a conical straw hat, black trousers, a ragged *ao-dai*. There was no way of telling how old she was. An old US Army musette bag stuffed with something hung from her left shoulder, and she had a bundle of what looked like rags in her other arm.

I watched her a full four minutes, I timed it, and she did not move. Then her shoulders heaved themselves up slowly and fell, as if she were drawing a breath, and she became motionless again.

I wondered if she could be dying, standing there. Instinctively, like some animal reacting, I took a thousand-piastre note out of my wallet and crossed the street and touched her on the shoulder.

Her hand came up. I put the bill in it and patted her on the shoulder. Only then did her head come up, and she looked at me with such a dumb, wordless despair that it was as if someone had thrown acid in my face. I have never seen such destroyed heart, such ravagement of spirit on a person's face. I turned and walked away, realizing belatedly that there had been a scrawny baby in the bundle.

I got as far as the corner before I could get myself stopped, or put my head in order. The baby didn't bother me. The baby didn't matter. It was the woman. I could not even put into thoughts what I was feeling. Most of us have defenses in our personalities. Usually, we have layer after layer of them. Even when we are dying, we can still put some last personality defense on our faces. This was a face from which the last, bottom layer of defense had been peeled like an onion.

I took the rest of the money I had with me, four thousand piastres, and walked back to her and put that in her hand with the other note. She did not even look at it, and raised her face again, and her face did not change. However much money it was, it would not be enough. She knew it, and I knew it. It might keep her going for a week, maybe even longer, that was all. Somewhere under her defenselessness some part of her seemed to be trying to tell me she appreciated my concern.

I walked away, wondering what kind of hope I'd hoped to give. There wasn't enough money to help her. Not now. The United States had not helped her. Neither had the French. The South Viets hadn't helped her, the North Viets hadn't helped her, the VC had not helped her. And what any of them or all of them might do for future generations would not do her any good at all.

She was all of Vietnam to me.

Hawaiian Recall

recall 4.a *Mil.* A call on the trumpet, bugle, or drum, which calls soldiers back to the ranks, camp, etc.

I hadn't planned it. But since I had to go on to New York anyway, I checked the fare and found it cost about fifteen dollars more to go on by Honolulu, than to go back the way I had come, via Paris. I had not been in Vietnam more than a week, before I knew I was going to do it. And once I had made up my mind, it seemed I had known all along that I would go. That I could not not go. A sounding of Recall.

The song *Jamaica Farewell* was much in my mind on the long trip from Saigon to Honolulu. It did not exactly approximate my situation, but it spoke of islands, of island weather, of lost youth, of the sea, of island populations, and I still thought about Hawaii that way.

I had left Honolulu in August of 1942, with elements of the 25th Division heading for Guadalcanal, a boy of twenty-one. I had not been back since. Before that, I had lived in Hawaii for three years, in the military, as an enlisted soldier. After The Great War II, I had spent four more years writing a novel about those three years. A not inconsiderable investment. Seven years.

The big Pan-Am 747 was only half full. After fifteen hours of it, passengers stretched out over banks of three and four seats. All of them were military personnel or military dependents leaving Vietnam. I myself was too keyed up to sleep.

The west coast of Oahu was intensely familiar as we approached it. I picked out Mt. Kaala in the Waianae Range. Then Barbers Point. Ewa Beach. Keahi Point, the Pearl Harbor entrance. Fort Kamehameha. They were all words as familiar to me as New York or Paris or Robinson, Illinois. Then we were low over Hickam Field, and I suddenly no longer knew where I was. Everything was built up, expanded, beyond my wildest imaginings. Even looking east toward Aliamanu Crater and the Tripler Army Medical Center, I did not recognize where I was. The plane landed. I got a taxi into town. And I still recognized nothing. Four-lane freeways. Six-lane freeways. Ritzy-looking modernistic restaurants. What I remembered as cane fields was now all housing development. It looked incredibly rich, after Vietnam.

No matter how fast you run, you can never catch up with the past. In the first place, the past is never the past when it is happening to you. Secondly, it rolls away from beneath you so slickly, so greasily, you have difficulty just staying on your feet. Sometimes you can get an inkling of it, when time seems to collapse, and you peer through a momentary hole in your future, and say, "Someday, I'll think back about this moment, and recall just exactly the way it was, and remember..." But you never quite do. And it never quite comes. When I first went there in 1939, the "Good Old Days" of Hawaii were 1910, or even 1920, when there were no transoceanic planes, and we did not have aircraft carriers, and there were no cars or almost none, and Honolulu traffic moved on clanging streetcars under the palms, slowly, leisurely, and one arrived only by ship, moving in slowly past Sand Island, to dock near the Aloha Tower, which was a "cultural" focal point then. In 1939 there was no way I could be a part of those "Good Old Days." And I had no way of knowing then that thirty years later my then-present would be the sweeter, quieter "Good Old Days" for 1973; that in pre-Pearl Harbor 1939 and '40 I was already living and participating in, without appreciating it, a leisurely non-jet, non-tourism, non-high-rise, non-international-airport Golden Age looked back on wistfully from 1973.

I had not been able to get into the old Royal Hawaiian, luxury symbol of my youth. So I was booked into the Sheraton-Waikiki, one of the new high-rise hotels that have sprouted in Waikiki, which was right next door to the Royal. When we pulled up to it on Kalakaua Avenue, I couldn't even find the old Royal. Then I saw its characteristic pink, off between the buildings. Most of its gardens were gone, to shops and airline offices and high-rise competition. It looked dwarfed and stunted among its neighbors. From my room on the twenty-fifth floor of the Sheraton I could look down on it, or down at the Sheraton pool, or off at Diamond Head and along the beach, or out to sea. The sheer richness of America was like a cold douche, after Saigon. I could have dwelt on this sourly, but after Saigon, and Hue, and Can Tho, I didn't feel sour. My social conscience didn't bother me at all. I was only animally grateful. The first thing I did was to have myself a real genuine American shower.

I decided the next thing to do was to hire myself a chauffeured car. It was eight-thirty in the morning and I hadn't been to bed in twenty-four hours but I could no more have slept than I could have flown. I had never driven in Honolulu. Only once or twice had I even had money enough to take a taxi—except for what we used to call "the jitneys," which took loads of us north to Schofield Barracks for fifty cents apiece after the last buses had left. There was a long line-up at the row of car-rental desks in the lobby.

There were two big conventions staying in the hotel, the beautiful half-white, half-Chinese girl told me, and I would have to wait forty-five minutes for my drivered car. I decided to use the time by having a drink at the beach bar of the Royal, and walked out to the street.

Only the Waikiki Theater and the Moana Hotel a half a block down were things I had ever seen before. I had difficulty finding the entrance to the Royal Hawaiian. Its profuse gardens had been cut down by sixty or seventy percent. The corner where Maggio had had his fist fight with the two MPs had disappeared completely. But once inside the entrance, I found I remembered, and that it looked about the same. The shops looked less expensive, though, and the lobby less formidably rich. It struck me forcibly suddenly, that I could walk into any of the shops and buy just about anything they had for sale. The beach patio had been changed and remodeled in some way I could not exactly define. Three huge jolly Hawaiian mama-sans joked along the tables with hotel clients they seemed to know. I bought my drink, a beer, drank it, and slunk back to the Sheraton. I remembered the times I had watched Air Force pilot officers drunk and fighting on the Royal Hawaiian's lawn after Midway—or was that Prewitt?

My driver was a young friendly hapa-Hawaiian who was maybe a third Japanese. When he turned his head and said, "Where do you want to go," I discovered I didn't know where I wanted to go. Some of the out-of-city places, like Schofield Barracks, Hanauma Bay, Makapuu Head, I was leaving till the next day and doing myself in a you-drive. But there were still lots of places in Honolulu proper I wanted to visit. But I found I could no longer remember many of the names.

Had I ever been in Hawaii? the driver wanted to know. His voice had the soft, slurring lilt that is so delicious in the Hawaiian English. I told him yes, I used to live there, a long time ago. In the War. Then I thought I better clarify, and cleared my throat. World War II, that is. "Well, you'll find us changed," he said. I could see his eyes watching me curiously in the mirror. Lamely, I told him to take me over into Kaimuki, the old Japanese section behind Diamond Head. There was a house up the hill I wanted to see there. But I couldn't remember the name of the street.

Did I mean Maunilani Heights? Yes, that was it. The street ran straight up...Wilhelmina Rise? he said. That was it. That was where I wanted to go.

The house was the house of Prewitt's hooker girlfriend Alma. It wasn't on Wilhelmina Rise itself, but on a street just off it. I couldn't remember the name of the street. But when I saw it on the street sign, I remembered: Sierra Drive. I had the driver turn off on it and drive past the house.

Wilhelmina ran straight up, up and up arrow-straight, and from up here you could see the whole of Waikiki and downtown Honolulu. Prewitt's hooker Alma had never actually lived in the Sierra Drive house. I did not know who had lived there. I had never been inside it. I had had a hooker girlfriend myself, who had served somewhat as the model for Alma and had lived not far away, and I had chosen the house for Alma myself because of having passed it so many times and having wanted to live there. I saw the driver's eyes watching me curiously in the rearview mirror again, and told him to take me downtown to the Army-Navy Y on Hotel Street.

If the house on Wilhelmina Rise was a sort of aching thrill to see again, the Army-Navy Y and Hotel Street area was the ache with the thrill excised. The whole area looked like some sort of ghost town. When I asked the driver, he said it had been like that for a long time. There were still some girls around at night, but they were pretty low types. I could do a lot better out near Waikiki. His car was free for the night, if I wanted to hire him.

It was amazing. The area had once been a swarming hive of bars, street vendors, tattoo parlors, shooting galleries, photo galleries, market shops, fruit and vegetable shops, and hooker joints occupying the rooms upstairs and labeled hotels. Now there was hardly a soul on the streets, and most of the shops and bars were shuttered and closed. Once it had been our Mecca, toward which we rose and prayed every morning, before Reveille. Compressed into a half-mile area down by the docks between the King's Palace and the little river, and bursting at the seams to break out, it had been the bottomless receptacle of our dreams and frustrations, and of our money. The payday payroll. Now it was all coming down soon, the driver said, and an urban reclamation would be built in its place.

I had him drive me around the old streets. I had forgotten most of their names. I had remembered King St. and Hotel St. But I had forgotten Fort St., Bishop St., Bethel St., Union St., Queen Emma St., Adams St. I had even forgotten Beretania St. and Nuuanu Ave. I looked at the corner bar, now closed, where Warden had come hunting for Prewitt when Prewitt was AWOL. The old Wu Fat's Chinese Restaurant was still there, still open, on its corner but it had not been repainted in a long time and its bright Chinese colors looked drab. The driver said it was coming down, too. Wu Fat's was where Maggio had begun his final rampage that ended in his going to the Stockade. Right next door to it had been the streetdoor entrance to the New Senator Hotel (I called it New Congress) where Alma worked. I saw the driver watching me again curiously in the mirror, and told him to take me past the Aloha Tower at the foot of Fort St., and then drive me back out to Waikiki to the Sheraton.

One of the biggest single differences was that in the old Hawaii the tourist business was incidental to a way of life, and that now the way of life was incidental to the tourist business. You saw this all over the island. The next morning, when I went down for my you-drive car, I found I had to take a hotel bus from the Sheraton back down Kalakaua almost to Ala Moana to pick up my little Dodge at a large house trailer converted into an office in a filling station parking lot. The two conventions and an unexpected influx of tourist parties had overtaxed the hotel's delivery service. The little bus was packed with families and quartets of couples, all going to pick up cars, and they had accents from all over the US. They had traveled, and rented cars, just about all over the world, and the wryly humorous complaints I heard about the bus showed they knew their way around.

It was good not to have someone eyeing me in the rearview mirror. Strangely enough, I felt a little like a man going off full of nervous guilt to meet some clandestine call girl or mistress. I planned to visit Hanauma Bay first, out of town out Kalanianaole Highway beyond Diamond Head at the foot of Koko Head. Hanauma Bay was where Prewitt was trying to get when he was killed on the Waialae Golf Course, which I drove past in a few minutes. Hanauma Bay was where the confrontation between Warden and Stark over Karen Holmes happened, and Stark chopped up his kitchen tent with his cleaver. Hanauma Bay had been my company's command post for almost a year after Pearl Harbor, until we left for Guadalcanal. After Hanauma Bay, I planned to drive the six miles on out to our old beach position at Makapuu Head, where I had spent so many isolated weeks. I had written one of my best short stories, *The Way It Is*, about Makapuu. Later, I had written a whole novel, *The Pistol*, with Makapuu as the principal setting. Then, in the afternoon, I was going to drive up to Schofield Barracks.

I could not help but feel I owned a small piece of all of them. A piece no real-estate agent could sell from under me.

But I did not get beyond Hanauma Bay that morning. By the time I left Hanauma Bay it was too late to go on, unless I wanted to miss my date at Schofield that afternoon. I hadn't meant to stay that long. I had driven up over the Koko Head saddle, and the blind V-shaped side-road cutoff to Hanauma was there just exactly as it had always been, except that now it was blacktopped. At the foot of it down the hill you ran in under the same canopy of thorn trees and longleaf pine over the bare soil. The old popcorn wagon from before the war, that we had made our CP field-telephone center, was no longer there. But the weathered clapboard GENTS and LADIES buildings we had used indiscriminately, one on either side of the road, were still there. I spotted in my mind's eye where Warden's—where our—CP tent had been, and on the other side of the road where Stark's kitchen tents had sat. I had never known a 1st/Sgt named Warden, and had never known a Mess/Sgt named Stark. It was confusing. Some new picnic tables and benches of concrete had been spotted around.

The parking lot was full of cars. New ramparts of field stone had been built along the edge of the forty-foot cliff, and a new auto road that had not been there before had been built down its face to the beach. I walked down. On the beach the old clapboard pavilion I remembered, where one of the key scenes between Pfc Mast and a Cpl named Winstock had taken place in *The Pistol*, had been torn down and replaced with a modernistic reinforced-concrete monstrosity. The old pavilion had had a dining room, but the new building had none. Hamburgers and chiliburgers were dispensed at a window. There seemed to be more palm trees on the grass than I remembered, but none of the longleaf pine trees seemed to be any bigger. Families of tourists and local picnickers in trunks and bikinis sunbathed on the grass or lay on the sand beach. Swimmers trumpeted and cavorted in the shallow water between the beach and the shallow reef just offshore.

In our day, after the War began, there was nobody. Deserted. The pavilion locked up. We had strung barbed wire all along the beach. Our company commander had got permission to put a gate of concertina in the wire, so we could swim. But without girl swimmers it had been much less fun, and gradually we had all but stopped.

I sat a long time on the grass. I was uncomfortable. I seemed to keep wanting to look around for something else to appear, or occur. Finally I put on my brand-new trunks and went to the spot where our concertina gate had been and waded out and swam to the reef. Even without a mask I could see the reef was exactly the same as I remembered. The hole we had blasted in it to enlarge the swimming area was still there. I swam back to the beach and lay on the grass, still wanting to keep looking around for something. I got dressed and ate a chiliburger, sitting on the raised concrete porch of the "new" building. Young kids yelled and pushed each other and played around me and down on the grass. Suddenly, without any preparation at all, tears were up behind my eyes. All that blood, all that sweat. How many men? Tears for thirty years, gone somewhere. Tears for a young idiotic boy in a "gook" shirt and linen slacks. It was after one o'clock when I pulled the car back up onto the V-shaped cutoff, and too late to go to Makapuu.

There was now a four-lane highway all the way to Schofield Barracks, but first you had to extricate yourself from all the freeways around Honolulu and Pearl Harbor. Once I was safely on Route 99 north and could look at the country, I could see that just about everywhere the pineapple fields I remembered had diminished and urban housing developments had increased. But when I went through the Main Gate—where the MP on duty hardly gave me a glance—everything looked the same as it had looked thirty years before. I might have moved backward in time. The main flagpole was the same pure white. The Post Library was the same building, in the same place. I turned right at the proper point, and drove down along the front of the four Infantry quadrangles that I knew so well, one of which I had lived in for two years. They had not been changed. I knew every shelf on the inside of the Post Library, too. It was there I had first picked up Thomas Wolfe's *Look Homeward, Angel*, and heard some "mystic" call telling me I was a writer. I wondered if they had changed the inside. I had called the Post PR officer the day before, and been given a number to call when I arrived. But I put off calling. I drove around the streets of the Post, remembering this, remembering that. There was lots I did not remember. Mainly, the beauty. Schofield Barracks is probably the most beautiful post the US Army has, or ever had. I had not remembered it. Long stretches of green lush lawn, with short palms and tall palms and spreading hardwoods thrusting up here and there out of its rolling expanses. I had not remembered it because I had never noticed it much. Had I not been too preoccupied, there were a lot of things on the Post I might have enjoyed. And backdropping it all, what I always thought of as The Pregnant Woman—Kole Kole Pass in the Waianae Range to the west. You could see her breasts, Mt. Kaala the highest point was her belly, Waianae Peak her knees, Peacock Flats her shins, and the cut at the pass made her long flowing hair, dropping straight from a jutting face-shaped ridge. She had always haunted me, and from up close, inside the confines of the Post, she haunted me anew. Immutable as the Post itself seemed immutable, she loomed over it no matter where you stood, no matter where you looked, reminding every soldier of the feminine. A cruel sculpture to be perpetually confronted by. I drove three times around the old Post Theater, also still unchanged, and its V-shaped parking lot with the old roofed-over open-air bus station for Honolulu at the bottom, catercorner to my old 27th Infantry quadrangle. Scene of so many lonely evenings thirty years before, when I had the money. I saw it had a James Garner moved playing. And found myself on Kole Kole Pass Road, headed toward the hills, and let the car run on, carrying me there.

I had marched in formation out that road so many times. Hoarse voices counting cadence. Up past the baseball diamond to the empty field beyond for close-order drill. On up, past the golf course for squad and platoon small-unit tactical problems. Beyond that were the ranges set against the hills—rifle, mortar, artillery. Danger-warning signs, though newer, still invited passers-by to stay on the road. Then as the road steepened and began to snake, climbing to the pass, I passed the old Stockade rock pile, hollowed into an amphitheater back into the mountainside. Overgrown with grass and weeds, it clearly had fallen into disuse. I had wanted to see that place, again.

At the top of the pass I got out, and talked with the chubby Marine guard from the Naval Ammunition Depot in the Waianae Valley down the other side, and stood looking off over Waianae Valley to the sea, and looked back down at the Post spread out on the plateau behind me. I had once marched up to Kole Kole alone— twice; two times—with a full field pack and an escorting noncom, over some stupid argument with my company commander. I had used the incident on Prewitt in the novel, and it had been reproduced in the film version. Now I no longer knew whether Prewitt had done it, or I had. After a while, I got back into the car.

I called the Post PR Office from an outdoor phone booth under the open-shed roof of the bus station in the theater parking lot. One of the phone booths had an OUT OF SERVICE sign on it. Under it some sour graffitist had lettered, "Don't you wish you were!"

I knew that once the other people came into it, it would change. But there was no way out of that. If I did not call, I could not visit the installations I wanted. It was nobody's fault. But once the PR people arrived, the past went out of it. Vanished in thin air. Disappeared. It was as though I held a tenuous cord in my hand, that could not survive conversations and references and talk about itself, and the interplay of personalities. It became a typical, polite, convivial visit of a writer to a modern Army post, 1973. I was taken to a scheduled parade of the division's service battalions, and introduced to the 25th Division commander, a young major general. I chatted with some of the officers' wives. Then I was taken to the division's Administrative Hq Company. The colonel there gave me an elaborately formal pass, as a half joke, entitling me to visit everything. I was taken up beyond the golf course to a new building, to visit one of the division's new Air Cav outfits. The "New Army" was everywhere much in evidence. A great store was set on the four-man barracks cubicle, as against the wide, open bays with rows of bunks as in my day. It was certainly pleasanter, more homelike. Finally, I was taken to the Hq Building of the 2nd Battalion, 27th Infantry—my old outfit—housed in my old 27th Regiment quadrangle.

It was into here that I had wanted to get, on my trip to Schofield. And it was here that would be—I thought—the culminating experience of my return. For two years this old quadrangle had been my home. I had slept on the second floor of the old 2nd Battalion barrack, which faced the Hq Building across the quadrangle square. Nowadays, in the modern streamlined division, which carried within it its own helicopter air transport, only one battalion of the regiment remained in active service. The other two were deactivated. And if the old quad had seemed the same on the outside, driving past, it was not the same inside. In the corner of the interior square the old regimental bandstand, which had also served us as a ring for the regimental boxing smokers, was gone. And most of the grass was gone. Trucks were parked everywhere, and men worked on them. In one corner a volleyball game was in progress on the packed earth. And the ground floor of our old 2nd Battalion barracks, which once housed the orderly rooms and mess halls for the four companies, was now one huge, nicely done, modern mess hall for the entire organization. There were other changes.

But when we came off the stairs onto the second floor of the Hq Building—despite the other people present—for a moment the past

appeared again. Absolutely nothing had changed here. The walls
and doors were still painted the same horrible cream green, and the
polished old concrete floor still gleamed. They might never have
been repainted since my day. The regimental trophy room was in
the same place. The administrative offices were the same. And the
colonel commanding's office down at the end was the same, his
desk in the identical same place, the US and regimental flags
behind his desk in their same stands. The only thing missing was
the guard orderly's desk outside the colonel's office. I had sat at the
desk the morning of Pearl Harbor, carrying messages for distraught
officers, wearing the pistol I was later able to get away with. The
initial sequence of *The Pistol* had taken place right here on this floor.
But was it Pfc Richard Mast who had been here, or was it me? Or
was it still a third unnamed, unnameable person? Where had it all
gone? I kept waiting for something to appear, to happen. For a
moment I felt actively dizzy.

Later, the young colonel walked me across the square to show me
the new mess hall. Everything that could be done had been done to
make eating pleasanter and more enjoyable, although, to me, the
troopers didn't appear any less disgruntled. The young colonel had
been a boy in grade school here back in 1940 when I served here, his
father an artillery officer. So had his adjutant. They grinned and he
said he thought maybe I had been a little hard on the old folks. In
any case, the old caste system was gone. You couldn't *make* these
youngsters do anything, you had to explain to them what you
wanted them to do, and make them understand it, and then lead
them. I had heard pretty much the same thing all over Vietnam.
We talked a bit about the "New Army." The two officers took me
upstairs to the second floor, and I stood in the spot where my old
bunk had been. The second floor here had not yet been remodeled
into the four-man cubicles, and the bunks stretched in rows across
the width and length of the barrack floor. I thought it looked
considerably cooler, this way. I stood and looked down at my old
bunk. Nobody came in through the open doors that I knew.

On our way back to the Hq Building the young colonel hollered
at two troopers who were out washing their car in the barracks
street. "I've got one down here that could stand a little polish, when
you're through there," he called. The two soldiers grinned. "Yeah?
Why don't you grab a sponge and come help with this one?" was
the answer that came back. The colonel grinned and winked at me.

Later, I went with a young sergeant who wrote for the Schofield paper, to meet some of the unhappy types, the malcontents, whom he knew and had worked with. There were five of them sitting around a four-man cubicle, playing cards on a blanket on the floor around a candle. The lights had been turned off. All but one of them wore mustaches, and all of them had hair longer than was usual. Their complaints, when the sergeant got them down to bare rock, were primarily that they wanted to wear their hair and their mustaches even longer. Why, I asked. "So we won't look so much like soldiers," one of the boys said glumly. "The girls here don't like soldiers." Mainly, it came out, they did not like the Army because they were so lonely. In thirty years the song had changed almost not at all. The past seemed to rise up and roar at me like a wind tunnel.

We talked about the Stockade. The new Stockade. They did not appear to be afraid of it, as we had been. Apparently it had been moved from its old environs, down closer in the Post proper, and now consisted of a rather pleasant area surrounded by a white picket fence, like a cottage. It appeared to be run on a semihonor system. The young PR sergeant offered to take me to see it, but added that it was rather late. There were only about seven guys there, working out summary courts, he said, and grinned. It was not like the old days. So instead we had some beer one of the boys had brought in, and talked about the Army. It was long after dark when I pulled the little car out onto the main road—past the MPs at the man gate, who did not even glance at me—and started back to Honolulu.

The next morning I drove out to Makapuu Head, which I had missed the day before. I was leaving that same night, and something kept telling me I shouldn't miss Makapuu. It too had played a very important part in my life, particularly after the War began. It had been at once the largest, the most primitive, and the most extended beach position of my company headquarters at Hanauma Bay. Being so far away, the food that got out to us there three times a day was always cold. There was no way to avoid it. I had spent over three months there after the War began.

Makapuu Head lay at the easternmost corner of Oahu. The main mountain range, the Koolau Range, ended there. And once you had turned that corner, you were on what was called the Windward

Side of Oahu, where the sea wind blowing in from the east never stopped. In both the story *The Way It Is* and the novel *The Pistol*, I had used that never ceasing wind as a conscious symbol of pressure on the men.

It was five or six miles from the Hanauma Bay cutoff, and almost all of the way bulldozers and earth-moving equipment were at work on either the landscape or the highway or both. The Lunalilo Freeway was obviously being extended this way, and the development was following it. The farms and cattle ranges I remembered had almost totally disappeared. I arrived at Makapuu depressed.

The Koolau Range ended at Makapuu in a huge cliff several hundred feet high. The old Kalanianaole Highway had been constructed down this cliff, leading to Waimanalo and Kaneohe. At the top of the fall there had always been a scenic overlook, out over Rabbit Island and the sea, where cars could park. Even in my day. But in my day, with the War, no cars had come. We had wished they would, knowing already that they couldn't, were not allowed. Now a steady stream of them arrived, as tourists pulled up, parked, got out to look, and then drove on.

But when I walked away from them and the constantly starting and stopping cars, on out onto the desolate little flat to seaward of the road, which further away led onto the destitute crags of Makapuu Point, they seemed to be no longer there. With the so-familiar, hard buffeting unceasing east wind in my face, I could no longer hear them in their protected spot. A curtain had dropped behind me, cutting me off from them, and with a kind of frightened, awed wonder I stood looking at a scene that had not changed one grass blade since I had last looked at it thirty years before. In front of me the thin soil covered with outcrops rose to the craggy cliffs of the Point. Not one outcrop had been disturbed. To the south looking out over the fall of land from the pass to the Kaiwi Channel, I could see the squared-off cleared spaces we had made to pitch our tents, all still there, exactly as we had made them. Everywhere around were the paths our feet and our picks had made, still faintly visible in the sparse grass. The only things missing were the men, and the tents themselves. And for a few moments every now and then from the corners of my eyes I thought I could see both—the men moving, the tents blowing, translucent like ghosts.

It is hard to give a full picture of the acute desolation of that place. The rocks are black and sharp and are everywhere, jutting up or just under the thin surface. Mostly it's because of that hard-flowing wind that never stops howling.

In November of 1941 my company had with our bare hands, and the aid of seven gasoline-driven jackhammers that would not shut off like pneumatic drills when you moved them, dug five pillboxes in the virgin rock up there, on those cliffs, and had floored them and walled them and roofed them, and apertured them, with concrete. Only one of them was visible from the road, and to see that one you had to know where it was. On December 7th we had been moved down here in trucks and occupied them with nothing but the machineguns and our rifles. And one canteen of water per man. I could no more not go look at them than I could have flown home via Honolulu without a stopover. My feet started carrying me up the complex of faded paths as surely as though they knew the way before my eyes did.

They were all there. All five of them. Somebody at some point had bricked the apertures shut, but most of them had been broken open. The hewn-rock stairs down into two of them had been blocked by rubble and trash, but by shouldering the steel doors of the other three I could get into those. I stood in each of them a long time, looking out and remembering times when late at night I had sat behind machineguns in all of them, staring out into the dark toward Rabbit Island and the beach that faced it.

When I came up out of the last one and started back down, I looked down and automatically placed my foot on a natural step in the rock that we had always used to climb in or out. It was still there, unchanged, uneroded, unchipped. And my foot still knew where it was. I stood staring down at it for several seconds, shocked, and when I looked back up and looked down the hill at the tourists and the clustered cars, it was as if I were back there in 1942, when the overlook was empty, peering forward into an unforeseeable future when it would be open and crowded with sightseers, as it was now. The only thing that was different was that I was alone, that there was nobody with me.

Foolishly, I began taking pictures. As if pictures could capture what was happening to me. In a way I felt I was bearing witness— bearing the witness I had come back to Hawaii to authenticate. But just exactly what it was—except a thumbing of my nose at time—I didn't know.

That night an old friend drove me out to the airport to say good-by. We sat in the lounge and talked about the old days at the university in Manoa Valley, when I had gone there. But we ticketholders rode out to the plane in a bus, and I could not see the airport building to wave good-by. The airport itself looked entirely foreign. As tired as the others, I climbed the steep stairs. I had come back hoping to meet a certain twenty-year-old boy, walking along Kalakaua Avenue in a "gook" shirt, perhaps, but I had not seen him.

Appendix: Unpublished Work From the 1940s

"They Shall Inherit the Laughter," Book Report of *The Red Badge of Courage*, Notes for *From Here to Eternity*

After being wounded on Guadalcanal, Jones was returned to the States for convalescence and reassignment in 1943. In November of that year, he was transferred to Camp Campbell, Kentucky, where he began working on *They Shall Inherit the Laughter*. Through the intervention of Lowney Handy, Jones received a medical discharge from the army on July 6, 1944, and returned home to Robinson, Illinois. In 1945, he had a completed manuscript ready to show to Ruth and Maxwell Aley, literary agents in New York City. After Maxwell Aley said the novel was interesting, but not publishable, Jones decided to take charge and presented the *Laughter* manuscript to Maxwell Perkins, legendary Scribner's editor. Perkins gave Jones genuine encouragement, but said that the novel needed considerable revision. Jones sent a revised manuscript to Perkins in January 1946; shortly thereafter he mentioned in a letter to him that he would like sometime to write a novel about the "old" peacetime army. Perkins liked the idea and offered a $500 advance. Jones immediately shelved *Laughter* and began what would become *From Here to Eternity*.

The *Laughter* manuscript was left with Lowney Handy when Jones left Illinois in 1957. It was rediscovered in the possession of Lowney's family, the Turners, by J. Michael Lennon and Jeffrey Van Davis while filming their 1985 documentary about the novelist's life and career, "James Jones: Reveille to Taps." The Turners donated the manuscript and other materials which comprise the Handy Writers' Colony Collection to Sangamon State University in Springfield, Illinois.

It is easy to see why Scribner's never published the novel—and why Perkins was attracted to it. *Laughter* is rambling and episodic in structure, self-indulgent and excessively bitter in tone, and extremely derivative of Dos Passos, Wolfe, Steinbeck, and even Emerson and the American transcendentalists. Toward the end, Jones borrows Tom Joad's "I'll be there" speech from *The Grapes of Wrath* and applies it to the returning American soldier. Still, it contains some fine writing and is fascinating as a kind of preview of Jones's literary career. It incorporates, moreover, early versions of some of the most memorable scenes from Jones's later work—for example, Landers's speech about "the soldier's responsibilities" to his Indiana hometown Elks Club in *Whistle*, "Mad" Welsh's desperate attempt to help the horribly wounded Tella in *The Thin Red Line*, and several of the major episodes in *Some Came Running*. In fact, *Laughter* is, to a large degree, an early, less successful version of *Some Came Running*. It focuses on Johnny Carter's return to small-town Endymion in Indiana's Wabash Valley. Carter is an intelligent, sensitive young veteran embittered by the absurdity of modern combat. Ultimately, he is "adopted" by an older, married woman, Corny Marion (based on Lowney Handy), who preaches an affirmative worldview devised equally from Emerson and Oriental mysticism. Carter is a prototype for Richard Mast of *The Pistol*, Dave Hirsh of *Some Came Running*, Geoffrey Fife of *The Thin Red Line*, and Marion Landers of *Whistle*. Ultimately, Johnny Carter is healed of his bitterness by Corny's affirmation and mysticism.

Two of the selections from *Laughter* that follow are flashbacks to the war and combat, while the other recounts Carter's intentionally subversive speech to the Endymion Rotary Club. Jones gave a similar speech in Robinson, Illinois, in 1944.

Following these excerpts is Jones's first extended piece of writing on combat, in which he compares his feelings while under attack on December 7 with those of Henry Fleming, the protagonist of

Stephen Crane's *The Red Badge of Courage.* Jones was twenty when he wrote it for an English class at the University of Hawaii, just before shipping out for Guadalcanal. Could he have imagined at the time that his own future writings would be compared favorably with Crane's? Given Jones's self-confidence, the answer is probably yes.

The final selection, also previously unpublished, consists of excerpts from Jones's notes for *From Here to Eternity.* They were written quite early in the novel's composition, probably before Perkins died in June, 1947. Those familiar with the novel will note that Jones had worked out most but not all of the details of the plot. Except for obvious spelling and typing errors, which have been corrected, the notes are given here as Jones wrote and typed them. A few names of actual people have been taken out. Prewitt's centrality (if there was ever a doubt) is reinforced by Jones's passionate comments on his hero's tragic situation.

[Johnny's First Kill; the Wounding of Shelley]

JOHNNY WAS SITTING QUIETLY, staring at his drink and listening abstractedly to Titan's voice as it ran on. He hardly knew who it was that spoke; actually he didn't hear beyond the first sentence. All he heard was, "like ducks in a shooting gallery," and the phrase leaped up and slapped him in the face. His mind cleaved onto it and was gone...... He is walking down the hill. Other men are walking down the hill. They are scattered haphazardly about like propaganda leaflets dropped from a plane. There is no formation to their moving. Some are close together, some too widely scattered, some far ahead, some far behind. They are aimless groups without purpose. They are simply men with rifles and they are walking down the hill.

There is lots of noise, so much noise that most of it is undistinguishable. The ears cannot encompass this great amount of noise. Now and then an individual sound rises above the mass. Perhaps the soft sh-sh-sh-sh-sh of a mortar shell coming down nearby; sometimes long, four or five seconds; sometimes short, a second and a half. And then its explosion. If it sounds like it will hit near, perhaps some of who hear it will collapse quickly to the ground. Then again perhaps they will not. It is too confused, everything is too confused, to be able to know whether it will land close or not. Perhaps a bullet will bzzzt fiercely by, too quickly come and gone to cause a reaction until it is long way past. Then the hearer will duck, will half-crouch, will jerk, will do nothing, according to how far the numbness has advanced inside him. The strain is much too great. It is already beginning to show in some. The blank faces and staring eyes. These faces are contrasted with the screwed-up faces and drawn half-open mouths of the others, whose fear has not yet grown strong enough to turn to numbness.

They are men with rifles and they keep walking down the hill. Further down the hill. None of them has fired a shot. The Japanese are in the jungle that grows partway up the hill; that is why they are walking down the hill with their rifles in their hands. There is nothing to shoot at. The tension is immense, and it seems they walk in complete silence, although the noise around them is a bedlam. Then as they get closer to the jungle, a man over on the left yells. "There's one! I see one!" His voice is shrill with excitement and disbelief. Half a dozen men fire a clip apiece in the direction of the excitedly pointing finger. It is a great discovery, greater to them than the discovery of radium or the sulfa drugs or of America. For a while walking down the hill they doubted whether there was anybody at all. They half-believed the Japanese had left their machineguns, rifles and mortars firing full blast and had gone away. Maybe back to Japan.

Then he sees it. He will never know why his eyes fastened upon it, for when he first looks, it seems nothing more than a dark blob of wood on the side of the tree. The tree is on the edge of the jungle, maybe fifteen yards away. Somehow his eyes have fastened themselves upon the innocent looking blob of wood and recognized it for a helmet. He is astounded; he does not believe it is a helmet. If it is, it is the first time he has ever seen a live Japanese. He leans forward and peers. Yes by Christ it is a helmet! He becomes excited and starts to shout, but a sly cunning creeps into his mind. If he shouts, the helmet might hear him and withdraw itself behind its tree more thoroughly. Suddenly he is afraid of this helmet, terribly afraid. If he does not shoot it now, it will certainly shoot him in a little while. The whole battle, the whole war becomes understandable, becomes centered upon this helmet, the top quarter of which is just visible behind the tree. This is the whole war; he and this helmet. If he gets the helmet first he will be safe. It all comes down to killing the helmet first. And he has it by surprise now. If he can only kill it, he will be safe forever. A rifle bullet shot direct will pass through a helmet easily. He sinks down to a kneeling position to be more sure his muzzle will not waver. Get him, or he'll get you. He aims very carefully. The two men on his left stop to watch him, trying unsuccessfully to see what he is aiming at. He takes up the slack and starts to squeeze the shot off. Just as he starts the squeeze the helmet moves. Carefully and slowly it raises itself, and a face appears below it. He is astonished. This is a Jap. He squeezes the shot off and in squeezing is more astonished to see how closely the dirty unshaved face beneath the helmet resembles the faces of the men around him in the tension and agony expressed upon it. The recoil slams his shoulder, already sore from continued firing. He keeps his eyes open as he was taught, and he sees the face open redly like a thrown tomato. He sees a piece of bridgework pop out of the mouth that the impact of the bullet jarred open. He pushes on the safety and jumps up shouting, "I got him!" I got him!" He starts to run the fifteen yards to the tree. Just then a mortar shell lands close by him. His body slams itself into the dirt harshly, independently, without his bidding. He lies there slightly stunned by the concussion of the explosion. It brings the war back to him. He remembers that there are no doubt other Japanese. For a few seconds the war was small, understandable, and individual like a prizefight. Now it is back as before. He is afraid again. Not individually, but largely, multiplely, of things he cannot see or foresee. He suddenly realizes that the fact that he has killed a Japanese means little or nothing. He gets back up and begins to walk toward the jungle as before, not noticing that his chin is bleeding from a deep cut where it hit the ground. Such things are unimportant......... He and Captain Rosen are standing side by side looking down at the dead Japanese. He looks at the dead Japanese and thinks without comprehending that this is the first man he had ever killed. It was like a prizefight. Get him or he'll get you. But he, the victor, looking down at the vanquished feels none of the feeling he used to feel back home when, after winning a tough fight, he stood looking down at his unconscious opponent. He does not feel excited or powerful or happy or heroic or thrilled. He only feels sad and a little foolish. He feels an understanding for this dead Japanese whose frightened face had looked so much like the faces of the men near him. He feels that this Japanese is like himself, a dogface fighting a war and afraid beyond all reasoning. He feels sad, terribly sad, and unhappy, and sorry for this dead Japanese. This was not right. It was too utterly final.

He wonders what this Japanese would have felt if the situation were reversed and the Japanese were looking down at his own dead body.

He looks at Captain Rosen who is Jewish and a lawyer and from Boston. His own feelings are mirrored in Rosen's face. For the first time since he had known the Captain, he feels friendly toward him and not antagonistic. The Captain does not have his privileges here. He is like the men in his company now for the first time. He is no longer an officer to be respected by order; he is a man to be liked by instinct.

The dead Japanese lies on his back sprawled out in the unnatural scarecrow fashion of death. The bullet entered his face just below the nose. It went slightly upward and split the upper lip and smashed the teeth that now stick out oddly, splintered and broken. The nose is pushed way over to one side. Thick, gluelike blood ran into the mouth until, overflowing sullenly, it runs out thickly at both corners to hang in strings down to the ground.

He thinks suddenly that it is an undignified way for any man to die.

The Captain sticks out his foot repugnantly and pushes the head. It lolls over to the side and then rolls back. The foot leaves a smudge of mud in the chin that is darker than the crusted dirt on the rest of the face.

"He's dead all right," Rosen says. "He's one Jap that won't make a booby trap out of himself." He pauses and slowly runs his hand over his week-old beard. "Well," he says slowly, "I guess you can cut a notch on your rifle, hunh?"

He does not answer the Captain but leans over and picks up the piece of bridgework that popped out of the mouth when the bullet hit. He sticks it between the brim of his steel helmet and the leather chin strap of the liner that runs up over it. He had seen marines with glass jars full of teeth with gold inlays in them. There is a wallet in one of the pockets of the shirt; he takes it, too. The wallet has a picture of a woman holding a baby and there is Japanese writing on the back of the picture. He sticks the wallet in his pocket. The rifle fire is getting heavy. He turns and walks away between the trees on down the hill toward the sound of firing with his rifle in his hands. . . . .

. . . . Somewhere in here he sees Shelley hit. A mortar shell, a ninety, explodes on the left, and shell fragments buzz unheard in the sound of the explosion. Shelley does not make a sound. He just stops walking and slowly, deliberately sets his rifle butt on the ground. Leaning on it, he slowly lowers himself to a sitting position. The acrid smell of burnt powder is strong; it coats lips and tongues; it burns eyes. Shelley drops his rifle and puts his hands between his legs. He sees bright blood running from Shelley's crotch, between his fingers to the ground. Shelley leans forward to watch the blood running from between his legs. It puzzles him for a moment; then he straightens up and stares straight ahead with no expression or movement on his face. Shelley begins to whimper like a frightened puppy; only louder, because he can hear Shelley's crying above the noise. He stands looking for a moment, until a bullet, like an angry Superman bee, buzzes by him and reminds him. Then he turns away to walk on down the hill through the jungle with his rifle in his hands. Shelley begins to curse and scream in the treble of a child. Looking back he sees Shelley start to puke, and puking over the front of his grimy uniform and crying at the same time, Shelley sounds like a grimly bubbling satire of Shep Field's "Rippling Rhythm."

A freak piece of shell fragment has entered Shelley's belly just below the navel and come out at his crotch taking his organs with it. When the corpsmen get there they do not bother to take Shelley back on a stretcher. They look at him and shake their heads and go on to the next man down the hill, leaving Shelley looking after them with a mute question in his eyes. The chaplain goes over to Shelley. Everybody likes the chaplain who is a good man, even if he is a chaplain. He has come up with the company of his own volition when he had not needed to come. The chaplain kneels down by Shelley, but Shelley curses him and tries to spit in his face.

"Fuck you!" Shelley says. "Fuck you and God and the United States! Get the fuck away from me!" The chaplain leaves him and

goes on to the next man. Shelley sits and watches his blood run
from him as life turns away to go on down the hill with its rifle in
its hands......

(from Chapter 8)

[Johnny's Speech to the Draftees]

AFTER A MOMENT, Bill Jacobs walked around the room over to the
other side where the long table was. He sat down at his place near
the head of the table. Johnny saw him leaning over and talking to
various people who were seated at the table. He noticed that the
men who had been at the bar were sitting at several different tables.
Apparently they were spreading the news. One of the men was
sitting at a table near Johnny with two heavily older women;
Johnny recognized one of them as a school teacher who had taught
him in grade school. The man leaned over toward Johnny and said,
"You tell them, son." Johnny grinned at him with bright-eyed
intensity and nodded. All right, they would be told. All part of the
game, the big game that was Endymion first, the rest of the United
States second, and the rest of the world last; never the reverse. He
was suddenly tremendously angry at their stupidity. Not only did
they insist on deluding themselves with their game, but they
insisted on dragging him, a bystander, into the farce. If they
wanted a show, by god, that was what they would get.

He inspected the large group of men at the long table. They were
of varying ages, but there was a common look of innocent cynicism
on their faces. None of them looked very enthusiastic.

He sat at his table and ate apple pie with icecream on it for
dessert, but it did not taste as good as the rest of the meal had
because his single-minded forgetfulness had been destroyed by Bill
Jacobs and his gang, who not only fought the war from the draft
board office but wanted the right to say what the war was being
fought for. After the pie, he mixed himself another drink and sat

watching the group of men in civilian clothes who sat around the long table.

Bill Jacobs made the introductory talk and call for attention. He introduced the Reverend Doctor Bryson. Reverend Bryson made a short talk to the effect that the young men at the table were going away to fight a war against oppression and greed for power and that God was behind them and championing their cause and that the fate of the church and the world was in their hands.

Tom Prentiss spoke, giving them the goodwill of the Rotary Club and voiced the hope that they would fight hard and well to preserve the American way of life, which was the best life yet devised on earth, and concluded with the thought that if the rest of the world had been taught more of the American way of life sooner there would have been no war.

After that Bill Jacobs made his speech, pointing out that this war was only a continuation of the last and that this time America was going to do the job right and finish it, instead of leaving it half-done like they did the last time.

"And now," Bill said with an air of expectancy, "you fellows have a special treat tonight. We've got with us a boy;" Bill laughed; "a *man*, I should say, but I never can remember how fast you fellows grow up;" a few of the men at the long table laughed with him; "we've got with us a man who has been through Guadalcanal and who has played his part in this adventure, as the ribbons on his shirt will say more eloquently than I ever could. He's reluctant to talk about himself, but I finally persuaded him to say a few words to you fellows. He's done and seen all the things you are about to do and see, so listen to him closely and maybe you can learn something from what he says. Johnny, come on up here and say hello."

Johnny stood up and walked up onto the raised organ stand where Bill Jacobs stood before the microphone. As he stood up, he felt his individuality slip curiously away from him. Bill Jacobs put his arm around Johnny and grinned at the long table. "Most of you fellows probably have known Johnny Carter all your lives, so he won't need any further introduction. I'll sit down and let him talk." Bill stepped down off the platform, sat down in his chair and looked expectantly up at Johnny. The draftees at the long table watched him with bored attention. Johnny stood in front of the mike, and there was a bright spotlight on the side of the stand that illumined him. He stood with his legs widespread, his arms hanging down along his thighs, his fists closed. In his tailored uniform he made a fine picture and the ribbons on his shirt glittered colorfully in the light. He stood quite still for several seconds after Bill Jacobs sat down. He looked down at the long table with no nervousness, not speaking.

When he spoke, his voice was coldly quiet and completely without emotion.

"I'm not reluctant to talk," he began, "but there is very little I can tell you guys. As Mr Jacobs said, most of you probably have known me all my life. I'm not talking to you as Johnny Carter whom you know. I'm talking as a soldier whom you don't know.

"These gentlemen have told you a number of things about this war. You have been told you are fighting for a number of things: democracy, freedom, to end oppression, and so on. There is one thing that you are fighting for that has not been mentioned. To me it is the most important. You are fighting for your life. These other statements may be true or not. There is a possibility they are not. True or not, they are general ideas, and the army is a particular life. When you are in the army, you will find it very hard to reconcile these general statements with the particulars of the life you'll live."

Johnny paused for a moment and looked around the room. Every face was turned toward him, and he could see the startled looks on a number of them. Bill Jacobs' mouth was hanging open, and the attention of the draftees was not bored. Johnny's eyes glittered savagely as he looked down at the long table.

"One other thing. Some of you may go overseas, and some of you may never get over. If you ever do, remember this. You must learn to hate. Brotherly love and mercy are all very fine back here. There they are worth nothing. You can not afford to think of mercy or sportsmanship or fair play. You will have to forget the code you've been taught. You are fighting to keep from being killed, and a dirty fighter kills a man just as dead and with less effort than a clean one. You can take no chances. When you are in combat, you are not fighting for freedom or anything else. You are fighting only to save your life. If you remember that, you will have every chance to get out alive that you can have. You may need them. Sometimes these chances are not very many. You have to learn to hate, because in hating without mercy you can kill better. And that is what you are for, if you're a soldier."

Johnny stopped talking abruptly and stepped off the stand. As he stepped to his booth he saw the face of the grade school teacher, contorted with a look of revulsion. She turned her face away and would not meet his eyes. He sat down in his booth and began to mix himself another drink.

There was a stillness in the Grille for several moments, and then people began to talk and move about, as if trying to refute the fact that there had been a lull. Johnny grinned to himself and sipped his drink. They wanted their war, but they wanted to select their own spices to kill its taste so it would fit into the game they played. They didn't want to know the true taste. The men in Europe had learned what was the game of war and what was the truth. The French and the Poles and the Greeks and the Russians had tasted it as it was. Their lives had been stripped of subterfuge and nonessential ideas. You couldn't select your own spices when you were starving. He looked over at the long table. Several of the draftees were looking at Bill Jacobs with derisive grins. Bill's face was expressionless, but tinged with red.

The draftees were herded out to catch their train, for them the first of a long line of herdings. The Grille settled back down to its former relaxation and enjoyment. The draftees were gone, like so many other groups of draftees; they were torn out of Endymion by the roots to be shuffled about and replanted all over the world, but their absence made no appreciable difference in the quiet laughter, fine drinks, good food, and people whose moods and memories hung outside beside their caps, except that now there was an invisible curtain of reproof drawn between Johnny Carter and the rest of the Grille.

People wandered over to his booth from time to time and were friendly and talked to him, but the invisible curtain was always present. Johnny grinned wryly to himself and did not try to penetrate it. Bill Jacobs came over for a moment and thanked him perfunctorily for talking to the selectees, but Bill looked at him coldly and did not offer to claim his drink. Johnny felt Bill had not liked what he said.

(from Chapter 10)

[Attu]

HE WAS GLAD when the orders came through to hold up the advance for the night. It was an unheard of thing, and because of its strangeness implied that a still stranger thing was coming: the end. He was very glad, as glad as he could be beneath the grey insolation of weariness that enveloped him. The front line, only a few hundred yards ahead, had been halted until tomorrow, because tomorrow would be the last day; tomorrow they would go into Chichagof for the cleanup. He squatted in the half frozen mud gratefully, his rifle between his legs to keep his behind off the wet muck, holding it with his hands like a kid on a broomstick. He had checked the guys to see they were all here, so he could relax, as much as was possible in this godforsaken place.

Smitty was sitting beside him, his head drooped forward and his shoulders hanging dispiritedly. Smitty's face, the parts of it that showed through his beard, hung in grey folds of weariness. His eyes were dull and his lips slack. Smitty was the sparkplug of the platoon, a PFC with six years Regular Army service, the man who never tired and couldn't get killed. If Smitty looked like that, how in the name of god must the rest of them look? George wondered. It seemed impossible that a few days over two could make such a scarecrow pitiful change in a man. He'd like to take the squad into a bar back home right now, just like they were. They probably wouldn't even be allowed to buy a beer.

They squatted like that, without speaking, waiting indifferently for the Staff; he had gone back to the CP a couple of hundred yards to the rear. He would have the details of the orders when he came back. Until then they just sat. In the last few days the periods of talking had grown shorter and shorter, and the long spaces of silence in between had grown longer, and if possible, more silent. It seemed that the eternal greyness that surrounded them had found a breach and had slipped in through it to fill their bodies and worm its way into their minds.

Eighteen days. It seemed there had never been anything before the eighteen days that had passed since they first hit the beach.

There was nothing else before, there would be nothing else after, except the eternal greyness. It was a good thing none of them knew what Attu or what combat was like before they got here. In that eighteen days none of them had had what you could call sleep, unless you could call squirming around and shivering in a wet cold slit trench, or lying stiffly on the wet tundra and feeling the wet slowly soak through your clothes. The Soldier's Handbook would call that sleep. George knew now why men wrote military textbooks. It was so they could stay out of combat.

After the first two days of confusion, of supposedly fighting the grey shadows that nobody saw, the company had been put on an ammunition-carrying detail. They had made an uncountable number of trips up with boxes and bandoleers of thirty calibre stuff, trips from Massacre Bay up the steep valley to the ever-further front. The men were triggerhappy anyway, and they fired at every shadow, even saw shadows where there were no shadows and fired at them too. It took a lot of ammo to supply them, and as the line fought its way inland, each trip up the steep slippery valley was longer than the last, and each trip back was longer than the trip up. Men falling with the heavy boxes, sliding back down; after the first fall they were never dry again, and there were a lot of broken bones and raw bruises. A long line of men moving like automatons back and forth in the dim grey light. Back and forth. Back and forth.

The squadleader had been hit in the head the first day. The Jap always tried to get the men who were directing movements. And George, as second, had inherited the squad. After one day of carrying the ammo, he had given up trying to keep them together. His mind would no longer work. But somehow or other, like sheep, the squad seemed to huddle together in the vast welter of men on the trail and at the beach, and then later the advance supply dump. How the outfit had finally found them God only knew.

For twelve days they had made the ever-lengthening trips with the ammo boxes, the round tricircular containers of mortar ammo. Finally it got to the point where they no longer had to think. They moved along the trail like wraiths without thought or feeling. Twelve days was almost two weeks, and in that time there had been no sleep except what they could snatch on their feet, moving the ammo along the eerie trail, mist-covered to the knees; or in some hole without even a shelterhalf, a raw grave into which the mists flowed and filled. They would walk back until somebody stopped them and put a box of ammo in their arms; then they would walk up toward the line until somebody else stopped them and relieved them of the burden. His mind could not grasp the truth of it, because there was nothing in the outside world to compare it to. People just didn't walk for twelve days without sleep. It was impossible.

The sleeping bags they had been issued so generously were supposed to come ashore later with shelterhalves and blankets, etc. Whether they came or not nobody knew, because nobody could find them in the vast welter of confusion at the beach. They saw no sleeping bags, but once George and his squad were commandeered by some frantic officer to unload a barge. They worked until the barge was almost unloaded of its boxes before some man broke one open thinking it might be food. The boxes contained condoms, case after case, box after box, of condoms. They quit working and sat down in the wet and laughed themselves silly; it was a bitter hungry laughter. The frantic officer cursed and stormed and had the rest of the barge's cargo dumped over the side.

—Once he had walked into a ration dump for a box of rations. There was nobody there. The stuff had just been dumped and left there; he was just lucky to stumble onto it. He had his rifle in his hands, the ever-present rifle that was always with him. Whether he carried a box of ammo, a can of water, or a box of rations on one shoulder, the rifle was always slung over the other. After a while the awkwardness of carrying it was gone and forgotten. It was like another, a heavier, more awkward arm. He stepped around a stack of C ration boxes and came face to face with a Jap. It was the first one he had seen close enough to distinguish his features. Always they were at a distance, like grey phantoms in the grey world.

The Jap was tearing open a C ration box. He had it part way open and was just getting out a can of meat and beans. George saw the label on the can, and for some reason it impressed itself upon his dulled stupid mind; it was the most vivid memory of the whole encounter. The Jap jumped up, as surprised as George. George looked at him for several seconds, not knowing what to do. The Soldier's Manual said nothing about the procedure when meeting a Jap in a US ration dump. The Jap raised his rifle with a slow movement like a sleepwalker, and George just watched him stupidly. Without thinking about it, he stepped in and hit the Jap on the mouth with his right fist. He was as big as three of the Jap, and the punch lifted the scrawny Jap clear off his feet; he dropped his rifle and lit on the back of his neck.

The Jap lay still for a moment, partially stunned, and George remembered he still held his own rifle in his left hand. He pointed it down at the Jap and fired it. He couldn't have missed.

The bullet hit the Jap someplace in the chest. It made no evident difference: no visible hole or blood. George couldn't even see a mark or hole in the wrinkled mess of his uniform. The Jap clutched his fingers in the tundra and made a wry face. He made no sound. His lips writhed back over his teeth as he looked at George. For the first time in the encounter a thought entered George's head. He hated the Jap. Here was this Jap stuffing his gut in a US ration dump, while George himself and the guys in the squad hadn't had food for God knows how long. No food, no sleep, no rest. And here was this Jap having himself a picnic.

George raised his rifle again and emptied the other seven rounds of the clip into the Jap's body. Then he jumped on the Jap's chest. He felt the chest wall of ribs give suddenly under his boots, his nice expensive leather boots that weren't worth a goddam. He took his rifle by the warm muzzle and rammed the butt of it down into the Jap's face several times. After that he sat down and dropped his rifle into the muck. He was very weak and gagged and gagged, but he had not had enough food to puke up anything.

He sat there a long time before he could regain the strength to pick up his rifle and a box of C rations. By that time he had forgotten the Jap, and he walked stupidly, ploddingly back to the beach. He didn't even tell his buddy Smitty about the Jap. It didn't seem to matter much. Once in a while his mind would dwell on it for a second and he would remember the label on the can of meat and beans and he would get scared. The Jap could just as easily have killed him.—

He and Smitty didn't say anything as they squatted. For a second he wondered what Smitty was thinking, but then the question faded and his mind went back to its confused series of meaningless pictures. They sat that way, cold as hell, till the Staff came back from the CP. Smitty used to be the company comic; his cracks would keep them going when nothing else could. On the transport Smitty had been chipper, and he used to imitate a club woman giving a report to her local Cultural Society in which she described the Island of Attu "where our boys are now fighting" as being rich in history and relics and how the Aleuts had named Massacre Bay for a big killing that took place there. Once Smitty had said the Bible was wrong about Hell: Hell was a cold place, not a hot one. Hell was Attu projected into Heaven.

George wondered if Attu was *really* the Hell of the Bible, and if the swirling shadows of mist that surrounded everything were not maybe the lost souls.

The Staff came back, plodding wearily through the deep mud that sucked hungrily at his boots, icy cold and soft. Once, as he walked toward them through the grey daylight that still lingered at 10 pm, he crossed a patch of snow. He was above them on the steep hill and on the windward side. At each step the wind caught a puff of the icy weightless crystals and swirled them around his figure like a full length halo. He plodded down to them in the lee, carrying his stolen Thompson gun slung with the butt up. The Staff was very paternal about his Thompson gun. When he squatted by George the muzzle dug into the mucky tundra. The Staff looked at it dully, cursed, and fired it into the air to clean the compensator. It was always a constant fight against rust, and the monotonous operation of cleaning and re-cleaning arms grew to be almost a penance for some obscure sin committed in civilian life.

"Battalion's set up back there," the Staff said to George and Smitty. "They say tomorrow's the cleanup. We got them all pocketed in a cul-de-sac. This here's the only way out of Chichagof. So we rest tonight," here the Staff snorted bitter laughter. "And tomorrow we clean it up; for good. We move in behind the line ahead as reserve."

"We bivouac here tonight," the Staff said, as if remembering what he had gone for.

Smitty cursed.

"What's the matter, Smitty?" the Staff said.

"We be better off to go on in tonight," Smitty said. "I don't like it. Whose orders, Staff?"

"Come down from division, I guess."

"I still don't like it. What about security?"

"Battalion's takin care of it."

"Balls," said Smitty. ". . . When this war's over, I'm gonna re-enlist into the Foreign Legion and git stationed in the middle of the Sahara Desert."

The Staff went away to see about the platoon.

"I'm gonna see what I can scrounge up," Smitty said to George. Due to his six years previous service, Smitty was the best thief in the regiment.

When Smitty came back, he had a bottle. "Officers," he said. He handed it to George who drank the fiery liquor deeply. Then he handed it around to the rest of the squad who squatted near.

"I found a pile of sleeping bags," Smitty whispered to George. "And there a coupla tents pitched right over there."

"How many bags?"

"Five or six," Smitty said.

"Go tell the Staff," George said. "I'll tell the cook." One of the company cooks, since there was no cooking to do, had volunteered to help out. He had joined the Staff's platoon. Everybody appreciated his gesture.

These were the first sleeping bags any of them had seen since the day they hit the beach. When they slept at all, they scrounged up a shelterhalf if they could. Usually they couldn't. So they were very pleased to see them.

George and Smitty hunted around near the pile of bags until they found enough for the whole squad. There were only nine left of the original fifteen. Within an hour they had spread themselves out in one of the abandoned tents Smitty had found. Smitty was a great guy. It was the first time they had really slept in eighteen days.

George felt himself sinking through layer after layer of black nothingness. It was as if he were sinking into layers of featherbeds, which opened to let him pass through and then closed again over the top of him. The world receded beyond the layers of blackness. There was no world.

For the first time that day he thought of Riley. In the bag he began to get warm and he could see in half-sleep, half-wakefulness Riley's wide smile, her competent hands that always knew everything. He felt awed at her glowing power that she was willing to use in ministering to him. He thought again that Riley was safe from war, and that fact seemed to justify his presence here a little more. As he fell deeper into sleep, the memory crystalized into dream, and he was in the house he planned. But the house was strange. In the bathroom the bathtub and commode were filled with snow, the hard icy snow of the north that never melts. He turned on the faucets but only snow came out, and he was forced to bathe in the freezingness of the snow. When he flushed the toilet, white snow swirled aroung the bowl of the commode. When he turned on the water in the washbasin to wet his toothbrush, snow came out of the faucet. He jaws and eyes ached with the iciness of it as he brushed his teeth. He hurried out of the bathroom into the livingroom, but in the livingroom the furniture was dusted with sifted snow. Young Jimmy was standing there in the center of the room, fully dressed, and shivering with blue face and hands. His very blood seemed blue. George thought at once to help him, and then discovered that he had left the bathroom stark naked. He was terribly embarrassed and worried about not having anything at all with which to help Jimmy because of being naked. Then Riley entered the room, and his embarrassment changed to shame. He tried to cover himself with his rifle but it was too small to provide cover. Riley paid no attention to Jimmy and she came to George. She touched his face and rubbed his shoulders with her warm hands, and George found himself fully clothed and warm. He was immensely grateful to Riley because she was not mad at him, but he could not speak; he was ashamed of his uniform, trailing muck into the livingroom of his nice house. He found an issue can of canned heat in his pocket and he gave it to Jimmy to warm himself. Then he gave Jimmy the rifle to show Riley his gratitude. Immediately he wished he had it back.

He awoke to the sound of a thousand screaming banshees. He unzipped the bag quickly and grabbed his rifle. When he got outside the tent, he saw about a million Japs. They were everywhere, and all of them were screaming and yelling. The noise was terrifying. He dropped down to one knee and began firing. They were firing rifles and light machineguns, and every now and then a grenade would boom out. Jesus Christ, he thought inarticulately, Jesus Christ. A spray of bullets hit the canvas tent with the sound of a zipper being whizzed open. His own terror made him frantic at the thought of being all alone. He screamed at the men in the tent, and the Staff came roaring out, firing his stolen Thompson gun like a wild Indian. Smitty crawled out and lay beside George. The rest of the men in the tent tumbled out haphazardly. Between clips George found out that the cook had never left his sack. He sat up just as the spray of bullets hit the tent, and he had been caught in the throat with one or several. The blood spurted all over the sack. "Oh God, help me," was all the cook could choke out.

Smitty looked at George through the silvery light of the

darkness. "I told you I didn't like this," Smitty said. "I had a hunch." His eyes were very wide and had a peculiar look in them that George had never seen before. "Some brasshat son of a bitch'll get the DSO out of this," Smitty said.

The Staff stuck a new clip into his Thompson gun. He was lying on the other side of Smitty. "Banzai," the Staff muttered. "Banzai, you cocksuckers." A bullet hit him just below his helmet brim, and he dropped his head forward. Smitty cursed and took his Thompson gun.

After that it became a nightmare. The screaming mob of Japs swept through like a wave, screaming, shooting, bayoneting, blowing grenades. In the shambles George lost Smitty. He must have moved off or back, because he could no longer see the tents. Twice he took ammo off dead bodies. He could see no live men around him; they must of all got away and ran, the live ones. Once three Japs rushed him and he shot one, kicked the second in the balls, and bayoneted the third. He shot the second one as he writhed on the ground, after he finally got his bayonet loose.

He was terrified at being all alone, and the only thought in his mind was to find the tents and Smitty. In the swirling mist he thought he caught a glimpse of them off to the right. There was not a live soul near him, and he started toward where he thought he saw the tents. It was then that the Jap concussion grenade hit his leg. It bounced from his thigh to the mucky tundra, and he saw it, red and black. By the time he focused his eyes, it exploded, blinding him, deafening him, shocking his nervous system into disintegration.

"Oh Christ," he sobbed. "Oh Jesus Christ. The dirty bastards blew my leg off. Oh Christ. Oh Jesus Jesus Christ."

He lay where he had fallen for a long time. Once for a little while he blacked out. Finally, because he could think of nothing else and because he was terrified at being alone in this deathlike silence with the noise of screaming and explosions in the distance, he started crawling toward the tent. Smitty could help him. He crawled on his left side, dragging his right leg. It made him sick to look at the mangled mess. There was no feeling in it, and the foot was turned around backwards, his own foot. The shin bones stuck out through the flesh and the remnants of his pantsleg that hadn't been blown off him. There was dirt and mud ground into the bone and flesh. It looked like a piece of raw beef, and it hung by only one little strip of flesh.

They'll cut off my leg. They'll cut off my leg. He kept thinking it until it became a song accompanied by a rhythm of his crawling body. He should take his sulpha pills, but his belt was gone and his first aid packet with it. He couldn't remember what had happened to it.

To hell with it. He was going to die anyway. He'd bleed to death, bleed to death alone, alone out here by himself, where there was nobody at all. He wanted to die. He wished the Japs would come and kill him off and get it over with. They'd cut off his leg anyway. George, you're going to die. George Schwartz is going to die. Even now the sentence had no meaning; he didn't know what it would be to be dead. But he didn't want to die.

He made it to the tent in the awesome silence. The wave of Japs had swept on, carrying the noise with it, and leaving a vast silence that was fearful by comparison. Smitty was still out in front of the tent. Smitty's leg was broken by a bullet, and he was sitting propped up on his hands. George called and Smitty turned to look at him slowly and without expression.

"I'm hit, George," Smitty said. "Where is everybody? They're all dead but us."

"The sons of bitches blew my leg off, Smitty," George said.

Smitty, sitting amidst the debree of carnage, gazed back at him. "Nobody's here," he said. "We're all alone." He shook his head slowly.

"They're going to have to cut my leg off, Smitty," George said.

After that George passed out, and once more he seemed to be sinking and sinking through layers of black felt that separated him from the world. They cushioned him against the half-frozen mud on which he lay. This was dying, then.

How long he lay out in front of the tent in the silence he did not know. Time lost its meaning. It had no meaning anyway. In the army nothing had any meaning. You weren't supposed to think, only do what you were told. What did the Soldier's Manual say about dying with your leg blown off? That possibility existed, but he could remember nothing in the Soldier's Manual that dealt with it.

Between periods of sinking into the folds of blackness, he thought about Riley. Each time he sank through another fold of the black felt, a huge gear seemed to grind somberly, slowing speed, relaxing him. It rubbed, like metal against stone. He reminded himself to write to Riley. He would write it all down in his notebook for her to read. A telegram from the War Department wasn't enough. It explained nothing, just like the Soldier's Handbook. Besides the telegram would go to his mother. Riley wouldn't get a telegram. She would have to go and see his mother, but then how would she know? Maybe his mother would write her. But then maybe she wouldn't. If Riley was his wife, *she* would get the telegram. But she wasn't. The dirty bastards sons of bitches. He was in the goddam army a whole year, and he couldn't even get a weekend pass to go home to marry Riley. Now she wouldn't get the telegram. Goddam them. Maybe...

George's mind ran on, arguing with itself hazily over the destination of the War Department telegram informing the world of his demise.

Then another bunch of Japs, a much smaller one now, came through the camp again, and George's mind awoke into crystal clear perception under the stimulus of fear. They came slowly down the line, prodding the bodies, bayoneting those who weren't yet dead. Some of them had bayonets fastened on the ends of sticks. They went into the abandoned tents, searching out every man who was not dead. George watched them come toward him slowly, jabbering excitely in their women's voices. When they got to Smitty, Smitty just sat and watched them stupidly, like a business man propped on the sand of a bathing beach on his holiday, watching the waves come in. They stopped in front of Smitty. Something about him seemed to make them mad, and they jabbered angrily. Smitty looked up at them expressionlessly, almost with curiosity. Then they stuck him. Pushed a bayonet into him slowly, deliberately, five times, until Smitty finally writhed on the ground, screamed once: "You yellow bastards!" and lay still. George clenched his hands helplessly. If he only had his rifle. He'd shoot them from where he lay. Why didn't he curse them for the bastards that they were? why didn't he do anything but just lay there?

They stood in front of Smitty for a minute, small figures in the rising mist, strange and foreign in the messy uniforms and rolled puttees, their queer-shaped helmets and dirty too-wide faces. They jabbered back and forth angrily among themselves, partly in English. Then they started coming on.

George shut his eyes. O Christ, he prayed, O Jesus; let them stick me through the heart the first time. He kept his eyes shut and held his breath. They stood in front of him, still arguing angrily in their jabber voices. One of them kicked him in the head and lights exploded in front of him, and their voices seemed to grow and fade, grow and fade. But he made no sound and tried to keep his muscles slack. They must have decided he was dead, because they went on and left him. He must look dead enough, all covered with blood and mud and his leg mangled, just hanging to him by a thin strip of flesh.

He heard someone behind him scream and then he passed out again. When he came to, his head ached where the Jap had kicked him, although his leg didn't hurt at all. This seemed funny to him, and he felt like laughing but nothing came. Far away and very faintly he could hear bells above the wind. They were playing the *Friendly Tavern Polka*, and he wondered why anybody would want to bring a jukebox up here. The tones of the bells were clear and above the wind. One of the high notes seemed a little flat.

"Hey, Smitty," George said. "Hear the bells? They're playing flat." Smitty played the guitar; he would get a kick out of this.

He wished he could have a good bath. He wished they'd come and get him. It wasn't decent for a man not to have a bath. A man shouldn't have to die dirty. Covered with blood and mud and snow and his own urine. That was no way for a man to die.

Attu, they would say, oh yes. That's one of the Aleutian Islands, isn't it? We've taken a new island. Attu. It's somewhere in the Aleutians. People don't take baths there.

George imagined Riley kept shaking him by the shoulder and giving him hell because he was dirty and had pissed his pants. He wanted her to stop, but the voice kept on. There were many voices. It was the Japs come back. He couldn't stand it, he thought. Oh Jesus Christ...A man hadn't ought to ever have to stand this. Then he realized the voices were American.

"I want a bath, Riley," he kept saying to the medic. "Don't let me die dirty."

In a haze he saw one medic look at his buddy and then turn his eyes away. The medic shook his head wearily, sadly.

(Chapter 19)

[A Book Report of *The Red Badge of Courage*]

Eng 262 James Jones 12 Oct 1942 Number I

BERT "YANK" LEVY in his book, *Guerrilla Warfare*, makes the following statement:

"Courage is the commonest of qualities. In my experience I have met very few real cowards, and they were probably sick men— nervously or psychologicially—"

The plot of Stephen Crane's novel, *Red Badge of Courage*, centers about the mental and physical reactions of a central character, Henry Fleming, to the various stimuli of war. In the barest essentials it deals with a boy who doubts his own courage before going into his first battle, flees in the midst of it and then becomes a hero in a minor sort of way. The whole plot hinges upon the fact that the boy feels he is a coward when he runs in the midst of his first battle.

Being a soldier living under the shadow of the possibility of going into battle at any time, I was naturally interested in the boy's doubting his own courage. I have had the same feeling many times. Even now, after being under fire, I sometimes wonder if I would stand up under battle: a bayonet fight, for example. With the thought of my own doubt in my mind I made a mental note to watch for the exact place in the story where the boy becomes afraid and flees; I wanted to study the causes of his fear. When I did find the spot, I was surprised to find that fleeing did not even seem logical to me under the circumstances. From my own experience and from what I have learned through talking to other soldiers and reading about the thing, the circumstances responsible for Henry's flight are almost exactly opposite to what I believe would cause flight.

The regiment of which Henry Fleming is a member is attacked by the enemy. The enemy advance almost to the regiment's line, and then they are forced back, are forced to withdraw to their old positions. In the interval following this attack the men of Henry's regiment congratulate themselves on their victory in repulsing the charge. Then, the enemy charges again. The men in the regiment are unable to believe that any living thing is capable of making another attack in the face of the previous repulse. Their imaginations build the Confederate forces up to supermen who are able to withstand shells and bullets as if they were rain. Crane describes in elaborate detail the reactions of young Henry when he sees the enemy begin their second charge:

.....“The youth stared. Surely, he thought, this impossible thing was not about to happen. He waited as if he expected the enemy to suddenly stop, apologize, and retire bowing. It was all a mistake.....

.....“Into the youth's eyes there came a look that one can see in the orbs of a jaded horse. His neck was quivering with nervous weakness, and the muscles of his arms felt numb and bloodless. His hands, too, seemed large and awkward, as if he was wearing invisible mittens. And there was a great uncertainty about his knee joints.....

.....“He began to exaggerate the endurance, the skill, and the valour of those who were coming. Himself reeling from exhaustion, he was astonished beyond measure at such persistency. They must be machines of steel. It was very gloomy struggling against such affairs, wound up perhaps to fight until sundown.....

.....“To the youth it was an onslaught of redoubtable dragons. He became like the man who lost his legs at the approach of the red and green monster. He waited in a sort of horrified listening attitude. He seemed to shut his eyes and wait to be gobbled.

“A man near him who, up to this time, had been working feverishly at his rifle suddenly stopped and ran with howls. A lad whose face had borne an expression of exalted courage, the majesty of him who dares give his life, was, at an instant, smitten abject. He blanched like one who has come to the edge of a cliff at midnight and is suddenly made aware. There was a revelation. He, too, threw down his gun and fled. There was no shame in his face. He ran like a rabbit.

“Others began to scamper away through the smoke. The youth turned his head, shaken from his trance by this movement, as if the regiment was leaving him behind. He saw the few fleeting forms.

“He yelled then with fright and swung about. For a moment, in the great clamour, he was like a proverbial chicken. He lost the direction of safety. Destruction threatened him from all points.

“Directly he began to speed toward the rear in great leaps....”

Crane uses here the psychology of the instinct to follow. Had not the man standing beside the youth run, the youth would probably have stayed to fight on. When he looked around and saw the others fleeing, he feared being left alone. With this fear came blind terror, causing him to forget everything in his desire to get to safety. It is safe to assume that imagination caused the retreat. The other men who fled were in the same state of mind as he: their imaginations had worked on them in such a way that they believed the charging enemy to be superhuman, that there was no possibility of stopping them.

It is hard for me to believe that these men, having weathered one charge and, consequently, become elated with the winey taste of victory, would suddenly lose all faith in their ability to stop the enemy. I should think it would work the other way round, that, having repulsed them once, the regiment would more surely believe itself capable of stopping them again. No matter how green the regiment might be in the ways of battle, it still seems impossible that they would think battles are won as simply and easily as that— merely repulsing a minor charge of the enemy.

Also, it is doubtful if the first man to run would have done so merely because the enemy were again attacking. Provided he were in this state of fear brought on by imagination, he would still be the first to run. He would not have the excuse of others running. The thought of how his comrades would ridicule and sneer at him would seem to be strong enough to overpower the desire to run. It is somewhat the same situation as the one in which Christ supposedly said: "Let him who is without sin among you cast the first stone." Nobody threw that first stone. Doubtless if someone had thrown the first one, others would have been quick to follow. The same thing applies here. I am inclined to think that each man that felt the impulse to flee would look around at the men near him and seeing them still fighting, would decide to remain. Thus none of them would be the first to run.

All this is supposing that while in the heat of combat men still possess the power to think along the many tangents of imagination. It has been my experience, and it is borne out by talking with others who have seen actual combat, that one does not have time to use one's imagination while fighting. What thinking is done— outside of necessary tactical and mechanical thinking—is done somewhat abstractly, done in a faraway, semi-conscious sector of the brain. This sort of thinking is certainly not conducive to imagination. Any boxer or football player can tell you the same thing. Before a game or a fight one sits and imagines all sorts of terrible possibilities. Even though death is unlikely, serious injury is very possible.

I use football and boxing, because I have had experience in both of these sports. I know that before a game or a bout I am so nervous that it takes every ounce of my will-power for me to sit still. Whenever I know I am about to participate in physical combat of any sort which includes the possibility of physical injury and the possibility of the humiliation of defeat, a sickly, drawn, hungry feeling seeps into the pit of my stomach. I feel as if I haven't touched food to my palate for at least two weeks, and I have a tremendous physical urge to urinate. Both sensations always come to me when I know beforehand that I am going into danger or combat of any sort. The sickly feeling of a clenched fist about my stomach makes me jumpy, and I make innumerable trips to the toilet in a futile effort to relieve myself. I keep wondering what in the name of Christ is holding up the proceedings, and wish the thing to be over with as soon as possible.

That is the hardest time of any combat, whether with guns, fists, or shoulder pads. It is then that one needs every ounce of courage one has. It is then that instinct whispers to you and says: "To hell with honor! To hell with what other people will think of you! To hell with the glory of winning, or of losing magnificently, for that matter! You don't want to get into this. You damned fool, what did you ever let yourself in for this for? You'd be a great one to lose an eye just for getting in a ring to make an impression on the women. Get out! Get out! It's almost too late." You almost do it, too—almost. But somehow, you always stick it out until it is time to climb into the ring or run out on the field.

Then, miraculously, these feelings drop from you like a shroud, and you are free. Your brain works clearly—at least, comparatively so, and your muscles lose their tenseness and are relaxed and smooth. Your only worry from then on to the end is showing the other guy you are better than he is. Usually, when losing, one seems to become possessed by a great rage, but it is a crystal rage, clean and sharp, seeing everything slowly and clearly. But never once, between rounds or during intervals between plays, do you become afraid again—either of injury or of losing. Your imagination has ceased to work.

Thus, it seems to me that if Henry Fleming was to run, he should have done so before the actual battle started. The slow walk across the fields without sound of firing or sight of enemy was the proper place for him to run. The only other time when he would be likely to run would have been after weeks or months of continuous fighting when the immense physical and mental strain might have cracked his nerve.

I have been under fire only once—December 7th—and in comparing my experience with that of Henry Fleming I found they were very similar, the only great difference being the element of anticipation. We had no idea at all that would be fighting until we were in the midst of it.

When the first bomb fell at Wheeler Field, most of my outfit were sitting at breakfast. We even thought the bomb was dynamiting! After several others fell, we finally rushed out into the street to see what was up. Most of us carried our coffee and our pint bottle of milk with us—milk is precious stuff in the army, even in peacetime. We worried more about somebody swiping our milk than the possibility of an attack. We stood in the road and gaped at the tower of smoke over Wheeler and did not even believe it was an attack when a great, tall, redheaded fellow came running up the road from the direction of Wheeler with his eyes as wide as dollars and his hair flying every which way like tiny licks of flame shouting, "Jesus Christ! It's the Japs! I seen the Rising Sun on their Goddam planes! It's the Japs, you damned fools! Well, don't just stand there, do something! Oh, Jesus Christ!" We still stood there with our coffee cups in one hand and our milk in the other like the silent, gaping demons carved immobile on a group of totem poles. It was only after a plane with the Rising Sun on its wingtips flew over us coughing .50 caliber slugs that spattered at our feet in the middle of the street that we woke up and realized what was happening. That's the main difference between my first action and Henry's. I didn't have time to worry about mine beforehand.

Apparently Crane thought that during the brief respite between the charges when there was little physical action required, a man's brain returned to its normal style of thinking complete with imagination. I disagree. It didn't work that way with me or with anyone I've talked to. The intense excitement and feeling of adventure didn't leave you between the waves of planes. It was there all the time the fighting was going on, and it was quite a while after the whole thing was over before your thinking processes dropped back to normal.

Some of us had grabbed what weapons and ammunition we could find and had climbed up through the attic to the roof of the barracks. On the roofs our moments of respite between waves of planes correspond to the lull experienced by Henry Fleming and his comrades. But there was no fear or imagination apparent in our case. It was more like the minute between rounds of a fight. You were too busy thinking about what you had done wrong the last round and how to correct it the next that you had no time to think about yourself at all except in an "expendable" sort of a way. You check your weapon (an automatic rifle in my case) to make sure the mechanism is in proper working order. You check the position of your full clips on the floor beside you to make sure of their position so you can reach them without looking and to be positive they are free from grit that might cause the gun to jam. Everything must be just right; one lost second and you may not get to fire at all at the next wave. Speed and smoothness in your action seems more important than life itself. You check and recheck these things and then recheck them again. You think back desperately to try and remember if there is anything you have forgotten. The sweat is rolling from you in a miniature Niagara and picks up soot from the chimneys and dirt from the seldom-cleaned roof until you would pass excellently for Al Jolson doing his Mammy act. But you don't even notice this until it is all over.

You are there, crouched on the bare roof, and there is little or no cover. The few chimneys have men behind them, and you may curse them loudly and subconsciously, but you don't even think of trying to crowd them out. You don't really expect to shoot down a plane, but you at least want the satisfaction of shooting at them. If you saw one fall, you'd probably stop firing and just kneel there with your mouth hanging open in astonishment.

Above and beyond your frenzy for checking everything and wholly unrelated to your brain—and yet somewhere in your brain—there is a great amazement at the fact that you—you, the guy you've lived with all your life, the guy who used to devour books like "Fix Bayonets!", "Beau Geste," "Through the Wheat," and "All Quiet on the Western Front," the guy who used to sweat away pounds over the outcome of a biology exam—are standing unconcernedly, even joyfully, on a barracks roof in Schofield Barracks in Hawaii in the middle of the Pacific Ocean firing real bullets at real Japs in real planes which are firing real bullets back at you. You'd known the war would start somehow, and yet you never really believed that you would be right in the midst of it with an excellent chance of getting killed—and here you are, right in the middle of the start of a war that will make history. You know it's true, but you don't believe it anyway.

Then a couple of planes come over, and you can see the goggled faces of the pilots and hear and see .50 caliber slugs bouncing off the roof beside you, and you start instinctively to fire again taking your leads calmly as if you were firing on the range. For the few seconds you can see the pilots you are in personal touch with them, and you hate them with the intensity of a poised stilleto—and yet you do not hate them, either. After they are gone you can't hate them at all, no matter how hard you try.

Our respites were quite similar to Henry Fleming's, but our reactions were entirely different. Crane elaborated the fact that the youth and his comrades believed their enemies to be fearless monsters to come back after having been beaten off. They imagined them to be irresistible and ran because in their fear they thought it useless to oppose them. Their case was not nearly as bad as ours. They were fighting men with guns; we were fighting planes that swooshed by in a couple of seconds and were gone. They had good cover and good targets; we were kneeling on a bare roof and made excellent targets while we shot at the hardest targets there are. If Crane's hypothesis is to be believed, our imaginations would have certainly led us to toss our guns aside and make tracks for the protection of the inside of the barracks. The fact that we didn't shows, to me, that Crane was wrong in supposing a man's imagination is able to function in the excitement and clear-cut confusion of actual combat.

[Notes for *From Here to Eternity*]

WHAT DO I want to say in this novel?

The first thing, *the main thing*, is I want to tell the story of the guys in the peacetime army. They are sons of bitches, but the fault is not theirs. The fault belongs to the society, the system under which they live—not only the economic system, but the moral system of righteousness.

This creates a natural problem: how to show them as the sons of bitches they are, and at the same time create sympathy for them with the reader.

To do this I have chosen the story of Prewitt. His story must be a tragedy, as the army is a tragedy.

—What is the nature of the story I want to tell? What is its tragedy? Here is one thing, I think: *these guys suffer from a hierarchy of arbitrary authority*. The authority generally means little to the officers who wield it; but it means the difference between a *good life* and a *bad life* to an EM.

The meaning of the army for me is one of personal degradation, a degradation that is inescapable once a man is hooked, a degradation rising directly out of the system of caste and privilege and arbitrary authority.

The most logical way to handle this then, is to show a man caught by the army. Prewitt. He is forced in by economic forces and once in cannot escape without sacrificing his self-respect and integrity, which he refuses to do.

I assert it is impossible to escape this degradation unless a man allows his own moral nature to be corrupted. This is a fact by the very nature of the army now, and will remain so until it is changed. All changes to date have been superficial; basically the army is still as it was before the war. Caste, Privilege, Favoritism, Politics, Arbitrary Authority.

I. Analysis Of Material

a. Naming its effect (*as is*)

My material is the peacetime army. The war has nothing to do with this material—except as it overshadows, unmentioned, the whole book. That was my first error in construction. The *effect* of the peacetime army (*as is*) is the tragedy and pathos which are implicit in the arid hopelessness of that way of life; and of the men who live it. These men were driven (by their own weakness, a fact I used to refuse to admit) into the army because of the depression that took their jobs and left them with a choice of insecurity and freedom on the bum, or security and serfdom inside the army.

Now I must define the arid hopelessness: One factor, a very important one, is the lack of women. The financial inability to marry or to maintain a woman is one cause. Another cause is that civilian women, except of the very lowest sort, were socially conditioned against having anything to do with soldiers (and rightly, from their viewpoint.) This lack is tremendously heightened by having to live within the confines of a world where women do not live and are seen only at a distance.

Another factor is the hierarchy of authority which destroys the individualities of the subordinates. Necessary in the army, yet it does not make the men like it because it is necessary. All of them to some extent, and many to the maximum, suffer from this blocking of desired action; yet their only choice is this, or else going back to a civilian life which is worse.

Still another, is the gross inefficiency of this hierarchy of authority, which makes suffering it still worse. The favoritism which forces a man to renounce his own integrity or else be discriminated against.

It is true that a great number of these men are so shiftless and ignorant that they will with cunning egoism suffer any degradation to get a meal and a bed (men like R———). It is also true that a great number of them seem to be more or less happily satisfied with their life, without having to be degraded; they succeed fairly well and are within normal limits content (men like Sgt C———).

But it is also true that there are men of superior abilities and basically good moral qualities who are deeply embittered through having to live in the presence of graft and frustration and inefficiency (men like Sgt W———). These men are, moreover, to be completely analytical, cynical about life in general as well as the particular of the army. The graft, inefficiency, frustration that is so open in the army is more subtly operative in most of the specific social forms, and these men are as bitter about that as they are the army. Therefore, putting the presence of their bitterness on a much higher plane, actually, than just the army.

—Yet, Tom [Uzzell, author of *The Technique of the Novel*] says (and rightly) that one theme is enough. "The dangers in being too philosophic are greater than in not being philosophic at all." My material is the peacetime army, and through portraying it to allude to the present army. The main point here is material; I could not do a proper job with the army of today because of all of the new elements which have entered in that I have not experienced. And material must come from your *own* experience.—

In addition to these types there are the Prewitt type, who have little power of reflection, who are unable to see the forces at work underneath, and who merely get along as best they can amid a chaotic social setup, which is not very well since they have nothing to have faith in besides themselves.

This material includes all the political corruption, rank favoritism, friendship before efficiency or justice, that is so prevalent in the army—then or now. At one time I hated these things—*mainly because I was not a recipient of them.* If I had been in position to accept the benefits from them, would I not have gladly taken them, like everybody else? No need to ask; of course I, or any other human, would. This is not cynicism, but analysis of human nature. This point is important, because in hating such things, I instinctively put myself first. *Indignation is false and selfish unless accompanied by sympathy and understanding.* Hence, one of the things that must come out is the contempt and hatred for these facts that I, for my own boosting, have written in.

—The best fashion to do this is to have a character the recipient of such favors—like Stark; which I've already done, so it's okay.

Another element, loneliness, which contributes to the sense of arid hopelessness in the army is the almost utter lack of intimate friendship. While men in the army are fairly closely acquainted at times with each other and each other's desires, I have hardly ever noticed a case of sacrifice of one friend for another. It just doesn't happen. For such transcendent friendship, I think a long term intimacy—perhaps from childhood, at least for years—is required. These men do not have opportunities to form such friendships, they are always moving, losing old faces, meeting suspicious new ones. They will do little favors for each other—like taking a man home when he is drunk—but real all-out friendship is almost nonexistent. And its lack and the awareness of it is terrible loneliness in the midst of many voices.

Now—the effect of the army *as is* is one of barrenness of most of the accepted values in life. It is defined by its *lacks*, rather than its positives—lack of women; lack of freedom; lack of pride in efficiency; lack of friendship; lack of money; lack of any kind of love or affection.

b. Classifying it (as to four kinds of emphasis)

Character: The general characteristics that grow out of such a life are: *Intense sexual frustration*, from lack of women (plus lack of money) which *drives a lot of men into abortive homosexuality*—usually with queers downtown. Lack of freedom drives them into a sort of *intense individual pride* that is disproportionate, so that they must turn all desires into the pride in their work. But the lack of efficiency often blocks this course, as in Prewitt's case, but leaving him with nothing but *pride in himself for something he can't do anymore*. The lack of friendship makes every man *distrustfully lonely*. The lack of money, accompanied with a surety of bed and board, has a peculiar degrading result; and it also, in order to get spending money at all or even for the dubious excitement of a good time in the midst of boredom and dullness turns many men to "playing the queers." The lack of love or affection usually result in a trait of *defensive cynicism*: "I don't need no love or affection to get along. To hell with it. All lies anyway."

Three main characters: Prewitt, Warden, Stark. Each of these three, in his own characteristic way, tries to rise above and defeat these social forces personified in the army. Prewitt, by trying to keep his pride and self-respect inviolate against all degradations; Warden, by an inverted pride trying to lie, cheat.

[From Here to Eternity]

Prewitt is the real protagonist in this book. It is with him that the main theme and main stream of action deals: the criminal theme as written to Perkins. The criminality is directly derived from an abnormally high personal pride. This pride is the result of an illusion about Adventure—(Not Adventure as portrayed in cannibals, combats, etc; but Adventure as signified by that absorption with pride above all else, that nothing must be allowed to interfere with the belief in that pride.) Prewitt has no illusions about Adventure in the physical world; but he does have an illusion about the Adventure of his Pride; (which actually as he never learns is *within* himself, not *without* in the actions of the material world upon his ideals.)

The main channel of the book is Prewitt's attempts to save his Pride in himself as an individual—he does it, or attempts it, by rebelling against and refusing anything to do with anything that seems to him to jeopardize his self-respect, his pride. Thus the book resolves itself into a perpetual conflict between Prewitt and Fate; it is his fate, as it is most every man's, that he must compromise with Fate in the end or be destroyed by Fate. Fate takes here the form of society; not only organized society but all human society, all life which is society. It is a conflict between Prewitt and life.

The conflict manifests itself in the first scene. Prewitt quits the Bugle Corps because he feels he must do it to save his pride, even tho he loves bugling. This is a sacrifice to his ideal. He is continually making such sacrifices:

1-He quits the Corps and goes to G Company. (This is his fate foreordained.)
2-He also quits Violet, because she will not accede to his own plan.

Here the plot thickens. In G Co Prewitt is immediately set in conflict with Capt Holmes's jockstrap setup.

Notes on PREWITT

Prewitt is gradually forced by external, irrational forces and his own inflexible honor into becoming a criminal.

The climax is tied in with the event of Pearl Harbor. When this occurs, Prew is over the hill, a fugitive, living with Alma in her Haleiwa apt to escape arrest. Against her advice, he goes back because "he is a soldier; he had to go back." He believes the reason he is wanted will be overlooked in this new crisis and need for men. It is not pure romance: realistically there is no other way open to him, except remaining hidden as he is indefinitely. And the war changes that.

When he goes back (walking toward beach positions, seeing the frantic movement etc.) he is stopped by MPs who have his name. (Perhaps because he has no papers.) They refuse to let him go on, and he runs. Then picturing himself as forever running he stops and goes back into bullets and is killed.

Here is an excellent person for Prew to kill: "Fatso," the Staff Sgt in charge of the Stockade under the Capt from Harlan. He could meet him in town some night. Here is another problem: I must have him kill Fatso in some extra-legal manner so that he is not discovered, is outside the law, for if he is discovered he will be brought to trial. There should be no witnesses. If Prew is wounded then he cannot go back without being suspected. He goes to Alma. Then later he can't go back because he is over the hill, also he fears being suspected because he went over the hill at time of murder.

Notes on HOLMES

Holmes courtmartials Prew (partially) because his company is about due for one, and so many are implicitly expected from each outfit every so often to show they are on their toes.

A scene in which Holmes asks Karen to be a little more congenial to Col Delbert. She asks don't he know Delbert is trying to make her. Holmes is shocked. Then he says it won't hurt to lead him on a little, she doesn't have to give in to him.

I have neither space nor material to show intimately a *good* officer. Therefore I must refrain from showing Holmes as a *bad* officer, unless I can offset him with a good one. He must be made pathetic and the victim of other circumstances just as he is the persecutor of Prew.

I want to do two scenes with Holmes and Delbert, in addition to the one in which Delbert orders him to win the championship again. One will be Delbert's "stag" at the Club apartment. The other will be at a dinner party at the Club in which Delbert tries to make Karen, and when she has to take Holmes home drunk, (scene already written with Lt Culpepper)

Holmes bust Ike later on to give Bloom Ike's rating.

The reason for Holmes's removal is War, and a Capt just forwarded in from States who has more official pull, just as they bump men in Harry's [Handy] plant for longevity. Delbert does

nothing to try to help Holmes out of this spot. (Use scene of B——
— at Haunauma Bay)

WARDEN

Warden is an efficiency expert. He loves the running of his
Company and will do anything to further its efficiency. Not for
credit, but for his love of it. In this he is stopped through Holmes.
Holmes plays politics and his fighting squad is his God.

Deliberately, with malice aforethought, Warden decides to se-
duce Holmes's wife in retaliation. *Irony*: they both fall in love.

Stark talks to Warden to show him where he had fallen down on
the job. Warden becomes a completely changed man, over a period
of time. Stark who has been put in the kitchen because of his
efficiency and who has maneuvered Prew into the kitchen because
of his efficiency, later talks to Warden because of lack of efficiency.
He tells Warden he is a fool because Karen has had other men in her
life and that's one of the ways she entertains herself, that she slept
with Wilson and another man, not here, at Biiss. Warden knows
this (Karen admits it), but he still holds a grudge, and gets Stark
busted because Stark went over his head and hired Prew, altho
basically part of his anger is about Karen. Ironically, the very
things he discusses with Capt Holmes and points out as true of
Prew are the things that later stand in his way when he tries to save
Prew from Stockade.

The basic problem of our age is the coordination of the
Individual to the Society—both men and nations of men—so that
the Individual does not become mechanized or enslaved by Society,
and the Society does not become mechanized or enslaved by the
Individual. Though they hate each other bitterly, the *Capitalist* and
the *Communist* are brothers; The *Nazi* and the *Religionist* are
brothers.

(1) The Company symbolizes Society.

(2) Holmes symbolizes the inept leaders of Society.

(3) Warden symbolizes the consecrated warriors who try to fight
all the evils of Society from within the framework and pattern of
Society, who use the very methods they fight in order to defeat
them, and who by the very height and compass of their vision

defeat themselves in the end and go down—altho the material victories they have accomplished remain behind.

(4) Prewitt symbolizes the *open* rebels against the Society who like Wardens perceive the evils of it and seek to hold themselves aloof from it and to withdraw from it, who are also defeated because such withdrawal is impossible.

(5) Stark symbolizes the business man who refuses to accept responsibility beyond his own immediate job, which when he is allowed to do it occupies him, gives him pride and satisfaction, and helps him to close his eyes to the evils the others cannot overlook.

(6) Gallowitz symbolizes the Nazis, who to escape their own inferiority attach themselves to a Leader and worship him, hoping to hitch a ride, and who to blind themselves to the evils about them (being unable to lose themselves in work because they have not the capabilities) accept their imperfect Leader as Perfection and hide behind this Beatific Vision.

Analysis.
Character: Love of the army, love of soldiering, pride in doing each man's own particular job, intense desire to maintain one's self-respect.

Complicaton: Entanglement and conflict with the army's system of caste, favoritism, politics, arbitrary authority.

Theme: The army will never be a satisfactory life until the tenets of its system are changed.

Desired Effect: Indignation and sorrow at the tragic, pathetic spectacle of talented men who are kept from realizing their talents in useful lives by the army's system.

The Plot:
The story of a man who is deprived of the work he loves, of the way of life he loves, and finally of his life—in an effort to retain his self-respect.

The main story must center around the situation in G Co— Holmes's favoritism and his boxing squad—which symbolizes the army system.

The plot is derived from the various attempts to force Prewitt into going out for the boxing squad. The whole situation is centered in the boxing squad—Warden's effort toward efficiency are all battles against the boxing squad which is inefficient. It, rather than the efficiency or welfare of the company is the dominating factor in the management of the company.

The basic intensification is to keep all the action, except when dealing with the women, within the Company. Leave the Officers' Club out. Instead of having Prew kill the headwaiter, have him kill a man in the Company—I imagine the best bet would be Henderson.

The *effect as is* of this material is one of tragedy, derived from the fruitless efforts of these men to seek and hold some value which will give purpose and meaning to their lives, and augmented by admiration for their courage as men who though frustrated and defeated will not give up hope. These men are first of all to be admired, but admiration is tempered by the knowledge of their faults, mainly getting drunk and overwhelming selfish interests— tho these interests may be altruistic.

The character classification is essentially the same in all: as stated above, pathetic efforts to grasp and hold some value, some realization of their own importance in life which will give them purpose and meaning. Each character cherishes a slightly different value: Holmes, his boxing squad; Warden, efficiency in his Company; Stark his kitchen; Gallowitz his rating; O'Hayer his money; Andy and Friday guitarplaying; Karen love; Prewitt bugling; Karelsen his cherished intellectuality. The values are in perpetual conflict, thus creating trouble and complications for all.

The complication classifications all arise from these conflicting desires for happiness. They all represent "social or man & man" clashes. Actually, the internal conflicts the action represents are attempts to choose between retaining self-respect and integrity or the cherished value.

Books by James Jones

From Here to Eternity. New York: Charles Scribner's Sons, 1951.
Some Came Running. New York: Charles Scribner's Sons, 1958.
The Pistol. New York: Charles Scribner's Sons, 1959.
The Thin Red Line. New York: Charles Scribner's Sons, 1962.
Go to the Widow-Maker. New York: Delacorte, 1967.
The Ice-Cream Headache and Other Stories. New York: Delacorte, 1968.
The Merry Month of May. New York: Delacorte, 1971.
A Touch of Danger. Garden City, N.Y.: Doubleday, 1973.
Viet Journal. New York: Delacorte, 1974.
WWII. New York: Grosset & Dunlap, 1975.
Whistle. New York: Delacorte, 1978.

About James Jones

Aldrich, Nelson. "The Art of Fiction XXIII: James Jones." *Paris Review* 20 (Autumn-Winter 1958–1959).

Bowers, John. *The Colony*, New York: E. P. Dutton, 1971.

Garrett, George P. *James Jones*. New York: Harcourt Brace Jovanovich, 1984.

Giles, James R. *James Jones*. Boston: G. K. Hall, 1981.

———. "Three Days in Byzantium." *Confrontation* 20 (Spring-Summer 1980): 3–25.

Hendrick, George, ed. *To Reach Eternity: The Letters of James Jones.* New York: Random House, 1989.

Jones, Kaylie. "James Jones's Hawaii." *Travel Holiday*, March 1990.

Lennon, J. Michael, and Jeffrey Van Davis. "James Jones: Reveille to Taps." Springfield, Illinois: Sangamon State University, 1984. Television documentary.

Lennon, J. Michael, and George Plimpton. "Glimpses: James Jones, 1921–1977." *Paris Review* 103 (Summer 1987).

McShane, Frank. *Into Eternity: The Life of James Jones*. Boston: Houghton Mifflin, 1985.

Morris, Willie. *James Jones: A Friendship*. Garden City, N.Y.: Doubleday, 1978.

Shaw, Irwin. "James Jones, 1921–1977." *New York Times Book Review*, June 12, 1977.

Styron, William. "A Friend's Farewell to James Jones." *New York Magazine*, June 6, 1977.

Wood, Thomas J., and Meredith Keating. *James Jones in Illinois: A Guide to the Handy Writers' Colony Collection*. Springfield, Illinois: Sangamon State University, 1989.